WORLD OF ANIMALS

INDEX

CUMULATIVE INDEX

Published 2006 by Grolier, an imprint of
Scholastic Library Publishing
Danbury, CT 06816

This edition published exclusively for the school
and library market

The Brown Reference Group plc.
(incorporating Andromeda Oxford Limited)
8 Chapel Place
Rivington Street
London
EC2A 3DQ

ISBN 978-0-7172-6214-4

**Library of Congress Cataloging-in-Publication
Data available upon request**

Editorial Director:	Lindsey Lowe
Project Director:	Graham Bateman
Art Director:	Dave Goodman
Picture Manager:	Becky Cox
Production Director:	Alastair Gourlay

Credits
Front Cover: Ardea: John Cancarosi br; Nature
Picture Library: Pete Oxford bl; Oxford Scientific
Films: David Fleetham tr, Stan Osolinski tl;
Premaphotos: Ken Preston-Mafham bc.

All artworks © The Brown Reference Group plc

Printed in China

WORLD OF ANIMALS

INDEX

CUMULATIVE INDEX

GROLIER

an imprint of

www.scholastic.com/librarypublishing

Find the Animal

World of Animals is a 50-volume library set that describes all the groups of living animals. Each 10-volume set within the library features a familiar animal group—mammals, birds, insects and other invertebrates, fish, and amphibians and reptiles. These groups also represent categories of animals that are recognized by scientists.

The Animal Kingdom

The living world is divided into five kingdoms, one of which (Kingdom Animalia) is the main subject of the *World of Animals*. Also included are those members of the Kingdom Protista that were once regarded as animals, but now form part of a group that includes all single-celled organisms. Kingdom Animalia is divided into numerous major groups called Phyla, but only one of them (Chordata) contains those animals that have a backbone. Chordates, or vertebrates as they are popularly known, include all the animals familiar to us and those most studied by scientists—mammals, birds, fish, and amphibians and reptiles. In all, there are about 38,000 species of vertebrates, while the Phyla that contain animals without backbones (so-called invertebrates, such as insects, spiders, and so on) include at least 1 million species, probably many more. To find which set of volumes in the *World of Animals* library is relevant to you, please see the chart below.

Main Groups of Animals

This chart shows the main groups of animals alive today. Volumes within the library that cover each major group are indicated below.

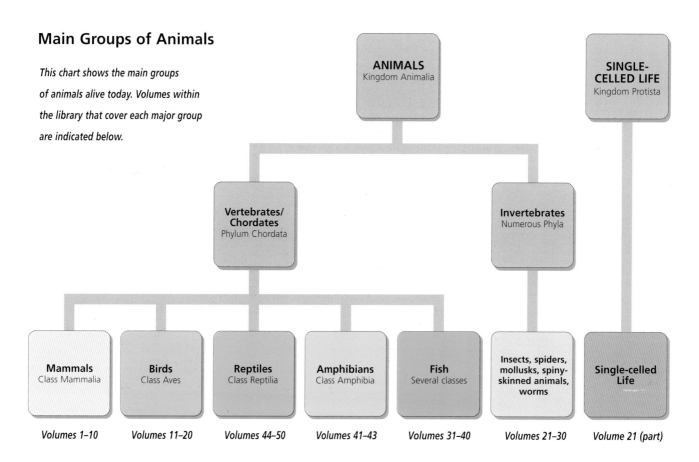

Cumulative Index

A **bold** number shows the volume and is followed by the relevant page numbers (e.g., **1:** 52, 74).

Common names in **bold** (e.g., **aardwolf**) mean that the animal has an illustrated main entry in the set. Underlined page numbers (e.g., **9:** 78–79) refer to the main entry for that animal.

Italic page numbers (e.g., **2:** *103*) point to illustrations of animals in parts of the set other than the main entry.

Page numbers in parentheses—e.g., **1:** (24)—locate information contained in At-a-Glance boxes.

Animals that have main entries in the set are indexed under their common names, alternative common names, and scientific names.

aardvark 1: *10;* **5:** (10), (12); **9:** 64, 65, (66), 67, 78–79
  African **9:** 65
aardwolf 2: 102, *103,* 110–111
aba aba 31: 82, 85, (108), 110–111
abalones **30:** 22, 23
  red **30:** *23*
Ablattara laevigata **25:** *30*
Ablatys taenionotus **39:** 67
Ablennes hians **38:** 73
Ablepharus **46:** 10, (11)
Abramis **34:** 46
  brama **34:** (87)
Abramites hyselonotus **38:** 21
Abraxas grossulariata **26:** 14–15
Abrocoma bennetti **8:** 30
Abrocomidae **8:** 31
Abronia **46:** 52, *52–53*
ABT-594 **43:** (80)
Aburria pipile **11:** 44
Abyssobrotula galatheae **36:** 24, (27)
Abyssocottidae **39:** 76–81
Abyssocottus gibbosus **39:** 78
acacia **6:** 87
Acalyptophis peroni **50:** (45), 46
Acantharia **21:** 13

Acanthaspis **24:** *38*
Acanthaster planci **30:** (102–103)
Acanthicus
  adonis **37:** 107
  hystrix **37:** 107
Acanthixalus spinosus **43:** 22
Acanthobdellae **21:** 94
Acanthocardia echinata **30:** 66
Acanthocephala **21:** 32,77
Acanthocerus **44:** 32, (40)
  atricollis **44:** *33*
Acanthochaenus luetkenii **39:** 12, *12*
Acanthocirrus retrirostris **21:** *85*
Acanthocleithron **37:** 71
Acanthoclonia paradoxa **22:** *32*
Acanthocoris sordidus **24:** (54)
Acanthocybium solandri **40:** 106
Acanthodactylus **45:** 58
  erythrurus **45:** (79)
Acanthopagrus berda **40:** 40
Acanthophis **48:** 61; **50:** 15
  antarcticus **48:** *16*
Acanthophorus **25:** *8–9*
Acanthophthalmus **34:** 100
Acanthoplus armativentris **23:** *15*
Acanthops falcataria **22:** *79*
Acanthopsis **34:** 13
Acanthopterygians 38: 50–51
  Who's Who **38:** (51)
Acanthorhodeus **34:** 66
Acanthorhynchus
  superciliosus **20:** 88, 94–95
  tenuirostris **20:** 88
Acanthosaura **44:** 32
  armata **44:** 35
  crucigera **44:** 35
Acanthosomatidae **24:** 14, (71)
Acanthuridae **40:** 9, 100–101
Acanthurus
  achilles **40:** 100, *100*
  coeruleus **40:** 101
  leucosternon **40:** 100, *101*
Acantopsis
  (Acantopsis) choirorhynchus **34:** 100
Acari **29:** 30–33
accentor 18: 36–37
  alpine **18:** 36, 37, *37*
  Himalayan **18:** 36, 37
  maroon-backed **18:** 36, *37*
  Radde's **18:** 36, *37*
  Siberian **18:** 36, *37*
Accipiter **15:** 42
  gentilis **15:** 8, 38–39, (48), (60); **18:** (34)
  nisus **15:** 8, 38
  striatus **15:** 8, 38; **18:** 39
Accipitridae **15:** 8, 12; **20:** 8, 11
Aceros
  cassidix **19:** 48
  nipalensis **19:** 48
  undulatus **19:** 48
Acestrorhynchidae **38:** 24–27
Acestrorhynchus
  falcatus **38:** 26, *26*

  falcirostris **38:** 26
  minimus **38:** 26
  nasutus **38:** 26
Acestrura bombus **16:** 44
Acharia **26:** 107
  stimulae **26:** 106
Achatina achatina **30:** *48*
Acheilognathinae **34:** 66–67
Acheilognathus **34:** 66
Achias australis **23:** *87*
Achiridae **39:** 92–95
Achirus
  achirus **39:** 92, *92*
  poropterus **39:** 92
Acinonyx
  jubatus **2:** 10, 26–29
  rex **2:** 29
Acipenser
  brevirostrum **31:** 67
  fulvescens **31:** (56), 60–61
  gueldenstaedti **31:** 52–53, (57), 66, 67
  nudiventris **31:** 56
  oxrhynchus **31:** (56), 58
  ruthenus **31:** 53, (56), 60, 62–63
  stellatus **31:** (57), *57,* 66, 67
  sturio **31:** 53, 58–59, 67
  transmontanus **31:** 52, 56
Acipenseridae **31:** (43), 48, 58, 60, 62, 64, 68
  subfamilies summary **31:** (52)
Acipenseriformes **31:** 52–57
Acipenserinae **31:** (52), 53, 58, 60, 62, 64
Acoela **21:** (81)
Aconaemys fuscus **8:** 30
Acontias **46:** 8, (11), 12
Acontinae **44:** (26); **49:** 25
acouchi **7:** *12*
  red **8:** 30
acraeas **26:** (55)
Acrantophis dumerili **48:** 54
Acrididae **23:** 10, 24–31
Acridotheres **18:** (41)
  cristallus **18:** 82
  ginginianus **18:** 82
  tristis **18:** 82, 88
Acris **43:** 32, 38
Acrobates pygmaeus **10:** 74, 84–85
Acrobatidae **10:** (76)
Acrocephalus **17:** 60
  arundinaceus **17:** 60; **20:** *49*
  palustris **18:** (41)
  schoenobaenus **17:** 60
  scirpaceus **17:** 60; **20:** (48)
Acrochordidae **48:** 9, 40; **49:** 65, (82); **50:** 49
Acrochordus
  arafurae **48:** 17, 40, *41,* 42–43
  granulatus **48:** 40; **50:** 37
  javanicus **48:** 40, *41*
Acrocinus longimanus **25:** 90
Acromis sparsa **25:** *102–103,* (103)
Acronicta aceris **26:** 96
Acrophylla titan **22:** *52, 55*

Acropoma japonicum **40:** 14
Acropomatidae **39:** (10), **40:** 12–19
Acrothoracica **28:** 9
Acryllium vulturinum **11:** 44
Acteon eloiseae **30:** 36
Actias luna **26:** 71
Actinaria **21:** 43, 56–61
Actinia equina **21:** 56, 59
Actinophrys **21:** 21
Actinopterygii **33:** 60, (61)
Actinote
    alcione **26:** 55
    pellenia trinitatis **26:** 13
Actinulida **21:** 43
Actitis
    hypoleucos **13:** 30, 44–47
    macularia **13:** 47
Aculeata **27:** 8, 10–11
Acutotyphlops **48:** 18
Adalia
    2-punctata **25:** 54–55, 56
    10-punctata **25:** 54–55
Adamas formosus **38:** 81
adaptive radiation **11:** (15), **44:** 12
addax **6:** 62
Addax nasomaculatus **6:** 62
adder 48: 25; **49:** 28; **50:** 9, 50, 80–85
    African night **50:** (21)
    Albany **50:** 68
    berg **50:** 62
    common death **48:** 16
    dance of the adders **50:** 83
    death **42:** 68; **48:** 61; **50:** 10, 15
    desert mountain **50:** 68
    European **49:** 52; **50:** 109
    forest night **50:** 57
    Gaboon (Gaboon viper) **48:** 8; **50:** 9, 51, 61, 64–65
    green night **50:** 56, 56–57
    habitat **50:** 80–81
    hibernation **50:** 82–83
    horned 48: (58); **49:** 33; **50:** 9, 50, 66–69
    hornsman (many-horned) **50:** 66–69
    hunting/foraging **50:** 84
    life span **50:** 84–85
    lowland swamp **49:** 33
    many-horned 49: (73); **50:** 50, 66–69
    mating **50:** 83–84
    Namaqua dwarf **50:** 69
    night 50: 50, 56–57
    northern **49:** 55
    nose-horned **49:** (73)
    Old World **50:** 15, 51, 53
    origin of name **50:** (82)
    Peringuey's **44:** 69; **50:** 69, (69)
    plain mountain **50:** 68
    red **50:** 68
    relatives **50:** (85)
    rhombic night **49:** 33
    South African horned **49:** (73)
    southern **50:** 68
    two-striped night **50:** 57

    variations **50:** 82
    West African night **50:** 56
    see also puff adder
Adejeania vexatris **23:** 104–105
Adelotus **42:** 92
    brevis **42:** 96
Adinia xenica **38:** 84
Adolfus **45:** 59
Adrianichthyidae **38:** 64–69
Adrianichthys kruyti **38:** 65
Aechmophorus
    clarkii **14:** 16
    occidentalis **14:** 16
Aegithalidae **17:** 70, 72
Aegithalos
    caudatus **17:** 70, 80–81
    concinnus **17:** 70
Aegla **28:** 87
Aeglidae **28:** 86
Aegotheles
    archboldi **15:** 78
    cristatus **15:** 78
Aegothelidae **15:** 78, 81
Aegypius monarchus **20:** 8
Aeoliscus **39:** 50, 51
    punctulatus **39:** 50, 51
    strigatus **39:** 50, 51
Aepyceros melampus **6:** 62, 86–87
Aepyprymnus rufescens **10:** 48
Aerodramus **15:** 76, 77
    amelis **15:** 70
    brevirostris **15:** 70
    elaphra **15:** 70
    fuciphagus **15:** 77
    leucophaeus **15:** 70
    unicolor **15:** 70, 76–77
Aeromys tephromelas **7:** 34, 36
Aeropetes tulbaghia **26:** 46–47
Aeshna
    cyanea **22:** 42, 43, 48
    juncea **22:** 51
Aesopia microcephalus **39:** 94–95
Aetalion reticulatum **24:** 95
Aetalionidae (Aethalionidae) **24:** (95)
Aetapcus maculatus **39:** 71
Aetheriidae **30:** 50
Aethia
    cristatella **12:** 98
    pusilla **12:** 98
    pygmaea **12:** 98
Aethiomastacembelus **33:** (106)
Aethopyga
    christinae **19:** 94
    mystacalis **19:** 94
Aetobatus **33:** (36)
    narinari **33:** 46–49
Aetomylaeus **33:** (36)
Aetoplatea **33:** (36)
afo (African arowana) **31:** 86
Africa, national parks/reserves **2:** 16, 31; **5:** 34
Afrixalus **43:** 18, 19, (20), 22
    fornasini **43:** (20), 103
Afronandus sheljuzhkoi **40:** 57

Afrotheres **5:** (10)
Afrotheria **9:** 10
Agalychnis **43:** 32, 61, (61), 100, 104, 107; **49:** 16, 105
    calcarifer **43:** 60, 62
    callidryas **42:** 35; **43:** 54, 58–63, 65, 67
    saltator **42:** 35; **43:** 58–63, 65, 67
    spurrelli **43:** 62–63, (62)
Agama **44:** 32
    aculeata **44:** 40–41
    agama **44:** 38–41
    atra **44:** 40, (40)
    mwanzae **44:** 39, (40)
    planiceps **44:** (40)
agamas 44: 24, 25, 28, 32–37
    amphiboluroid **44:** 34
    Australian species **44:** 34
    green tree **44:** 33
    ground **44:** 40–41
    horned **44:** 32, (37)
    Mwanza flat-headed **44:** 39
    Mwanza rock **44:** (40)
    Namibian rock **44:** (40)
    origins **44:** 34
    pygmy **44:** (37)
    red-headed rock 44: 38–41
    relationships **44:** 34
    relatives **44:** (40)
    rock **44:** 32, (40)
    Southeast Asian species **44:** 35–36
    southern rock **44:** 40, (40)
    toad-headed **44:** 32, 33–34, 36, 36
    tree **44:** 32, 33, (40)
    whorl-tailed **44:** 32, 36
Agamidae **44:** 20, 25, 32, 80
agamids **49:** (71)
Agamyxis pectinifrons **37:** 78–79
Agapostemon **27:** 11
Agathemera **22:** 56–57
age, calculation of **31:** (61), **34:** (37)
Agelaius
    cyanopus **18:** 74
    phoeniceus **18:** 74, 79
    thilius **18:** 74
    tricolor **18:** 74
Agelas conifera **21:** 36
Agelena labyrinthica **29:** 94, (96), 97
Agelenidae **29:** 40, 94–97
Agelenopsis aperta **29:** 95
Agkistrodon **50:** (89), (97)
    bilineatus **50:** (89), 96
    contortrix **50:** 9, 53, 86–89
    himalayanus **50:** 50
    piscivorus **49:** 80; **50:** 55, 88–89, (89)
Aglais urticae **26:** 42–43
Aglaophenia cupressina **21:** 46–47
Aglyptodactylus **43:** 100
Agonidae **39:** 76–81
Agonostomus monticola **38:** 53
Agonus cataphractus **39:** 79
agouti 7: 8, 10, 12, 14; **8:** 28
    black **8:** 8–9
    Central American **8:** 30

common 8: <u>42–43</u>
spotted (common) **8:** <u>42–43</u>
Agouti
paca **8:** 30
taczanowskii **8:** 30
Agoutidae **7:** *12*
Agraulis vanillae **26:** *53*
agriculture **1:** 46; **2:** 21, 28, 44, 69, 77, 79
Agrilus discolor **25:** *48*
Agriocharis ocellata **11:** 44, 81
Agriotes ustulatus **25:** *42*
Agriphila tristella **26:** *103*
Agrostichthys parkeri **35:** 108
Agulla **22:** *100–101*
nixa **22:** *100*
Ahaetulla **49:** 18, (73)
nasuta **48:** 12; **49:** <u>18–19</u>
Ailuridae **2:** (99)
Ailurinae **1:** 20
Ailuroedus
crassirostris **19:** 100
melanotis **19:** 100
Ailuropoda melanoleuca **2:** 82, <u>98–101</u>
Ailurops ursinus **10:** 74
Ailurus fulgens **1:** 20, <u>30–31</u>; **2:** (99)
aimara **38:** 25
Aipysurus **50:** 44, (45)
eydouxii **50:** 48
laevis **50:** *44–45*, 46, 48–49
air sacs **12:** 47, 51, (54); **20:** (18)
aircraft, bird strikes **14:** (62)
Aix
galericulata **14:** 52, <u>76–77</u>
sponsa **14:** 52, <u>70–71</u>
Ajolote **41:** (61)
ajolote 46: <u>110–111</u>
akepa **20:** 98
akialoa, Kauai **20:** *99*
akiapola'au **20:** 98, *99*
Akysidae **37:** 93
Alaemon alaudipes **18:** 22
alarm **11:** 24, (54); **14:** 8, (12), 30; **18:** (51)
alarm calls **4:** 46, 57, 89, 100; **6:** 79; **7:** 53, 111; **8:** 51, 55, 99
American Sign Language **4:** 13, (16), 27
mechanical sounds **13:** 51; **18:** (10)
response to noise **11:** 58
social gestures **19:** (19)
unison **14:** 86–87
alates **27:** 44
Alauda
arviensis **18:** 22, <u>24–27</u>, 28–29
gulgula **18:** 22
razae **18:** 22
Alaudidae **18:** 22
Alaus corpulentus **25:** *44*
albacore **40:** 107
albatross 11: (9), (13); **12:** 30; **13:** 109
Amsterdam wandering **12:** 28, 32
Antipodes wandering **12:** (34)
black-browed **12:** 28, 62

Gough wandering **12:** 28, 32
gray-headed **12:** 28, *29*
Laysan **12:** 28
light-mantled **12:** 28
royal **12:** 28, 32
sooty **12:** 28
Tasmanian shy **12:** 28
wandering 12: 28, <u>32–37</u>
Albatrossia pectoralis **36:** 29, (30)
albino **8:** (84)
Albulidae **33:** (62)
Albuliformes **33:** 62, (62)
alburn **34:** (87)
Alburnus alburnus **34:** 81, (87)
Alca torda **12:** 98, <u>110–111</u>
Alcedinidae **14:** 100
Alcedo
atthis **14:** 100; **18:** 13
pusilla **14:** 100
Alcelaphus
buselaphus **6:** 62
lichtensteinii **6:** 62
Alces
alces **6:** 10, <u>14–19</u>
alces alces **6:** 15
alces americanus **6:** 15
alces andersoni **6:** 15
alces gigas **6:** 15
alces shirasi **6:** 15
Alcidae **12:** 98
Alcyonaria **21:** 43
Alcyonium digitatum **21:** *62*
alder psyllids **24:** *96, 96–97*
alderflies 22: <u>98–99</u>; **27:** *26–27*
European **22:** *98*
Aldrovandia affinis **33:** *96–97*
Alectoris rufa **11:** 44
Alectura lathami **11:** 44
Alepisauridae **35:** 80, <u>100–101</u>
Alepisaurus
brevirostris **35:** 100, *101*
ferox **35:** 80, 100, *100*
Alestes baremoze **38:** 30
Alestidae **38:** <u>30–31</u>
Aleuroscalabotes felinus **45:** 13
Aleuroscalobotinae **45:** 8
alevins (salmon) **35:** *54*
alewife **36:** (101)
Aleyrodidae **24:** *98–99*
alfonsino **39:** 21
algae and salamander eggs **41:** (58)
algae eater 34: 11, 12, 89, 90, 100
Borneo **34:** (92)
captive-bred **34:** 93
Chinese 32: 107, **34:** 12, 88, <u>90–93</u>
Indian **34:** 90
ornamental golden Chinese **34:** *92–93*
spotted **34:** (92)
Alicia mirabilis **21:** *58–59*
Alima **28:** *41*
Alle alle **12:** 98, <u>102–103</u>
Alleculidae **25:** (73)
Allenbatrachus grunniens **36:** *58–59*

Allenopithecus nigroviridis **4:** 40
Allgalathea elegans **28:** (89)
alligator
albino American **47:** *102*, (102)
Allegheny (hellbenders) **41:** (12), 14, 30, <u>32–35</u>
American 47: 54, 94, <u>100–105</u>
Chinese **47:** *94*, (101)
habitat **46:** 50
mutant **47:** (102)
skin tagging **47:** 105
Alligator
mississippiensis **47:** 54, 94, <u>100–105</u>
sinensis **47:** *94*, (101)
Alligatorinae **47:** 95
Allocebus trichotis **4:** 96
Allocyttus niger **39:** 24
Alloeostylus diaphanus **23:** *101*
Allophryne ruthveni **43:** (29)
Allophrynidae **42:** 10; **43:** (29)
allopreening **14:** 41
allospecies **14:** 67
Alopex lagopus see *Vulpes lagopus*
Alopias
pelagicus **32:** 83
superciliosus **32:** 83
vulpinus **32:** <u>82–83</u>, 83
Alopiidae **32:** (12), (74), <u>82–83</u>
Alopochen aegyptiacus **14:** 52, <u>64–65</u>
Alosa **36:** (101)
alosa **36:** *100–101*
fallax **36:** (101)
pseudoharengus **36:** (101)
sapidissima **36:** (101)
Alouatta
fusca **4:** 72, <u>74–75</u>
palliata **4:** 72
seniculus **4:** 72
alpaca **5:** 92, 93, 105, (106)
Alpaida cornuta **29:** *111*
Alsophis **49:** (39)
antillensis **48:** (77)
Aluterus scriptus **39:** *102*, 104
Alydidae **24:** (56)
Alytes **42:** 30, 30–31; **43:** (11)
cisternasii **42:** *30*
muletensis **42:** *31*, (31)
obstetricans **42:** <u>32–33</u>
amakihi **20:** 98
Amaralia **37:** 92
Amaryllis philatelica **28:** 45
Amarynthis meneria **26:** *36–37*
Amauris ochlea **26:** *59*
Amaurobiidae **29:** <u>52–53</u>
Amaurobius similis **29:** *52, 52–53, 53*
Amazilia rutila **16:** 44
saucerrottei **16:** 44
amazon 16: (14), 28
orange-winged **16:** 22
red-necked **19:** (33)
St. Vincent 19: 12, <u>30–33</u>
vinaceous **16:** 22
yellow-crowned **19:** 12
Amazona

amazonica **16:** 22; **19:** 28
arausiaca **19:** (33)
guildingii **19:** 12, 30–33
ochrocephala **19:** 12
ornatus **16:** 22
Amazonsprattus
scintilla **36:** 98
Ambassidae **40:** 9, 20–21
Ambassis
ambassis **40:** 20
gymnocephalus **40:** 21
productus **40:** 21
amberfish **30:** 110–111
ambergris **3:** 89
Amblonyx cinereus **1:** 32, 70–71
Ambloplites **40:** 26
cavifrons **40:** 26
interruptus **40:** 26
Amblycereus holosericeus **19:** 78
Amblycipitidae **37:** 11
Amblydoras hancocki **37:** 76–77, 79, (81)
Amblyglyphidodon aureus **40:** 82–83
Amblyodipsas **49:** 106
concolor **49:** 107
Amblyomma **29:** 31
Amblyopsidae **36:** 18, 18–19
Amblyopsis
rosae **36:** 19
spelaea **36:** 18
Amblyornis
inormatus **19:** 100
macgregoriae **19:** 100
Amblypygi **29:** 26–27
Amblyraja **33:** (26)
Amblyrhynchus cristatus **44:** 15, 29, 81, 82, 90–95
Ambulyx moorei **26:** 69
Ambystoma **41:** 56
barbouri **41:** 56
californiense **41:** 56, 67, (67)
cingulum **41:** 57
dumerilii **41:** 63
gracile **41:** 44, 57, (58)
jeffersonianum **41:** 56, 57, (57)
laterale **41:** 57, (57), 58
lermaense **41:** 63
mabeei **41:** 56
macrodactylum **41:** 56, 59
maculatum **41:** 56, 57, 58
mexicanum **41:** 27, 28, 29, 56, 59, 60–63; **46:** (111)
opacum **41:** 57, 59
platineum **41:** (57)
talpoideum **41:** 56, 58, 92
tigrinum **41:** 28–29, 56, 64–67
tremblayi **41:** (57)
Ambystomatidae **41:** 27, 29, 44, 56, 88
Ameba proteus **21:** 13, 18, 19
amebas
and allies 21: 18–21
reproduction **21:** 14
shelled, reproduction **21:** 14
tests (shells) **21:** 20, 21

Ameca splendens **38:** 106–107, 109
ameca
silvery-gold **38:** 106–107
Ameiurus **37:** 15, (21)
catus **37:** 14
melas **37:** 20
natalis **37:** 20
nebulosus **37:** 16, 20
Ameiva **45:** 82, 83, 85
ameiva **45:** 86–87
major **46:** (67)
ameiva
common (jungle racer) **45:** 82, 86–87
Martinique giant **46:** (67)
amelanism **49:** (29), 46–47, (47)
American Sign Language **4:** 13, (16), 27
Amia calva **31:** (72), 73, 80–81
Amiidae **31:** (43), (72), 75, 80
Amiiformes **31:** 72–75
Amitermes meridionalis **22:** (64)
Ammodorcas clarkei **6:** 62
Ammodytidae **39:** 28
Ammomanes deserti **18:** 22
Ammophila
alberti **27:** 13
laevigatum **27:** 80–81
pubescens **27:** 77
Ammotragus lervia **6:** 62
Amolops **42:** 17; **43:** 82, 84
Amorena undulata **30:** 35
Amphelocoma coerulescens **49:** 96
Amphibia **41:** 8
amphibians 41: 8–19
anatomy **41:** 10–11
ancestors **41:** 13–14
conservation **41:** 14–16
decline of species **41:** 16–17
definitions **41:** (8)
eggs **41:** 10
encouragement for **41:** 19
fertilization **41:** (10)
as pets **41:** 18–19
size **41:** (17)
skin breathers **41:** (12)
amphiboluroids **44:** 34
Amphiglossus **46:** 8
astrolabe **46:** 10
Amphioxiformes **31:** 24–25
Amphioxus **31:** 24
Amphipoda **28:** 34, 44–45
Amphiprion **40:** 82
frenatus **40:** 80
Amphisbaenia **46:** 102, 103
alba **46:** 104–105, 105, 107
fulginosa **46:** 102, 106–107
amphisbaenians **41:** 20, (61); **44:** 8, 9
Amphisbaenidae **46:** 102, 103, 104
Amphitrite johnstoni **21:** 97
Amphiuma **41:** 38–39
means **41:** 26–27, 38, 38–39
pholeter **41:** 39
tridactylum **41:** 39
amphiumas 41: 26, 27, 38–39

Amphiumidae **41:** 26–27, 27
amplexus **42:** (12), 13
Amulius longiceps **24:** 13
amur
white **34:** 52
Amyciaea lineatipes **29:** 69
Amycta quadrangularis **26:** 110
Amytornis
striatus **18:** 60
woodwardi **18:** 60
Anabantidae **37:** (54), **40:** 9, 58–59, 60
Anabas
cobojius **40:** 58
testudineus **40:** 58, 58, 59, 60
Anablepidae **38:** 90–93
Anableps anableps **38:** 90, 91
Anacanthobatidae **33:** (9), 26, (26)
Anacanthobatis **33:** (26)
anaconda 48: 44, 45, 64–67, 107
breeding **48:** 66–67
De Schauensee's **48:** 45, 67
green **48:** 45, 64
human victims **48:** 65–66
size **48:** 64–65
yellow **48:** 45, 67
Anaea fabius **26:** 39
Aname grandis **29:** 48–49
Anapsida **44:** 10
Anapsidacea **28:** 34, 36
Anarhynchus frontalis **13:** 8, 26–29
Anartia amathea **26:** 10, 44
Anas
acuta **14:** 52
americana **14:** 52, 72–75
clypeata **14:** 52
laysanensis **14:** 67
melleri **14:** 67
platyrhynchos **14:** 52, 66–67
rubripes **14:** 67
superciliosa **14:** 69
undulata **14:** 67
Anaspides tasmaniae **28:** 37
Anastomus lamelligerus **14:** 32
Anatidae **12:** 66; **14:** 52
Anatinae **12:** 66; **14:** 64, 80
anchoveta **36:** 90
anchovy 36: 33, 87, 90–95, 97
Argentine **36:** 94
declining stocks **36:** 95
European **36:** (88), 92–93, 94, 94
fisheries **36:** 94
Japanese **36:** 94
northern **36:** 92–93
northern Pacific **36:** 90–91, 94
Peruvian **36:** 34, 91, 94
whiskered **36:** (92)
Ancistrus **37:** 106
Ancylocranium **46:** 102
Ancyluris aulestes **26:** 34
Andara **30:** 53
Andigena laminirostris **19:** 56, 70
Andrena
haemorrhoa **27:** 92–93
nigroaenea **27:** 93

nitida **27:** *94*
Andrenidae **27:** 92–95
Andreolepis **31:** 42
Andrias
   davidianus **41:** (17), *30–31*, 31, (31)
   japonicus **41:** (17), 30–31
Androphryne rattrayi **43:** 87
Aneides **41:** 68
   aeneas **41:** 72
Anelosimus eximius **29:** (101)
Anelytropsis papillosus **45:** 13
anemonefish **40:** 9, 80, 81, (81), 82, 83
   spine-cheek **40:** 81
angel *see* angelfish
Angelastes niger **11:** 44
angelfish 32: 106, **38:** (40), **39:** (10),
   40: 23, (47), 50–53, 54, 68, (71), 79,
   100
   altum angel **40:** 78
   barred **40:** (52)
   bicolor **40:** (52)
   blackspot **40:** (52)
   blacktail **40:** (52)
   Cocos **40:** 50
   conspicuous **40:** (52)
   diamond **40:** 79
   Eibl's **40:** (52)
   emperor **40:** *52*
   Fisher's **40:** (52)
   flameback **40:** (52)
   gold-headed marble **40:** *76*
   Herald's **40:** 51
   Japanese **40:** 50, (52), (53)
   Japanese swallow **40:** 51
   keyhole **40:** 51
   king **32:** *68*
   koi **40:** 79
   lemonpeel **40:** *50–51*, 51
   Leopold's angel **40:** 78
   masked **40:** 50, 51
   midnight **40:** 23
   multicolor pygmy **40:** (52)
   orange **40:** (52)
   pearl-scaled **40:** 51
   purplemask **40:** (52)
   pygmy **40:** (52)
   regal **31:** *12*, **40:** *50*
   resplendent **40:** 50, (52)
   rusty pygmy **40:** 51
   scalare **40:** 78
   silver **40:** 78
   yellowhead **40:** 50
anglerfish 36: 8, (10), 11, 12, 13, (14),
   60, 64, 66, 67, 73
   black **32:** 107
   bulbous **36:** 83
   clown **36:** 67, *67*
   deep-sea 36: 74–83
   fanfin **36:** 82
   humpback **36:** *74*
   Mediterranean **32:** 107
   nonparasitic male **36:** 81, 83
   parasitic male **36:** (80), *80*, 81, 82, 83
   two-rod **36:** 83

warty **36:** 67, *67*
   whipnose **36:** *76, 80–81*, 81, 83
Angolosaurus **45:** 98, 100
Anguidae **44:** 25, (26), 28, (105); **45:** *99*;
   46: 50–55
Anguilla **33:** *66*, 91
   anguilla **33:** 60, 64, *66–67*, 68, *68*,
   71, **39:** 10
   rostrata **33:** 64, 70; **39:** 10
Anguillidae **33:** (62), 68–73
Anguilliformes **33:** 62, (62)
Anguinae **46:** 50, 51–52
Anguis
   cephallonica **46:** 51, (56)
   fragilis **44:** (26); **46:** 50, 51, 56–59,
   (61)
angwantibo **4:** 106, *106*
Anhinga **12:** 44
ani **20:** 47
   greater **20:** 46
Aniculus elegans **28:** *94–95*
Aniliidae **48:** 9, 28, 31, (35)
Anilius scytale **48:** 9, 28, *30*, 31, 34–35
animal farming **2:** (97)
animals
   animal kingdom 21: 28–33
   classification **21:** (28)
   diploblastic **21:** 30, 42
   first 21: 34–35
   larval types **21:** 31–32
   multicellular **21:** 30–31
   spiny-skinned 30: 90–93
   symmetry in **21:** 30
   triploblastic **21:** 30–31
Anisochromis
   kenyae **40:** 22
   mascarenensis **40:** 22
anisodactylism **18:** *18*, (18)
Anisomorpha buprestoides **22:** *52–53*,
   57
Anisoptera **22:** 42
Anisozygoptera **22:** 42
Annelida **21:** 32, 77, 94–97
   fossils **21:** 96–97
   locomotion **21:** (96)
Annie **40:** 22
Anniella **44:** (26); **46:** (55), (60), (61)
   geronomensis **46:** 54, 64–65
   pulchra **46:** 54, 64–65
Anniellinae **46:** 50, 54
anoa, lowland **6:** 62
Anobiidae **25:** (53)
Anobium punctatum **25:** (53)
Anodonta cygnea **30:** *60*
Anodonthyla **42:** 104
Anodontiglanis dahli **37:** 68
Anodorhynchus hyacinthinus **19:** 12
Anodus
   elongatus **38:** 16
   orinocensis **38:** 16
anole 44: 24, 25, 81; **49:** 105, *105*
   Cuban **44:** 106, (107)
   Cuban brown **44:** *80*
   green 44: 106–107

Anolis **44:** 80, 81; **48:** 46
   carolinensis **44:** 106–107
   sagrei **44:** *80*, 106, (107)
Anomalepidae **48:** 9, 18, 19, (35)
Anomalepis **48:** 18
Anomalopidae **35:** (88), **39:** 9, 16–21
Anomalops katoptron **39:** 17
Anomalopus **46:** 11
Anomaluridae **7:** *12*, (19)
Anomiidae **30:** 59
Anomochilidae **48:** 9, 28, 30
Anomochilus **48:** 28, 30
Anomura **28:** 56, 58
Anopheles **23:** (49)
Anopia **21:** 77
Anoplogaster
   brachycera **39:** 16
   cornuta **39:** 8, 16, *16*, *17*
Anoplogastridae **39:** 16–21
Anoplopomatidae **39:** 53
Anops **46:** 102
anostomid
   big-mouthed **38:** 20
   funny-mouthed **38:** 20
   gold-ringed **38:** 20
   peculiar-mouthed **38:** 20
Anostomidae **38:** 20–21
Anostomus anostomus **38:** *20*, 21
Anostraca **28:** 16–18
Anotheca spinosa **43:** 39, *39*, (76)
Anotopteridae **35:** 80, 98–99
Anotopterus
   nikparini **35:** 99
   pharao **35:** 99
   vorax **35:** 99
Anous
   minutus **12:** 74
   stolidus **12:** 74
   tenuirostris **12:** 74
Anoxypristis **33:** 16, (16)
   cuspidata **32:** 108, 110
Anser
   anser **14:** 52
   brachyrhynchus **14:** 52
   caerulescens **14:** 52
   indicus **14:** 52
Anseranas semipalmata **14:** 52
Anserinae **14:** 80
Ansonia **42:** 56, 57, 60
ant lions **22:** 90, 95–96
Antaresia **48:** 82
   childreni **48:** 84–85
   maculosus **48:** *15*
   perthensis **48:** 80, 85
antbird 19: 65, 72–75, (82)
   chestnut-backed **19:** 72, *74*
   white-plumed **19:** 72, *72–73*, 75
anteater 1: 9, 14; **9:** 64–67
   banded *see* numbat
   giant 9: *64*, 65, 68–71
   marsupial *see* numbat
   short-nosed spiny *see* echidna, short-
beaked
   silky **9:** 65, 66

Antechinomys laniger **10**: 27
antechinus 10: 11, 25, 20,(25), 27
  agile **10**: 41
  brown 10: 27, 40–41
  dusky **10**: 27
  sandstone **10**: 27
Antechinus
  stuartii **10**: 27, 40–41
  swainsonii **10**: 27
Antedon bifida **30**: *94*
antelope 5: 10, *11*, 12, 13; **6**: 60–63
  American pronghorn **2**: 26; **6**: 63
  four-horned **6**: 60, 62
  pronghorn 6: *60*, 62, (63), 110–111
  pygmy **6**: 60, 62
  roan **6**: 62
  royal **6**: *60*, 62
  sable **6**: 62
  Tibetan **6**: 62
Antennariidae **36**: 64–69
Antennarius **36**: 66
  avalonis **36**: 64
  biocellatus **36**: 64
  commerson **36**: 66
  maculatus **36**: 67, *67*
  multiocellatus **36**: 64
  sanguineus **36**: *14–15*
Anthaxia nitidula **25**: *46*
Antheraea
  eucalypti **26**: *72*
  oculea **26**: *73*
Anthia hexasticta **25**: *18–19*
Anthias **40**: 15
  squamipinnis **40**: *16*
Anthidium manicatum **27**: *89*
Anthochaera paradoxa **20**: 88
Anthocoridae **24**: (35)
Anthonomus grandis **25**: (110)
Anthophora plumipes **27**: *96–97*
Anthophoridae **27**: 96–101
Anthozoa **21**: 43, 62–67
Anthracoceros
  coronatus **19**: 48
  malayanus **19**: 48
anthrax **23**: 103, 108
Anthrax seriepunctata **23**: *70*
Anthrenus verbasci **25**: 53
Anthreptes
  malacensis **19**: 94
  reichenowi **19**: 94
Anthribidae **25**: 104
Anthuridea **28**: 34
Anthus
  campestris **17**: 44
  leucophrys **17**: 44
  novaeseelandiae **17**: 44
  petrosus **17**: 44, 50–51
  pratensis **17**: 44, 50; **20**: (48)
  rubescens **17**: 44
  spinoletta **17**: 44, 50
  spragueii **17**: 44
  trivialis **17**: 44
Antiantha expansa **24**: *92–93*
Antidorcas marsupialis **6**: 62, 96–97

Antigonia **39**: *24*
  capros **39**: 25, *25*
  indica **39**: 25
Antilocapra americana **6**: 62, 110–111
Antilocapridae **6**: 63, 110
Antilope cervicapra **6**: 62
anting (behavior) **18**: (92)
Antipatharia **21**: 43
antishark net **32**: 63
antivenom **50**: (11), 16, 61
antlers **6**: 9, 12, (15), 24–25, 34, 38, 40, *60*
antpitta **19**: 72, (74)
  chestnut-crowned **19**: 72
  tawny **19**: 72
ants 9: 64, 66, 69, 76; **27**: 8–13, 40–57; **44**: 48, 84, 103
  alates **27**: 44
  army **27**: 54–56
  bullet **27**: *41, 56–57*
  caterpillars and **26**: 31–33, 36–37
  cow-killer velvet **27**: *38–39*
  Cremastocheilus beetles inhabiting ants' nests **25**: (86)
  crickets living in ants' nests **23**: (19)
  defense, chemical **27**: 42
  driver **27**: *45*
  fire **49**: (103)
  green tree **27**: *48–49*
  harvester **27**: *40–41*, 52
  honeydew supplies **27**: (48)
  honeypot **27**: 52
  jet black **27**: *47*
  leaf-cutting **27**: *44*, 50–51
  nests **27**: 44–47, 51–52
  plants and **27**: (46)
  red **27**: *49*
  scent trails **27**: (45)
  slave-making **27**: 49–50
  sociability **27**: 40
  tandem running **27**: (45)
  termite-slaying **27**: 43
  treehoppers and **24**: (93)
  velvet **27**: 38–39
  weaver **27**: *40–41, 42–43*, 52–54
  western harvester **27**: *52*
  white *see* termites
antshrike 19: 72, 73, (74)
  barred 19: 72, 76–79
  black **19**: 72
  bluish-slate **19**: 72, 74
  giant **19**: 72
  great **19**: 72
antthrush **19**: 72, (74)
  rufous-breasted **19**: 72
antvireo **19**: 72, (74)
  plain **19**: 72
antwren **19**: 72, 74, (74)
  short-billed **19**: 72
  streaked **19**: 72
  white-flanked **19**: 72
Anura **41**: 8; **42**: 8, 10; **43**: 100
anurans **42**: (8)
Anyphaena accentuata **29**: *42–43*, (81)

Anyphaenidae **29**: (81)
Aonyx
  capensis **1**: 32
  cinereus see Amblonyx cinereus
  congicus **1**: 32
Aorichthys
  aor **37**: 26, 27
  seenghala **37**: 26, 27
Aotus
  nigriceps **4**: 72
  trivirgatus **4**: 72, 84–85
Apalharpactes **19**: 34
  mackloti **19**: 34
  reinwardtii **19**: 34
Apaloderma **19**: 34
  aequatoriale **19**: 34
  narina **19**: 34
Apalone spinifera **47**: 60–61
apapane **16**: 76, *76*; **20**: 98
Aparallactinae **49**: 106
Aparallactus **49**: 106, 107, 108–109
Apaturinae **26**: 40
ape
  ape family 4: 12–13
  Barbary *see* macaque, Barbary
  red *see* orangutan
Apeltes quadracus **39**: 34
Aphanius **38**: (89)
  dispar **38**: 86
  fasciatus **38**: 89
  mento **38**: 89
Aphasmida **21**: 77
Aphelocoma coerulescens **18**: 90
Aphididae **24**: 14, 100–105
aphids 24: 14, 100–105; **25**: 57; **27**: 49
  bean **24**: *102*
  cabbage **24**: *105*
  defense **24**: 103, 105
  feeding **24**: 100–101, 102–103
  life cycle **24**: 101–102
  lupin **24**: *14*
  peach-potato **24**: *100*
  rose-root **24**: *103*
Aphis fabae **24**: *102*
  breeding **24**: 101–102
Aphonopelma seemannii **29**: *46–47*
Aphredoderus sayanus **36**: 16, 20–21
Aphrocallistes vastus **21**: *39*
Aphrodes bifasciatus **24**: 86
Aphrodite aculeata **21**: *99*
Aphyocharax
  anchovia **38**: 35
  anisitsi **38**: *34–35*, 35
  halecinus **38**: 35
Aphyonidae **36**: 26, 27
Aphyonus gelatinosus **36**: 27
Aphyosemion **38**: (79), 81
  bivattatum **38**: *78*
  gardneri **38**: 80, *82–83*
  gardneri nigerianum **38**: 80
  ossingi **38**: *80–81*
Apicomplexa **21**: 13, 26–27
Apidae **27**: 102–113
Apiomeris flaviventris **24**: *40*

Apioscelis bulbosa **23:** *33*
Apis
　mellifera **27:** *102, 112*
　mellifera scutellata **27:** (111)
Apistogramma **40:** 70
Apistus carinatus **39:** 65
Aplacophora **30:** 9
Aploactinidae **39:** 11, <u>68–71</u>
Aploactisoma milesii **39:** 70
Aplocheilichthys **38:** 105
　brichardi **38:** 103
　rancureli **38:** *104*
　spilauchen **38:** 103
Aplocheilidae **38:** <u>78–83</u>
Aplocheilus **38:** 81
　lineatus **38:** *79*
Aplochiton **35:** (34)
　taeniatus **35:** 34
Aplochitoninae **35:** (34)
Aplodinotus grunniens **40:** 19
Aplodontia rufa **7:** 28
Aplodontidae **7:** *12*, 28, 29
Aplonis
　atrifusca **18:** 82
　metallica **18:** 82
Aplopeltura **49:** 90, 91
　boa **49:** 16, 90
Aplysia punctata **30:** *36–37*
Aplysiomorpha **30:** 18, 37
Apocrita **27:** 8, 10–11, *12*
Apoda **41:** 20
Apodemus sylvaticus **7:** <u>78–79</u>
Apoderus coryli **25:** *109*
Apodidae **15:** 70
Apodora papuana **48:** 82
Apogon
　imberbis **40:** 30
　maculatus **40:** 30, *30*
Apogonidae **40:** <u>30–31</u>
apollos (swallowtail butterflies)
　26: <u>16–21</u>
apostlebird **20:** 100
Appaloosa **5:** 59
Aprasia **45:** 50
Aprosmictus erythropterus **16:** 22
Apseudomorpha **28:** 34
Aptenodytes
　forsteri **12:** 8, <u>12–17</u>
　patagonicus **12:** 8, 12; **13:** 109
Aptera fusca **22:** *70*
Apteronotidae **31:** (108), **33:** 100, (100), 101
Apteronotus **33:** 101
　albifrons **33:** <u>102–103</u>
Apterygidae **11:** 16
Apterygota **22:** 30
Apteryx **20:** (14), 42
　australis **11:** 16, <u>36–39</u>
　haastii **11:** 16
　owenii **11:** 16
Aptychotrema **33:** (27)
Apus
　apus **15:** 70, <u>72–75</u>
　barbatus **15:** 70

　caffer **15:** 70
　pacificus **15:** 70
　pallidus **15:** 70
Aquila
　chrysaetos **11:** 14; **15:** 8, <u>44–49</u>
　heliaca **16:** 100
　verreauxii **15:** 8
Ara
　ararauna **19:** 12
　chloroptera **19:** *24–25*, 28
　cyanoptera **19:** (29)
　macao **16:** 22; **19:** 12, <u>24–29</u>
Aracana aurita **39:** 106
aracari
　fiery-billed **19:** 56
　green 19: 56, <u>66–67</u>
　lettered **19:** 56, *59–60*
Arachnida **29:** 8, 9
arachnids 29: <u>14–15</u>
　anatomy **29:** 14–15
Arachnocoris **24:** 36–37
arachnology **21:** (33)
Arachnothera
　flavigaster **19:** 94
　magna **19:** 94, <u>98–99</u>
　robusta **19:** 94
Aradidae **24:** <u>50–51</u>
Aradus depressus **24:** 50
Arafura granulatus **48:** (41)
Aral Sea **35:** (70)
Aramidae **14:** 82
Aramus guarauna **14:** 82, <u>90–91</u>
Araneidae **29:** <u>106–111</u>
Araneomorphae **29:** 38, 41
Araneus **29:** *44*
　diadematus **29:** *110–111*
arapaima 31: 82, 83, 86, <u>88–91</u>
Arapaima gigas **31:** 82, 86, <u>88–91</u>
Aratinga
　auricapilla **16:** 32–34
　jandaya **16:** 32
　solstitialis **16:** 22, <u>32–35</u>
Arcas imperialis **26:** *31*
Archaeobatrachia **42:** 10, 34
archaeocetes **3:** 56
Archaeogastropoda **30:** 18, <u>22–25</u>
Archaeonycteris **1:** *8*
Archaeopteryx **11:** *10*, (10); **20:** (67)
Archboldia
　papuensis **19:** 100
　sanfordi **19:** 100
Archelon **47:** 9
Archeognatha **22:** 30, (37)
archerfish 38: 50, **40:** 9, <u>44–45</u>
　banded **40:** 45
　common **40:** 45
　largescale **40:** *44*, 45
　primitive **40:** 45
　smallscale **40:** 45
　western **40:** 45
Archiacanthocephala **21:** 77
Archiannelida **21:** 77, 94, 96
Archidoris pseudoargus **30:** *38*
Archilochus

　alexandri **16:** 44
　colubris **16:** 44, <u>52–55</u>
Archocentrus nigrofasciatus **40:** 70
Archosargus probatocephalus **40:** 40
Archosauria **44:** 18
Arcidae **30:** 50, 53
Arctia caja **26:** *88, 90*
Arctictis binturong **1:** 88
Arctiidae **26:** <u>88–91</u>
　sound production **26:** (91)
Arctocebus **4:** 106
　aureus **4:** 106
　calabarensis **4:** 106
Arctocephalus
　gazella **3:** 9
　pusillus **3:** 9, <u>16–17</u>
Arctogalidia trivirgata **1:** 88
Arctonyx collaris **1:** 32
Arctophilornis africana **14:** 96
Arctozenus risso **35:** 99
Ardea
　cinerea **14:** 20, <u>24–27</u>
　goliath **14:** 20, 65
　herodias **14:** 20; **18:** 80
　purpurea **14:** 20
Ardeidae **14:** 20
Ardeotis
　arabis **11:** 84
　australis **11:** 84, <u>86–87</u>
　kori **11:** 84, 86; **17:** (12)
　nigriceps **11:** 84
Arenaria **13:** (70)
　interpres **13:** 30, <u>68–71</u>
Arenophryne **42:** 92
　rotunda **42:** 92, 95, 97, <u>98–99</u>; **43:** 16
Argentina
　sialis **35:** 22
　silus **35:** 22, *22, 23*
　sphyraena **35:** 23
argentine 35: 8, *8–9*, <u>22–23</u>, 101
　greater **35:** 22, *22, 23*
　North Pacific **35:** 22
Argentinidae **35:** <u>22–23</u>
Argentinosaurus huinculensis **3:** 98
Argiope
　argentata **29:** *106–107*
　bruennichi **29:** 106
　versicolor **29:** <u>44–45</u>
Argonauta **30:** 72
Argonauta
　argo **30:** (89)
　nodosa **30:** *89*
argonauts **30:** 84, (89)
Argopecten irradians **30:** *8*
argus
　crested **11:** 44
　great **11:** 44
Argusianus **11:** 45
　argus **11:** 44
Argynnis paphia **26:** *12*
Argyroneta aquatica **29:** (110)
Argyropelecus
　aculeatus **38:** 29

affinis **35**: *80–81, 90, 91*
gigas **35**: *90*
hemigymnus **38**: *29*
Arhynchobatidae **33**: (9), 26, (26)
Arhynchobatis **33**: (26)
Arhynchobdellae **21**: 94
Ariidae **37**: 64–65
Arilus **24**: *42–43*
Ariolimax californicus **30**: *49*
Ariopsis felis **37**: *64*
Aristotle **21**: 8, (28)
Aristotle's lantern **30**: 93, 106
Arius **37**: 64
fuscus **37**: *65*
graeffei **37**: *65*
jatius **37**: *65*
maculatus **37**: *65*
sciurus **37**: *65*
seemanni **37**: *65*
truncatus **37**: *65*
Arixeniina **22**: (59)
Arjin Shan Lop Nur Nature Reserve
5: (102)
Armadillidium vulgare **28**: *46*
armadillo 9: 64–67
common **9**: 65
giant **9**: 65
lesser fairy **9**: 65
long-nosed (nine-banded)
9: 65, 74–77
nine-banded 9: 65, 74–77
southern naked-tailed **9**: 65, *66*
three-banded **9**: 64
Armophorea **21**: 13
armorhead 40: 54–55
pelagic **40**: 55
Arnoldichthys spilopterus **38**: *31*
Aromobates **43**: 68
nocturnus **43**: 68, 72–73
Arothron **39**: 109
hispidus **39**: 109
meleagris **39**: 109
nigropunctatus **39**: 109
stellatus **39**: 109
arowana 31: 82, 83, 97, 99, 101, 105
African (Nile) 31: 83, 86–87
black **31**: 83, 93, 95
feeding habits **31**: (94)
as food in Amazonia **31**: (95)
silver **31**: 83, *84–85, 92*, 93, *93, 94,
95, 95*
South American 31: 86, 92–95
Arrhenodes minutus **25**: *112*
arrowtail **36**: 52
Artamidae **20**: 100
Artamus
cyanopterus **20**: 100
fuscus **20**: 100
maximus **20**: 100
minor **20**: 100
monachus **20**: 100
personatus **20**: 100, 108–109
Artemia salina **28**: *19*
Arthroleptella **43**: 82, 87

Arthroleptidae **42**: 10; **43**: 12, (15), (17)
Arthroleptides **43**: 87
Arthroleptinae **43**: 12
Arthroleptis **43**: 12
adelphus **43**: *12, 13*
affinis **43**: *14*
wahlbergi **43**: 12–15
Arthropoda **21**: 32
arthropods 22: 8–13
anatomy **22**: 9–11
classification **22**: 8
relatives **22**: 12
Articulata **21**: 69, 70, 71; **30**: 94–97
artiodactyl **1**: *8*; **8**: 102
Artiodactyla **1**: *10*; **5**: (10), 12, 66; **6**: 52
Arvicola terrestris **7**: 98–99
Ascalopteryx **22**: 97
Ascaphidae **42**: 10
Ascaphus
montanus **42**: 16, (17)
truei **41**: 16, 42–44, (45); **42**: 16–17,
45
Ascaris suum **21**: *90*
Ascidiacea **31**: 22–23
Ascidinidae **39**: 29
Asellota **28**: 34
Asian bumblebee (catfish) **37**: 27, 28,
29, 89
Asilidae **23**: 62–67
Asilus crabroniformis **23**: 66–67
Asio otus **15**: 50
asity **20**: 74
Schlegel's **20**: 74
velvet **20**: 74
asp **50**: (78), (85)
Bibron's burrowing (Bibron's stiletto
snake) **49**: 106, 110–111
Duerden's burrowing **49**: *107*
Aspatha gulans **19**: 42
Aspidelaps **50**: 14, (25)
Aspidites
maculosus **48**: (105)
melanocephalus **48**: 80, 86–87; **50**:
(35)
ramsayi **48**: 80, *81*, 86, (105)
Aspidomorpha punctata **25**: *100*
Aspidontus taeniatus taeniatus **40**: *90,
91*
Aspidoras **37**: 99
Aspilia **4**: (29)
Aspitrigla cuculus **39**: *56*
Aspredinichthys **37**: 92
Aspredinidae **37**: 92–93
Aspredo **37**: 92
aspredo **37**: *92*
Asprocottus abyssalis **39**: 77
ass 5: 42, (44)
African **5**: 42
Asian wild 5: 56–57
Asiatic **5**: 42
domestic **5**: 57
Assa **42**: 92
darlingtoni **42**: 92, *97*; **43**: (11)
Astacidea **28**: 56, 70–79

Astacopis gouldi **28**: (71)
astartes **30**: 62
Asteroidea **30**: 91, 98
Asterophryinae **42**: 104
Asterophrys turpicula **42**: 104
Asterorhombus fijiensis **39**: (90)
Asterozoa **30**: 91, 98–103
Astraea undosa **30**: *24*
Astrapia
mayeri **19**: 106
splendidissima **19**: 106
astrapia
ribbon-tailed **19**: 106
splendid **19**: 106
Astroma **23**: (33)
Astronesthes gemmifer **35**: (88), *88–89*
Astroscopus **31**: (108)
Astrotia stokesii **50**: (45), 46
Astyanax
jordani **38**: 8, 35, 36, *36*
mexicanus **38**: 8, 35, 36
Astylosterninae **43**: 12, (15)
Astylosternus **43**: 12
Ateleopodidae **35**: 78
Ateleopodiformes **35**: 78, (79)
Atelerix
albiventris **9**: 12, 20–21
algirus **9**: 12, *13*
frontalis **9**: 21
Ateles
belzebuth **4**: 72
geoffroyi **4**: 72, 76–77
Atelopus **41**: 17; **42**: 56, 57, 58, 60,
74–75; **43**: 73
flavescens **42**: 74
ignescens **42**: 57, 74
oxyrhynchus **42**: 60
varius **42**: 74
zeteki **42**: 58, *75*, (75)
Athecanephria **21**: 77
Athene noctua **15**: 50
Atherina presbyter **38**: *60*, 62
Atherinidae **38**: 50, 52, 56, 60–63
Atherinopsis californiensis **38**: 63
Atheris **50**: 91
acuminata **50**: 59
ceratophorus **50**: 52, 59
hispida **50**: 9, 50, 52, 58–59
katangensis **50**: 59
nitchei **50**: *51*
Atherurus
africanus **8**: 12
macrourus **8**: 12
Atilax paludinosus **1**: 98
Atlantoraja **33**: (26)
Atlapetes tricolor **16**: 62
Atopochilus **37**: 73
Atopocottus tribranchius **39**: 77
Atractaspididae **48**: 9, 15; **49**: 106
Atractaspininae **49**: 106
Atractaspis **49**: 106, 110; **50**: 9, (21),
(35)
bibroni **49**: 110–111
duerdeni **49**: *107*, 111

irregularis **49:** 110
microlepidota **49:** 110
Atractosteus **31:** 72, 74, (77)
  spatula **31:** 74, <u>76–77</u>
  tristoechus **31:** *74–75*, (77)
  tropicus **31:** 74, (77)
Atrax robustus **29:** *48*
Atrichornis
  clamosus **11:** 104, <u>110–111</u>
  rufescens **11:** 104
Atrichornithidae **11:** 104
Atrophacanthus japonicus **39:** 99
Atta **27:** 51
  bisphaerica **27:** *51*
  cephalotes **27:** *44, 50–51*
attacks **38:** 12
  by eels **33:** (81)
  by sawfish **33:** 17
  by sharks **32:** (24–25), *24–25*, (54), (89), **33:** 34, 36
  on stingrays **33:** 34, 36
Attacus
  atlas **22:** 11
  edwardsi **26:** *70*
Attelabus nitens **25:** 109
Atteva punctella **26:** 112
Atyidae **28:** (64)
Atympanophrys **42:** 34
Atypidae **29:** <u>50–51</u>
Atypus affinis **29:** *50*
Aubria **43:** 82
Auchenipterichthys thoracatus **37:** *82–83*
Auchenipteridae **37:** <u>82–83</u>
Auchenoglanis
  ngamensis **37:** 29
  occidentalis **37:** *24–25*, 29
Auchenorrhyncha **24:** 8, 10, 12, 13
auk 12: 31, 74, 83, 103
  auk family 12: <u>98–101</u>
  great **12:** 101
  little *see* dovekie
auklet **12:** 31, 98, 101
  Cassin's **12:** 98, 101
  crested **12:** 98, *98*
  least **12:** 98, 101
  parakeet **12:** 98, *100*
  rhinoceros **12:** 98, *98*, 101
  whiskered **12:** 98, *98*
Aulacorhynchus prasinus **19:** 56
Aulastomatomorpha **35:** *9*
Aulichthys japonicus **39:** 29
Aulopiformes **35:** 80
  families summary **35:** (79)
Aulopus purpurissatus **35:** *78–79*
Aulorhynchidae **39:** 10, 26, <u>28–29</u>
Aulorhynchus flavidus **39:** *28*, 29
Aulostomidae **39:** 11, 26, <u>48–49</u>
Aulostomus
  chinensis **39:** *48*, 49
  maculatus **39:** *48–49*, 49
  strigosus **39:** 49
Aulotrachichthys **39:** 21
Aurelia aurita **21:** *50*

auritus **40:** 74
aurochs **6:** 63
Australia, mammals introduced into **2:** 80; **5:** (97); **8:** 72
Austrelaps superbus **50:** 15
Austrodromidia octodentata **28:** *111*
Austrolebias **38:** (79)
Austropotamobius pallipes **28:** *75*
Autographa gamma **26:** *95*
autohemorrhagy **48:** 78
Automolus dorsalis **20:** 80
autotomy **46:** (17)
  caudal **44:** 22, 30, 81
autotrophs **21:** 9
Avahi
  laniger **4:** 96
  occidentalis **4:** 96
aversion, innate **50:** (24), 26
avocet 13: 29, <u>72–75</u>, (74), (84)
  American **13:** 72, *73*
  Andean **13:** 72
  pied 13: 72, <u>76–81</u>, 84, 85; **18:** (56)
  red-necked **13:** 72
Avocettina **33:** 87
  gilli **33:** 87
  infans **33:** 86
Axis
  axis **6:** 10
  porcinus **6:** 10
axolotl 41: 18, 27, *28*, 29, 56, 58, 59, <u>60–63</u>; **46:** (111)
Axolotus pisciformis **41:** 61
aye-aye 4: 96, 97, <u>102–103</u>
Aythini **12:** 66
Aythya **12:** 70; **14:** 53
  americana **14:** 72
  ferina **14:** 52
  fuligula **14:** 52
  marila **12:** 66
ayu **35:** *26*, 29, *29*
  Ryukyu **35:** 29
Azemiopinae **50:** 50, (57)
Azemiops feae **50:** 50, *57*, (57)

B

babbler **17:** 60; **18:** (50)
babirusa 5: 74, 75, <u>86–87</u>
baboon 4: 8, 40, 42, 42–43
  Chacma **4:** *56–57*
  gelada 4: 40, 42, 43, <u>62–63</u>

hamadryas 4: 40, 43, <u>58–59</u>
  long-tailed *see* mangabey
  olive **4:** *10–11*
  sacred (hamadryas) **4:** 40, 43, <u>58–59</u>
  savanna 4: 40, 42–43, <u>54–57</u>
  yellow (savanna) **4:** 40, 42–43, <u>54–57</u>
Babyrousa babyrussa **5:** 74, <u>86–87</u>
Baccha obscuripennis **23:** 77
Bachia **45:** (85)
backswimmers 24: <u>24–27</u>
badger 1: 34
  American 1: 32, <u>76–77</u>; **2:** (60)
  European 1: 32, 34, *35*, <u>78–81</u>
  hog **1:** 32
  honey 1: 32, <u>82–83</u>
  Indian ferret **1:** 32
  Palawan stink **1:** 32
Badis badis **40:** 56, *57*
Baetis rhodani **22:** *39*
Bagarinae **37:** (51)
Bagarius yarelli **37:** (51)
Bagrichthys
  hypselopterus **37:** *26–27*
  macracanthus **37:** 27
bagrid *see* catfish, bagrid
Bagridae **37:** <u>22–29</u>, 89
Bagroides melapterus **37:** 27
Bagrus docmak **37:** 25
baiser **35:** 73
"bait-balling" **36:** 102
baitfish **34:** (79)
Baja California **46:** (110)
bak wan gam si **34:** (65)
bak wan san ue **34:** (65)
Balaena mysticetus **3:** 55, <u>110–111</u>
Balaeniceps rex **12:** 45; **14:** 32
Balaenicipitidae **14:** 32
Balaenoptera
  acutorostrata **3:** 55, <u>106–107</u>
  bonaerensis **3:** 107
  musculus **3:** 55, <u>98–101</u>
Balanoglossus **21:** 79
Balantiocheilos **34:** <u>54–57</u>
  melanopterus **34:** 57
Balanus nubilis **28:** 25
Baleaphryne muletensis **42:** (31)
Balearica pavonina **14:** 82, <u>88–89</u>
Balearicinae **14:** 88
Balistapus undulatus **39:** *101*, 103
Balistes vetula **39:** 103
Balistidae **39:** 8, 11, 96, <u>100–105</u>
Balistoides conspicillum **39:** 103, *104–105*
Balitoridae **34:** 9, 10, 14, 15, (88), 89, 108
bamboo **2:** 98–99, 100; **4:** 97
bandfish
  crested **35:** 104
bandicoot 10: (10), 24, 25, 27
  eastern barred **10:** *8–9*
  giant **10:** 27
  golden **10:** 27
  large short-nosed (northern) **10:** <u>46–47</u>

long-nosed **10**: 27
mouse **10**: 27
northern 10: _46–47_
northern brown (northern)
   10: 27, _46–47_
pig-footed **10**: 27
rabbit-eared _see_ bilby
Raffray's **10**: 27
rufous spiny **10**: 27
Seram Island **10**: 27
striped **10**: 27
western barred **10**: 27
banteng **6**: 62
barb 34: 20, _22–29_, 81, **37**: 8
African blind **34**: 24
Asoka **34**: 24
banded **34**: 27
Bandula **34**: 22, 23, 24
black ruby **34**: 22, 24
blind cave **34**: (28)
cherry **34**: 22, _23_, 24
Chinese **34**: 28, 29
clown **34**: _29_
Congo blind **34**: (28)
Cuming's **34**: 22, 24, (27)
dwarf **34**: 28
endangered **34**: (29)
five-banded **34**: 27
golden **34**: 28, _28_, 29
golden dwarf **34**: 29
golden tinfoil **34**: _27_
green **34**: 28, 29
half-striped **34**: 29
hex **34**: 27
Indian glass **38**: 29
large-scaled **34**: 19
leaping **34**: _18–19_, **38**: 29
lemonfin **34**: _12–13_
Martenstyn's **34**: 24
Puntius **34**: (26)
rosy **34**: _22_, (27)
round-banded **34**: 27
six-banded **34**: 27
Stoliczk's **34**: (27)
striped **34**: 27
Sumatra **34**: _24_, 26
tic-tac-toe **34**: (27)
ticto **34**: (27)
tiger **34**: 20, 24, _24–25_, 25, 26, 27
tinfoil **34**: 13, 26, _26_, 28
barbel 34: 25, 88, **36**: 24
Caspian **34**: 31
Caucasian **34**: 31
Euboean **34**: 31
European 34: 24, 27, _30–31_
Greek **34**: 31
Iberian **34**: 31
Mediterranean **34**: 31
Peloponnesian **34**: 31
Po **34**: 31
red-tailed **34**: 31
southern **34**: 31
Thracian **34**: 31

Turkish **34**: 31
barbet 19: _56–59_
black-spotted **19**: 56
blue-throated **19**: 56
crested **19**: 56
double-toothed **19**: 56, _57_
great **19**: 56
many-colored **19**: 56, _57_
naked-faced **19**: 56
prong-billed **19**: 56, 70
red-and-yellow **19**: 56, _57_
red-headed 19: 56, _68–69_
toucan 19: 56, _70–71_
Barbodes **34**: 24, 25, (26), 28
schwanenfeldii **34**: 26
see also Barbus
Barbonymus **34**: 28
schwanenfeldii **34**: _13_
see also Barbus
Barbourisiidae **39**: _12–15_
Barbourula **42**: 24, 26
Barbousia rufa **39**: 13
barbudofish **35**: 110
Barbus **34**: _22–29_, (26), 27
albanicus **34**: 31
asoka **34**: 24
bandula **34**: 22
(Barbodes) schwanenfeldii **34**: _26_, 28
barbus **34**: 24, 25, 27, _30–31_, **37**: 8
bocagei **34**: 31
brachycephalus **34**: 31
caninus **34**: 31
ciscaucasicus **34**: 31
comizo **34**: 31
cumingii **34**: 22
cyclolepis **34**: 31
esocinus **34**: 19
euboicus **34**: 31
graecus **34**: 31
guiraonis **34**: 31
haasi **34**: 31
martenstyni **34**: 24
meridionalis **34**: 31
microcephalus **34**: 31
nigrofasciatus **34**: 22
"Odessa" **34**: (27)
peloponnesius **34**: 31
plebejus **34**: 31
prespensis **34**: 31
(Puntius) conchonius **34**: _22_, (27)
(Puntius) cumingi **34**: (27)
(Puntius) everetti **34**: _29_
(Puntius) gelius **34**: 29
(Puntius) hexazona **34**: 27
(Puntius) johorensis **34**: 27
(Puntius) partipentazona **34**: 27
(Puntius) pentazona **34**: 27
(Puntius) rhomboocelatus **34**: 27
(Puntius) semifasciolatus **34**: 28, 29
(Puntius) stoliczkanus **34**: (27)
(Puntius) tetrazona **34**: 20, _24–25_, 26
(Puntius) ticto **34**: (27)
(Puntius) titteya **34**: _23_
schuberti **34**: _28_

sclateri **34**: 31
steindachneri **34**: 31
stoliczkae **34**: (27)
tetrazona **34**: 24
ticto stoliczkanus **34**: (27)
ticto ticto **34**: (27)
titteya **34**: 22
tyberinus **34**: 31
bare-eye **19**: 72
black-spotted **19**: 72, _73_
Barilius **34**: 65
bakeri **34**: 65
Barisia **46**: 52
imbricata **46**: _51_
bark stripping **8**: 24
barklice 22: _86–87_
barnacle zone **28**: (27)
barnacles 3: _57_, 92, 102, 108;
   28: 10, _22–27_
acorn **22**: _8_; **28**: _22_
commensal **28**: _26_
giant acorn **28**: _25_
goose **28**: _24–25_, (24), _27_
parasitic **28**: _26_
reproduction **28**: 26–27
Baroniinae **26**: 16–17
barracuda 32: 67, **38**: 52, **39**: 109,
   40: 9, _102–103_
chevron **40**: _103_
great **40**: 102, _102–103_
Guachanche **40**: 102
Guinean **40**: 102
red **40**: 102, 103
yellowstripe **40**: 102, _102_
barracudina 35: 80, _98–99_
ribbon **35**: 99
slender **35**: 98
barramundi
Indo-Pacific silver **40**: 14
barreleye 35: _24–25_
Barygenys **42**: 104
Baryphthengus
martii **19**: 42
ruficapillus **19**: 42
Basiliscus **44**: 30, 34
basiliscus **44**: 26
plumifrons **44**: 26, 81, _86–87_, 98;
   48: (58)
vittatus **44**: 87
basilisk 44: 25, 30, 81
Central American **44**: 34
plumed 44: 81, _86–87_, 98; **48**: (58)
South American **44**: 26
striped **44**: 87
basket stars 30: _98–103_
basketfish **39**: 106
Basommatophora **30**: 18, 45–46
bass 39: (10), **40**: _12–19_
blackmouth **40**: 15
European sea **40**: 14, 15
largemouth **34**: 97, **40**: 26, (27),
   _28–29_
Roanoke **40**: 26
sea **40**: 9, 12

smallmouth **31:** 79
striped **37:** 18
striped sea **40:** 14
temperate **40:** 12
Bassaricyon
 alleni **1:** 20
 gabbii **1:** 20
Bassariscus
 astutus **1:** 20
 sumichrasti **1:** 20
basslet **40:** 22, 24
 fairy **40:** 53
 hidden **40:** 23
 Rose Island **40:** 23
 spiny **40:** 25
 yellow **40:** 24
 yellowbar **40:** 24
bat 1: *8, 10,* 14; **7:** 12, (37); **9:** 80–87
 African slit-faced **9:** 82, 84
 American false vampire **9:** 86
 American little brown **9:** 87
 American pallid **9:** 84
 bat families **9:** 86–87
 Bechstein's **9:** 80–81
 Brazilian (Mexican) free-tailed
  9: 82, (83), 84–85, *86,*
  100–103
 bulldog (fisherman) **9:** 87, 108–109
 Daubenton's **9:** 87
 diadem roundleaf **9:** *86*
 disk-winged **9:** 87
 Egyptian fruit **9:** 86
 Egyptian rousette 9: 92–93
 false vampire 9: 82, 98–99
 fisherman 9: 108–109
 free-tailed **9:** 87
 fruit **9:** 58, 80, 81, 86
 funnel-eared **9:** 87, *87*
 greater false vampire (false vampire)
  9: 82, 98–99
 greater horseshoe **9:** 86
 guano (Mexican free-tailed) **9:** 82,
  (83), 84–85, *86,* 100–103
 hairy big-eyed **9:** *85*
 hairy-legged vampire **9:** 94
 hammerheaded **9:** 80, 86
 horseshoe **9:** 80, 87
 house (Mexican free-tailed) **9:** 82,
  (83), 84–85, *86,* 100–103
 Indian greater false vampire (false
  vampire) **9:** 82, 98–99
 Kitti's hog-nosed **1:** *11,* (11); **9:** 38,
  80, 86
 lesser bulldog **9:** 108
 lesser horseshoe 9: 106–107
 lesser long-nosed **9:** *84–85*
 little brown 9: 83, 104–105
 long-eared 9: 110–111
 long-tongued **9:** 86
 Mexican free-tailed 9: 82, (83),
  84–85, *86,* 100–103
 mouse-tailed **9:** 86
 mustached **9:** *87*
 New World leaf-nosed **9:** 87

 New Zealand short-tailed **9:** 86–87
 Old World false vampire **9:** 82, 87
 Old World leaf-nosed **9:** 87
 Old World sucker-footed **9:** 87
 rousette **9:** 86
 sheath-tailed **9:** 87
 slit-faced **9:** 87
 spear-nosed **9:** 84, *87*
 spectacled **9:** 87
 thumbless **9:** 87
 vampire 9: 84, (85), 94–97
 whispering (long-eared) **9:** 110–111
 white-winged vampire **9:** 94
 see also flying fox; pipistrelle
Batanota **25:** *101*
Batara cinerea **19:** 72
Batazonellus fuliginosus **27:** *60–61, 61*
bateleur 15: 8, 36–37
batfish 36: (14), 70–73, 76
 pancake **36:** *70*
 red-lipped **36:** *12–13*
 reticulated **36:** *72–73*
 shortnose **36:** 70, *72–73*
bathing **11:** 11; **14:** 8
Bathophilus
 brevis **35:** 89
 filifer **35:** 89
 nigerrimus **35:** 89
 pawneei **35:** 89
Bathyergidae **7:** *12;* **8:** 9
Bathyergus
 janetta **8:** 56
 suillus **8:** 56
Bathylutichthyidae **39:** 76–81
Bathylutichthys taranetzi **39:** 81
Bathynellacea **28:** 34, 36
Bathyraja **33:** (26)
Bathysaurus **35:** 96
 ferox **35:** 96
 mollis **35:** 96
Bathysolea profundicola **39:** (93)
Batis molitor **17:** 66
batis, chinspot **17:** 66
Batocera parryi **25:** 90–91
Batocnema coquereli **26:** *67*
batoids **33:** 10, 11, 12, 13
Batrachocottus
 multiradiatus **39:** 78
 nikolskii **39:** 78
Batrachoglanis raninus **37:** 87
Batrachoides gilberti **36:** *56*
Batrachoididae **36:** 54–59, **39:** 54
Batrachomoeus **36:** 54
Batrachoseps **41:** 68, 73
Batrachostomus cornutus **15:** 78
Batrachuperus **41:** 36, (37)
 gorganensis **41:** 36
 persicus **41:** *37*
 pinchonii **41:** *26–27,* 36
Batrachylodes **43:** 86
bats, fruit **45:** (42)
Battus philenor **26:** *18, 20–21*
Bdelloidea **21:** 69
Bdeogale

 crassicauda **1:** 98
 jacksoni **1:** 98
beach fleas 28: 44–45
bear 2: 9; **5:** 9
 American black 2: 82, 90–93
 Andean **2:** 82, *83*
 Asian black **2:** 82, *83*
 bear family 2: 82–83
 big brown (brown) **2:** 82, *83,* 92,
  94–97
 brown 2: 82, *83,* 92, 94–97
 dancing **2:** (97)
 "dawn bear" **2:** 82
 grizzly 2: 82, *83,* 92, 94–97
 koala *see* koala
 Malaysian sun **2:** 82
 native Australian *see* koala
 panda *see* panda, giant
 polar **2:** 9, 82, 84–89; **3:** 83
 skunk *see* wolverine
 sloth **2:** 82, *83*
 spectacled **2:** 82, *83*
 sun **2:** 82, *83*
beardfish 35: 82, 110–111
 Atlantic **35:** 110, 111
 Japanese **35:** 110
 Pacific **35:** *111*
 silver eye **35:** 110
 stout **35:** 110, *110,* 111
Beatragus hunteri **6:** 62
beaver 7: 8, 9, *10,* 11, *12,* 13
 American 7: 28, 29, 30–33
 beaver family 7: 28–29
 Canadian (American) **7:** 28, 29, 30–33
 Eurasian **7:** 28, 29
 mountain **7:** *12,* 14, 28, (29)
 mountain beaver family 7: 28–29
 swamp *see* coypu
bedbugs 24: 34–35
Bedotia **38:** 55, (56)
 geayi **38:** 56, *57*
 madagascariensis **38:** 56, *57*
 marojejy **38:** 56
Bedotiidae **38:** 54–59
bee-eater 14: 103; **17:** 8–9; **19:** 42
 blue-bearded **17:** 8, *8*
 carmine **11:** *84;* **17:** 8, (12)
 Eurasian (European) **17:** 8, 10–13
 European 17: 8, 10–13
 little **17:** 8, *9*
 Sulawesi **17:** 8, *8*
 swallow-tailed **17:** 8
 white-fronted **17:** 8, *9*
 white-throated **17:** 8
bees 27: 8–13
 carpenter 22: *35;* **27:** 96–101
 creeping willow **27:** 90
 digger 27: 96–101
 and flowers **27:** (105)
 forked-tongue **27:** 89–90
 hairy-legged mining **27:** *90–91*
 **honeybees and relatives
  27:** 102–113
 leaf-cutter and relatives 27: 84–91

leaf-cutting (leaf-cutter) **27**: <u>84–91</u>
masked **27**: 89–90
mason **27**: 84, 87–88
mining 27: <u>92–95</u>
orchid **27**: 102–103
pygmy flower **27**: *11*, (95)
red mason **27**: *85, 88*
stingless **24**: 107–108; **27**: 102, 108–109
wool-carder **27**: 84, 88–89
beetles 25: <u>8–15</u>
anatomy **25**: 8–12
antennae **25**: (10)
asparagus **25**: *98*
bee **25**: *86–87*
betsy (bessbugs) **25**: (75)
blister 25: <u>62–67</u>
bombardier **25**: (18)
brown tiger **25**: *20*
burying (carrion) **25**: <u>28–31</u>
cardinal (fire-colored) **25**: <u>60–61</u>
carpet **25**: 53
carrion 25: <u>28–31</u>
caterpillar hunters **25**: 16, *17*
cellar **25**: 68
chafer *see* chafers
checkered 25: <u>40–41</u>
churchyard **25**: 68
click 25: <u>42–45</u>
cockchafer **22**: *35*
cock-tail (rove) **25**: 32–33
Colorado potato **25**: *103*
comb-clawed **25**: (73)
darkling 25: <u>68–73</u>
deathwatch **25**: *53*, (53)
digestive system **25**: 12
diving 25: <u>24–25</u>
drugstore **25**: (53)
dung **2**: 76–77; **25**: 76–77, (78), 81
eggs **25**: 12
elephant **25**: 87, *88–89*
European bee-wolf **25**: *40*
European pot-bellied emerald **25**: *13, 99*
European wasp **25**: *95*
false blister **25**: (61)
feeding **25**: 8, 12, 13
fire-colored 25: <u>60–61</u>
fireflies 25: <u>36–37</u>
fleet-footed tiger **25**: *12*
flower **25**: 85–87
forked fungus **25**: 70
furniture **25**: (53)
glowworms **25**: (35)
Goliath **25**: *85–87*
green tiger **25**: *22*
ground 25: <u>16–19</u>
hairy fungus **25**: (52)
handsome fungus **25**: (52)
harlequin **25**: *90*; **29**: (21)
Hercules **25**: *76, 87*
hide **25**: (81)
ironclad **25**: *73*
jewel 25: <u>46–49</u>

ladybug **24**: *104–105*; **25**: <u>54–59</u>
larder **25**: 53
leaden tortoise **25**: *14–15*
leaf 25: *13*, <u>96–103</u>
long-horned 25: *8–9*, <u>90–95</u>
metallic wood-boring (jewel) **25**: <u>46–49</u>
mint leaf **25**: *96, 97*
museum (carpet) **25**: 53
Neptune **25**: *86–87*
net-winged 25: <u>38–39</u>
oil **25**: *62*
patent-leather (bessbugs) **25**: (75)
pleasing fungus 25: <u>50–53</u>
reproduction and growth **25**: 12–14
rhinoceros **25**: 87
rove 25: <u>32–33</u>
scarab **25**: <u>76–89</u>
sexton (carrion) **25**: <u>28–31</u>
soldier 25: <u>34–35</u>
speckled-bellied fungus **25**: *51*
splendor (jewel) **25**: <u>46–49</u>
stag 22: 32; **25**: <u>74–75</u>
thick-legged flower **25**: *61*
tiger 25: <u>20–23</u>
Titan **25**: 90
tortoise **25**: *96, 100, 101, 102–103*
undertaker (carrion) **25**: <u>28–31</u>
Vedalia **25**: (56)
waltzing (whirligig) **25**: <u>26–27</u>
warty leaf **25**: *96–97*
water (diving) **25**: <u>24–25</u>
water scavenger **25**: (26)
wharf borer **25**: (61)
whirligig 25: <u>26–27</u>
see also weevils
behavior (fish) **31**: 17
head bending **34**: (19)
beira **6**: *60, 62*
bellbird **19**: 83
three-wattled **19**: 80, 83
bellowfish **39**: 50, 51
Belone belone **38**: 73
Belonesox belizanus **38**: 96
Belonidae **38**: <u>70–75</u>
Belonogaster juncea **27**: *11*
Belontia **40**: 61
hasselti **40**: 63
signata **40**: 63
Belontiidae **40**: <u>60–63</u>
Belostomatidae **24**: (21)
beluga 3: 55, <u>80–83</u>; **31**: 52, 53, (56), (57), <u>64–67</u>
Bembix **27**: *80*
Bembras japonica **39**: 73
Bembridae **39**: 11, 53, <u>72–73</u>
Benthobatis **33**: (20)
marcida **33**: 22
berrypecker, flock 18: <u>68–69</u>
crested 18: 68, 69, <u>72–73</u>
tit **18**: 68, *68*, 69
Berycidae **39**: 21
Berytidae **24**: (49)
bessbugs **25**: (75)

Betta **40**: 61
imbellis **40**: 63
macrostoma **40**: 62
picta **40**: 62
splendens **38**: 76, **40**: 60, *60*
unimaculata **40**: 61
betta
crescent **40**: 63
Javan **40**: 62
marine **40**: 24, *24*, 25
one-spot **40**: 61
peaceful **40**: 63
bettong
burrowing **10**: 48, *51*
Tasmanian **10**: *8*
Bettongia lesueur **10**: 48
Bias flammulatus **17**: 66
bib **36**: 38, *44–45*
Bibio
hortulanus **23**: *54–55*
marci **23**: *54, 55*
Bibionidae **23**: <u>54–55</u>
bichir 31: <u>44–51</u>, 52, 74, 75
armored **31**: *48–49*
barred **31**: *48–49*
fins **31**: (47)
Nile **31**: *51*
ornate **31**: *44–45*, 50
Senegal **31**: *46–47*, 50
shortfin **31**: *44*
species summary **31**: (51)
bightfish
port and starboard **39**: 20
bigscale **39**: 12, 13, 14
crested **39**: 13
yawning **39**: 13
Bilateria **21**: 30, 32
bilby 10: <u>44–45</u>
greater **10**: 27, 44, *45*
lesser **10**: 27, 44
bilharzia/ziasis **21**: (83); **30**: 21, 46
biliverdin **43**: 28, (35)
billfish **40**: 107, 108, 109, 110
bills **11**: 12–13
bent **13**: 26, (29)
of birds of prey **11**: *12*; **15**: 8, *8*
casques on **19**: (49), 50, 52, *53, 54*
colored **19**: 60–61
crossed mandibles **16**: 76, *77*
differences between sexes **20**: 100
of finches **16**: 76, *76, 77*
hooked **15**: 28, *29*
of hummingbirds **16**: (45)
lamellae on **13**: 78
lined with spines **12**: (105)
mobile mandible **19**: *12*
of parrots and cockatoos **16**: 22, *23*, (23)
pronged **19**: 70, 71
receptors in **13**: 30
serrated **19**: 42, 51, *60–61*
toothlike projections on **19**: 101
used for climbing **16**: 22, 84–86
bill-wrestling **12**: (107); **19**: (62)

binary fission **21:** 14, 25
binturong **1:** 88, *89*, *90*, 91
biological control *see* pest control
bioluminescence **28:** 29; **35:** *84–85*, (88), **36:** 29, 79, (79)
biomedical research *see* medical research
bipedalism **4:** 10
Bipedidae **46:** 103, 104, 105
Bipes **46:** 102, 110, (110)
   biporus **41:** (61); **46:** 104, 110–111
bird of paradise 19: (91), 106–109
   blue **19:** 106, (108)
   crested **19:** 106
   emperor **19:** 106
   greater **19:** 106, 108
   king **19:** 106, 108
   King of Saxony **19:** 106, (108)
   MacGregor's **19:** 106, 108
   magnificent **19:** 106
   Raggiana 19: 106, 110–111
   twelve-wired **19:** 106, *109*
   Wilson's **19:** 106, *107*
birds 11: 8–15
   definition **11:** 8
   external features **11:** *8*
   size **11:** (9), 11
   skeleton **11:** *8–9*, 9–11
birds of prey 14: (62); **15:** 8–13; **17:** (109), 111
   eyesight **15:** (49)
   feet **11:** 10; **18:** *18*, (18)
   numbers of prey and **15:** (34)
   size differences **15:** (48)
   strengthening prey populations **15:** (27)
birds, evolution **44:** *10*
birdwings (swallowtail butterflies) **26:** 16–21
   Queen Alexandra's **26:** 16, *16*
Birgus latro **28:** (100)
bishop, red **16:** 100, *101*
bison
   American 6: 60, 62, 64–69
   European **6:** 62, (66), *67*
   wood **6:** 68
Bison
   bison **6:** 62, 64–69
   bison athabascae **6:** 68
   bonasus **6:** 62, 66
Biston
   betularia **26:** (75)
   strataria **26:** *74*
Bitia hydroides **49:** 15
Bitis **50:** 51, 62
   albanica **50:** 68
   arietans **48:** 109; **49:** (67); **50:** (8), 9, 14, 58, 60–63
   armata **50:** 68
   atropos **50:** 62
   caudalis **48:** (58); **49:** 33, (73); **50:** 9, 66–69
   cornuta **49:** (73); **50:** 66–69
   gabonica **48:** 8; **50:** 9, 51, 61, 64–65
   inornata **50:** 68

   nasicornis **49:** (73); **50:** 52, 65
   olduvaiensis **50:** 63
   peringueyi **44:** 69; **50:** 51, 66, 69, (69)
   rubida **50:** 68
   xeropaga **50:** 68
Bittacus italicus **22:** *109*
bitterling 34: 66–67
   Amur **34:** 66
   Hong Kong **34:** *67*
   rosy **34:** *67*
bittern 14: 20
   American 14: 20, 30–31; **15:** *18*
   dwarf **14:** 20, *23*
bivalves 30: 50–53
   anatomy **30:** 50–52
   attachment to surfaces **30:** (52)
   primitive **30:** 53
   rock boring **30:** (66)
Bivalvia **30:** 9, 10, 50–53
black prince **38:** 110
black widow **38:** 41
   Carribean **36:** 27
blackbird 14: (50)
   American blackbird family 18: 74–75, (80), (81)
   austral **18:** 74, 75
   Eurasian **18:** 44, *44*
   Forbes's **18:** 74, 75
   melodious **18:** 74, 75
   red-breasted **18:** 74, *75*
   red-winged **18:** 74, 75, *75*, 79, 80
   rusty **18:** 74, *75*
   tricolored **18:** 74
   unicolored **18:** 74
   yellow-headed **18:** 74, 80
   yellow-winged **18:** 74, 75
blackbuck **6:** *61*, 62
blackcap **17:** 60, *60*
blackchin
   Pacific **35:** 82, 103
blackdragon
   Pacific **35:** 89
black-eye, olive **18:** 68, *68*
blackfish
   Alaska **35:** 20, *20*, 21, *21*
blackpoll **17:** 88, (93)
blacktail **35:** 66, (68)
bladderworm **21:** *84*
Blanus **46:** 102, 105, 108
   cinereus **46:** 102, 108–109
Blaps mucronata **25:** 68
Blarina brevicauda **9:** 28, 30–33
Blastocerus dichotomus **6:** 10
Blattodea **22:** 30, 68–73
bleak **34:** 81, (87)
Blenniidae **39:** 28, **40:** 9, 90–93
blenny 31: 73, **36:** 27, **39:** 28, **40:** 9, 90–93
   black-headed **40:** 93
   blackfaced **40:** 93
   blackline fang **40:** 91, *91*
   bluelined sabre-toothed **40:** 91
   carpet eel **40:** 22
   combtooth **40:** 90, 91

   convict **40:** 23, 24
   eel **40:** 22, 25
   "other" blennies **40:** (91)
   Red Sea mimic **40:** 91
   sabre-toothed **40:** 90, 91
   scale-eating **40:** *90*
   tompot **40:** *92–93*, 93
   yellow **40:** 93
Blepsias cirrhosus **39:** 80
Blicca bjoerkna **34:** (87)
blind fish **34:** (28), **36:** 19, **37:** (89), **38:** 8, 35, 36, *36*, (39), 41
blind snakes 44: 15; **48:** 18–21, 105; **50:** 15, 48
   Bibron's **48:** 20
   Brahminy 48: 19, 20, 24–25
   dawn **48:** 18
   Diard's **48:** 20
   early (dawn) **48:** 18
   plains slender (Texas thread snakes) **48:** 20, 22–23
   Schinz's beaked **48:** *20–21*
   Schlegel's **48:** 19, 20
   Sulu **48:** 20
blind worms (slow worms) **44:** 28; **45:** *99*; **46:** 50, 51, 56–59, (61)
blindcat **37:** (19), 21
   Mexican **37:** 16, 21
   toothless **37:** 15, 16, 21
   widemouth **37:** 16, 21
blindfish
   gelatinous **36:** 27
bloater (whitefish) **35:** 38, 41
bloaters **36:** 111
blockhead **40:** 68
   African **40:** 68–69
blood, countercurrent heat exchange **12:** 9
bloodsuckers (garden lizards) **44:** 32, 35, (37), 46–47
bloodworms **21:** 103; **23:** *51*
blubber **3:** 34, 58, 72, 84, 85, 89, 91, (101)
"blue" fish **38:** (73)
blue flash **40:** 68
bluebird 18: 45
   eastern 18: 44, 54–57
   mountain **18:** 54
   western **18:** 54
bluebuck **6:** 63
blue-eye **38:** 59
   cape **38:** 59
   glass **38:** (56)
   horny **38:** (56)
   red-finned **38:** (56), 59
blues (gossamer-winged butterflies) **26:** 28, 29
   Adonis **26:** *29*, *30*
   imperial **26:** *31*
   large **26:** *28*
   pygmy **26:** 28
bluethroat **18:** 44, (50), (56)
Boa
   constrictor **48:** 44, 48–53

dumerili **48:** 46, 54–55
madagascariensis **48:** 46, 55
mandrita **48:** 46, 55
Boaedon **49:** 68
boafish **35:** 85
boar, **wild 5:** 74, 76–79
boarfish **39:** 10, 22, *24*, 25, **40:** 54
  big-spined **40:** 55
  common **39:** 25, *25*
  deepbody **39:** 25, *25*
  giant **40:** 55
  longfin **40:** 55
  longsnout **40:** 55, *55*
  Richardson's **40:** 55
  striped **40:** 55
  yellow-spotted **40:** 55
boas
  Amazon tree **48:** *45*
  Arabian sand **48:** 47
  banana **48:** 47
  black-tailed dwarf (Cuban wood
    snake) **48:** 78–79
  boa constrictor (common boa) **48:** 44,
    46, 48–53
  boas and relatives 48: 44–47
  burrowing **48:** 44
  Calabar ground **48:** 17, 46, 69, 72
  central Baja rosy **48:** *72–73*, 73
  clouded **48:** 50
  coastal rosy **48:** 73
  common 48: 44, 46, 48–53
  constriction **48:** 44, 51–52, 71, 75
  Cooke's tree **48:** *46*
  Cropan's **48:** 45
  Cuban **48:** 45, 78
  desert rosy **48:** 73
  distribution **48:** (50)
  Dumeril's 48: 46, 54–55
  dwarf **48:** 44, 47, 79
  East African sand 48: 74–75
  Egyptian (East African) sand **48:**
    74–75
  emerald tree 48: 56–59, 96; **50:** 91
  Haitian vine **48:** 45
  Kenyan (East African) sand **48:** 74–75
  locomotion, rectilinear **48:** 51
  Madagascan ground **48:** 46
  Madagascar tree **48:** 46
  Mascarene **48:** 47
  Mexican rosy **48:** 73
  Mona Island **48:** 45–46
  New Guinea ground **48:** 60, (61)
  Pacific **48:** 46, (61)
  Pacific ground 48: 46, 60–61
  Pacific tree **48:** 46, 60, (61)
  Panamanian dwarf **48:** *47*
  Puerto Rican **48:** 85
  racer **48:** (77)
  rainbow 48: 45, 62–63
  red-tailed **48:** 50
  reproduction **48:** 17
  rosy 48: 46, 68, 70–73
  Round Island 48: 47, 76–77, 79
  Round Island keel-scaled (Round

  Island) **48:** 47, 76–77, 79
  rubber 48: 16, 46, 68–69, 72
  sand **48:** 8, 44, 46–47
  spurs **48:** (49)
  Tanzanian (East African) sand **48:**
    74–75
  tree **48:** 45
  "true" **48:** 44
  viper **48:** 46, 60, 61
boat traffic **3:** 50, 51, 65, 79, 103
bobcat 2: 10, 38–39, 40
bobolink **18:** 74, 75, *75*
bobwhite, **northern 11:** 44, (46),
  50–51
bocaccio **39:** 64, 65
body temperature **1:** 9–12
  control of **5:** (17); **9:** 24, 67, 72, 82,
    (90); **10:** 69
  desert animals **5:** 95–96
  see also hibernation; torpor
Bogertophis **49:** 10, (43)
Boggi (stump-tailed skinks) **46:** 9, *10*,
  14, 15, 44–47
Boidae **48:** 9, 44, 80
Boiga **49:** 11, (22)
  blandingi **49:** 22–23, (39)
  dendrophila **49:** (22), (39)
  irregularis **49:** 20–23
Boinae **48:** 44, 45–46
Boisea trivittata **24:** *58*, 58–59
Bolbometopon muricatum **40:** 88, *88*
Bolitoglossa **41:** 27, 68, 69, 76–79
Bolitoglossini **41:** 71
Bolitotherus cornutus **25:** 70
Bolyeria multocarinata **48:** 47
Bolyeriidae **48:** 9, 44, 47, (77)
Bombay duck **35:** 79, 94, (96)
Bombina **42:** 24
  bombina **41:** (92); **42:** *24–25*, 25, (25)
  lichuanensis **42:** 26
  maxima **42:** *25*, 26
  orientalis **41:** 18, *19*; **42:** 9, 26, 28–29
  variegata **42:** (25), 26, *26–27*, *27*
Bombinatoridae **42:** 10, (22), 24
Bombus
  hortorum **27:** *106–107*
  lucorum **29:** *33*
  pascuorum **27:** *105*
  pratorum **27:** *106*
  terrestris **27:** 104–105
Bombycidae **26:** 78–79
Bombycilla
  cedrorum **18:** 30, 32, 41
  garrulus **16:** (84); **18:** 30, 32–35
  pallidiceps **18:** 32
  japonica **18:** 30
Bombycillidae **18:** 30
Bombycillini **18:** 30
Bombyliidae **23:** 68–71
Bombylius major **23:** 68
Bombyx mori **26:** 78
bommaloe macchli **35:** (96)
bonito **40:** 106
  Atlantic **40:** 106

bonobo 4: 12, 34–35
bontebok **6:** 62
bonxie *see* skua, great
bony fish **31:** (10), *15*, **33:** 60–61
  Who's Who **33:** (61)
bonytongue fish 31: 82–85, 90, 110
booby **12:** 44, 45, (46), 47, 48, 63
  Abbott's **12:** 44, 47
  blue-footed **12:** 44, *46*, (46); **18:** (56)
  brown **12:** 44
  masked **12:** 44
  Nazca **12:** 44
  red-footed **12:** 44, *45*, 47
Boodontinae **49:** 8, 12–13
booklice 22: 86–87
  winged **22:** *86–87*
boomslang 43: 103; **49:** 36–39, (51),
  (71); **50:** 17
  African **49:** 11
  juvenile African **48:** *12*
Boophis **43:** (59), 100, 101
bordallo **34:** 78
Boreogadus saida **36:** 39
Borhyaenidae **10:** 26, 36
Bos
  frontalis **6:** 62
  grunniens **6:** 74–75
  javanicus **6:** 62
Boselaphus tragocamelus **6:** 62
Bostrychia hagedash **14:** 32
Botaurus lentiginosus **14:** 20, 30–31;
  15: *18*
Bothidae **39:** 11, 84, 87, 88–91
Bothragonus swanii **39:** 80
Bothriechis **50:** 54, 59, (90)
  lateralis **42:** 82
  schlegelii **48:** (97); **49:** (51), (73), 105;
    50: 9, *10–11*, 50, 59, 90–91, (111)
Bothrochilus boa **48:** 82
Bothrops
  ammodytoides **50:** 50
  asper **50:** (8), 9, (52), 92–93
  atrox **48:** 109; **50:** (8), *11*, 52–53, 92
  lanceolatus **50:** 50, (93)
Bothus
  ocellatus **39:** 88
  pantherinus **39:** 86–87
botia **34:** 78
  redtail **34:** (104), *104–105*
  see also loach
Botia **34:** 100, 102, 103, (104), 106,
  108
  dario **34:** *105*
  helodes **34:** (104)
  lohachata **34:** (104)
  macracanthus **34:** 14, 102–105
  modesta **34:** 14, (104), *104–105*
  sidthimunki **34:** (104)
  striata **34:** (104)
boto *see* dolphin, Amazon
Botrylloides magnicoecus **31:** 23
boubou **15:** 104–105
  southern **15:** 104, *106–107*
Boulengerella **38:** 25, (26)

cuvieri **38**: 25
lateristriga **38**: 26
lucius **38**: 26
maculata **38**: (26), *27*
Boulengerina **50**: 14
Boulengerochromis microlepis **40**: 68
Boulengerula **41**: 21, 22
Bovidae **6**: 9, 60–63
bovine tuberculosis **1**: 81
bowerbird 11: 14; **19**: 108
    Archbold's **19**: 100, 102
    bowerbird family 19: <u>100–103</u>
    fawn-breasted **19**: 100
    flame **19**: 100
    gardener **19**: 102
    golden **19**: 100, 102
    golden regent **19**: 100
    great **19**: 100, *103*
    MacGregor's gardener **19**: 100
    regent **19**: 100, *101*
    Sanford's **19**: 100
    satin 19: 100, <u>104–105</u>
    tooth-billed **19**: 100, 102, 103
        Vogelkop gardener **19**: 100,
100–101, 102
    western **19**: 100
    yellow-breasted **19**: 100, 102
bowers **19**: *100–101*, 101–102, *102*,
104–105
bowfin 31: 43, 47, <u>72–75</u>, <u>80–81</u>
boxfish 39: 11, 96, 97, <u>106–107</u>, 110
    black-spotted **39**: 107
    blue-spotted **39**: 107
    cube **39**: 107
    Pacific **39**: 107
    polkadot **39**: 107
    spotted **39**: *106–107*, 107
    white-spotted **39**: 107
    yellow **39**: 107
Brachaeluridae **32**: (12), (30), 32
Brachaelurus waddi **32**: 45
brachiation **4**: 38, 72
Brachinus **25**: (18)
Brachionichthydae **36**: 67
Brachionichthys politus **36**: *64–65*
Brachionus **21**: *68*
Brachiopoda **21**: 32, 69, <u>70–71</u>
Brachiosaurus **44**: *10–11*
Brachycaudus cardui **24**: *100–101*
Brachycephalidae **42**: 10, (79)
Brachycephalus ephippium **42**: *79*, (79)
Brachycera **23**: 36, 39
Brachychalcinus orbicularis **38**: 35
Brachydanio **34**: 63
    "*frankei*" **34**: 63
    rerio **34**: 63
Brachygalba
    albogularis **17**: 20
    lugubris **17**: 20
    salmoni **17**: 20
Brachylagus idahoensis **8**: 64, (93)
Brachylophus **44**: 80
Brachyomus octotuberculatus **25**: *106*
Brachyophidium **48**: 28

Brachypelma smithi **29**: *46*
Brachyplatystoma filamentosum **37**: 87
Brachypteraciidae **15**: 86, 87
Brachyramphus
    brevirostris **12**: 98
    marmoratus **12**: 98
Brachyrhamdia imitator **37**: 86
Brachysynodontis **37**: 71
Brachytarsophrys **42**: 34, (89)
Brachyteles arachnoides **4**: 72
Brachytrupes orientalis **23**: *19*
Brachyura **28**: 56, 58, <u>102–113</u>
Bradypodion **44**: 25, 56, 61, <u>62–63</u>; **49**:
    36
    predators of **44**: (63)
Bradypterus baboecala **17**: 60
Bradypus
    torquatus **9**: 65
    variegatus **9**: 65, <u>72–73</u>
Bradytriton **41**: 68
brains **18**: 8
Brama brama **40**: 35
brambling **16**: 76
Bramidae **40**: <u>34–35</u>
Branchiopoda **28**: 9, <u>16–21</u>
    feeding **28**: 19–20
    locomotion **28**: 19
Branchiostoma **31**: 24
    caribaenum **31**: 24
    lanceolatum **31**: 24
branding, freeze branding **8**: (84)
Branta
    canadensis **14**: 52, <u>60–63</u>
    sandvicensis **14**: 52
Brassolidae **26**: <u>48–49</u>
Brazil, forestation in **4**: 90–91
breaching **3**: 96, *96–97*, *103*, 104, 109;
    32: 85, (88), **33**: (47), *51*
bream 34: 46, (87), **40**: <u>40–41</u>
    collared large-eye **40**: 41
    emperor **40**: 40
    longface emperor **40**: 40, *40–41*
    redfin dwarf monocle **40**: 41
    slender emperor **40**: 41
    small-toothed whiptail **40**: 41
    threadfin **40**: 40, 41
    whiptail **40**: 40, 41
    white **34**: (87)
    see also seabream
breeding **11**: 14; **31**: 19
    captive **19**: (32), 54
        by dominant birds **11**: 24, *24*;
            19: 9; **20**: 39, (66), 110–111
        double clutching **13**: 57
        explosive **42**: 40–41, 44–45, 59, 96;
            43: 36, 61, *93*, 94
        helpers **17**: 81; **18**: 60–61, 63, 93;
    20: (66), 69, 73
    K strategists **7**: 14; **8**: 21
    R strategists **7**: 14
    selective **5**: (43), 74; **6**: 63
    synchronized **3**: 20–21; **6**: 83, 88;
        7: 57; **8**: 79; **10**: 41
        see also captive breeding;

reproduction; inbreeding; interbreeding
rain calls **43**: 58
    selective **49**: (47), 51
breeding mound **7**: *18*
Bregmaceros **36**: 53
Bregmacerotidae **36**: <u>52–53</u>
Brentidae **25**: <u>112–113</u>
Brentus **25**: *113*
    anchorago **25**: *113*
Brephidium exilis **26**: 28
Breviceps **42**: 93, 95, 105, 106, (107),
    (111)
    adspersus **42**: <u>106–107</u>
    namaquensis **42**: *107*
Brevicipitinae **42**: 104
Brevicoryne brassicae **24**: *105*
Breviraja **33**: (26)
Brevisiana **24**: *82*
Briána **34**: 31
brill **39**: 90
bristlehead, Bornean **20**: 100
bristlemouth
    elongated **35**: *82–83*
bristlenose **37**: 106, (107)
    chubby **37**: *108–109*
bristletails **22**: (37)
bristlyskin **39**: 15
brittle stars 30: <u>98–103</u>
broadbill
    African **20**: 74
    black-and-red **20**: 74, *75*
    black-and-yellow **20**: 74
    broadbill family 20: <u>74–75</u>
    dusky **20**: 74
    green **20**: (78)
    lesser green 20: 74, <u>76–79</u>
Brochis **37**: 99
brocket, red **6**: 10, *11*, *13*
bromeliads **4**: (90)
    tank **41**: 76
Bronchocela **44**: 32, 35, (47)
    cristatella **44**: *33*, (47)
brood patches **12**: 15, (45)
brood/nest parasitism **12**: 71; **14**:
    54, 71, 73, 94–95; **16**: 71, 90,
    91; **17**: 20–21, 93, 103;
    18: 75; **20**: 46, (48), 49–53,
    50–51, 55, 86
Brookesia **44**: 25, 56, 57, 58, (59),
    64–65
    minima **44**: 25, 56
    peyrierasi **44**: *25*, 57
    stumpffi **44**: <u>64–65</u>
    superciliaris **44**: 64–65
Brosme **36**: 39
Brosmophysis marginata **36**: 27
brotula **36**: 23, 24, 26
    abyssal **36**: *24*, (27)
    deepwater **36**: 26
    false **36**: 26, 27
    livebearing **36**: 26, 27
    many-whiskered **36**: *25*
    red **36**: 27
Brotula multibarbata **36**: 25

brotulid, dusky **36:** *26*
Brotulina fusca **36:** *26*
brown bear **35:** (64), *64*
browns (satyrs) **26:** 46–47
browsing **5:** 12, 13, 38; **6:** 9
brumby *see* mustang
Brunei beauty **40:** 62
brush turkey **11:** 48, 49
    Australian **11:** 44
brush-finch, tricolored **16:** 62
Bryozoa **21:** 32, 69, 72–73
Bubalornis **16:** (104)
Bubalus
    depressicornis **6:** 62
    mindorensis **6:** 62
Bubastis **2:** (12)
bubble nests **40:** *61*, (62)
bubble netting **3:** 104
"bubblenetting" **36:** *102–103*
Bubo **15:** 56, (60), 62
    bubo **11:** *13*; **15:** 50
    sumatranus **15:** 50
    virginianus **15:** 34, 50, 56, 62–63
bubonic plague **7:** 14, 76–77; **22:** (113)
Bubulcus ibis **6:** (73); **14:** 20
Buccinum **30:** *32*
    undatum **30:** *19, 32*
Bucconidae **17:** 22; **19:** 56
Bucephala **12:** 66
    clangula **14:** 52, 78–79; **18:** (57)
    islandica **14:** 78
Buceros
    bicornis **19:** 48, 52–55
    hydrocorax **19:** 48
    rhinoceros **19:** 48
Bucerotidae **19:** 48
Bucerotiformes **18:** 48
Bucorvidae **19:** 48
Bucorvus
    abyssinicus **19:** 48
    leadbeateri **11:** *12*; **19:** 48
budding **21:** 14
budgerigar 16: 22, 23, 26–31, (35), 37
Budorcas taxicolor **6:** 62, 108
Buergeria **43:** 100
Buergeriinae **43:** 100
buffalo 1: *15*; **34:** 99
    African 6: 60, 62, 70–73
    bigmouth **34:** 99
    North American **34:** 89
see also bison, American
buffalohead **40:** 68
Bufo **41:** 8, 18; **42:** 56, 68
    alvarius **42:** 44, 57, (65)
    americanus **42:** *60–61*, 68
    asper **42:** 58, (65)
    blombergi **42:** (38), 56, (65)
    brongersmai **42:** 71
    bufo **41:** (17); **42:** *11*, 12, (18), 56, 62–63
    bufo spinosus **42:** (65)
    calamita **42:** *57, 59, 71*
    canorus **42:** 73
    danatensis **42:** 71

dapsilis **42:** 56
debilis **42:** 44, 57
gariepensis **42:** 57
gutteralis **42:** 56
juxtasper **42:** (65)
marinus **42:** 12–13, 64–69; **46:** 85; **50:** 43
mauritanicus **42:** 71
melanochlorus **42:** (38)
melanostictus **42:** 56
microscaphus **42:** 57
paracnemis **42:** (65)
periglenes **41:** *14–15*; **42:** 12, 73
quercicus **42:** 59
robinsoni **42:** 57
superciliaris **42:** (38), 56
typhonius **42:** (38), 56, *57*
viridis **42:** 55, 70–71
Bufonidae **42:** 8, (8), 10, 56; **43:** 73
bugs 22: *31*; **24:** 8–15
    assassin 24: 10, *13, 14, 15*, 38–43; **27:** *39*
    backswimmers 24: 24–27
    bark 24: 50–51
    bedbugs 24: 34–35
    box elder **24:** (59)
    broad-headed **24:** (56)
    burrower **24:** (66)
    capsid (plant) **24:** 8, 30–33
    cochineal **24:** (109)
    cone-nose **24:** *41*
    cotton-stainers (stainers) **24:** 48–49
    creeping thistle lace **24:** *28–29*
    damsel 24: 36–37
    definition **24:** 8
    eastern box elder **24:** *58, 59*, (59)
    eggplant lace **24:** (29)
    families **24:** 8
    feeding **24:** 12–13
    fire (stainers), **24:** 48–49
    flag-footed (leaf-footed) **24:** *8–9*, 14, 52–57
    flat (bark) **24:** 50–51
    flower **24:** (35)
    fulgorid (lanternflies) **24:** *12*, 72–77
    fungus (bark) **24:** 50–51
    giant shield **24:** (64)
    giant water **24:** 20–21, (21)
    golden egg **24:** 55–56
    green capsid **24:** *30–31*
    ground (seed) **24:** *11*, 44–47
    harlequin **24:** *70*
    lace 24: 28
    leaf (plant) **24:** 8, 30–33
    leaf-footed 24: 8–9, 14, 52–57
    lightning (fireflies) **25:** 36–37
    litter **22:** 72
    marsh damsel **24:** *36–37*
    Mexican bed **24:** *41*
    minute pirate **24:** (35)
    peanut **24:** 76
    peanut-head **24:** 76
    pill **28:** 46, 48
    pinching (stag beetles) **25:** 74–75

plant 24: 8, 30–33
platAspid stink **24:** (63)
red (stainers) **24:** 48–49; **29:** (32)
ripple 24: 18–19
scentless plant 24: 58–59
scuttle (whirligig beetles) **25:** 26–27
seed 24: *11*, 44–47
shield-backed 24: 70–71
shield (stink) **24:** *10*, 14, 60–69, (71)
shore **24:** (23)
short-horned **24:** *76–77*, (77)
sow **28:** 46
spider **24:** (33)
spittlebugs 24: 78–79
squash (leaf-footed) **24:** 8–9, 14, 52–57
stainers 24: *11*, 48–49
stilt **24:** (49)
stink 24: *10*, 60–69
"Sultan" **24:** (54)
thorn **24:** *90, 90–91*, 93–94
thunder (thrips) **22:** 84–85
tip-wilter (leaf-footed) **24:** *8–9*, 14, 52–57
toad 24: 22–23
tortoise **24:** *70*
true *see* true bugs
water measurers **24:** (19)
water scorpions 24: 20–21
water striders 24: 16–17
western box elder **24:** (59)
wheel **24:** *42–43*
woundwort stink **24:** *67*
bulbul 17: 111; **18:** 69
    bulbul family 16: 56–57
    common (garden) **16:** 56, 57, 58–61
    garden 16: 56, 57, 58–61
    gray-cheeked **16:** 56
    Philippine **16:** 56
    red-eyed **16:** 56, *56–57*
    red-vented **16:** 56, *56*, 57
    red-whiskered **16:** 56, *56*
    spectacled **16:** 56, (61)
    white-spectacled **16:** 56
bullfinch **16:** 76
    Eurasian **16:** 76, (87)
bullfrog 42: 9
    African **42:** (89); **43:** 87
    American 41: (65); **42:** (89); **43:** 82, 83, *83*, (85), 88–91
    Asian **42:** 104
    crowned **43:** 84
    giant African 43: 52, 98–99, 103
    Indian **43:** 84
    Knudsen's **42:** *76–77*
    South American 42: 90–91
bullhead **37:** 14, 15, 16, 17, (21), **39:** *76, 77*, 80
    black **37:** 20
    brown **37:** *15, 16*, 20
    yellow **37:** 20
Bullomorpha **30:** 18
bullrout **39:** 67
Bulweria bulwerii **12:** 28

bumblebees (honeybees) **27:** 102, 103–108
buff-tailed **27:** *104–105*
carder **27:** *105*
garden **27:** *106–107*
white-tailed **29:** *33*
see also catfish, bumblebee
bummalo **35:** (96)
bumphead **40:** 68
Bungarus **50:** 14, (35)
flaviceps **50:** 21
Bunocephalus **37:** 92
amaurus **37:** *93*
coracoideus **37:** *92*
Bunolagus monticularis **8:** 64
bunting 16: 62–63; **17:** 89; **18:** 44
corn **16:** 62, *63*
indigo **16:** 62, 63
McKay's **16:** 62
meadow **20:** *49*
painted 16: 62, 72–75
reed **16:** 62
snow 16: 62, 64–65
buntingi **38:** 64, 67, 69
black **38:** (68)
duckbilled **38:** 65, 67
Popta's **38:** 65
poso **38:** 65
Sarasin's **38:** 65
sharp-jawed **38:** (68)
Buphagus
africanus **6:** (73); **18:** 82
erythrorhynchus **18:** 82
Buprestidae **25:** 46–49
buprestins **25:** 46
burbot **36:** 38, (51)
Burhinidae **13:** 90, 91
Burhinus **13:** 91
capensis **13:** 90
magnirostris **13:** 90
oedicnemus **13:** 90
senegalensis **13:** 90
superciliaris **13:** 90
vermiculatus **13:** 90
Burramys parvus **10:** 74
burrfish **39:** 108
burrows **7:** 26–27; **9:** 44–45, 67; **10:** 99; **12:** 106-107; **13:** (103); **15:** (101), 102; **18:** (11); **19:** 45
ground destabilization **7:** 49, 50, 59; **8:** 29, *57*, 66–67; **9:** 77; **10:** 99
see also tunnels
bush baby 4: 106–107
Demidoff's 4: 106, 110–111
bush fires **15:** (93)
bush squeakers 43: 12–15
bush viper 50: 51, 52, 58, 91
acuminate **50:** 59
hairy 50: 9, 52, 58–59
Mount Kenya **50:** 58, 59
rough-scaled (hairy) **50:** 9, 52, 58–59
Shaba **50:** 59

spiny (hairy) **50:** 9, 50, 52, 58–59
Usambara **50:** 52, 59
bushbuck **6:** 62
bushfish 40: 58–59
banded **40:** 59
Petheric's **40:** 59
tailspot **40:** 59
bushmasters 50: (8), 50, 54, 63, 65, 94–95
black-headed **50:** 94
bushmeat trade **4:** 27, 32, 40, 53, 61, 85; **5:** 87; **6:** 59, 66, 72
bushpig **5:** 74, *75*
bush-robin **18:** (50)
bush-shrike **15:** 104, 105
fiery-breasted **15:** 104
four-colored **15:** 104
gray-headed **15:** 104, *104*
olive **15:** 104
bushtit **17:** 70, *70*
bustard 11: (9), 40, 92; **14:** 90
Arabian **11:** 84
Australian 11: 84, 86–87
black-bellied **11:** 84, 85, *85*
bustard family 11: 84–85
crested **11:** 84, 85
great 11: 84, 88–91
great Indian **11:** 84
houbara **11:** 84
kori **11:** 84, *84*, 85, 86
little **11:** 84
Nubian **11:** 84
Vigors' **11:** 84, 85
butcherbird **20:** 101
black **20:** 100
black-backed **20:** 100
black-headed **20:** 100
gray **20:** 100, *101*
Louisiade **20:** 100
pied **20:** 100, 101
silver-backed **20:** 100
Buteo buteo **15:** 8; **17:** (13)
Butorides striatus **14:** 22
butterflies 26: 8–15
African monarch **26:** 60
alfalfa **26:** 22
American monarch **26:** *58*
anatomy **26:** *10*, 11–12
Aracne checkerspots **26:** *44–45*
army-ant (ithomiids) **26:** 56–57
Artemesia swallowtail **26:** *16–17*
blue morpho **26:** 50
brimstone **26:** *22–23*
brush-footed 26: 11, *11*, 38–45
buckeye **26:** *41*
classification example **21:** (8)
coolie **26:** *10, 44*
eggs **26:** 12–13, (13)
gossamer-winged 26: 28–33
green-lined charaxes **26:** *38–39*
gulf fritillary **26:** *53*
life cycle **26:** *13*
milkweed 26: 58–61
mimicry **22:** 34

monarch **21:** (8); **26:** *15*, 60, *61*
owl 26: 48–49
painted lady **26:** *38–39*
passion-flower (longwings) **26:** 52–55
pipevine swallowtail **26:** *20–21*
puddling **26:** (15), *16–17*
pupae **26:** 14–15
red admiral **26:** *38*
silver emperor **26:** *41*
silver-washed fritillary **26:** *12*
six-tailed brush-foot **26:** *37*
swallowtail 26: 16–21
tiger swallowtail **26:** *21*
whites *see* whites
wing colors **26:** (11)
see also caterpillars
butterfly fish 39: (10); **40:** 46–49, 54, 100
African 31: 82, 83, 84, 100–101
brown-banded **40:** 46
chevron **40:** 46
copperband **40:** *46*
Eritrean **40:** *48*
foureye **40:** *46–47*, 47
Indian **40:** 46
orange-face **40:** 46
raccoon **40:** *48–49*
threadfin **40:** 46
threeband **40:** 46
triangular **40:** 46
butterfly lions **22:** 90, *96*
button quail 11: 92–93; **14:** 82
barred **11:** 92, *92*
painted **11:** 92, *93*
yellow-legged **11:** 92
buzzard **15:** (9), 12; **17:** (13)
Eurasian **15:** 8, *10*
honey **15:** 8, 13
byssus threads **30:** (52), 59, 63, (65)
Bythitidae **36:** 26, 27

C

Cabassous unicinctus **9:** 65
cabezón **32:** 102; **39:** 76, 80
Cacajao **4:** 72
calvus **4:** 72, 80–81
melanocephalus **4:** 72
Cacatua galerita **16:** 22
Cacatuidae **16:** 22; **19:** 12
cachorro **38:** 26, 27, (27), 87

Amazonian **38:** 26
spotted **38:** 26, *26*
Cacicus
　cela **18:** 74
　chrysonotus **18:** 74
　chrysopterus **18:** 74
　holosericus **19:** 78
cacique **18:** 74, 75
　golden-winged **18:** 74
　mountain **18:** 74
　yellow-billed **19:** 78
　yellow-rumped **18:** 74
cacomistle **1:** 20, 21
Caenolestes **10:** 14
　caniventer **10:** 14
　fuliginosus **10:** 14
Cacophis **50:** 14
Cacosternum **43:** 87
　capense **43:** 87
Cactospiza
　heliobates **20:** 96
　pallidus **20:** 96
caddisflies 22: 102–103
　great red sedge **22:** *102*
Caecilia **41:** 21
　tentaculata **41:** *22*
　thompsoni **41:** (17)
caecilians 41: 8–9, 14, (17), 20–23
　Asiatic yellow-striped **41:** *9*
　blue-ringed **41:** (20), 20–21
　burrowing characteristics **41:** 20–21
　color range **41:** 21
　feeding **41:** 23
　Koh Tao **41:** 21
　locomotion **41:** 22–23
　reproduction **41:** 23
　respiration **41:** 22
　rubber (South American aquatic) **41:** 21, 24–25
　sensory tentacles **41:** 21–22
　on the Seychelles **41:** (23)
　South American aquatic 41: 21, 24–25
Caeciliidae **41:** 21
Caecobarbus geertsi **34:** 24, (28)
Caecomastacembelus **33:** (106)
Caecorhamdia
　brasiliensis **37:** (89)
　urichi **37:** (89)
Caenolestidae **10:** 16
Caenorhabditis elegans **21:** (90)
Caepaea nemoralis **30:** 19
Caerostris mitralis **29:** *108*
caerulein **43:** (56)
cage birds **18:** (40)
caiman
　black 47: 106–107
　broad-nosed **47:** *96–97*
　common **47:** 94, 106
　Cuvier's smooth-fronted **47:** *94–95*
　fossils **47:** 94
Caiman
　crocodilus **47:** 94, 106
　latirostris **47:** *96–97*

neivensis **47:** 94
Cairnsichthys rhombosomoides **38:** 57
Calabaria **48:** 46
Calais (click beetle) **25:** *44*
Calamaria **49:** 16
　lumbricoidea **50:** 21
　vermiformis **49:** 8
Calamarinae **49:** 8, 16
Calandrella
　brachydactyla **18:** 22
　raytal **18:** 22
Calanoida **28:** 9
Calephelis perditalis **26:** *34*
calf fish (dogfish) **32:** 22, 47
Calidris **13:** 30, 33
　alba **11:** 15; **13:** 30
　alpina **13:** 16, 30, 52–55, *64–65*
　canutus **13:** 30, 55, 64–65
　fuscicolis **13:** 30
　maritima **13:** 30
　melanotos **13:** 30, 62–63
　minuta **13:** 30, 56–57
Caligo
　atreus **26:** *48*
　memnon **26:** *49*
　opsiphanes **26:** *48*
Caligus rapax **28:** *30*
Callaeas cinerea **20:** 100, 102–103
Callaeidae **20:** 100
Calliactis parasitica **21:** *60*; **28:** (97)
Callicebus
　moloch **4:** 72
　personatus **4:** 72
　torquatus **4:** 72
Callichthyidae **37:** 96–103
Callichthys **37:** 101, 103
　callichthys **37:** *96*, 101
Callimico goeldii **4:** 86
Calliophis **50:** 14, (25)
　gracilis **50:** 21
　schlegelii **50:** 21
Callipepla gambelii **11:** 44
Calliphora
　vicina **23:** *108–109*
　vomitoria **23:** *108*
Calliphoridae **23:** 108–111
Callisaurus draconoides **44:** 82
Callithrix
　argentata see *Mico argentata*
　geoffroyi **4:** 86
　humilis see *Mico humilis*
　jacchus **4:** 86, 92–93
　pygmaea see *Cebuella pygmaea*
Callixalis pictus **43:** 19–20
Callophrys rubi **26:** *28–29*
Callopistes **45:** 82, 83
　maculatus **45:** *82–83*, 84
Calloplesiops altivelis **40:** 24, *24*
Callorhinus ursinus **3:** 9, 14–15
Callorhynchidae **33:** (55)
Callorhynchus **33:** 58
　callorhynchus **33:** 58
　capensis **33:** 58
　milii **33:** 58–59

Callosciurus
　nigrovittatus **7:** 36
　notatusisi **7:** 36
　prevosti **7:** 36
Calloselasma rhodostoma **50:** 9, 50, 96–97
Calophysus macropterus **37:** 84, 91
Caloprymnus campestris **10:** 48
Calopteryx splendens **22:** *45*
Calosoma
　scrutator **25:** *17*
　sycophanta **25:** 16
Calotes **44:** 32, 35, (37)
　calotes **44:** *46–47*
　versicolor **44:** 35, (37), 46–47
Calumia godeffroyi **40:** 97
Calumma **44:** 56
　brevicornis **44:** 60
　nasuta **44:** 61
　parsonii **44:** 61, 66–67
Caluromys
　derbianus **10:** 14
　philander **10:** 14
Caluromysiops irrupta **10:** 14
Calyptocephalus gratiosus **25:** *37*
Calyptomena viridis **20:** 74, 76–79
Calyptommatus **45:** (85)
Calyptraeidae **30:** 29–30
Calyptura cristata **19:** 80
calyptura, kinglet **19:** 80, 83
Camarhynchus
　parvulus **20:** 96
　pauper **20:** 96
　psittacula **20:** 96
Cambaris monongalensis **28:** *58*
camel 5: *8*, 9, 12
　Arabian (dromedary) **5:** 92, 93, 94–99, 102
　Bactrian 5: 92, 93, (98), 100–103
　camel family 5: 92–93
　domestication **5:** (98)
　dromedary 5: 92, 93, 94–99, 102
　one-humped (dromedary) **5:** 92, 93, 94–99, 102
　two-humped (Bactrian) **5:** 92, 93, (98), 100–103
camelids **5:** 92–93
Camelus
　bactrianus **5:** 92, 100–103
　dromedarius **5:** 92, 94–99
　ferus (*bactrianus*) **5:** 92, 100–103
camouflage **11:** 12; **15:** (60), 80, (80), *81*; **31:** *79*; **33:** 22–23, 42–43, *43*; **35:** *96–97*; **36:** 68–69; **37:** (72); **39:** (42)
camouflage see coloration, cryptic
Campellolebias **38:** (79)
　brucei **38:** 82
　chrysolineatus **38:** 82
　dorsimaculatus **38:** 82
Campephilus principalis **18:** 8, 14
Camponotus detritus **27:** *42–43*
Camposcia retusa **28:** *110–111*
Camptorhynchus labradorius **12:** 69

Campylomormyrus
  cassaicus **31:** 107
  rhynchophorus **31:** *106, 108–109*
Campylorhamphus falcularius **17:** 28
Campylorhynchus
  brunneicapillus **17:** 52, 56–59
  chiapensis **17:** 52, (57)
  griseus **17:** 52, (57)
  yucatanicus **17:** 52, (57)
canary **16:** 76
canastero, creamy-breasted **20:** 80
Cancer gracialis 2: *12–13*
candirú **37:** (91), *94*, 95
candlefish **35:** (28)
Candoia **48:** 46
  aspera **48:** 46, 60, (61)
  bibroni **48:** 46, 60, (61)
  carinata **48:** 46, 60–61, (61)
Canephora unicolor **26:** *110*
Canidae **1:** 20
Canis
  dingo **2:** 50, 80–81
  familiaris **2:** 50, (53)
  latrans **2:** 50, 58–61
  lupus **2:** 50, 54–57
  lupus dingo (*C. dingo*) **2:** 50, 80–81
  mesomelas **2:** 50, 62–63
  simensis **2:** 50
cannibalism
  frogs **43:** (22), 99
  lobsters and crayfish **28:** 76
  mantids **22:** 77–78
  salamanders **41:** 105, (107)
  shrimps and prawns **28:** 66
  snakes **48:** (66); **50:** 72
  tadpoles **42:** 13
  web spinners **22:** 82
Cantharidae **25:** 34–35
cantharidin **25:** 62, (63), 65
Cantharis rustica **25:** *34*
Canthesancus gulo **24:** *38*
Canthigaster **39:** 109
  callisterna **39:** 109
  rostrata **39:** 109
  valentini **39:** (102), *108*
cantil **50:** (89), 96
capelin **35:** 26, *26–27*, 28, *28*
capercaillie **11:** 44, *45*
Caperea marginata **3:** 55
Capholymma stygia **25:** *95*
Capito niger **19:** 56
Capitonidae **19:** 56, 57
Capoëta **34:** 24, 25, (26), 28
  see also Barbus
Capra
  aegagrus **6:** 62
  ibex **6:** 62, 106–107
  ibex caucasica **6:** 106
  ibex cylindricornis **6:** 106
  ibex ibex **6:** 106
  ibex nubiana **6:** 106
  ibex sibirica **6:** 106
  ibex walie **6:** 106
Caprellidae **28:** 34

Caprellidea **28:** 34
Capreolus capreolus **6:** 10, 38–39
Capricornis
  crispus **6:** 62
  sumatraensis **6:** 62, 108
Caprimulgidae **15:** 78
Caprimulgiformes **15:** 78, *80*
Caprimulgus **20:** 74
  carolinensis **15:** 78
  europaeus **15:** 78; **18:** 12
  vociferus **15:** 78, 82–83
Caprodon longimanus **40:** 15
Caproidae **39:** 10, 22–25
Caprolagus hispidus **8:** 64
Capromyidae **7:** *12*; **8:** 31
Capromys pilorides **8:** 30, 52–53
Capros aper **39:** 25, *25*
captive birds **16:** (28), (34), (35), 98–99
  breeding **18:** (40); **19:** (32), 54; **20:** 18–21
  mimicry **18:** (41), 89
captive breeding **1:** 45, 47, 54, (55), (59), 71; **2:** (23), (29), 59, 100; **4:** (17), 87, 90–91, 98, 101; **5:** 26, 65; **6:** 91; **7:** 15; **42:** (53); **49:** (47)
  alligators **47:** (101)
  frogs **43:** 54, 73, 80
  giant galliwasps **46:** 67
  Gila monsters **46:** 79
  reptiles **44:** (16–17)
  tortoises **47:** 88
captivity **1:** 22, 29, 65; **3:** 59, 65, 71, 74; **4:** 27, 78; **6:** *42–43*, 58, 66, 91; **9:** 21; **10:** 83; **41:** 61, (62); **42:** (29)
capuchin **4:** 10, 72, 83
  brown **4:** 72, 73
  weeper **4:** 72
  white-faced **4:** 72
capuchinbird **19:** 80, 83
capybara 7: 8, *12*, 28; **8:** 8, 9, 10, 28, 48–51
  farms **8:** (50)
Carabidae **25:** 16–19
caracal **2:** 10, *11*
Caracanthidae **39:** 11, 53, 68–71
Caracanthus
  maculatus **39:** 68, *68, 69*
  madagascariensis **39:** 68
  typicus **39:** 68
  unipinna **39:** 68
caracara 15: 11, 12
  crested 15: 8, 24–27
carajota
  South American **38:** 73
Carangidae **40:** 34–35
Caranx
  hippos **40:** *34*
  ignobilis **40:** 34
carapace **47:** *10–11*
Carapidae **36:** 22–23
Carapus **36:** *22–23*
  acus **36:** 23
  homei **36:** 23

Carassius **34:** 80
  auratus **34:** 43
  auratus auratus **34:** 8, 16, 31, 42–51, 43, 80
  auratus buergeri **34:** 44
  auratus gibelius **34:** 43, 44, (44)
  auratus grandoculis **34:** 44
  auratus langsdorfii **34:** 44
  carassius **34:** 43, 44, (44)
  cuvieri **34:** 44
  gibelius **34:** 42, 43, 44
caravaning **9:** 39
Carcharhinidae **32:** (12), (42), 55, 66, 68–73, 93
Carcharhiniformes **32:** 42–45
Carcharhinus
  albimarginatus **32:** 51
  amblyrhynchos **32:** 22, 48–51
  amblyrhyncoides **32:** 50
  amboinensis **32:** 20
  leucas **32:** 22, 52–55
  limbatus **32:** 15, 22
  longimanus **32:** 24, 66
  melanopterus **32:** 50
  nicaraguensis **32:** 53
  perezi **32:** (18), *54*
  plumbeus **32:** (18), 22, 55
  wheeleri **32:** 50
  zambezensis **32:** 53
Carcharias
  borneensis **32:** 25
  limbatus **32:** 25
  obscurus **32:** 25
  plumbeus **32:** 25
  taurus **32:** 19, *23*, 25, 35
Carchariidae **32:** (74)
Carcharodon carcharias **32:** 10, *11*, 12, 43, 54, 60, 77, 84–89
carcinology **21:** (33)
Carcinus maenas **28:** *102*
Cardellina rubifrons **17:** 88
Cardiidae **30:** 50, 65–67
cardinal (red cardinal, northern cardinal) **16:** 62–63, 66–71
cardinalfish 40: 30–31
  Banggai **40:** 31, *31*
  fistulose **40:** 30
  large-toothed **40:** 30
  pyjama **40:** *30–31*
  red-colored **40:** 30
  red-spotted **40:** *30–31*
Cardinalinae **16:** 62
Cardinalis cardinalis **16:** 62, 66–71
Cardioglossa **43:** 12
Cardium edule **30:** *62–63*
carduelines **16:** 77, 78–79, 81
Carduelis
  carduelis **16:** 76
  chloris **16:** 76
  flammea **16:** 76
  pinus **16:** 76
  tristis **16:** 76, 80–81
Caretta caretta **47:** *8–9, 15*, 16–17, 54
Carettochelyidae **47:** 9, 28, 58

Carettochelys insculpta **47**: <u>58–59</u>
Caria mantinea **26**: *34–35*
Cariama **19**: 8
   cristata **11**: 92, <u>94–95</u>
Cariamidae **11**: 92
caribou 6: 10, 12, <u>20–25</u>
Caridea **28**: 56, <u>60–69</u>
Carinotetraodon
   lorteti **39**: 109
   travancoricus **39**: 109
Carlia **46**: 8, 10
Carnegillea strigata **38**: *28*, 29
carnero **37**: 95
Carnivora **1**: *10*, 18; **2**: 8
carnivores 1: *10*
  large 2: <u>8–9</u>
  small 1: <u>18–19</u>
  teeth **1**: *15*
carp 31: 63, **34**: 10, <u>16–19</u>, 80, **37**: 8,
   (36), **40**: (96)
  Amur **34**: 35
  bronze **34**: 43, (44)
  common 34: 8, *8–9*, 16, 18, <u>32–41</u>,
   44, 46, 83, **37**: 18
  common, species names **34**: (35)
  crucian **34**: 42, 44, (44)
  "cunning" **34**: *9*
  European **34**: 32
  gibel **34**: 42, 43, 44, (44)
  gold crucian **34**: 42
  golden **34**: 42
  grass 34: 18, <u>52–53</u>, 71
  highland **38**: 106
  leather **34**: *33*, 34, 40
  mirror **34**: *33*, 34, 40
  native **34**: 42
  Prussian **34**: 42, 43, 44, (44)
  silver **34**: 18, 88
  see also koi
"Carp Farcie" **34**: 37
"Carpe à la Maitre d'Hotel" **34**: 37
Carpiodes **34**: 95
  carpio **34**: 95, 99
  cyprinus **34**: 95, 99
  velifer **34**: 95, 99
carpione **35**: (69)
Carpococcyx renauldi **20**: 46
Carpodacus rubicilla **16**: 76
Carpodectes nitidus **19**: 80
carpsucker **34**: 99
  highfin **34**: 95
  river **34**: 95
carrion feeders **13**: (71); **14**: (36), (39);
  20: (14)
Carterodon sulcidens **8**: 30
cartilaginous fish 31: (10), *14*, 42, **32**:
  <u>8–9</u>, **33**: <u>8–15</u>, <u>54–57</u>, **36**: 97
Casarea dussumieri **48**: 47, <u>76–77</u>, 79
cascarudo **37**: 101, 103
Casella astromarginata **30**: *20–21*
Casmerodius albus **14**: 20
Cassiopeia frondosa **21**: 53
cassowary 11: 18, 19
  Bennett's **11**: 16

double-wattled (southern) **11**: 16,
  <u>28–33</u>
  one-wattled **11**: 16, *17*
  southern 11: 16, <u>28–33</u>
Castor **7**: 28
  canadensis **7**: 28, <u>30–33</u>
  fiber **7**: 28castoreum **7**: (31)
Castoridae **7**: *12*, 28
Casuariidae **11**: 16
Casuarius
  bennetti **11**: 16
  casuarius **11**: 16, <u>28–33</u>
  unappendiculatus **11**: 16
cat (fish)
  duck-billed **31**: 70
  shovel-billed **31**: 70
  spoonbill **31**: 70
  see also catfish
cat 2: 9
  African wildcat **2**: *12*
  Asiatic golden **2**: 10, *13*
  blackfooted **2**: 10, *13*
  cat family 2: <u>10–13</u>
  domestic **2**: 9, 10, (12), 49
  European wildcat **2**: *12*
  jungle **2**: 10, *13*
  leopard **2**: 10, *13*
  miner's *see* raccoon, ringtail
  saber-toothed **2**: 10
  sand **2**: 10, *13*
  tiger **2**: 10, *12*
  wildcat 2: 10, *13*, <u>48–49</u>
Catacanthus anchorago **24**: *60*
Catacola amatrix **26**: 92
Catagonus wagneri **5**: 88
catamount *see* puma
catarrhines **4**: 11
catatonia **10**: (20)
catbird **19**: 100, 101, 102–103
  black **18**: 36, *37*
  gray **18**: 36, *37*
  green **19**: 100
  spotted **19**: 100
caterpillar hunters **25**: 16, *17*
caterpillars **26**: 13–14
  Amycta quadrangularis **26**: *110*
  butterfly **27**: *48–49*
  California tent caterpillar moth **26**: 86
  Caligo opsiphanes **26**: 48
  cinnabar moth **26**: *90*
  cloudless sulfur **26**: *24–25*
  cup moth **26**: *107*
  danaid **26**: *58–59*
  Eucylodes **26**: (76)
  European drinker moth **26**: *85*
  European feathered thorn **26**: *76*
  European large elephant hawk
   moth **26**: 68
  European puss moth **26**: *82*
  European sycamore moth **26**: 96
  Euthalia **26**: 42
  geometrid **26**: (76)
  gypsy moth **26**: (101)
  Heliconius sara **26**: 55

hieroglyphic moth **26**: *97*
ithomiid **26**: 56
lackey moth **26**: *86*
Lirimiris **26**: *82*
Lycaenidae **26**: 30–31
monkey slug **26**: *106*
mottled umber **26**: *77*
Naprepa **26**: *82*
Narathura **26**: *32–33*
narrow-bordered five-spot burnet
moth **26**: *109*
noctuid **26**: 95–97
notodontids **26**: 81–83
Oiketicus elongatus **26**: *111*
orchard swallowtail **26**: *18–19*
owlet moth **26**: *97*
pipevine swallowtail **26**: *18*
plume moths **26**: 102–103
Prepona antimache **26**: *40*
red dagger wing **26**: *42–43*
saturniid **26**: 72–73
silkworm moths **26**: *79*
skippers **26**: *64*
small tortoiseshell **26**: *42–43*
sphinx moth **26**: 67–69
swallowtail **26**: (19), *20*
western tussock moth **26**: *100*
wood-boring **26**: 104–105
yponomeutid **26**: 112–113
catfish 31: 42, (95), **33**: 20, 100, **37**:
  <u>8–13</u>
  African bumblebee **37**: 71
  African glass **37**: (34), *39*, 40
  African shoulder-spot **37**: 41
  African walking **37**: 54, *54–55*, 55
  African wood **37**: 22
  air-breathing **37**: 11
  airsac 37: 11, 30, <u>56–57</u>
  aluminium **37**: 22, *23*
  Amur dragon **37**: 29
  angler **37**: 58, (59)
  antenna 37: 29, <u>84–89</u>, 104
  Aristotle's **37**: 30, 32
  armored 37: <u>96–103</u>
  Asian glass **37**: *31*, (34), 40
  Asian hillstream 37: <u>48–51</u>
  Asian red-tailed bagrid **37**: 28, *28–29*
  Asian stinging **37**: 10
  Asian walking **37**: <u>52–55</u>, 55
  bagrid 37: 11, <u>22–29</u>, 38, 39
  banded bagrid **37**: 28, 29
  banjo 37: 11, 59, <u>92–93</u>
  belly sucker **37**: 50, (51)
  big-eyed miji **37**: 22
  black spiny **37**: 107
  black tandan **37**: <u>66–67</u>
  blue **37**: *18*, 20, 65
  blue whale **37**: <u>90–91</u>
  Boldatov's **37**: 32
  Bornean glass **37**: (34)
  broad-headed **37**: 50
  bulldog **37**: 107
  bullhead *see* bullhead
  bumblebee **37**: 27, 28, 29, (69), 87,

89
Burmese frogmouth **37:** (59)
butter **37:** *38*, 40, 41
butterfly **37:** 48, *48–49*
callichthyid armored **37:** 96, 97
candy-striped **37:** 40
cave **37:** 55
channel **34:** 97, **37:** 14, *14*, 16, 17, 18, 20, *20*, (21), (44)
cheetah **37:** 48, (51)
chocolate **37:** (59)
clown **37:** *48*, (51)
Congo **37:** (34)
Congo glass **37:** 40, *40–41*
coral **37:** 66, *66*, 67, *68–69*, (69), **40:** 24
croaking **37:** 10
Debauwi **37:** 40
dolphin **37:** *76*, 77, 78, (78), 79
driftwood 37: 12, 77, 82–83
dwarf anchor **37:** 48, (51)
dwarf marbled **37:** 88
eel **37:** 55
eeltail **37:** 66, 68
electric 31: (108), **37:** 60–63
electric, species summary **37:** (62)
European **37:** 30, *30*
false Siamese shark **37:** 41
family differences **37:** (32)
flagtail **37:** 100, 101, 103
flat-headed **37:** 50
flathead **37:** 16, 20, 21
flathead eel **37:** 55
fork-tailed **37:** 64
fossil **37:** 56
freshwater **32:** 55
frogmouth 37: 58–59, (59)
frying pan **37:** *92*
ghost glass **37:** *31*, (34)
giant **37:** 8, 11, 32, *42*, 45
giant glass **37:** *36–37*
giant moth **37:** 48
giant river **37:** (51)
giraffe **37:** *24–25*, 28, 29
glass 37: 30, *31*, (34), 36, 37, 39, 40, *41*
golden tiger shark **37:** *43*
golden-yellow bodied **37:** 22
grass cutter **37:** *38*, 40, 41
gray **37:** 28
Guinea **37:** *24*, 27, 29
Hancock's talking **37:** *76–77*, 79
hardhead sea **37:** *64*
imitator **37:** *86*
Indian **37:** *50–51*
Indian frogmouth **37:** *58*, 59
iridescent shark *see* shark, iridescent
jaguar **37:** 77
large-headed walking **37:** 55
liver **37:** 56, *56–57*
long-striped glass **37:** 41
long-tailed banjo **37:** 26
long-whiskered **37:** 8, 10, 26, 27, 84, 85

madtom *see* madtom
Malarmo antenna **37:** 87
Malayan glass **37:** *34–35*
Malaysian **37:** (59)
Mekong **37:** 32, *42*
milk-drinking **37:** (26)
moth **37:** 48
mottled **37:** 22
"noisy cats" **37:** (29)
North American freshwater 37: 14–21
pajama-striped bagrid **37:** 28, 29
parasitic 37: 11, 84, (91), 94–95
parasitic subfamilies **37:** (94)
pencil **37:** 94
peppered **37:** 96, *97*
phantom glass **37:** *31*
pirate **37:** 84
"plecostomus" **38:** (40)
poor man's glass **37:** (34)
porthole **37:** *100–101*, 101, 103
pygmy **37:** 11
red-tailed **37:** 29, *84*, 87
salmon **37:** 64
saltwater **37:** 67
scarlet **37:** *10–11*
schilbeid 37: 30, (34), 38–41, (40)
sea 37: 64–65
self-protection **37:** 10
shark 37: 38, 42–47, 64, 65
shovelhead **37:** 21
shovelmouth **37:** 26, 27
shovelnose **37:** 26, 27, *85*
Siamese shark **37:** 41
slender armored **37:** *96*, 101
slender banjo **37:** 92
smaller ghost glass **37:** (34)
smallmouth electric **37:** *60–61*
spiny dwarf **37:** 11, 97
spiny-headed **37:** 94
squarehead **37:** 58, (59)
squeaking **37:** 10, 11, 29, 70
stick **37:** 110
as "stingers" **37:** 8
stinging **37:** 56, 66
stream **37:** 93
striped **37:** *12, 38*
stripetail **37:** 101
sturgeon **37:** 87
suckermouth **34:** 109
suckermouth armored 37: 11, 97, 104–111
suckermouth armored, subfamilies **37:** (106)
talking 37: 10, 26, 29, 76–81
tandan 37: 29, 66–69
thorny **37:** 76, 97
toothless **37:** *68*
torrent **37:** 11
twig **37:** 110
two-spot pink bagrid **37:** *22*
upside-down 37: 8, 11, 70–75, **39:** (86)
Vaillant's butter **37:** (34), *34–35*

venom **37:** 10, 17
"vulture of the water" **37:** 84, (86)
walking 37: 30, 43, 52–55
West African glass **37:** (34), 40
whale 37: 11, 84, 90–91
whiptail **37:** (49), (51), 110
white **37:** 14, 16, 20
white-edged bumblebee **37:** 88
white-spot spiny **37:** 107
Who's Who **37:** (13)
yellow **37:** 21
Catharacta **12:** 17, 76; **16:** (26)
  antarctica **12:** 74
  chilensis **12:** 74
  maccormicki **12:** 74
  skua **12:** 9, 43, 74, 92–95
Cathartes **20:** (14)
  aura **15:** 24; **20:** 8, 12–15, 17
  burrovianus **20:** 8
  melambrotus **20:** 8
Cathartidae **15:** 8, 12; **20:** 8
Catharus guttatus **18:** 44
Cathedra serrata **24:** 72–73
Cathimeris hymenaea **27:** 36–37
Catlocarpio siamensis **34:** 19
catopra **40:** 57
Catoprion **38:** (45)
  mento **38:** 44–45
Catoptrophorus semipalmatus **13:** 30
Catostomidae **34:** 9, 10, 12, (88), 89, 94, 96–99, 100
Catostomus **34:** 99
  catostomus **34:** 12, 94
  commersoni **34:** 98–99
  latipinnis **34:** 98
  microps **34:** 96
cattle 1: 15; **5:** 9, *11*, 12; **6:** 60–63; **8:** 62
  humped zebu **6:** 63
  humpless **6:** 63
cattle rearing **4:** 79
Caudacaecilia **41:** 21
caudal autotomy **44:** 22, 30, 81
Caudata **41:** 8, 27
Caudiverbera **42:** 76
Caulophryinidae **36:** 74–83
Caulophryne **36:** 82
Cauricara eburnea **25:** 69
Causinae **50:** 50, 56
Causus **50:** (21), 50, 56–57
  rhombeatus **49:** 33
cavefish 36: 8, 18–19, 21
  distribution of **36:** (19)
  northern **36:** *18*
  Ozark **36:** 19
  swamp-dwelling **36:** 18, 19
Cavia
  aperaea **8:** 39
  porcellus **8:** 30, 38–41
  tschudii **8:** 39
caviar **31:** 55, 56, (57), 63, 64, (66), 71; **39:** 57, 83
Caviidae **7:** 12
Caviomorpha **7:** (8); **8:** 28, 31

cavy 7: 11, *12*, (14)
  Brazilian **8:** 39, *41*
  cavies and relatives 8: <u>28–31</u>
  common yellow-toothed **8:** 28, 30
  domestic *see* guinea pig
  Patagonian *see* mara
  Peruvian **8:** 39
  rock **8:** 30
  southern mountain **8:** *10–11*, 30
cavylike rodents 8: <u>8–11</u>
Cebidae **4:** 72, 84
Cebuella pygmaea **4:** 86
Cebus **4:** 72
  apella **4:** 72
  capucinus **4:** 72
  olivaceus **4:** 72
Celaenia kinbergi **29:** (108)
celestial **34:** 49
Celestus **46:** 52, <u>66–67</u>
Celeus elegans **18:** 8
cellulose **4:** 41, 75; **5:** 11–12, 70;
  6: 8; **7:** 103; **8:** 49; **28:** 49
centipedes 22: <u>22–25</u>
  defense **22:** (24)
  European common **22:** *22–23*
  house **22:** *9, 22*
Centrarchidae **40:** <u>26–29</u>
Centriscidae **39:** 11, 26, <u>50–51</u>
Centriscops **39:** 50
  humerosus **39:** 50, *50*
Centriscus **39:** 50
  scutatus **39:** *50–51*
Centrocercus urophasianus **11:** 44,
  <u>70–73</u>
Centrolene **43:** 28
Centrolenella **43:** 28
Centrolenidae **42:** 10; **43:** 28, 101
Centrophoridae **32:** (12), 26, (92)
Centrophryne spinulosa **36:** 83
Centrophrynidae **36:** <u>74–83</u>
Centropodinae **20:** 46
Centropomidae **40:** <u>12–19</u>
Centropomus **40:** 13
Centropus
  phasianinus **20:** 46, <u>62–63</u>
  senegalensis **20:** 46
Centropyge
  aurantonotus **40:** (52)
  bicolor **40:** (52)
  eibli **40:** (52)
  ferrugata **40:** 51
  fisheri **40:** (52)
  flavissima **40:** *50–51*, 51
  heraldi **40:** 51
  interruptus **40:** 50
  joculator **40:** 50
  multicolor **40:** (52)
  multifasciata **40:** (52)
  nigriocellus **40:** (52)
  nox **40:** 23
  resplendens **40:** 50
  tibicen **40:** 51
  venustus **40:** (52)
  vrolikii **40:** 51

Centroscyllium
  excelsum **32:** 94
  fabricii **32:** 94
  granulatum **32:** 94
  kamoharai **32:** 94
  nigrum **32:** 94
  ornatum **32:** 94
  ritteri **32:** 94
Centroscymnus coelolepis **32:** 93, 97
Cephalocarida **28:** 9, (14)
Cephalochordata **21:** 32
Cephalophus **6:** 62, 80
  dorsalis **6:** 62
  monticola **6:** 62
Cephalopoda **30:** 9, 10
cephalopods 30: <u>72–73</u>
Cephalopterus
  glabricollis **19:** 86
  ornatus **19:** 80, <u>86–87</u>
  penduliger **19:** 86
Cephaloscyllium **32:** 57
  fasciatum **32:** 58
  isabellum **32:** 59
  laticeps **32:** 59
  nascione **32:** 59
  sufflans **32:** 58
  umbratile **32:** <u>58–59</u>
  ventriosum **32:** 59
Cephalosilurus albomarginatus **37:** 88
Cepphus grylle **12:** 98, <u>108–109</u>
Cerambycidae **25:** <u>90–95</u>
Ceramius tuberculifer **27:** 69
Cerastes
  cerastes **48:** *9, 12;* **49:** (73); **50:** 9, 51,
    58, <u>70–71</u>, 77, 103
  gasperettii **50:** 71
  vipera **50:** 71
Ceratias **36:** 82a
  holboelli **36:** (76), 77
Ceratiidae **36:** <u>74–83</u>
Ceratitis capitata **23:** (90)
Ceratobatrachus **43:** 82
  guentheri **42:** (38); **43:** 86
Ceratocoris cephalicus **24:** *63*
Ceratodontidae **31:** (33), <u>38–41</u>, **33:** 63
Ceratophora **44:** *13, 32, (37)*
Ceratophryinae **42:** 76, 87
Ceratophrys **41:** 18; **42:** 36, (38), 76; **43:**
  86, 99
  cornuta **42:** *76–77*
  cranwelli **42:** 87
  ornata **42:** *86–87*
Ceratopogonidae **23:** (52)
Ceratosaurus **44:** *10–11*
Ceratotherium simum **5:** 28, <u>30–35</u>
Cerberus rynchops **49:** 15
Cercartetus **10:** 74
  concinnus **10:** 74
  nanus **10:** 74
Cercocebus
  galeritus **4:** 40
  torquatus **4:** 40
Cercopidae **24:** <u>78–79</u>
Cercopis vulnerata **24:** *78*

Cercopithecidae **4:** 40
cercopithecines **4:** 40, *40–41*, 42, 43
Cercopithecus
  aethiops **4:** <u>44–47</u>
  cephus **4:** 40
  neglectus **4:** 40
Ceriantharia **21:** 43
Ceroplastes **24:** *106–107*
Cerorhinca monocerata **12:** 98
Certhia
  americana **17:** 82
  brachydactyla **17:** 82, 86
  familiaris **17:** 82, <u>84–87</u>
Certhiaxis cinnamomea **20:** 80
Certhidea olivacea **20:** 96
Certhiidae **17:** 82; **18:** 64
Certhilauda albescens **18:** 22
Cerura vinula **26:** *82*
Cervidae **6:** 9, 10, 12
Cervus
  canadensis **6:** 10, <u>26–29</u>
  canadensis manitobensis **6:** 27
  canadensis nannodes **6:** 27
  canadensis nelsoni **6:** 26
  canadensis roosevelti **6:** 27
  elaphus **6:** 10, 26, <u>30–33</u>
Ceryle rudis **14:** 100
Cestoda **21:** 77, 81, 82–83
Cestraeus goldiei **38:** 53
Cetacea **1:** *10;* **5:** (10)
cetaceans **3:** 54–59
Cetomimidae **39:** 9, <u>12–15</u>
Cetomionus picklei **39:** (15)
Cetopsidae **37:** 11, 84, <u>90–91</u>
Cetopsis coecutiens **37:** *90–91*
Cetorhinidae **32:** (12), (74)
Cetorhinus maximus **31:** 70, **32:** 12, 22,
  38, 76, <u>78–81</u>, 93
Cettia cetti **17:** 60
Ceuthophilus brevipes **23:** *21*
Chaca
  bankanensis **37:** (59)
  burmensis **37:** (59)
  chaca **37:** *58, 59*
chachalaca **11:** 48
  plain **11:** 44
Chacidae **37:** <u>58–59</u>
Chacophrys **42:** 87, 88–89
Chaeropus ecaudatus **10:** 27
Chaetoderma penicilligera **39:** *97*
Chaetodipus penicillatus **7:** <u>22–23</u>
Chaetodon
  auriga **40:** 46
  baronessa **40:** 46
  capistratus **40:** *46–47*, 47
  larvatus **40:** 46
  lunula **40:** *48–49*
  mitratus **40:** 46
  modestus **40:** 46
  paucifasciatus **40:** *48*
  triangulum **40:** 46
  trifascialis **40:** 46
Chaetodontidae **39:** (10); **40:** <u>46–49</u>, 51,
  54, 100

Chaetodontoplus conspicillatus **40**: (52)
Chaetognatha **21**: 32, 77, 79
Chaetomys subspinosus **8**: 30
Chaetonotoida **21**: 69
Chaetorhynchus papuensis **17**: 106
Chaetostoma **37**: 107
  thomsoni **37**: 107
Chaetura
  brachyura **15**: 70
  martinica **15**: 70
  pelagica **15**: 70
  vauxi **15**: 70
chafers **25**: 82, *85*
  flower **25**: *85*
  pine **25**: *82*
chaffinch 16: 76, 77, 78–79
  Canary Islands **16**: 76
Chaga's disease **8**: 27; **21**: 17; **24**: 46
chain chorusing **5**: 71
Chalarodon **44**: 80
Chalcides **44**: (26); **46**: 8
  chalcides **46**: 20–23
  ocellatus **46**: 20, *22–23*
Chalcidoidea **27**: (23)
Chalcophaps indica **16**: 12
Chalcopsitta atra **20**: 36
Chalicodoma
  parietinum, nests **27**: (88)
  siculum, nests **27**: (88)
Chamaeleo **44**: 56, 78
  bitaeniatus **44**: 61
  calyptratus **44**: 59, 70–71
  carpenteri **44**: 58
  dilepis **44**: *58*, 60, *60*, 60–61; **49**: 36
  ellioti **44**: 61
  gracilis **44**: 56
  hoehnelii **44**: 56, *57*, 58
  jacksonii **44**: 28, 58, 72–73
  montium **44**: 58, *58*
  namaquensis **44**: 68–69
  parsonii cristifer **44**: 66
  pfefferi **44**: 58
  pumilus **44**: 62
  rudis **44**: 56
  senegalensis **44**: 56
  xenorhinus **44**: 58
Chamaeleonidae **44**: 25, 56
Chamaesaura **45**: (81), 98
chameleon fish 40: 56–57
chameleons 44: *25*, 25, 28, 29, 30, 56–61; **49**: 36, (71), 73
  African dwarf 44: 62–63
  African pygmy (western pygmy)
    44: 65, 78–79
  American (green anoles) **44**: 106–107
  coarse **44**: 56
  color **44**: 59, 60–61
  defense **44**: 60
  dwarf **44**: 25, 56; **49**: 36
  feeding and diet **44**: 59–60
  flap-necked **44**: *58*, 60, *60*, 60–61;
    49: 36
  graceful **44**: 56
  ground **44**: 25, 56

habitat **44**: 56–57
high-casqued **44**: 56, *56–57*, 58
Jackson's 44: 28, 58, 72–73
Knysna dwarf **44**: 62
leaf (western pygmy) **44**: 57, 65,
    78–79
lesser **44**: 59
myths **44**: (59)
Namaqua 44: 68–69
Natal midlands dwarf **44**: *62–63*
Oustalet's **44**: 56, 57
panther 44: 74–77
Parson's 44: 61, 66–67
Pfeffer's **44**: 58
physical features **44**: 57–58
reproduction **44**: 60–61
sail-fin **44**: 58, *58*
Senegal **44**: 56
senses **44**: 28–29, 58
short-horned **44**: 60
Smith's dwarf **44**: 63
stump-tailed 44: 25, 57, 60, 64–65
tails **44**: 58
tongue-testing **44**: 59
two-lined **44**: 61
veiled 44: 59, 70–71
western pygmy 44: 65, 78–79
Yemen (veiled) **44**: 59, 70–71
Chamoideae **30**: 50
chamois **6**: 62
  European **6**: 108
  Pyrenean **6**: 62
Chanda ranga **40**: 20
Channa
  argus **40**: 65
  asiatica **40**: 64
  bleheri **40**: 65
  gachua **40**: 64
  marulia **40**: 65
  micropeltes **40**: 65
  orientalis **40**: *64–65*, 65
  striata **40**: *64*
Channallabes apus **37**: 55
Channidae **40**: 64–65
char 35: 9, 46–47, (51), 66
  Alpine **35**: 47
  Arctic **35**: 46, 47, *47*
  brook **35**: 46, 47, 67
  East Siberian **35**: 46
  head-spotted **35**: 46
  Honshu **35**: 46
  long-finned **35**: 47
  sea **35**: 46
  white-spotted **35**: 46, 47
Characidae **33**: 100; **38**: 8, 34–47
  subfamilies summary **38**: (34)
Characidium **38**: 33, *33*
  fasciatum **38**: 32
  rachovii **38**: 33
Characiformes
  families summary **38**: (11)
characin 34–35
  African red-eyed **38**: *31*
  banded darter **38**: 32

blackband predator **38**: 24, 25
blind **38**: 8
blind cave **38**: 8, 35, 36, *36*, (39), 41
flying **38**: 28
gar *see* gar characin
pike *see* pike characin
Rachov's **38**: 33
subfamilies summary **38**: (34)
sucker **38**: 17
swordtail **38**: 11, 35
Characodon
  audax **38**: 110
  garmani **38**: 110
  lateralis **38**: 110, (111)
characodon
  bold **38**: 110
  Parras **38**: 110
characoids 38: 8–11
  Who's Who **38**: (11)
Charadrii **11**: (103); **14**: 98
Charadriidae **13**: 8, 30
Charadriiformes **12**: 74, 98
Charadrius **13**: 8–9
  bicinctus **13**: 8, 27
  hiaticula **13**: 8, 18–19
  pecuarius **13**: 8
  vociferus **13**: 8
charal, Mexican **38**: (63)
Charax gibbosus **38**: 35
Charaxes
  candiope **26**: 38–39
  subornatus **26**: 40
  rajahs **26**: 39–40
Charina
  bottae **48**: 16, 46, 68–69, 72
  reinhardtii **48**: 17, 46, 69
  trivirgata **48**: 46, 68, 70–73
Charis chrysus **26**: 37
charms **3**: 61; **8**: 67; **9**: 79
Charniodiscus **21**: *35*
Charonia tritonis **30**: *27*
Chascanopsetta lugubris **39**: 91
Chasmistes **34**: 99
  brevirostris **34**: 96
  cujus **34**: 96
  muriei **34**: 96
chat **17**: (76)
  yellow-breasted **17**: 88, *88*
chat-shrike **15**: 104
Chauliodus **35**: 86
  danae **35**: 86, (86)
  sloani **35**: *84–85*, 86, (86), *87*
Chaunacidae **36**: (73)
cheetah 2: 9, 10, 26–29
  king **2**: 29
Cheilodipterus macrodon **40**: 30
Cheiramoeca leucosterna **15**: 94
Cheirodon **38**: 41
  interruptus **38**: 35
Cheirogaleus
  major **4**: 96
  medius **4**: 96
Chela **34**: 19
  caeruleostigmata **34**: *18–19*, **38**: 29

laubuca **38:** 29
Chelicerata **22:** 9
chelicerates 29: *8–9*
Chelidae **47:** 9, 28, 83
Chelidonichthys
  lastoviza **39:** 57
  lucerna **39:** 57
Chelidoptera tenebrosa **19:** 56
Chelisoches bimammatus **22:** (59)
Chelmon rostratus **40:** 46
Chelodina oblonga **47:** *32–33*, 38
Chelon labrosus **38:** 53
Chelonia **44:** 11, 18; **47:** 8
  mydas **47:** *18–21*, 73
chelonians **47:** 8–11
Cheloniidae **47:** 12
Chelorrhina polyphemus **25:** *84–85*
Chelus fimbriatus **47:** 10, *34–37*
Chelydra serpentina **47:** 47, (50), *52–55*
Chelydridae **47:** 9, 28
chemical poisoning *see* pollution
chemosynthesis **21:** 93
Cherax destructor **28:** *78*
Chersina **47:** 80
chevrotain **5:** *8;* **6:** 10
  greater Malay *see* deer, greater mouse
  Indian spotted **6:** 10
  water **6:** 10
chewing the cud **6:** 8
chickadee 18: 64
  black-capped 17: 70, *74–79*
  boreal **17:** 70, (78)
  Carolina **17:** 70, 74, 75, (78)
  chestnut-backed **17:** 70, (78)
  mountain **17:** 70, (78); **18:** 67
chiffchaff **17:** 60, 62, 64, (64)
chiggers **29:** (32)
Chilara taylori **36:** 25
Chilatherina **38:** 57
  sentaniensis **38:** (56)
Chilidonias
  hybridus **12:** 74
  leucopterus **12:** 74
  niger **12:** 74, 88
chillipepper **39:** 64
Chilocoris renipustulatus **25:** *58*
Chilodus
  gracilis **38:** *21*
  punctatus **38:** *20*, 21
Chiloglanis **37:** 73
Chilomeniscus **49:** (63)
  cinctus **49:** 25
  palarostris **50:** (25)
Chilopoda **22:** 14, *22–25*
Chilorhinophis **49:** 106
Chilorhinus suensonii **33:** *76*, 77
chimaera 31: 42; **33:** *54–57*
  deepwater **33:** (56)
  leopard **33:** (56)
  long-nose **33:** 56
  purple **33:** 54
  research priority **33:** (56)
  short-nose **33:** 57
  Who's Who **33:** (55)

Chimaera
  monstrosa **33:** *56–57*
  panthera **33:** (56)
Chimaeridae **33:** 54, (55); **36:** 85
Chimaeriformes **33:** 54, (55)
chimpanzee 4: *11*, 12, 13, *28–33*; **5:** 9
  common **4:** 12
  pygmy *see* bonobo
China, Imperial Hunting Park **6:** 44, 45
chinchilla 7: *12;* **8:** 10, 28, *36–37*
  fur **8:** (10)
  short-tailed **8:** 37
Chinchilla lanigera **8:** 30, *36–37*
chinchilla rat **8:** 31
  Chilean **8:** 30, *31*
  common **8:** 30
Chinchillidae **7:** *12*
Chinese grass **34:** 52
chinook **35:** (65)
Chioglossa **41:** 88
  lusitanica **41:** 93, *93*
Chionactis **49:** 62, (63)
  occipitalis **49:** *24–25*
  palarostris **49:** 25
Chionidae **13:** 90, 93
Chionis
  alba **13:** 90, *108–111*
  minor **13:** 90
chipmunk 7: 15, 18
  eastern 7: 34, *48–49*
  Siberian **7:** 48
Chirindia **46:** 104
Chirixalus **43:** (76), 100
Chirocentridae **36:** *96–97*
Chirocentrus dorab **36:** *96*
Chirocephalus diaphanus **28:** *19*
Chiromantis **43:** 100, (103)
  petersi **43:** (66)
  xerampelina **43:** (20), (66), *102–103*
Chironectes minimus **10:** 14
Chironectus
  dorab **36:** 96
  nudus **36:** 96
Chironex fleckeri **21:** 52, (54)
Chironius vicenti **48:** (77)
Chironomidae **23:** *50–53*
Chironomus **23:** *50*
  plumosus **23:** 51
Chiroptera **1:** *10;* **9:** (86)
Chiropterotriton **41:** 68
Chiroptes
  albinasus **4:** 72
  satanas **4:** 72
Chiroxiphia
  caudata **19:** 80
  linearis **19:** 80
chiru **6:** 62
chital **6:** 10, *13*, 45
Chitala
  lopis **31:** *102*
  ornata **31:** *102–103*
chitons 30: 9, *14–15*
  lined **30:** *15*
chivato **35:** 111

Chlamydera **19:** 100, 102
  cerviniventris **19:** 100
  guttata **19:** 100
  lauterbachi **19:** 100
  nuchalis **19:** 100
Chlamydia psittaci **10:** 95
Chlamydomonas **41:** (58)
Chlamydosaurus **44:** 32, (42)
  kingii **44:** 30, 32, 34, *42–43*
Chlamydoselachidae **32:** (98)
Chlamydoselachus anguineus **32:** 10, 100
Chlamydotis undulata **11:** 84
Chlamyphorus truncatus **9:** 65
Chlamys hastata **30:** 59
Chlopsidae **33:** (62), *76–77*
Chlopsis
  bicolor **33:** 76, *76–77*, 77
  bidentatus **33:** 77
  longidens **33:** 77
Chloridops kona **20:** 98
Chlorocebus aethiops **4:** 40
Chlorocharis emiliae **18:** 68
Chlorohydra viridissima **21:** 47
Chloropipo holochlora **19:** 80
Choanocytes **21:** *34*, 37
Choanoflagellates **21:** 34–35
Choanoflagellida **21:** 13
Choerodon **40:** 84
  fasciatus **40:** *85*
cholera **23:** 103
Choloepus
  didactylus **9:** 65
  hoffmanni **9:** 65
Chologaster **36:** 19
  agassizi **36:** 18, 19
  cornuta **36:** 18, 19, *19*
Chondrichthyes **33:** 8
Chondrodactylus **45:** 10
  angulifer **45:** 30, (39)
Chondropython viridis **48:** 94
Chordata **21:** 32
Chordeiles minor **15:** 78
Choridactylus **39:** 66, 67
  multibarbus **39:** 67
chorionic gonadotrophin (HCG) **42:** (55), (69)
Chorthippus brunneus **23:** *24–25*
chough 18: 93
  red-billed **20:** 104
  white-winged 20: 100, *104–107*
chozchori **8:** 29
Chromacris colorata **23:** *9*
chromide **40:** 68
  orange **40:** 69
Chromileptis altivelis **40:** 16
Chromis **40:** 80
Chromodoris **30:** *42–43*
  quadricolor **30:** *40–41*
Chrotogale owstoni **1:** 88
Chrysaora fuscescens **21:** *54–55*
Chrysemys
  picta **47:** *66–69*
  scripta **47:** *70–71*

Chrysichthys
  auratus **37**: 22
  furcatus **37**: 22
  grandis **37**: 22
  helicophagus **37**: 22
  longipinnis **37**: 22
  ornatus **37**: 22
  sianenna **37**: 22
  stoppersii **37**: *23*
Chrysididae **27**: *34–35*
Chrysis ignita **27**: *35*
Chrysobatrachus cupreonitans **43**: 20
Chrysochloridae **9**: 9
Chrysochroa fulminans **25**: *46–47*
Chrysococcyx cupreus **20**: 46
Chrysocyon brachyurus **2**: 50
Chrysolampis mosquitus **16**: 44
Chrysolina menthastri **25**: *96, 97*
Chrysolophus
  amherstiae **11**: 44, 56
  pictus **11**: 44, 56
Chrysomelidae **25**: *96–103*
Chrysopa (Chrysoperla) **22**: 90
  carnea **22**: *90–91, 92*
Chrysopelea **43**: (62); **44**: (45); **49**: 11,
  27
  ornata **49**: *11*
  paradisi **49**: *26–27*
Chrysopidae **22**: 90
Chrysops caecutiens **23**: *58, 61*
Chrysospalax trevelyani **9**: 40
Chthalamus entatus **28**: 23
Chthonerpeton **41**: (24)
chub
  bigeye **34**: (71)
  Black Sea **34**: 78
  creek **34**: *78–79*
  Dnieper **34**: 78
  European **34**: 68, *73*, 77, 78, 79
  flame **34**: 74
  lined **34**: (71)
  pale **34**: 65
  redeye **34**: (71)
  spotfin **34**: (71)
chuckwallas **44**: 52, (54), *54*, 82
  American **44**: 30, 34
  San Esteban **44**: *54*
  spiny **44**: *54–55*
chuck-will's-widow **15**: 78
chulengo **5**: 109
Chunga **19**: 8
  burmeisteri **11**: 92
Cicada orni **24**: *83*
cicadas 24: *80–85*
  anatomy **24**: 80
  cold-blooded **24**: 80–81
  escape behavior **24**: 80
  life cycle **24**: 83–84
  noise-producing **24**: 81–82, (82)
  periodical **24**: (84)
  warm-blooded **24**: 80–81
Cicadella viridis **24**: 86
Cicadellidae **24**: *86–89*
Cicadidae **24**: *80–85*

cichlid 37: 73, 74, 75; **39**: 8, (10); **40**:
  12, *68–79*
  African rift lake **40**: 72, (78)
  angel *see* angelfish
  Balzani **40**: 72
  blue gold-tip **40**: 73
  butterfly **40**: *74–75*
  convict **40**: 70
  goby **40**: 68
  horseface **40**: 74
  Malawi **40**: *70*
  as milk drinkers **40**: (71)
  pearl **40**: 70, *74*
  pike *see* pike cichlid
  ram **40**: *74–75*
  snail shell nests **40**: (73)
  Tanganyika giant **40**: 68
  zebra **40**: 70
Cichlidae **39**: 8, (10); **40**: 11, 12, *68–79*
Cicindela
  aurulenta **25**: *23*
  campestris **25**: *20, 22*
  cincta **25**: *12*
  hybrida **25**: *20–21*
  versicolor **25**: *21*
  reproduction **25**: 23
Cicindelidae **25**: *20–23*
Cicinnurus
  magnificus **19**: 106
  regius **19**: 106
  respublica **19**: 106
Ciconia
  abdimii **14**: 32, (39)
  ciconia **14**: 32
  nigra **14**: 32
Ciconiae **14**: 32
Ciconiidae **14**: 32
Ciconiiformes **14**: 20
Ciliata **36**: (37)
ciliates 21: *22–25*
  reproduction **21**: *14*
  slipper **21**: *22–23*
  usefulness to humans **21**: (25)
Ciliophora **21**: 13, *22–25*
Cimex lectularius **24**: *34, 34–35*
Cimicidae **24**: *34–35*
Cinclidae **14**: 108
Cinclocerthia rufucauda **18**: 36
Cinclodes fuscus **20**: 80
cinclodes, bar-winged **20**: 80
Cinclus
  cinclus **14**: 108
  leucocephalus **14**: 108
  mexicanus **14**: 108, *110–111*
  pallasii **13**: 104; **14**: 108
  schultzi **14**: 108
cindirú **37**: (91)
Cinnyris
  habessinicus **19**: 94
  jugularis **19**: 94
  regius **19**: 94
  superbus **19**: 94
Ciona intestinalis **31**: *22*
Circia **22**: *53*

Circus cyaneus **13**: 14; **15**: 8
Cirrhitichthys falco **40**: 66
Cirrhitidae **40**: *66–67*
Cirrhitus rivulatus **40**: 66
Cirripedia **28**: 9, *22–27*
cisco 35: 9, *38–41*
  Arctic **35**: 40
  blackfin **35**: 41
  Bonneville **35**: 39, 40
  deepwater **35**: 41
  least **35**: 41
  longjaw **35**: 41
  sardine **35**: 41
  shortjaw **35**: *40*, 41
  shortnose **35**: 41
Cissa chinensis **18**: 90
Cissomela pectoralis **20**: 88
Cisticola **17**: 60, 61
  juncidis **17**: 60
cisticola, zitting **17**: 60, *60*
Cistothorus palustris **17**: 52
Citellus tridecemlineatus see
  Spermophilus tridecemlineatus
CITES *see* Convention on International
  Trade in Endangered Species
  of Wild Fauna and Flora
Citharidae **39**: 86
Citharinidae **38**: *12–15*
citharinids 38: *12–15*
  bone structure **38**: (15)
Citharinus **38**: 13
  citharus **38**: 12, *12–13*
Cithraichthys sordidus **39**: 90
civet 1: 98
  African **1**: 88
  African palm **1**: 88
  banded palm **1**: 88, 90, *90*, 91
  civet family 1: *88–91*
  common palm 1: 88, 90, *90*, *94–95*
  golden palm **1**: 88
  Hose's palm **1**: 88
  Indian **1**: 90
  Jerdon's palm **1**: 88
  large Indian **1**: 90
  large spotted **1**: 88
  Lowe's otter **1**: 88
  Malayan **1**: 88, *90*
  masked palm **1**: 88
  Oriental **1**: 88, *90*
  otter **1**: 88, 91
  Owston's banded **1**: 88, 91
  palm **1**: 90, 91
  small Indian **1**: 88
  small-toothed palm **1**: 88
  Sulawesi palm **1**: 88
civet oil **1**: (91)
Civettictis civetta **1**: 88
clades **21**: 11
cladistics **21**: 11
Cladonia rangiferina **6**: 23
Cladorhynchus leucocephalus **13**: 72
Cladoselache **32**: 101
clams 30: *62–71*
  bean **30**: *68–69*

coral **30:** *67*
file **30:** *51*
giant **30:** 62, (65)
hard-shelled **30:** 68
harvesting **30:** (69)
soft-shelled **30:** 62
zigzag razor **30:** *71*
Clangula hyemalis **12:** 66, 70–71; **14:** 53
Clarias
  batrachus **37:** *52, 53*, 54
  cavernicola **37:** 55
  gareipinus **37:** *54–55*, 55
  macrocephalus **37:** 55
Clariidae **37:** 11, 30, (32), 43, 52–55
clasping organs **32:** *9*
classification
  natural **21:** 10
  see also taxonomy
clay, helping digestion **19:** (28)
cleaner fish **33:** 51
cleaner mimic **40:** 90
cleaner shrimp **32:** *45*, **33:** (82), *82*
cleaner wrasse **33:** (82)
clegs (horseflies) **23:** 58–61
Cleidopus gloriamaris **39:** 20
Clelia **49:** 16
Clemmys
  guttata **47:** 76–77
  insculpta **47:** *30*
Cleridae **25:** 40–41
Clethrionomys gapperi **7:** 94–95
Climaciella **22:** *93*
cline **17:** (87)
clingfish **32:** 66
Clinidae **40:** (93)
Clitellata **21:** 77, 94
clompers **5:** 58
clownfish **21:** (61); **40:** 80, 81
  tomato **40:** *80*
Clupanodon **36:** 87
Clupea
  harengus **36:** (88), *98–99*, 105
  pallasii **36:** *89*, 105
  sprattus **36:** 106
Clupeacharax anchoveoides **38:** 35
Clupeidae **35:** 22, **36:** 50, 88, 94, 98–111
Clupeiformes **36:** 84–89
Clyomis laticeps **8:** 30
Clytoceyx rex **14:** 100
Clytomyias insignis **18:** 60
Clytus arietis **25:** *95*
Cnemidophorus **45:** 82, *82–83*, 83; **50:** 105
  deppei **45:** *90–91*
  tigris multiscutatus **45:** *90*
  uniparens **45:** 83, 88–91
  vanzoi **45:** 85
Cnemophilinae **19:** 106, (109)
Cnemophilus macgregorii **19:** 106
Cnidaria **21:** 32, 42, 43
coalitions **2:** 28
coati 1: 19, *20*, 21
  mountain **1:** 20

ringtailed 1: 28–29
  white-nosed **1:** 20, 29
coatimundi *see* coati, ringtailed
coat-of-mail fish **39:** 18, 20
Cobanilla **26:** 98–99
cobia **40:** 32, 33
Cobitidae **34:** 9, 10, 13, 14, *14–15*, (88), 89, 108
Cobitis
  larvata **34:** 89
  taenia **34:** *88–89*, 89, 100, 101, 102
Cobitoidea **34:** 88–89
  families summary **34:** (88)
cobra 48: 15; **50:** 9
  African water **50:** 14
  Asiatic **50:** (29)
  black-necked spitting **50:** *31*
  black spitting **50:** 32
  Cape 50: 9, 12, 32–33
  Central Asian **42:** 71; **50:** (29)
  cobra family 50: 12–15
  false water **49:** 16
  hoods **50:** 14
  Indian 48: *16*; **50:** (8), 9, 28–31, 42, 43
  king 50: (8), 9, *12–13*, 34–35
  monocled **50:** 28
  rinkhals **43:** 99
  spectacled (Indian) **48:** *16*; **50:** (8), 9, 28–31, 42, 43
  spitting **44:** 41; **49:** 100; **50:** 10, 14, (29), (30)
  tree **50:** 14
Coccidae **24:** 106–111
Coccidia **21:** 13
Coccinella
  7-punctata **25:** *54, 57*; **27:** *29*
  9-notata **25:** *54–55*
Coccinellidae **25:** 54–59
Coccothraustes coccothraustes **16:** 76, 86, 88–89
Coccus hesperidium **24:** *107*
Coccyzinae **20:** 47
Coccyzus
  americanus **20:** 46
  erythropthalmus **20:** 46
cochineal insects **24:** (109)
Cochranella **43:** 28
Cociella crocodila **39:** 72
cockatiel 16: 22, (35), 36–37
cockatoo 16: 22–25
  palm **19:** 12, *13*
  sulfur-crested **15:** *25*; **16:** 22
cockchafers, European **25:** *11, 83*
cockles 30: 62–71
  bloody **30:** 53
  common **30:** *62–63*
  creeping **30:** *64*
  dog **30:** 53
  prickly **30:** *66*
cock-of-the-rock 19: 83
  Andean **19:** 80, *81*, 88, (91), (92)
  Guianan 19: 80, 88–93
cockroaches 22: 68–73

American **22:** 9, *68, 69*
giant burrowing **22:** *72*
lesser **22:** 69
reproduction **22:** 70–73
wood **22:** *71*
cod 31: 42; **36:** 8–15, 32, 33, 38–51, 103; **39:** 75
  "Antarctic cod" **36:** (50)
  Arctic **36:** 39, 51
  Atlantic **31:** 36; **36:** *8–9*, *38*, *38–39*, 39, 40, 42, 43, 44, 49, 50, 51
  butterfly **39:** 60, (61)
  "coral cod" **36:** (50)
  deep-sea 36: 52–53
  eel **36:** 53
  eucla **36:** 53
  families summary **36:** (9)
  freshwater **36:** (51)
  gadiform **36:** (10)
  "Maori cod" **36:** (50)
  moray **36:** 53
  morid **36:** 52
  Murray **36:** (50); **40:** *13*, 14
  origins of **36:** (10)
  Pacific **36:** 42, 51
  pelagic **36:** 37, 52
  poor **36:** *50–51*
  potato **40:** 15
  swimming motion **36:** (14)
  true **36:** (10)
  Who's Who **36:** (9)
Cod Wars **36:** (47)
codlet **36:** 53
codling **35:** 101, **36:** 52
  southern **36:** *34–35*
  tadpole **36:** *52*
coelacanth 31: 15, 32, 34–37, 42, 45, 46, (47), 48; **32:** 101; **38:** (110)
Coelacanthus **31:** 35
Coeliades keithloa **26:** *64*
Coeligena **16:** (45)
  iris **16:** 44
Coelodonta **5:** *28*
Coenagrion puella **22:** *44–45*; *49*
Coendou **8:** 12
  mexicanus **8:** 12, 26–27
  prehensilis **8:** 12
coendou *see* porcupine, tree
Coenobita rugosus **28:** 99
Coenocorypha pusilla **13:** 30
Coenothecalia **21:** 43
coffinfish **36:** (14), (73)
Coiidae **40:** 36–37
Coius
  campbelli **40:** 36
  microlepis **40:** 36
  quadrifasciatus **40:** 36
Colaptes
  campestris **18:** 8
  rupicola **18:** 8
Coleoidea **30:** 9, 72
Coleonyx **45:** 13, (18), 19, 63
  variegatus **45:** 18–19; **48:** (39)
Coleophrys **36:** 70

Coleoptera **22:** 30
see also beetles
Colias eurytheme **26:** *22*
Coliidae **20:** 68
Coliiformes **20:** 68
Colinus virginianus **11:** 44, (46), 50–51
Colisa **40:** 61, (62)
lalia **40:** 63
Colius
castanotus **20:** 68
colius **20:** 68
leucocephalus **20:** 68
striatus **20:** 68, 70–73
Collembola **22:** 26, 28–29
Colletes cunicularius **27:** *90*
Colletidae **27:** 89–90
Collocalia unicolor see *Aerodramus unicolor*
colobines **4:** 40, 41–42
colobus 4: 10, 40, 40–42, 68–69, 69, 75
Angola (black-and-white) **4:** 40, 68–69
black **4:** 42
black-and-white 4: 40, 68–69
red **4:** 41–42, 68
satanic black **4:** 40
western red **4:** 40
white-epauleted black (black-and-white) **4:** 40, 68–69
Colobus **4:** 40
angolensis **4:** 40, 68–69
satanus **4:** 40
Colocongridae **33:** (62)
Coloptychon rhombifer **46:** 52
color **11:** 11, 12
caecilians **41:** 21
chameleons **44:** 59, 60–61, 74–76, *76–77*, 78–79
changes in courtship **14:** 23, 25
green tree pythons **48:** 95–96, (97)
leaf frogs **43:** 67
lizards **44:** 29–30; **46:** 52, *52–53*, 71, (77)
iridescent **19:** 34
melanistic **17:** (38)
ontogenetic change **49:** 38, 42
pigmentary **14:** (50); **16:** 38, (41); **19:** 34–36
rain frogs 42:82 **42:** *82–83*
reptiles **44:** 12
sandfish **46:** 37
seasonal differences **11:** 12
sexual dichromatism **19:** 22
skinks **46:** (13), (17)
snakes **49:** 38, 42; **50:** 64, 86
structural coloration **18:** (80)
treefrogs **43:** 34–35, (35)
Tyndall scattering **43:** (35)
see also coloration; dimorphism; polymorphism
coloration
aposematic (warning) **22:** 33–34
cryptic **42:** 82, *82–83*; **43:** 67; **44:** 12,

29–30, 78–79; **46:** (77)
disruptive **50:** 64, 86
flash **42:** 82
gravid **44:** *76–77*, 82, 89, 109
threat **46:** 47
see also color
Colossoma **31:** 91; **38:** 46
macropomum **38:** 35, 45, *47*
Colostethus **43:** 68, 70, (72), 73
flotator **43:** 70
Colotois pennaria **26:** *76*
Colpodea **21:** 13
Coluber **49:** (13)
constrictor **49:** 10, 29, 59
gemonensis **49:** 29
hippocrepis **49:** 29
viridiflavus **49:** 28–29
Colubridae **48:** 8, 9, 15, *16*; **49:** 8, (13)
colubrids 48: 15, 109; **49:** 8–17, (39)
Madagascan **49:** 13–14
as pets **49:** 10–12
Colubrinae **49:** 8, 10
colugo 1: *10*; **7:** (37); **8:** 108–111
Malayan **8:** 109, *109*, 110, *110–111*
Philippine **8:** *108–109*, 109, 110
Columba **16:** 13
livia **16:** 12, 16–19; **18:** (81)
palumbus **18:** (10)
Columbidae **16:** 12
comb jellies 36: 95; **21:** 42, 44–45
warty **21:** *42*
comber **40:** (16)
combfish **39:** 75
longspine **39:** 75
shortspine **39:** 75
combtail **40:** 61
Ceylonese **40:** 63
Malay **40:** 63
Comephoridae **39:** 53, 76–81
Comephorus **39:** 78
baikalensis **39:** 79
dybowskii **39:** 79
comet **34:** 49; **40:** 24, 25
sarassa **34:** *49*
commensalism **7:** 14; **21:** 17, 39; **28:** 25–26, 65, (88), 109–112
"Common Agricultural Policy" **18:** (26)
changes in **18:** (26)
communication **1:** (23); **3:** (83); **4:** (56), 74, 79, 85, 99–100; **5:** 13, 15, 19, (24), 44, (49), 79; **7:** 53, 101; **8:** 16, 42, 51; **9:** 61; **10:** 80; **11:** (54)
competitive exclusion **11:** (15)
conches **30:** 26, (27)
condor 11: (9); **15:** 8, 24; **20:** (11)
Andean **15:** 8; **20:** 8, *16*
California 15: 8; **20:** 8, 16–21
Condylura cristata **9:** 40, 48–51
Conepatus
chinga **1:** 32
mesoleucus **1:** 32
coney *see* pika, American
Conger

cinereus **33:** *92–93*
conger **33:** *88, 89,* (93)
myriaster **33:** *90–91*
oceanicus **33:** (93)
Congiopodidae **39:** 11, 68–71
Congiopodus
kieneri **39:** 71
spinifer **39:** 71
torvus **39:** 71
Congridae **33:** (62), (72), 88–93
Congrogadus subduscens **40:** 22
Conidae **30:** (33)
Coniophanes fissidens **42:** 82
Coniophis **48:** (35)
conjugation **21:** 25
Connochaetes
gnou **6:** 62, 82
taurinus **6:** 62, 82–85
Conolophus
pallidus **44:** 97
subcristatus **44:** 81, 96–97
Conopidae **23:** 82–83
Conopophagidae **19:** 75
Conops quadrifasciata **23:** *83*
Conopsis **49:** (63)
Conraua **43:** 82
goliath **41:** *17*, (17); **42:** 8; **43:** 84, 90
conservation **1:** 47, (59), 75; **2:** 33, 55, (88), 100; **3:** 15, 19; **4:** 35; **5:** 26, 39, 63; **6:** 25, 64; **7:** 45, 77; **9:** 85; **10:** (77), (95), (101); **11:** 69; **12:** 85; **13:** 73, (77); **15:** 35; **18:** (26), (57); **41:** 14–16, 24, 73, 83; **47:** (73), 88, 104; **49:** (75); **50:** (107)
see also protection
constellationfish **35:** 90
constrictors
in Australia **48:** 84
boas **48:** 44, 51–52, 71, 75
pythons **48:** 80, 86, 92, 100
snakes **49:** 16
Constrictotermes cyphergaster **22:** (64)
Contopus cinereus **17:** 30
conure
golden-capped **16:** 32–34
jandaya **16:** 32
sun 16: 22, 32–35
Conuropsis carolinensis **16:** 23
Conus
geographicus **30:** (33)
textilis **30:** (33)
Convention on International Trade in Endangered Species of Wild Fauna and Flora (CITES) **1:** 17; **19:** 54; **31:** 37, 61, (66), 67; **34:** (28); **39:** 46; **40:** (18)
convergence **21:** 11
convergent evolution **9:** 10, 40; **10:** 36, (52); **43:** 104, 108–109; **44:** (26), (49); **48:** (58); **49:** (18); **50:** 59
convict fish **39:** 75
Cooloola Monster **23:** (11)
Cooloolidae **23:** 11

31

coon hunting **1:** 26
coonskins **1:** (23)
coot **14:** 25
    common **14:** 82, 92
Copella arnoldi **38:** 8, 22, *23*
Copepoda **28:** 9
copepods 28: 28–31
    feeding **28:** 30
    parasitic **28:** (30)
Cophixalus **42:** 104
Cophotis ceylanica **44:** (37)
Cophylinae **42:** 104, 108
Copilia **28:** *28–29*
Copiphora rhinoceros **23:** *11, 12–13,* 14
copperhead 50: 9, 50, 53, 86–89
    Australian **50:** 15
    Chinese (100-pace snake) **50:** 50, 96,
        (97)
    hibernation **50:** 88
coppers (gossamer-winged butterflies)
    26: 28, 29
    American **26:** *28*
coppicing **7:** 106
coprophagy **8:** 51, 62; **46:** (19)
Copsychus sechellarum **18:** 44
coquette
    frilled **16:** 44, *44*
    peacock **16:** 44
    white-crested **16:** 44
Coracias **15:** 86
    caudata **15:** 86, (93)
    garrulus **15:** 86, *88–89,* 90, (92)
    spatulata **15:** 86
Coraciidae **15:** 86
Coraciiformes **18:** (18); **19:** 42, 48
Coraglanis **37:** 51
Coragyps atratus **20:** 8, 12
coral hopper **28:** *45*
coral reefs **21:** 64–66
coral snakes 41: 21; **48:** 9, 16, 34, 35;
    49: (55), 62; **50:** 9, 10, 12–13, 14,
    15, 21, (25)
    African **50:** 14
    American 50: 9, 12, 22–27
    Arizona **49:** 25
    Asian **49:** 16; **50:** (35)
    Australian **50:** (25)
    brown Malaysian **50:** 21
    Colombian **50:** 23
    eastern **50:** *23*
    false (South American pipe snakes)
        48: 28, *30,* 31, 34–35;
        49: 16, (63); **50:** 24, 26
    Malaysian **50:** (25)
    Malaysian blue 50: 9, 20–21
    pink-headed **50:** 21
    regal **50:** 23
    Sonoran **50:** *22, 25,* (25)
    South African **50:** (25)
    Spix's **50:** 23
    striped Malaysian **50:** 20
    Venezuelan **50:** 23
Corallimorpharia **21:** 43
Corallus **48:** 45

caninus **48:** 56–59, 96; **50:** 91
cropanii **48:** 45
enhydris cookii **48:** *46*
hortulanus **48:** *45*
corals 21: 62–67
    bleaching **21:** (66)
    brain **21:** 65
    coral shapes **21:** 62–64
    plate **21:** *65*
    soft **21:** *63,* (64)
    staghorn **21:** *65, 66*
    sunflower **21:** *62*
    tube **21:** *62*
Corcoracidae **20:** 100, 104
Corcorax melanorhamphos **20:** 100,
    104–107
Cordulegaster boltonii **22:** 46
Cordylidae **44:** 25, (26), 28; **45:** (81), 98,
    98–100
Cordylochernes scorpioides **29:** *20–21,
    21,* (21)
Cordylosaurus subtessellatus **45:** 98, 100
Cordylus **44:** 27; **45:** 98, 98–99, 103,
    (103); **49:** (69)
    cataphractus **45:** 104–105
    giganteus **45:** *99*
    niger **45:** 102–103
Coregonus **35:** *38–41,* (41)
    albula **35:** 38, 40
    alpenae **35:** 41
    autumnalis **35:** 40
    autumnalis autumnalis **35:** 40
    autumnalis migratorius **35:** 40
    clupeoides **35:** 38, 40, *41*
    hoyi **35:** 38, 41
    huntsmani **35:** 41
    johannae **35:** 41
    kiyi **35:** 38
    lavaretus **35:** *38,* 40
    nigripinnis **35:** 41
    oxyrinchus **35:** 38, *39*
    pennantii **35:** 40
    reighardi **35:** 41
    sardinella **35:** 41
    stigmaticus **35:** 38, 40
    zenithicus **35:** *40,* 41
Coreidae **24:** 14, 52–57
Coris aygula **40:** *84*
coris, clown **40:** *84*
Corixidae **24:** (27)
cormorant 12: 44, 48–49; **13:** 109,
    110; **14:** 10, 25
    double-crested **12:** 44
    flightless **12:** 44, *48,* 49
    Galápagos (flightless) **12:** 44, *48,* 49
    great 12: 44, 60–61
    guanay **12:** 44
    pygmy **12:** 44
    red-faced **12:** 44
cornetfish 39: 11, 26, 48–49
    Atlantic **39:** 49
    bluespotted **39:** 49
    Pacific **35:** 101, **39:** 49
    red **39:** 49

Corniger spinosus **39:** (20)
Coronatae **21:** 43
Coronella austriaca **48:** 87
Corriola **26:** 93
Corucia **46:** 8
    zebrata **46:** 9, 13, 15, 16–19
coruro **8:** 29, 30
Corvidae **18:** 90
Corvinella corvina **15:** 104
Corvus **18:** 90, 92, 108
    brachyrhynchos **18:** 39, 90
    capensis **18:** 90
    caurinus **18:** 90
    corax **13:** (36); **18:** 90, 100–103;
        20: 23
    corone **18:** 90, 105–106
    frugilegus **18:** 90, 108–109
    monedula **18:** 90, 106
    moneduloides **18:** 90
    splendens **18:** 90
Corydalus **22:** 98–99
Corydon sumatranus **20:** 74
corydora **37:** (98)
    adolfo's **37:** *99*
    banded **37:** 98, *98*
    bronze **37:** 99, *102*
    peppered **37:** 99
    "winking" **37:** (98)
Corydoradinae **37:** 96
Corydoras **37:** 96, 99
    adolfoi **37:** *99*
    aeneus **37:** 99, *102*
    barbatus **37:** *98*
    paleatus **37:** 96, *97*
    pygmaeus **37:** 11
Corynopoma riisei **38:** 11, 35, 48, *48*
Coryphaena
    equiselis **40:** 33
    hippurus **40:** 33, 103
Coryphaenidae **40:** 32–33
Coryphaenoides
    armatus **36:** (31)
    rupestris **36:** 30, (30)
Corythaeola cristata **16:** 38, 42–43
Corythaixoides leucogaster **16:** 38
Corytophaninae **44:** 80
Cotesia glomerata **27:** *10,* 25
cotinga 19: 76, 80–83, (82), (83)
    lovely **19:** 80
    snowy **19:** 80
    swallow-tailed **19:** 80, *80*
Cotinga amabilis **19:** 80
Cotingidae **19:** 80
Cotinus pyralis **25:** *36–37*
Cottidae **39:** 11, 76–81
Cottinella boulengeri **39:** 77
Cottocomephridae **39:** 76–81
cotton bollworms **9:** 103
cotton spinners **30:** (113)
cottonmouth **49:** 80; **50:** 55, *88–89,*
    (89), (111)
cotton-stainers (stainers) **24:** 48–49
cottontail 8: 62
    desert **8:** 64, *67,* (93)

Dice's **8**: (93)
eastern 8: 64, 90–93
Mexican Guerrero **8**: (93)
New England **8**: (93)
Omilteneor **8**: (93)
swamp **8**: (93)
Cottunculus microps **39**: 80
Cottus **35**: 44
  asperrimus **39**: (78)
  echinatus **39**: (78)
  extensus **39**: (78)
  gobio **39**: 76, *76, 77*
  greenei **39**: (78)
  leiopomus **39**: (78)
  paulus **39**: (78)
  princeps **39**: (78)
  tenuis **39**: (78)
Coturnix coturnix **11**: 44
coua, crested **20**: 46
coucal 20: 46
  pheasant 20: 46, 62–63
  Senegal **20**: 46, *46*
cougar *see* puma
countershading **37**: (72)
courser 13: 90–91, 93, 100–101
  bronze-winged **11**: 98, 99
  Burchell's **11**: 100-101
  courser family 11: 98–99
  cream-colored 11: 98, 100–103
  double-banded **11**: 98, *98*, 99
  Indian **11**: 98
  Temminck's **11**: 98, 99, *99*
  three-banded **11**: (103)
courtship **11**: 14
  aerial **12**: 59; **13**: 47, 50–51; **14**: 106;
    15: 34, 37, 47, 85, *85*, (92);
    16: 54; **19**: 39; **20**: (35), (79)
  bobbing **20**: (79)
  bowing **16**: *15, 18*
  bowing and billing **12**: (107)
  calls **11**: 24; **12**: 79; **14**: 86–87;
    20: (44)
  chasing **16**: 97; **19**: 47; **20**: (59)
  color changes in **14**: 23, 25
  cooperative **12**: (64)
  coordinated **20**: (35)
  dance **14**: 19, 86, 89
  displays **11**: *24*, (49), 54–55, 58–59,
    63, 75, 87, 90; **12**: 109; **14**:
    29, 47–48, 65, 68, 78–79, *99*;
    15: 37, *37*; **19**: 105
  "ecstatic" **12**: *21*, 23
  feeding **11**: (49); **16**: *28*, (29), (71);
    17: *18*, (76), 87; **18**: 56
  female aggression **14**: 96
  gifts **12**: *52*, 75; **14**: 106; **16**: *28*, (29);
    17: *12, 22*; **18**: 34–35, 50, 62;
    19: 53; **20**: 59, (59)
  jumping **16**: 99
  leks **11**: 48; **13**: 33; **15**: 85; **16**: 47,
    57; **19**: 82, (91); **20**: (44)
  peering **16**: (92)
  prancing **14**: *88–89*
  rituals **11**: 30; **12**: (34), 88–89;

13: (84); **14**: 19, *26–27*, (26),
    65, 73
  songs **13**: 33; **18**: 39, 40
  spinning **20**: 74, (79)
Cous cristata **20**: 46
cow killers **27**: 38
cowbird **17**: 93, 103, 105; **18**: 74, 75
  brown-headed **16**: 71; **18**: 74, 75, 79
  giant **18**: 74, 75
  shiny **18**: 74; **20**: 86
cowcod **39**: 65
cowfish 39: 96, 97, 106–107
  longhorn **39**: *106*, 107, *107*
  striped **39**: 106
cowries **30**: 26, (27)
coyote 1: 77; **2**: 50, 58–61
coypu 7: *12*; **8**: 9, 11, 31, 44–47
  South American **8**: (46)
crabs
  anemone hermit **28**: *97*
  arrowhead **28**: *103*
  Atlantic mole **28**: *92, 93*
  blue swimming **28**: *113*
  Christmas Island **28**: 107
  coconut **28**: (100)
  decorator **28**: *110–111*
  elegant hairy hermit **28**: *94–95*
  fiddler **28**: *112–113*, (113)
  ghost **28**: *56–57*
  giant coconut **28**: *100–101*
  graceful **28**: *12–13*
  hermit 28: 94–101
  horseshoe 29: 8, 10–11
  Japanese giant spider **28**: 104
  land hermit **28**: 99–100
  mole 28: 90–93
  oyster **28**: 111–112
  Pacific mole **28**: 90
  pea **28**: 111–112
  porcelain 28: 86–89
  Puget Sound king **28**: *98*
  robber **28**: *100–101*
  Sally Lightfoot **28**: *103*
  sand (Pacific mole) **28**: *90*
  shore **22**: *8*; **28**: *102, 108*
  soldier **28**: *109*
  South Sea porcelain **28**: *88–89*
  sponge **28**: *111*
  stone **28**: (98)
  true *see* true crabs
Cracidae **11**: 44, 48
Cracticus
  argenteus **20**: 100
  cassicus **20**: 100
  louisiadensis **20**: 100
  mentalis **20**: 100
  nigrogularis **20**: 100
  quoyi **20**: 100
  torquatus **20**: 100
crane 11: 92; **14**: 82–83; **19**: 8
  black crowned 14: 82, 88–89
  common **14**: 82
  sandhill **14**: 82, 86
  sarus **14**: 82

wattled **14**: 82, *83*
  whooping 14: 82, 84–87
  wood buffalo **14**: *87*
Crangon crangon **28**: *60*
Craniata **21**: 32
Craseonycteridae **9**: 86
Craseonycteris thonglongyai **9**: 38
Crassinarke **33**: (20)
Crassostrea virginica **30**: 56
Craterocephalus **38**: 63
  fluviatilis **38**: (63)
Crax rubra **11**: 44
cray, Australian shovel-nosed **28**: *12*
crayfish 28: 70–79
  American spiny-cheeked **28**: *75*
  blue **28**: *58*
  freshwater **28**: (75), *78*
  Louisiana **28**: *8–9*
  sense of gravity **28**: (77)
  signal **28**: *72–73*
  size **28**: (71)
  Tasmanian **28**: (71)
  white-clawed **28**: *75*
  yabby **28**: *78*
Creadion carunculatus **20**: 100
creeper, Hawaiian **20**: 98
Cremastocheilus **25**: (86)
Crenichthys **38**: 106, 110
  baileyi **38**: 111
  nevadae **38**: 111
Crenicichla **37**: (108); **38**: (40); **40**: 70
Crenimugil crenilabis **38**: 53
Crenuchidae **38**: 32–33
Crenuchus spilurus **38**: 32, *32*
Crepidula **30**: 29–30
  fornicata **30**: *30–31*
crestfish 35: 82, 104–105
  unicorn **35**: 82, 104
cria **5**: 107
cribo (indigo snake) **49**: 11, 52
crickets 23: 8–11, 16–19
  ant-guest **23**: (19)
  black **23**: *16*
  bush *see* katydids
  camel **23**: (21)
  cave **23**: (21)
  defense **23**: 19
  European water **24**: *18, 18–19*
  families **23**: 8
  4-spotted tree **23**: *16–17*
  Jerusalem (king) **23**: 20–21
  king 23: 20–21
  leaf-rolling **23**: 21
  mating **23**: 16–19
  mole 23: 22–23
  pygmy mole (sand) **23**: (35)
  sagebush **23**: (14)
  sand (pygmy mole) **23**: (35)
  "singing" **23**: 16–17
  water (ripple bugs) **24**: 18–19
Cricosaura **45**: 54
Crinia **42**: 92, 93–94
Crinifer **16**: 41
  zonurus **16**: 38

Criniger bres **16**: 56
Crinoidea **30**: 91, 94–95
Crinozoa **30**: 91, 94
Crioceris asparagi **25**: *98*
Cristiceps aurantiacus **40**: (93)
croaker **40**: 12
crocodile 44: *13*
    African dwarf **47**: *94–95*, 96
    American **47**: 94, *94*, 96–97
    estuarine (saltwater) **47**: 94, 95,
        108–109
    evolution **44**: *10*
    Indo-Pacific (saltwater) **47**: 94, 95,
        108–109
    Johnston's **47**: 95, 109
    mugger **47**: *94*
    New Caledonia **47**: 95
    Nile 47: 40, 94, 108, 110–111
    saltwater 47: 94, 95, 108–109
    slender-snouted **47**: *94*
crocodilefish **39**: 72
crocodilians 47: 94–97
Crocodilurus lacertinus **45**: 82, 83–84
Crocodylia **44**: 8, 9; **47**: 95
Crocodylidae **47**: 95
Crocodylinae **47**: 95
Crocodylus
    acutus **47**: 94, *94*, 96–97
    cataphractus **47**: *94*
    johnstoni **47**: 95, 109
    niloticus **47**: 40, 94, 108, 110–111
    palustris **47**: *94*
    porosus **47**: 94, 95, 108–109
Crocuta crocuta **2**: 102, 108–109
Croesus septentrionalis **27**: *20–21*
crop raiding **5**: 23–24, 41, 72, 91;
        6: 13, 78, 81; **7**: 100, 105;
        8: 18–19; **9**: 85, 91
Crossarchus
    alexandri **1**: 98
    ansorgei **1**: 98
crossbill **11**: 15; **16**: 76–77, *77*
    parrot **16**: 76, *76*
    red **16**: 76, (84); **18**: (34)
Crossocheilus siamensis **34**: 18, 56, 88
Crossodactylus **42**: 78
crossopterygians **41**: 13
Crossoptilon **11**: 45
    auritum **11**: 44
Crossorhinidae **32**: (30)
Crotalinae **50**: (11), 50, 53
Crotalus **50**: 101
    adamanteus **50**: (8), (55), 65, 103
    atrox **50**: *8*, (8), 9, 42, 98–103
    catalinensis **50**: (102)
    cerastes **48**: 11–12, (58); **50**: 9, 51,
        54, 55, 66, 70, 104–105
    durissus **50**: 54
    horridus **50**: 88
    lepidus **50**: *99*, 100
    lepidus klauberi **49**: (71)
    mitchelli **50**: 99
    ruber **50**: (102), *103*

    scutulatus **50**: 99, 103
    tigris **50**: 99
    tortugensis **50**: (102)
Crotaphatrema **41**: 21
Crotaphytidae **44**: 88
Crotaphytinae **44**: 80, 88
Crotaphytus **44**: 84, 108
    collaris **44**: 81, 88–89
    dickersonae **44**: 88
    vestigium **44**: 88
Crotophaga major **20**: 46
Crotophaginae **20**: 47
croucher
    coral **39**: 68, 71
    pygmy coral **39**: 68
    spotted **39**: 68
    spotted coral **39**: 68, *68, 69*
crow 12: 69; **13**: 19; **14**: 25; **15**: 19,
        95; **17**: 108, (109), 111;
        18: 63; **19**: 108
    American **14**: 74; **18**: 39, 90; **19**: 93
    Cape **18**: 90, *91*
    carrion **18**: 90, 92, 105–106
    crow family 18: 90–93
    house **18**: 90, (93)
    New Caledonian **18**: 90
    northwestern **18**: 90
    paradise **19**: 106, 108
crucifix fish **37**: 64
Cruriraja **33**: (26)
Crustacea **22**: 9
crustaceans 28: 8–15
    anatomy **28**: 12–14, *15*
    classification **28**: 14
    development **28**: 14
    scientific names **28**: (11)
crypsis **46**: (73)
cryptic (hidden) species **41**: (51)
Cryptobatrachus **43**: 41, (45)
cryptobiosis **21**: 90; **23**: 53
Cryptoblepharus **46**: 8
    boutonii **46**: 10
Cryptobranchidae **41**: 27, 36
Cryptobranchus **41**: 34
    alleganiensis **41**: (12), 30, 32–35
    fuscus **41**: 33
Cryptocercidae **22**: 69–70
Cryptodira **47**: 9, 9–10, *10–11*
Cryptolepas rhachianecti **28**: 26
Cryptomys
    damarensis **8**: 56
    hottentotus **8**: 56
    mechowi **8**: 56
Cryptophyllobates **43**: 68
    azureiventris **43**: 72
Cryptoprocta ferox **1**: 88, 96–97
Cryptopsaras couesi **36**: 77
Cryptothylax gresshoffi **43**: 22
Cryptotis parva **9**: 28
Crypturellus
    saltuarius **11**: 40
    soui **11**: 40
    undulatus **11**: 40

Ctenidae **29**: 86–87
Ctenizidae **29**: (49)
Ctenocephalides
    canis **22**: *110*
    felis **22**: 110, *112–113*
Ctenochromis horei **37**: 75, **40**: 59
Ctenodactylidae **7**: *12*, 108
Ctenodactylus
    gundi **7**: 108, 110–111
    vali **7**: 108
Ctenoides ales **30**: *51*
Ctenoluciidae **38**: 24–27
Ctenolucius **38**: 25
    hujeta **38**: *24–25*, 25
Ctenomyidae **7**: *12*; **8**: 9
Ctenomys
    frater **8**: 30
    validus **8**: 30
Ctenopharyngodon idellus **34**: 18,
        52–53, 71
Ctenophora **21**: 32, 42, 43, 44–45
Ctenophorus **44**: 32, 34
Ctenopoma **40**: 58, 59
    kingsleyae **40**: 59
    petherici **40**: 59
Ctenops nobilis **40**: 62, 63
Ctenosaura **44**: 90, (101)
    quinquecarinata **44**: *101*
    similis **44**: (101)
Ctenotus **46**: 8
Ctenus **29**: 86
Cubanichthys
    cubensis **38**: (89)
    pengelleyi **38**: (89)
Cubozoa **21**: 43, 50–55
cuckoo 17: *61*; **18**: 8, (18), 60, 63;
        19: 37; **20**: 46–47
    African emerald **20**: 46
    black-billed **20**: 46, 47
    channel-billed 20: 46, 54–55
    common 16: 71; **20**: 46, 48–53
    coral-billed ground **20**: 46, *47*
    European (common) **16**: 71; **20**: 46,
        48–53
    Old World **20**: 46
    yellow-billed **20**: 46, 47
cuckoo-roller **15**: 86, 87
cuckoo-shrike **17**: 111
"cuckoo spit" **24**: (79)
cuckoo-spit insects (spittlebugs)
        24: 78–79
Cuculidae **20**: 46
Cuculinae **20**: 46
Cuculus canorus **16**: 71; **17**: *61*;
        20: 46, 48–53
cucumber fish **36**: 22
    Mediterranean **36**: 23
cui-ui **34**: 96
Culea inconstans **39**: 35
Culicidae **23**: 46–49
Culiseta annulata **23**: *46, 47, 49*
culls **3**: 15, 43, 45, 67; **6**: 32, 66;
        8: 81; **10**: (95)

Cumacea **28:** 9, 34, 50–51
cumaceans 28: 50–51
    classification **28:** 50–51
Cumberland River system **34:** (77)
Cuon alpinus **2:** 50
Cuora flavomarginata **47:** 29
Cupiennius getazi **29:** 87
Curaeus
    curaeus **18:** 74
    forbesi **18:** 74
curassow **11:** 48
    crestless **11:** 44
    great **11:** 44, 48
    razor-billed **11:** 44
Curculio venosus **25:** 104
Curculionidae **25:** 104–111
curimata 38: 18–19
    diamond spot **38:** 18
Curimatidae **38:** 18–19
curlew 13: 30
    beach stone- *see* thick-knee, beach
    Eskimo **13:** 30, (32), (33)
    slender-billed **13:** 30, (33)
    stone *see* thick-knee, Eurasian
    western 13: 30, 32, 40–43
currawong
    black **20:** 100
    gray **20:** 100
    pied **20:** 55, 100
cursorial animals **2:** 50
Cursorius
    coromandelicus **11:** 98
    cursor **11:** 98, 100–103
    littoralis **11:** 100
    rufus **11:** 98, 100–101
    temminckii **11:** 98
cuscus 10: 76, (77)
    admiralty **10:** 74
    bear **10:** 74
    common spotted (spotted) **10:** *12–13*, 82–83
    ground **10:** 74
    mountain **10:** 74
    peleng **10:** 74
    small Sulawesi **10:** 74
    spotted 10: *12–13*, 82–83
    waigeou **10:** 74
cusk eel 36: 24–27, 8, 11, 23, 52, 53
    Atlantic striped **36:** 25
    Cuban cave **36:** 27
    Pacific spotted **36:** 25
    pink **36:** 24, 25
    reef **36:** *25*
cusk eel liver **36:** 25
cuskfish **36:** (10), 39, (51)
cutaneous respiration **41:** 8, (12), 33, 68–69; **42:** 10; **43:** 13–14
Cuterebra **23:** *97*
cuttlefish 30: 73, 76–83
    giant **30:** *78*
    giant Australian **30:** *77*
    as hunters **30:** (78)
cuy *see* guinea pig

Cyamidae **28:** 34
Cyanea capillata **21:** *50–51*
Cyanocitta **18:** (98)
    cristata **16:** 71; **17:** 103; **18:** 39, 90, 94–99
    stelleri **18:** 90, (97)
Cyanolimnas cerverai **14:** 82
Cyanophenus **9:** 86
Cyanoramphus
    auriceps **16:** 22
    novaezelandiae **16:** 22
Cyclarhis gujanensis **17:** 98
Cyclemys
    dentata **47:** 78–79
    spengleri **47:** 79
Cycleptus elongatus **34:** 13, 94, 99
Cycliophora **21:** 32, 69
Cyclodomorphus gerrardii **46:** 14
Cyclommatus tarandus **25:** *74–75*
cyclomorphosis **28:** (17)
Cyclopes didactylus **9:** 65
Cyclopoida **28:** 9
Cyclops **28:** *28*; **41:** 80
Cyclopteridae **39:** 53, 82–83
Cyclopterus lumpus **39:** 82, *82, 83*
Cyclorana **42:** 40; **43:** 32, 33, 34
    australis **43:** 52–53
    platycephala **42:** 54
Cyclorrhapha **23:** 39, 40
Cyclorrhynchus psittacula **12:** 98
Cyclosa insulana **29:** *106–107*
Cyclotyphlops **48:** 18
Cyclura **44:** 80, 82
    collei **44:** 16–17
    cychlura **44:** *80–81*
Cydnidae **24:** (66)
Cyema atrum **33:** *64*, (95)
Cyematidae **33:** (62), (95)
Cygnus
    atratus **14:** 52, 56
    buccinator **14:** 52
    melanocorypha **14:** 52, 56
    olor **11:** 14; **14:** 52, 56–59; **18:** (81)
Cylindrophiidae **48:** 9, 28
Cylindrophis **48:** 30
    ruffus **48:** 32–33; **50:** 21
Cymbacephalus beauforti **39:** 72, *72–73*
Cymbirhynchus macrorhynchos **20:** 74
Cymolutes lecluse **40:** *87*
Cynictis penicillata **1:** 98
Cynipidae **27:** 32–33
Cynipoidea **27:** (23)
Cynisea **46:** 105
Cynocephalidae **8:** 108
Cynocephalus **45:** (42)
    variegatus **8:** 109
    volans **8:** 109
Cynogale
    bennettii **1:** 88
    lowei **1:** 88
Cynoglossidae **39:** 92–95
Cynoglossus **39:** 94
Cynolebias **38:** (79)

Cynomys ludovicianus **7:** 34, 56–59
Cynopoecilus melanotaenia **38:** 82
Cynops **41:** 88, 91, (95)
    ensicauda **41:** (95)
    orientalis **41:** (95)
    pyrrhogaster **41:** 94–95
    wolterstorffi **41:** (95)
Cyphocharax spilurus **38:** 18
Cyprichromis leptosoma **40:** 68
Cypridina **28:** 32
Cyprinella **34:** 68–71
    alvarezdelvillani **34:** 69
    bocagrande **34:** 69
    formosa **34:** 69
    lutrensis **34:** 53, *68*, 71, 97
    monacha **34:** (71)
    panarcys **34:** 69
    prosperpina **34:** 69
    santamariae **34:** 69
    venusta **34:** *70*, (71)
    xanthicara **34:** 69
Cyprinidae **34:** 9, 10, 12, *13*, 16–19, 54, 34: 63; **34:** 68, 72, 81, 85, 88, **38:** 106, **40:** (96)
    subfamilies summary **34:** (16)
Cypriniforms 34: 8–15
    bone structure **34:** (10)
    Who's Who **34:** 9
Cyprinodon **38:** (89)
    diabolis **38:** 86, *87*
    inmemoriam **38:** 87
    macularis macularis **38:** *87*
    radiosus **38:** 89
    salinus salinus **38:** 87
    variegatus **34:** 72, **38:** 87
Cyprinodontidae **38:** 86–89
Cyprinus **34:** 34, (35)
    acutidorsalis **34:** 35
    barbatus **34:** 35
    carpio **34:** 34, (35), 38, **37:** 8, 18
    carpio carpio **34:** 8, *8–9*, *10–11*, 16, 18, 32–41, 44, 46, 83, **38:** 106
    carpio chilia **34:** 35
    carpio haematopterus **34:** 35
    carpio viridiviolaceus **34:** 35
    daliensis **34:** 35
    ilishaetomus **34:** 35
    intha **34:** 36
    longipectoralis **34:** 35
    mahuensis **34:** 36
    megalophthalmus **34:** 35
    micristius **34:** 35
    multitaeniata **34:** 35
    pellegrini **34:** 35
    yilongensis **34:** 35
    yunnanensis **34:** 36
Cypseloides
    cryptus **15:** 70
    fumigatus **15:** 70
    major **15:** 70
cypselurid **38:** *72*
Cypselurus **38:** 71
Cypsiurus parvus **15:** 70

Cyrtodactylus **45:** 10, (10)
   peguensis **45:** *10*
Cyrtonyx montezumae **11:** 44
Cysteodemus armatus **25:** *62–63*
cysts **21:** 14
cytology (33)
Cyttus australis **39:** 22

D

dab **39:** 90, *90–91*
Daboia russeli **50:** (8), 9, (11), 72–73
dace 34: 72–79
   blackside **34:** 73, 74, 75, (77)
   common **34:** *73*, 77, 78, 79
   Danilevskii **34:** 78
   European **34:** 77
   finescale **34:** 73
   Makal **34:** 78
   mountain redbelly **34:** 74
   northern redbelly **34:** 73
   southern redbelly **34:** 73, *74*, 75
   Syr-darya **34:** 78
   Tennessee **34:** 74
   Turskyi **34:** 78
   Ukliva **34:** 78
   Zeravshan **34:** 78
Dacelo **11:** 109
   leachii **14:** 100
   novaeguineae **14:** 100; **18:** 63
Dacne bipustulata **25:** *50*
Dactylobatus **33:** (26)
Dactylomys dactylinus **8:** 30
Dactylopsila
   tatei **10:** 74
   trivirgata **10:** 74
Dactyloptena
   macracantha **39:** 57
   orientalis **39:** *55*, 57
Dactylopteridae **39:** 53, 54–57, 66
Dactylopterus volitans **39:** *54*, 56
Dactylopus coccus **24:** *109*
Dactylotum **23:** *24–25*
daddy-longlegs 29: 22–25
   crane flies 23: 42–45
   defense **29:** 23–24
   mating **29:** 24
   pale-saddled **29:** *24*
   splay-legged **29:** *23*
Daector **36:** 59
Dagetella sudamericanus **31:** 49

daggertooth 35: 80, 98–99
   North Pacific **35:** 99
   South Ocean **35:** 99
Dalatias licha **32:** 25, 94–95
Dalatiidae **32:** (12), 26, 47, (92), 94–95
Dallia pectoralis **35:** 20, *20*, 21
Dama dama **6:** 10, 40–43
Damaliscus
   lunatus **6:** 62, 88–89
   lunatus jimela **6:** 88
   lunatus korrigum **6:** 88
   lunatus lunatus **6:** 88
   lunatus tiang **6:** 88
   lunatus topi **6:** 88
   pygargus **6:** 62
Damon variegatus **29:** *15*
damsel *see* damselfish
damselfish 40: 53, 80–83
   four-striped **40:** *81*
   golden **40:** *82–83*
damselflies 22: 42–51
   azure **22:** *44–45*, 49
   demoiselle **22:** *45*
   reproduction **22:** 45–51
Danacetichthys galatheus **39:** 14
Danaidae **26:** 58–61
Danaus
   chrysippus **26:** *20*, 60
   plexippus **21:** (8); **26:** *15*, 58, 60, *61*
dance **14:** 19, 86, *89*; **18:** 41
danio 34: 60–65
   barred **34:** 64
   Canton **34:** (65)
   Chinese **34:** (65)
   leopard **34:** *61*, 63, 64
   zebra **34:** 60, *60*, 63, 64
Danio **34:** 63
   "frankei" **34:** *61*, 63
   pathirana **34:** 64
   rerio **34:** 60, *60*, 63, 64
Danionella **34:** 19
   translucida **34:** 18
Dapediidae **31:** (72), 73
Daphnia **28:** *16, 17, 21;* **41:** 62, 80
   magna **28:** *11*
   reticularia **28:** 20
Dardanus
   gemmatus **28:** *97*
   pedunctulatus **28:** *99*
Darevskia **45:** 58
   saxicola **45:** 89
Dario **40:** 56
darter 12: 44, 45, 48; **40:** 18
   banded **38:** 33
   South American 38: 32–33
   watercress **40:** 18
dartfish **40:** 99
Daruma sagamia **39:** 77
Darwin, Charles **21:** 10
Dascyllus **40:** 80
   melanurus **40:** *81*
Dasia **46:** 8, 9
dassie, rock *see* hyrax, rock

Dasyatidae **33:** (9), 34, (34)
Dasyatis **32:** 55, **33:** (34)
   americana **33:** *14–15, 37*
   brevicaudata **33:** *8–9*
   pastinaca **33:** 40–41
   sabina **33:** 11
Dasycercus cristicauda **10:** 27
Dasykaluta rosamondae **10:** 27
Dasymutilla **27:** 38
   occidentalis **27:** *38–39*
Dasypeltis **49:** 11, 91; **50:** 58, 77
   atra **49:** (35)
   fasciata **49:** *30, 32–33*, (35)
   inornata **49:** (35)
   medici **49:** 33, (35)
   palmarum **49:** (35)
   scabra **49:** 30–35, (67), 68
Dasypoda altercator **27:** *90–91*
Dasyprocta punctata **8:** 30, 42–43
Dasyproctidae **7:** *12*
Dasypus novemcinctus **9:** 65, 74–77
dasyure
   broad-striped **10:** 27
   narrow-striped **10:** *25*, 27
   red-bellied **10:** 27
   short-furred **10:** *25*, 27
Dasyuridae **10:** 24, 36
Dasyuromorphia **10:** 24
Dasyurus
   albopunctatus **10:** 27
   hallucatus **10:** 27, 32–33
Datnioides
   pulcher **40:** 36
   undecimradiatus **40:** 36
Daubentonia madagascariensis **4:** 96, 102–103
davatchan **35:** 46
DDT **9:** 103
dead man's fingers **21:** *62*
dealfish **35:** 106
death, omens of **13:** (43)
Decapoda **28:** 9, 34, 56–59; **30:** 72, 76–83
decapods **28:** 56–59
Decapotoma
   catenata **25:** *65*
   lunata **25:** *62*
Declining Amphibian Population Task Force (DAPTF) **41:** 16–17
decorated sino **37:** *8–9*
deer 5: *8*, 9, 10, 12
   barking *see* muntjac
   black musk **6:** 10
   black-tailed (mule) **6:** 10, 34–37
   Chinese water **6:** 10
   deer and relatives 6: 10–13
   dwarf musk **6:** 10
   fallow 6: 10, 12, 13, 40–43
   greater mouse 6: 10, 48–49
   Himalayan musk 6: 10, 50–51
   hog **6:** 10
   Key **49:** 97
   lesser mouse **6:** 10, 48
   marsh **6:** 10, *12*

mouse *see* chevrotain
mule 6: 10, <u>34–37</u>
muntjac *see* muntjac
musk **6:** 10
pampas **6:** 10, *12*
Père David's 6: 10, 13, <u>44–45</u>
red 6: 10, 12, 13, <u>30–33</u>
roe 6: 10, 12, <u>38–39</u>, *60*
Siberian musk **6:** 10
sika **6:** 12
spotted **6:** 10, *13*
tufted **6:** 10
white-tailed **6:** 10, *13*, 18, (36)
see also brocket
deer parks **6:** 13, *42–43*, 47
deforestation **1:** 21, 31, 48, 51, 71;
  2: 58–59; **3:** 61; **4:** (17), 27,
  32, 37, 61, 69, 73, 75, 81, 90;
  5: 20; **6:** 49, 51; **9:** 23, 91; **41:**
  (45), 73; **42:** 14, 71, (97); **44:**
  78; **46:** 52, 72; **48:** (54); **50:**
  19, 35
see also habitat destruction
degu **8:** 29, *31*
  Bridge's **8:** 30
  mountain **8:** 30
dehydration **5:** 95–96
Deilephila elpenor **26:** *68*
Deinacrida rugosa **23:** *20*
Deinagkistrodon acutus **50:** 50, (97)
Deinopidae **29:** <u>54–55</u>
Deinopis **29:** *54–55, 55*
  guatemalensis **29:** *54*
Deinosuchus **47:** 94
Delias nigrina **26:** *23*
Delichon urbica **15:** 94
Delma **45:** 50
  nasuta **45:** *52–53*
Delphacidae **24:** (75)
Delphinapterus leucas **3:** 55, <u>80–83</u>
Delphinus
  capensis **3:** 69
  delphis **3:** 55, <u>68–69</u>
Deltistes **34:** 99
  luxatus **34:** 96
Demansia **50:** 14
Dendroaspis **50:** (8), 9, 12, 14, <u>16–19</u>
  augusticeps **50:** 16, *16*
  jamesoni **50:** 16
  polylepis **50:** 9, 14, 16, *18–19*
  viridis **50:** 16, *16–17*
Dendrobates **43:** 68, 71, (71), 72, (72),
  80, 81
  abditus **43:** 68
  auratus **43:** 70, *70*, 77
  azureus **43:** 71, *77*
  bombetes **43:** 68, 72
  granuliferus **43:** (76)
  histrionicus **43:** (76)
  imitator **43:** 73
  lamasi **43:** (71)
  lehmanni **43:** (71), (76)
  leucomelas **43:** 68–69, (71), 73
  minutus **43:** 68

pumilio **43:** 70, (71), <u>74–77</u>, 80, 111
  reticulatus **43:** (71)
  speciosus **43:** (71), (76)
  tinctorius **43:** *70–71*, (71), 73, (80)
  variabilis **43:** *73*
  virolinensis **43:** 68
Dendrobatidae **42:** 10, 13, 58, (89);
  43: (11), 39, 68, (72), 108; **44:** 104
Dendrobranchiata **28:** 56, 57–58
Dendrocincla
  fuliginosa **17:** 28
  merula **17:** 28
  tyrannina **17:** 28
Dendrocitta formosae **18:** 90
Dendrocoelum lacteum **21:** *82*
Dendrocolaptes certhia **17:** 28
Dendrocolaptidae **17:** 28
Dendrocopos
  major **18:** 8
  syriacus **18:** 8
Dendrocygna viduata **14:** 52, <u>80–81</u>
Dendrohyrax **8:** 102
  arboreus **8:** 103
  dorsalis **8:** 103
  validus **8:** 103
Dendroica **17:** (91)
  castanea **17:** 88, (93)
  coronata **17:** 88
  kirtlandii **17:** 88
  petechia **17:** 88, 93
  pinus **17:** 88, (93)
  striata **17:** 88, (93)
  tigrina **17:** 88, 93
Dendrolagus
  bennettianus **10:** 48
  goodfellowi **10:** 48, <u>66–67</u>
Dendronanthus indicus **17:** 44
Dendrotriton **41:** 68, 69
Dendroxena maculata **25:** *28*
Dentalium elephantinum **30:** *16, 16–17*
Dentatherina merceri **38:** 59, (59)
Dentatherinidae **38:** 55, (59)
Dentcipitidae **36:** 84
Denticeps clupeoides **36:** 84, 88
Denticipitidae **36:** 88
Deraeocoris ruber **24:** *30, 32–33*
Derbidae **24:** (77)
Derichthyidae **33:** (62)
Dermacentor **29:** *32*
Dermaptera **22:** 30, <u>58–61</u>
Dermatemydidae **47:** 9, 28
Dermatemys mawii **47:** <u>62–63</u>
Dermatophagoides **29:** *30–31*
Dermestes lardarius **25:** 53
Dermochelyidae **47:** 9, 12
Dermochelys coriacea **47:** 9, <u>24–27</u>
Dermogenys pusilla **38:** *76–77, 77*
Dermolepida albohirtum **25:** *85*
Dermoptera **1:** *10*; **8:** 108
desman 9: 9, 11, <u>40–43</u>
  Pyrenean 9: *11*, 40, <u>52–53</u>
  Russian **9:** 40, 42, 43, *53*
Desmana moschata **9:** 40
Desmodema polystictum **35:** 106, *107*

Desmodus rotundus **9:** <u>94–97</u>
Desmognathinae **41:** 68, 70
Desmognathus **41:** 68
  aeneus **41:** 70
  fuscus **41:** 69, 86
  imitator **41:** *72–73*, 73
  monticola **41:** (75)
  ocoee **41:** (75)
  quadramaculatus **41:** <u>74–75</u>
deuterostomes **21:** 31
Deuterostomia **21:** 32
development stages, insects **22:** 31
devil dogs (hellbenders) **41:** (12), 14, 30,
  <u>32–35</u>
devil, Tasmanian 10: (24), 27, <u>28–31</u>
devilfish **40:** 25
dewfish **37:** 67, (68)
dhani (danio) **34:** (62)
dhole **2:** 50, *51*
Diachlorus ferrugatus **23:** *61*
Diadectes **41:** *13*
Diadema setosum **30:** *106*
Diadophis punctatus **49:** 16, <u>94–97</u>; **50:**
  14, (35)
dialects of whale pods **3:** 63
Dianema **37:** 98
  longibarbis **37:** *100–101*, 101
  urostriata **37:** 100, 101
diapause **25:** (52)
  embryonic **10:** 12–13, 57, 63, 69, 71,
  73, 85
Diaphus ostenfeldi **35:** *102–103*
Diapsida **44:** *10*
diarrhea
  hiker's **21:** 17
  infantile **23:** 103
diastema **7:** 10, *11*; **8:** 60
  see also reproduction
Dibamidae **44:** 25, (26), 28; **45:** 8, 13
Dibamus **45:** 13
dibatag **6:** *61*, 62
dibbler **10:** 27
Dibranchus **36:** 70
Dicaeidae **18:** 69
Dicamptodon **41:** <u>40–45</u>
  aterrimus **41:** 40, (51)
  copei **41:** 40, 40–41
  ensatus **41:** 40, *40, 42–43*, 44, *44–45*,
  (51); **42:** 17
  tenebrosus **41:** 40, *40–41*, 45, (51)
Dicamptodontidae **41:** 27, 51
Dicentrarchus labrax **40:** 14
Diceratiidae **36:** <u>74–83</u>
Dicerorhinus sumatrensis **5:** 28
Diceros bicornis **5:** 28, <u>36–39</u>
Dichopetala **23:** *14*
dichromatism, sexual **23:** 25; **44:** *60–61*,
  61, 67
Dicksonia **21:** *34–35*
dicoumarol **7:** 75
Dicraesaurus **44:** *10–11*
Dicranopalpus ramosus **29:** *23*
Dicrodon **45:** 82, 83, 84
Dicroglossinae **43:** 82, 84–85

Dicruridae **17:** 106
Dicrurus
   adsimilis **17:** 106, 111
   atripennis **17:** 106
   bracteatus **17:** 106
   caerulescens **17:** 106
   forficatus **17:** 106, 110–111
   fuscipennis **17:** 106
   leucophaeus **17:** 106
   macrocercus **17:** 106
   megarhynchus **17:** 106
   paradiseus **17:** 106
   remifer **17:** 106
Dictynidae **29:** (53)
Dictyoptera aurora **25:** *38*
Didelphidae **10:** 14, 16
   common *see* opossum, Virginia
Didelphis
   albiventris **10:** 14
   virginiana **10:** 14, 18–23
Didinium **21:** *23*
digestion **11:** *9*, (21); **19:** (28); **20:** 65–66
   external **29:** 15
Digononta **21:** 69
dik-dik
   Kirk's **6:** *60*, 62
   Salt's **6:** 62
dikkop
   spotted **13:** 90, (93)
   water **13:** 90, (93)
dimorphism **14:** (22); **17:** (37); **42:** 72–73, 82; **43:** 85; **45:** 106; **49:** 14, (51) sexual **3:** 87; **41:** 57; **43:** (21); **44:** *32–33*, 67, 71, 81, *88–89*; **46:** 87; **49:** 38, (71)
dingo 2: 50, 80–81; **10:** (30), 37
Dinomyidae **7:** *12*
Dinomys branickii **8:** 30
Dinornis maxima **11:** (9)
dinosaurs **3:** 98; **44:** 10, *10–11*, 18
Diodon **39:** 108
   holocanthus **39:** 109
   liturosus **39:** *108–109*
Diodontidae **39:** 11, 96, 97, 108–109, 110
Diomedea
   amsterdamensis **12:** 28, 32
   dabbenena **12:** 28, 32
   epomophora **12:** 28, 32
   exulans **12:** 28, 32–37
Diomedeidae **12:** 28, 30
Diopsidae **23:** 86–87
Diopsis **23:** *86*
Diphthera festiva **26:** *94–95*, 97
Diplobatis **33:** (20)
Diplodactylidae **44:** 25; **45:** 8, 11–12, (36), 48
Diplodactylus **45:** (10)
   ciliaris **45:** *44*, 45
   elderi **45:** 12
   taenicauda **45:** 44–45
Diplodus
   sargus sargus **40:** 40

   vulgaris **40:** 40
Diplogale hosei **1:** 88
Diploglossinae **46:** 50, 52
Diploglossus **46:** 52, 55, 66–67
   bilobatus **46:** *66–67*
   fasciatus **46:** 52
   lessonae **45:** 63
Diplomesodon pulchellum **9:** 28
Diplomys labilis **8:** 30
Diplopoda **22:** 14, 16–21
Diplospinus multistriatus **35:** 101
Diplostraca **28:** 9, 18
Diplura **22:** 26, (27)
Dipluridae **29:** 48–49
dipnoan **31:** 32
Dipodidae **7:** *12*
Dipodomys ordii **7:** 24–25
Diporiphora **44:** 32, 34
   superba **44:** 34
dipper
   American 14: 108, 110–111
   brown **13:** 104; **14:** 108, *108*
   dipper family 14: 108–109
   European **14:** 108, *108*
   rufous-throated **14:** 108
   white-capped **14:** 108, *108*
Diprotodontia **10:** 25, 75, (94)
Dipsadinae **49:** 8, 16, (99)
Dipsas **49:** 8, 16, 90, 91, 98–99
   articulata **49:** 99
   bicolor **49:** *16–17*, *98–99*
   indica **49:** 98
Dipsochelys
   dussumieri **46:** (67)
   hololissa **46:** (67)
Dipsosaurus dorsalis **44:** 82
Diptera **22:** 30; **23:** 36–41
Dipturus **33:** 26, (26)
   batis **33:** *12–13*, *27*, 30–31
Diretmidae **39:** 21
Dirphia **26:** 70
Discocyrtus **29:** *23*
Discodeles **43:** 82, 86
Discoglossidae **42:** 10, 14, 25, 30
Discoglossus **42:** 30, 30–31
Discopyge **33:** (20)
discus **37:** (108), **40:** 68, 78, 79
   blue **40:** 79
   brown **40:** 79
   green **40:** 79
   Heckel **40:** 79
   pompadour **40:** 79
   turquoise **40:** (71), *71*
diseases **1:** 26, 87
   from parasites **21:** 17
   from ticks and mites **29:** (32)
   rodent-borne **7:** 14
Dismorphia amphione **22:** *34*
Dispholidus typus **43:** 103; **48:** *12*; **49:** 11, 36–39, 51, (71); **50:** 17
displays **11:** (72), 88–89
   butterfly flight **13:** 13–14, 57, 84, 96
   distraction **11:** 25; **13:** (74); **15:** 85; **16:** 61

feigning injury **11:** 25; **13:** 17, 24, 33, 37, (46), (54), (61); **15:** 85
   piping **13:** 96
   ritual **12:** (46), *56*; **14:** 19, *26–27*, (26), 47
   social gestures **19:** (19)
   threat **11:** *57*, *96*, 97; **13:** 78–79; **14:** *57*, *62–63*; **17:** 77; **19:** *92*
   see also courtship; territorial behavior
Disteira **50:** (45)
distemper **3:** 41
   canine **2:** 79
Distichodus
   decemmaculatus **38:** 14
   lusosso **38:** 14
   mossambicus **38:** 14
   rostratus **38:** 14
   sexfasciatus **38:** 14, *14*
distichodus
   dwarf **38:** 14
   long-nosed **38:** 14
   longsnout **38:** 14
   six-lined **38:** 14, *14*
   sixbar **38:** 14, *14*
Distoechurus pennatus **10:** 74
diver **12:** 45
   black-throated *see* loon, Arctic
   great northern *see* loon, common
   red-throated *see* loon, red-throated
   white-billed *see* loon, yellow-billed
Dives dives **18:** 74
diving-petrel **12:** 29, 31
   common **12:** 28, *31*
   Peruvian **12:** 28
   South Georgia **12:** 28
dobsonflies 22: 98–99
dodo **15:** (11)
dog 1: 15; **5:** 9
   African hunting (African wild) **2:** 9, 50, 53, 78–79
   African wild 2: 9, 50, 53, 78–79
   bush **2:** 50, 53
   dog family 2: 50–53
   domestic **2:** 9, 50, (53)
   painted hunting (African wild) **2:** 9, 50, 53, 78–79
   raccoon **2:** 50
   see also prairie dog
dogfish 32: 10, 46–47, 57
   bareskin **32:** 94, 95
   black 32: 47, 94–95
   chain **32:** 46
   combtooth **32:** 94, 95
   granular **32:** 94, 95
   highfin dogfish **32:** 94
   large-spotted **32:** 46
   lesser spotted **33:** 30
   ornate **32:** 94, 95
   Pacific black **32:** 94
   spiny **32:** *16–17*, 55, *92–93*, 94, 102
   whitefin **32:** 94, 95
   see also shark
dojo **34:** 107
Dolatettix **23:** *34–35*

Dolichoderus **24:** *108;* **27:** *9, 44*
Dolichonabis limbatus **24:** *36–37*
Dolichonyx oryzivorus **18:** 74
Dolichopodidae **23:** (75)
Dolichopteryx **35:** 24
  longipes **35:** 24
Dolichopus wahlbergi **23:** *75*
Dolichotis patagonum **8:** 30, 32–35
Dolichovespula media **27:** *66–67*
dollarbird *see* roller, Eastern broad-billed
dolly varden **35:** 46, 47
  southern **35:** 46
Dologale dybowskii **1:** 98
Dolomedes **29:** *9*
  albineus **29:** *89*
  triton **29:** *88–89*
dolphin 1: *10;* **3:** 54–59; **5:** (10)
  Amazon 3: 55, 60–61
  bottlenose 3: 55, 66, 72–75
  clymene **3:** 76
  common 3: 55, 68–69, 71
  dusky **3:** 71
  Fraser's **3:** 71
  Ganges **3:** 55, (61)
  hourglass **3:** 71
  Indus **3:** 55, (61)
  La Plata **3:** 55, (61)
  long-beaked (spinner) **3:** 55, 76–77
  long-beaked common **3:** 69
  Pacific white-sided 3: 55, 70–71
  pink (Amazon) **3:** 55, 60–61
  Risso's **3:** 71
  river **3:** (61)
  rollover (spinner) **3:** 55, 76–77
  short-beaked common **3:** 69
  short-snouted spinner **3:** 76
  spinner 3: 55, 76–77
  spotted **3:** *56–57, 77*
  white-beaked **3:** 71
  white-sided **3:** 71
  Yangtze river **3:** 55, (61)
dolphinaria **3:** 71, 74
dolphinfish **40:** 32, 103
  common **40:** 33
  Pompano **40:** 33
domestication **2:** 53; **5:** (43), (45), (98),
  105–106, 107; **6:** 25, 63;
  8: 38–39, 40, (72); **11:** (63),
  (81); **14:** (68); **16:** 16–17
  see also cat, domestic; dog, domestic
domino **40:** 80
Donacidae **30:** 68–70
Donax
  deltoides **30:** *63*
  gouldii **30:** *68–69*
donkey
  domestic **5:** (45)
  wild **5:** *44–45*
dorab **36:** 96
doradid
  Hancock's **37:** *76–77,* 79
Doradidae **37:** 76–81, 77, 97
Doratifera vulnerans **26:** *107*
Dorcatragus megalotis **6:** 62

dorcopsis
  gray **10:** 48
  white-striped **10:** 48
Dorcopsis
  hageni **10:** 48
  luctuosa **10:** 48
Dorcopsulus
  macleayi **10:** 48
  vanheurni **10:** 48
Dormitator maculatus **40:** 97
dormouse 7: 11, *12,* 13, 15, 17, 19
  African **7:** 103
  Asiatic garden **7:** 102
  Chinese **7:** 102
  Chinese pygmy **7:** 103
  common (hazel) **7:** 102, 103,
    106–107
  desert **7:** 102
  dormouse family 7: 102–103
  edible 7: (14), 102, 104–105
  fat (edible) **7:** (14), 102, 104–105
  forest **7:** 102
  garden **7:** 102, *102–103*
  hazel 7: 102, 103, 106–107
  Japanese **7:** 102, *102*
  masked mouse-tailed **7:** 102
  Oriental **7:** 103
  Roach's mouse-tailed **7:** 102
  Setzer's mouse-tailed **7:** 102
  spectacled **7:** 102
  spiny **7:** 103
  woolly **7:** 102
Doru lineare **22:** *59*
dory 39: 22–25
  John Dory 39: 9, 10, 22, *22,* 23, *23*
  mirror Dory **39:** 23
  "other dories" **39:** (25)
  silver Dory **39:** 22
  silvery John Dory **39:** 23
Dorylus nigricans **27:** *45*
Doryrhamphus **39:** *45*
Dosidicus gigas **30:** *82*
dotterel, Eurasian **13:** 8, 9, *9*
dottyback 40: 22–25
  double-striped **40:** 23
  lyretail **40:** *23*
  midnight **40:** 23
  royal **40:** 22, 24
douroucouli *see* monkey, Northern night
dove
  beautiful fruit **16:** 12, 13
  collared **16:** 12
  crimson-capped fruit **16:** 12, 13
  diamond **16:** 12, *13*
  green-winged **16:** 12
  laughing **16:** 12; **19:** 97
  many-colored fruit **16:** 12
  mourning 16: 12, 20–21
  rock (feral pigeon) **16:** 12, 16–19
  wompoo fruit **16:** 12
  zebra **16:** 12, *13*
dovekie 12: 98, (98), 100, 102–103
dowitcher 13: 30
  long-billed **13:** 58, 59

  short-billed 13: 30, 58–61
Doxocopa laure **26:** *41*
Dracaena **45:** 82, 83
  guianensis **45:** 83–84, 92–93
  paraguayensis **45:** 83–84, *92–93,* (93)
Draco **43:** (62); **44:** 32
  melanopogon **44:** 45
  volans **44:** 30, 44–45
Draculin **9:** 97
dragon
  tawny **37:** 27
dragon fish (dragonfish) 31: 82, 83,
  84, 86, 90, 93, 95, 96–97, 99, 101,
  35: 78–83, **39:** 60
  barbeled 35: *80,* 84–90
  black **35:** *86–87,* 89
  gold **31:** 96
  green **31:** 96
  rainbow **31:** 97
  red **31:** 97
  scaleless black **35:** (88), 89
  scaly **35:** 85
  short **39:** *36*
  silver **31:** 96
  Sumatran red **31:** 96
  winged **39:** 36
dragonflies 22: 42–51
  eastern amberwing **22:** *47*
  flame skimmer **22:** *42–43*
  4-spotted skimmer **22:** *50–51*
  giant **42:** 19
  golden-ringed **22:** *46*
  reproduction **22:** 45–51
  ruddy darter **22:** *46*
  southern hawker **22:** *42, 43, 48*
  spangle skimmer **22:** *26–27*
Drapetisca socialis **29:** *113*
dread (behavior) **12:** 89
dreamer **36:** 83
Dreisseniidae **30:** 60, (61)
Drepanididae **20:** 98
Drepanis pacifica **20:** 99
Drepanorhynchus reichenowi **19:** *94*
Drepanornis albertisi **19:** 106
drill **4:** 40, 42
drinking by sucking **16:** (18), 90, 94
Dromadidae **13:** 90, 93, 101
Dromaiidae **11:** 16
Dromaius novaehollandiae **11:** 16,
  26–27, 34
Dromas ardeola **13:** 76, 90, 100–103
dromedary *see* camel, dromedary
Dromiacea **28:** 56
Dromiciops gliroides **10:** 14
Dromicus biserialis **48:** 14
drongo 17: 24, 76
  ashy **17:** 106, 108–109
  black **17:** 106, *109*
  Ceylon crested black **17:** (108)
  Comoro **17:** 106
  crested 17: 106, 110–111
  drongo family 17: 106–107
  fork-tailed **17:** 106, *107,* 109, (109),
  111

greater racket-tailed **17:** 106, 108, *108*, (108)
lesser racket-tailed **17:** 106, (108)
New Ireland **17:** 106, 108
Papuan mountain **17:** 106, 108
shining **17:** 106, 109
spangled **17:** 106, (108)
white-bellied **17:** 106, *106*
Drosophila melanogaster **23:** *92–93*
Drosophilidae **23:** 92–93
drought **4:** 63; **5:** 34, 94
drug testing **4:** 13, 93
drum 39: 54; **40:** 12–19
freshwater **40:** 19
red **40:** 19
drumming **13:** 51; **18:** (10)
Drupa rubusidaeus **30:** *33*
Drymarchon corais **49:** 11, 52
Drymornis bridgesii **17:** 28
Dryocopus
    martius **18:** 8
    pileatus **18:** 8, 14–19
Dryomys
    laniger **7:** 102
    nitedula **7:** 102
    sichuanensis **7:** 102
Dryoscopus cubia **15:** 104
Duberria **49:** 13
    lutrix **49:** (93)
    variegata **49:** (93)
duck 11: *12*; **14:** 52, 53, 54; **15:** 19, 34
American black **14:** 67
black-headed **14:** 54
Falkland steamer **12:** 66, 67
flying steamer **12:** 66
harlequin **12:** 66, *69*
Labrador **12:** 69
Laysan **14:** 67
long-tailed 12: 66, 70–71; **14:** 53
Magellanic steamer **12:** 66
mandarin 14: 52, 76–77
Pacific black **14:** 69
pintail **14:** 52, *53*
ruddy **14:** 52, *53*, 54
sea 12: 66–73
steamer- **12:** 66, 68
tufted **14:** 52, *53*
velvet scoter **14:** 52, *53*
white-faced whistling- 14: 52, 80–81
white-headed steamer **12:** 66
wood 14: 52, 70–71
Ducula **16:** 13
    aenea **16:** 12
Dugesiella hentzi **42:** 110
dugong 1: *10*; **3:** 46–47, 52–53; **5:** (12)
Dugong dugon **3:** 47, 52–53
duiker
bay **6:** 62
blue **6:** 62
bush (common) **6:** 62, 80–81
common 6: 62, 80–81
forest **6:** 80
Duliticola **25:** *39*

Dulus dominicus **18:** 30; **19:** 43
Dumetella carolinensis **18:** 36
dump nesting *see* brood/nest parasitism
Dunkleosteus **33:** 62
dunlin 13: 16, 30, 33, 52–55, *64–65*
dunnart 10: 27
    common 10: 38–39
    fat-tailed **10:** *25*, 27
    Gilbert's **10:** 38
    Kangaroo Island **10:** 38
    little long-tailed **10:** 38
    red-cheeked **10:** 27
dunnock 18: 36, 37, 42–43; **20:** (48), *49*
duos **16:** (61)
Duplicidentata **8:** 61
Dusicyon australis **2:** 50
dust-bathing **18:** *26*; **20:** (107)
Duvernoy's gland **49:** (39)
Dynastes hercules **25:** *76*
Dyscophinae **42:** 104, 108
Dyscophus
    antongilii **42:** 104, 105, 108–109
    guineti **42:** 109
    insularis **42:** 109
Dysdera crocata **29:** *59*
Dysdercus
    flavidus **24:** *48–49*
    mimus **24:** *11*
Dysderidae **29:** 38, (59)
dysentery
    amebic **21:** 20
    bacterial **23:** 103
Dysithanmus mentalis **19:** 72
Dysodius lunatus **24:** *51*
Dysodonta **30:** 9, 50, 54–55
Dysphania contraria **26:** *75*
Dytiscidae **25:** 24–25
Dytiscus marginalis **25:** *24, 24–25, 25*

E

eagle 11: 13, (13); **12:** 69; **15:** 8, (9), 10, 11, 12–13, 50
African fish- **20:** 28
American harpy 15: 8, 40–43
bald 15: 8, 10, (21), 30–35
black (Verreaux's) **15:** 8, *9*
fish **15:** 10, 40
golden 11: 14; **15:** 8, 44–49
imperial **16:** 100

Isidor's **15:** 8, *12*
martial **15:** 8, 10, 12
Steller's sea **15:** 8, 10, 30
Verreaux's **15:** 8, *9*
vulturine fish- *see* vulture, palm-nut
white-tailed sea **15:** 30
ears, owls' **15:** 52–53, 64
earthcreeper 20: 80, 82
Bolivian **20:** 80
Patagonian (scale-throated) **20:** 80, 82–83
scale-throated 20: 80, 82–83
eartheater **40:** 70
Paraguay **40:** 72
earthworms 21: 102–105
ecological importance **21:** (104), 105
giant Gippsland **21:** (105)
earwigs 22: 58–61
European **22:** *58–59, 60–61, 61*
linear **22:** *59*
sand **22:** *60*
striped **22:** *60*
tawny **22:** *58*
Ecdysozoa **21:** 32
Ecdyzoa **21:** 69
Echeneidae **40:** 9, 32–33
Echeneis naucrates **33:** 51, **40:** *32, 33*
echidna 1: 14; **8:** 12; **10:** 105
long-nosed **10:** 105, 110
short-beaked 10: 105, 110–111
Echidna
    catenata **33:** 81
    rhodochilus **33:** 81
Echidnocephalus **33:** 96
Echimyidae **7:** *12*; **8:** 31
Echimys pictus **8:** 30
Echinocardium caudatum **30:** *108*
Echinoderes **21:** *79*
Echinodermata **21:** 32; **30:** 90, 91
echinoderms **30:** 90–93
Echinoidea **30:** 91, 104–109
echinoids
    camouflage **30:** *108*
    irregular **30:** 104, 108
    regular **30:** 104
Echinomacrurus
    mollis **36:** (30)
Echinoprocta rufescens **8:** 12
Echinops telfairi **9:** 24
Echinorhinidae **32:** (12), 47, (92)
Echinorhinus **32:** 55
Echinosorex gymnura **9:** 12, 22–23
Echinotriton **41:** 88, 91, 101
    andersoni **41:** *92*
Echinozoa **30:** 91
Echinus esculentus **30:** *105*
Echiodon drummondi **36:** 22
Echis **49:** 33, 34; **50:** 14, 52, 53, 58, 74–77, 103
    carinatus **50:** (8), 74, *74*, 77
    coloratus **50:** 74, 75
    ocellatus **50:** 75
    pyramidum **50:** 77
Echiura **21:** 32, 77, 78

echolocation **9:** 8, 28, 32, 37, 80–81, 92–93, 99, 106, 109, 110–111; **15:** 76–77, 78, 81
Echymipera
 clara **10:** 27
 rufescens **10:** 27
echymipera, Clara's **10:** 27
Eciton burchelli **27:** *55, 56*
Eclectus roratus **19:** 12, 22–23
ecology **21:** (33)
ecotones **6:** 86
ecotourism **33:** 39
Ecsenius gravieri **40:** 91
Ectinolobia buqueti **25:** *49*
Ectobius panzeri **22:** 69
Ectomocoris **27:** *39*, (38)
Ectopistes migratorius **13:** 15
ectoplasm **21:** 14
ectotherms **44:** 8
Ectreposebastes imus **35:** 101, **39:** 66
Edentates **9:** 64, *64*
Edessa rufomarginata **24:** *60–61*
Edilia
 obscura **40:** 14
 vittata **40:** 14
eel **31:** 26, **33:** 60, 62–67, **39:** 10
 American 33: 64, 66, 68–73, **39:** 10
 American conger **33:** (93)
 Asian swamp 33: 108–109
 avocet snipe **33:** *86*
 belted spiny **33:** 110
 bicolored false moray **33:** 76, *76–77, 77*
 black (South American aquatic caecilians) **41:** 21, 24–25
 bobtail snipe **33:** (95)
 Bombay swamp **33:** 106
 chain moray **33:** 81
 collared **33:** 77
 conger 33: (72), 88–93
 conger (amphiumas) **41:** 38–39
 Congo (amphiumas) **41:** 38–39
 curtailed snipe **33:** *64*, (95)
 cusk *see* cusk eel
 cutthroat 33: 65, 84–85
 deep-sea spiny **33:** 107
 deepwater arrowtooth **33:** *84*
 ditch (amphiumas) **41:** 38–39
 dragon moray **33:** 83, *83*
 Edward's spaghetti **33:** 74, *74, 74–75, 75*
 eel-like fish 33: 62–67
 electric 31: 108, (108), 111, **33:** 20, 100, 104–105
 European 33: 60, 64, 66, *66–67*, 68–73, **39:** (10)
 European conger **33:** *88, 89*, (93)
 false moray 33: 76–77
 families summary **33:** (62)
 fire **33:** *110–111*
 freshwater moray **33:** 81
 Fryer's false **33:** 77
 garden **33:** (92), *92*
 giant moray **33:** 79, *79*

 gray-face moray **33:** 79
 guineafowl moray **40:** 24, 25
 gulper 31: 42, **33:** 64, 65, *65*, 94–95
 harlequin sea **33:** 81
 Kaup's arrowtooth **33:** 85, *85*
 leaf-nosed moray **33:** 82
 lesser spiny **33:** *110*
 long-fin African conger **33:** *92–93*
 marbled swamp **33:** 106
 margined snake **33:** (66)
 moray 31: *17*, 29, **32:** 51, 59, 67, **33:** 64, 78–83, **39:** 109
 Napolean snake **33:** *85*
 navigation **33:** (70)
 peacock eye spiny **33:** *107*
 pelican 33: 94–95
 ribbon **33:** *63*, 82
 rice **33:** 109
 rubber (South American aquatic caecilians) **41:** 21, 24–25
 sand *see* sand eel
 seagrass **33:** 76
 Sicilian (South American aquatic caecilians) **41:** 21, 24–25
 slender conger **33:** (91)
 snake **33:** (66)
 snipe 33: 64, *64*, 65, 86–87
 snub-nosed parasitic **33:** 65, 85
 spaghetti 33: 74–75
 spiny 33: 96, 106–107, 110–111, **39:** (10)
 spotted moray **33:** *82*
 starry moray **33:** 81
 swallower 33: 94–95
 swamp 33: 106–107, **39:** (10)
 undulated moray **33:** *60, 78*
 white-spotted spiny **33:** *110*, 111
 worm **33:** 74
 zebra moray **33:** *80*
eel blenny *see* blenny
eel pout **36:** 27
"eel skin" **31:** 29
Efferia benedicti **23:** *62–63*
eft **41:** (89)
 red (eastern newt) **41:** 86, *88–89*, 91, 98–99
Egernia **46:** 8, 10
 stokesii **46:** 8, 24–25
egg brooding **48:** (83)
egg cases **32:** 27, (41), *43, 46*
 blue skate **33:** *27*, 30
egg-laying mammals 10: 104–105
eggs **11:** *14;* **35:** 63, **36:** *106–107*, 107, **37:** (12), (110)
 laying in other bird's nests *see* brood/nest parasitism
 numbers laid **15:** (61)
 relative clutch mass **44:** 104–105
 use in rites and rituals **11:** (25)
egret 6: (73)
 cattle **14:** 20, 22, 23
 great white **14:** 20, *21*
 little 14: 20, (22), 28–29
 reddish **14:** 20, 22

 Swinhoe's **14:** 23
Egretta
 ardesiaca **14:** 20
 caerula **14:** 20
 eulophotes **14:** 23
 garzetta **14:** 20, 28–29
 rufescens **14:** 20
 eider 12: 66, *66*, 70; **14:** 52, 53, 54
 common **12:** 66, (69), 72, 73
 king 12: 66, 72–73
 spectacled **12:** 66
 Steller's **12:** 66
eiderdown **12:** (69)
Eidolon **9:** 86
Eigenmannia **33:** 101
 virescens **33:** *101*
Eimer's organs **9:** 45, (50)
Eira barbara **1:** 32
Eisenia foetida **21:** *105*
El Niño **3:** 22; **36:** (95), **38:** 37; **44:** (94)
Elachistodon westermanni **49:** (35)
elaenia **17:** 30
 mountain **17:** 30
Elaenia frantzii **17:** 30
eland 5: *13*
 common **6:** *60*, 62, 76
 giant 6: 62, 76–77
 Lord Derby's (giant) **6:** 62, 76–77
Elanoides forficatus **15:** 8
Elanus caeruleus **44:** 41
Elaphe **48:** 58; **49:** 10, (39)
 bairdi **49:** (43)
 flavirufa **49:** (43)
 guttata **49:** 10, (43), 46–47
 guttata rosacea **49:** 47
 hohenackeri **49:** 45
 lineata **49:** 45
 longissima **49:** 45
 obsoleta **48:** *17*, (97); **49:** 40–43; **50:** 88
 quatuorlineata **48:** (97); **49:** 10, 45
 scalaris **49:** 45
 situla **49:** 44–45, (51)
 taeniura **48:** 85
 vulpina **49:** (43)
Elaphodus cephalophus **6:** 10
Elaphrosaurus **44:** *10–11*
Elaphurus davidianus **6:** 10, 44–45
Elapidae **48:** 9, 15, *16*, 35; **50:** 9, 12
Elapinae **50:** 12, 12–13, (39)
Elapsoidea **50:** 14
Elasmucha grisea **24:** 71
Elassoma
 alabamae **40:** 29
 evergladei **40:** 28
 okatie **40:** 29
 okefenokee **40:** 29
 zonatum **40:** 29
Elassomatidae **40:** 26–29
Elateridae **25:** 42–45
electric fish **31:** (108), 111, **33:** 11, 20–23, 24, 25, 100, 102, 103, 104–105, **37:** 60–63
electrocution **4:** 67

Electron
  carinatum **19:** 42
  platyrhynchum **19:** 42
electronic sensors **31:** *71*, **32:** 15
Electrophoridae **33:** 100, (100)
Electrophorus electricus **31:** 108, (108), 111, **33:** 20, 104–105
Eledone cirrhosa **30:** *85*
Eleotridae **40:** 94–99, (96)
elephant 1: 10, *10*; **5:** 8, (10), 11, (12)
  African 5: 14, 15, 16–21, 26
  Asian 5: 14, 15, 16, 22–27
  circus elephants **5:** *24*, (24)
  elephant family 5: 14–15
  family units **5:** *15*
  forest **5:** 14, *14–15*
  savanna **5:** 14, 15
elephant fish 31: 85, **33:** 58–59, **36:** 85
  Cape **33:** 58
  see also elephantnose
elephant shrew 1: *10*; **9:** 10, 58–59
  black and rufous **9:** 59, *59*
  checkered **9:** *58–59*, 59
  four-toed **9:** 59, *59*
  golden-rumped 9: 59, 62–63
  North African **9:** 59, *59*
  short-eared **9:** 59, *59*
elephantiasis **21:** 91
elephantnose 31: 82, 85, 106–109, *107*, 110, 111, **37:** 60
  Angolan **31:** 107
  blunt-jawed **31:** *106–107*, 107
  electric fish **31:** (108)
  Peter's **31:** 106, 107, (109), *109*
  see also elephant fish
Elephantulus rozeti **9:** 59
Elephas maximus **5:** 14, 22–27
Eleutherodactylus **41:** (17); **42:** 9, 76, 80–85; **43:** 12, 107; **49:** 105
  abbotti **42:** *80*
  acuminatus **42:** *81*
  altae **42:** 82
  antillensis **42:** 82
  bufoniformis **42:** 81
  coqui **42:** 81, 82
  cubanus **42:** 76
  gaigae **42:** 82; **43:** (73)
  gulosus **42:** 81
  jasperi **42:** 85, (85)
  johnstonei **42:** 81
  limbatus **42:** 81
  martiniquensis **42:** 85
  megacephalus **42:** 81
  mimus **42:** (38)
  noblei **42:** *82–83*
  planirostris **42:** (80), 81
Elgaria **46:** 52, (69)
  coerulea **46:** 50, 69
  multicarinata **46:** 68–69
Eliomys
  melanurus **7:** 102
  quercinus **7:** 102

elk 6: 10, 26–29
  eastern **6:** 26
  Irish **6:** 10
  Manitoba **6:** 27
  Merriman **6:** 26
  North American **6:** 12
  Rocky Mountain **6:** 26–27
  Roosevelt's **6:** 27
  Siberian **6:** 15
  Tule **6:** 27
  see also moose
Elminia
  albicauda **17:** 66
  longicauda **17:** 66
Elopichthys bambusa **34:** 16, 19
Elopidae **33:** (62)
Elopiformes **33:** 62, (62)
Elopomorpha **33:** 62–67
  families summary **33:** (62)
Elphidium **21:** *21*
elvers **33:** 66–67
Elysia **30:** 42
Emballonuridae **9:** 87
Emberiza **16:** 62
  calandra **16:** 62
  cioides **20:** 49
  citrinella **16:** 62
  schoeniclus **16:** 62
Emberizidae **16:** 62, 100; **20:** 96
Embia ramburi **22:** *82–83*
Embioptera **22:** 30, 82–83
Embiotocidae **40:** 9, 12–19
emblems
  of fertility **14:** (39)
  of luck **11:** 66; **14:** (39)
  of marital fidelity **19:** 51
  national **14:** (15); **15:** 27, 30; **18:** 38; **19:** 39; **20:** 84
  of organization **13:** (77)
embryology **21:** (33)
embryonic diapause **10:** 12– 13, 57, 63, 69, 71, 73, 85
Emerita
  analoga **28:** *90*
  talpoida **28:** *92, 93*
Emersonella niveipes **27:** *29*
Emoia **46:** 8
  atrocostata **46:** 14
emperor *see* bream
Empetrichthys **38:** 106, 110
  latos latos **38:** 110
Empididae **23:** 72–75
Empis
  livida **23:** *74*
  stercorea **23:** *72–73*
  tessellata **23:** 72
  trigramma **23:** 73
emu 11: 16, 19, 26–27, 34, 40
Emus hirtus **25:** *32*
emuwren, mallee **18:** 60
Emydidae **47:** 9, 28
Emydocephalus **50:** 44, (45)
  annulatus **50:** 46, *46–47*, 48
  ijimae **50:** 48

Emydura
  krefftii **47:** 38–39
  macquarii **47:** *30*
  signata **47:** 38
Emys orbicularis **47:** 72–73
Encheliophis **36:** 22
Enchonopa concolor **24:** *95*
Endomychidae **25:** *52*
endoplasm **21:** 14
Endoprocta **21:** 32, 69
endoprocts **21:** (72)
endothermy **48:** 102–103
Engraulidae **36:** 90–95, 97
Engraulis
  anchoita **36:** 94
  encrasicolus **36:** (88), *92–93*, 94, *94*
  japonica **36:** 94
  mordax **36:** *90–91*, 94
  ringens **36:** 34, *90*, 91, 94
Enhydra lutris **1:** 32, 72–75
Enhydrina schistosa **50:** (45), 47
Enhydris **49:** 64, (65)
Enneacanthus **40:** 26
  gloriosus **40:** 26
Enopia **21:** 77
Enoplida **21:** 89
Enoplometopus occidentalis **28:** *58–59*
Enoplosidae **40:** 54–55
Enoplosus armatus **40:** 54, *54*, 55
Ensatina **41:** 68
  eschscholtzii **41:** *70–71*, 72, 92
Ensifera ensifera **16:** 44, 48–51
Ensis siliqua **30:** *68, 70*
Entimus granulatus **25:** *105*
entomology **21:** (33)
Entomyzon cyanotis **20:** 88, 92–93
Eoacanthocephala **21:** 77
Eoanilius **48:** (35)
Eobania vermiculata **30:** *46*
Eohippus **5:** 42
Eolophus roseicapillus **16:** 22
Eomanis waldi **9:** *64*
Eopsetta jordani **39:** 90
Eos squamata **19:** 12
Epalzeorhynchos **34:** 54–57
  bicolor **34:** *17*, 18, 55
  frenatus **34:** *54–55*, 56
  kalopterus **34:** 54, *54*
epaulette **40:** 18
Ephalophis greyi **50:** 44, (45)
Ephemera danica **22:** *39, 41*
Ephemeroptera **22:** 30, 38–41
epibatidine **43:** (80)
Epibolus pulchripes **22:** *18–19, 19*
Epicaridea **28:** 34
Epicharis **27:** *97*
Epicrates
  angulifer **48:** 45, 78
  cenchria **48:** 45, 62, 62–63
  chrysogaster **48:** (63)
  exsul **48:** (63)
  gracilis **48:** 45
  inornatus **48:** 85
  moensis **48:** 45–46

Epicrionops **41:** 21
Epigonichthys **31:** 24
Epimachus fastuosus **19:** 106
Epimenia **30:** *12–13*
Epinephelus
  lanceolatus **40:** (10), 15
  tukula **40:** *15*
Epipedobates **43:** 68, (71), 72
  femoralis **43:** (73)
  tricolor **43:** 72, *72–73*, 73, (80)
Epiplatys **38:** 81
  annulatus **38:** 81
epitokes **21:** (101)
Eptatritus stouti **31:** *27*
Equidae **5:** 42
Equus
  asinus **5:** 42, 57
  burchelli **5:** 42, 46–51
  caballus **5:** 42, 58–61
  caballus przewalskii (*E. przewalskii*)
    5: 42, 54–55
  grevyi **5:** 42, 52–53
  hemionus **5:** 42, 56–57
  przewalskii **5:** 42, 54–55
  quagga **5:** 48
  zebra **5:** 42
Erannis defoliara **26:** *77*
Ercinidae **30:** 50
Erebia aethiops **26:** *46*
Eremalauda starli **18:** 22
Eremitalpa granti **9:** 40, 56–57
Eremophila alpestris **18:** 22, 28–29
Eremopterix
  grisea **18:** 22
  nigriceps **18:** 22
Erethizon dorsatum **8:** 12, 20–25
Erethizontidae **7:** *12*; **8:** 12
Eretmochelys imbricata **47:** (15), 22–23
Eretmodus cyanostictus **40:** 74
Ereuniidae **39:** 76–81
Erimyson **34:** 99
Erinaceidae **9:** 9, 11
Erinaceus
  concolor **9:** 12
  europaeus **9:** 12, 14–19
Eristalis
  nemorum **23:** *78*
  tenax **23:** *76*, 78
Eristias acutirostris **40:** 55
Erithacus
  alkahige **18:** (50)
  komadori **18:** (50)
  rubecula **11:** (49); **18:** 44, 46–51,
    52, 54
ermine **1:** 112
  see also stoat
Erosa erosa **39:** 59
Erotylidae **25:** 50–53
Erotylus maculiventris **25:** *51*
Erpetoichthys **31:** 48
  calabaricus **31:** 44, 49, 50
Erpeton tentaculatum **49:** 15, 64–65,
  (73)
Erycinae **48:** 44, 46–47, 68, 75

Erymnochelys madagascariensis **47:**
  41–42
Eryops **41:** *13*
Eryphanis polyxena **26:** *49*
Erythrinidae **38:** 24–27
erythrinu **38:** 25
Erythrocebus patas **4:** 40
Erythrolampus **50:** 26
Erythrura **16:** 90
  gouldiae **16:** 90, 92–95
  trichroa **16:** 90, (92), 96–97
Eryx **48:** 46
  colubrinus **48:** 74–75
  conicus **48:** 44
  jayakari **48:** 47
Esacus **13:** (93)
  magnirostris **13:** 90, 106–107
  recurvirostris **13:** 90
Eschemeyer nexus **39:** 69
Eschrichtidae **3:** 92
Eschrichtius robustus **3:** 55, 92–97
escolar
  roudi **35:** 101
  striped **35:** 101
escuerzo (Bell's horned frog) **42:** 86–87
Esocidae **35:** 10–19, (12), **36:** 33, **38:** 27
Esociformes **35:** 8, (9)
Esox **35:** (12)
  americanus americanus **35:** 16
  americanus vermiculatus **35:** 16,
    16–17
  lucius **31:** 78, **35:** *10–11*, 11, *12–13*,
    (14), (17), *18–19*,
    37: 18, **38:** 27
  masquinongy **35:** 10, (14), 17
  niger **35:** *14–15*, 18
  osseus **31:** 78
  papyraceus **35:** (17)
  reichertii **35:** 18
  tiemani **35:** (17)
Esox lucius **35:** 15
estivation **7:** 19; **9:** 13, 21; **30:** 47; **44:**
  9–10
Estrilda nonnula **16:** 90
Estrildidae **16:** 62, 90, 92
Etheostoma nuchale **40:** 18
Ethiopia, geladas in **4:** 63
Ethmostigmus **22:** *24–25*, 25
ethology **21:** (33)
Etmopteridae **32:** 92, 94
Etmopterus
  perryi **32:** 92
  pusillus **32:** 93
  spinax **32:** *19*
Etroplus **40:** 68
  maculatus **40:** 69
Eubalaena
  australis **3:** 108–109
  glacialis **3:** 55
Eublepharidae **44:** 25; **45:** 8, 13
Eublepharinae **45:** 8
Eublepharis **45:** 13, 63
  macularius **44:** 22; **45:** (10), 14–17
Eubucco bourcierii **19:** 56, 68–69

eucalyptus **10:** 95–96, *96*
Euchilichthys **37:** 73
Euchiloglanis **37:** 51
Eucinostomus melanopterus **40:** 37
Euclichthyidae **36:** 52–53
Euclichthys polynemus **36:** 53
Eucrossorhinus dasypogon **32:** 36–37
Eucylodes **26:** (76)
Eudromia
  elegans **11:** 40, 42–43
  albida **11:** 42
  multiguttata **11:** 42
Eudromias morinellus **13:** 8
Eudyptes **12:** 10
  chrysocome **12:** 8, 26–27
  chrysolophus **12:** 8, 20; **13:** 109,*111*
  pachyrhynchus **12:** 8
  sclateri **12:** 8
Eudyptula minor **12:** 8, 24–25
Eugerres plumieri **40:** 37
Euglossa **27:** *102–103*, 103
Eugonycha **25:** 99
eukaryotes **21:** 9, *10*
eulachon **35:** (28)
Eulalia viridis **21:** *98*
Eulamellibranchia **30:** 9, 50, 62–71
Eulemur **4:** *96*
  coronatus **4:** 96
  macaco **4:** 96
  mongoz **4:** 96
Eulophidae **27:** 25
Eulyes amaena **24:** *39*
Eumalacostraca **28:** 9, 34
Eumastacidae **23:** 32–33
Eumeces **46:** 8, 9, (15)
  fasciatus **46:** *13*, 26–27, 61
  lagunensis **46:** *12–13*
  laticeps **46:** *14–15*
  obsoletus **46:** (13)
  schneideri **46:** 10, 28–29
  septentrionalis **46:** 61
  taylori **46:** (13)
Eumecichthys fiski **35:** 82, 104
Eumenes fenestralis **27:** *64*
Eumetazoa **21:** 30, 32, 69
Eumetopias jubatus **3:** 9, 18–19
Eumorphus micans **25:** *52*
Eunectes
  deschauenseei **48:** 45, 67
  murinus **48:** 64–67, 107
  notaeus **48:** 45, 67
Eunice viridis **21:** *101*
Eunomota superciliosa **19:** 42
Euoticus
  elegantulus **4:** 106
  pallidus **4:** 106
Euphagus carolinus **18:** 74
Euphausia superba **28:** 54–55
Euphausiacea **28:** 9, 34, *52–55*
Euphylictis **43:** 85
Euplectes
  jacksoni **16:** 100
  orix **16:** 100
Eupleres goudotii **1:** 88

Euplotes **21:** *24*
Eupodotis
    afra **11:** 84
    melanogaster **11:** 84
    ruficrista **11:** 84
    vigorsii **11:** 84
Euproctus **41:** 27, 88, *88–89*, 92, (97)
    asper **41:** 96–97
    montanus **41:** 96, (97)
    platycephalus **41:** 96, (97)
Euprymna tasmanica **30:** *80–81*
Euptilotis neoxenus **19:** 34
Euroscaptor parvidens **9:** 40
Eurostopodus diabolicus **15:** 78
Eurota sericaria **26:** *90*
Eurotamandua **1:** *9*
Euryapsida **44:** *10*
Eurycea **41:** 27, 29, 68, 70, 71, 73, (81), 82
    bislineata **41:** *71*, (81)
    guttolineata **41:** 80–81
    longicauda **41:** 80
    nana **41:** (83)
    neotenes **41:** (81), (83)
    quadridigitata **41:** *69*
    rathbuni **41:** (83)
    robusta **41:** 73, (83)
    sosorum **41:** 73, (81), 82–83
    tynerensis **41:** (81)
Eurycephalus otaitensis **39:** *72*
Eurydactylodes **45:** 12
Eurygaster
    maura **24:** *70*
    testudinaria **24:** *70*
Eurylaimidae **20:** 74
Eurylaimus ochromalus **20:** 74
Eurynorhynchus pygmeus **13:** 30, 48–49
Eurypegasus
    draconis **39:** 36, *36*
    papilio **39:** 36, 37
Eurypharyngidae **33:** (62), 94–95
Eurypharynx pelecanoides **33:** 64, *65*, *94*
Eurystomus **15:** 86
    azureus **15:** 86
    glaucurus **15:** 86, 92
    gularis **15:** 86, 92
    orientalis **15:** 86, 90–93
Eurytides agesilaus **26:** *18*
Euryzygomatomys spinosus **8:** 30
Euscyrtus bivittatus **23:** *18*
Eusphyra blochii **32:** 69
Eustenogaster calyptodoma **27:** *67*
Eusthenopteron **41:** *13*
Eutaeniophorus festivus **39:** 15
Euthalia **26:** 42
Eutheria **10:** (10)
Euthrix potatoria **26:** *85*
Eutoxeres aquila **16:** 44
Evanioidea **27:** (23)
Evarcha arcuata **29:** *74*
Evechinus chloroticus **30:** *104*
Everglades' ecosystem **33:** 108, 109
Evermannichthys metzelaari **40:** (99)

evolution **1:** *10;* **11:** 8, (10)
    convergent (parallel) **9:** 10, 40; **10:** 36, (52); **11:** 40; **12:** 98; **19:** 57; **20:** (11); **43:** 104, 108–109; **44:** (26), (49); **48:** (58); **49:** (18); **50:** 59
    by natural selection **20:** 96
    of mammals **1:** *10*
    of rodents **7:** *12*
Exocoetidae **38:** 50, 70–75, 77
Exocoetus volitans **38:** *70*
Exostoma **37:** 51
Extatosoma tiaratum **22:** 57
extermination **6:** 64–66
external digestion **29:** 15
Eybrachyura **28:** 56
eye diseases **23:** 103
eyelight fish **39:** 18
eyes **32:** 15, 16, *50*, **38:** 90, (93), *93*, **39:** (104), **40:** (48)
    of birds of prey **15:** 9, (49)
    false **31:** 80, **40:** (48)
    nictitating membrane **32:** 45, *50*, 74
    for night vision **15:** 51
    slit **12:** 97
    third eyelid **14:** 109
Eysarcoris fabricii **24:** *67*

F

fa (African arowana) **31:** 86
facial expression **4:** (56), 100
facultative endothermy **48:** 102–103
fairy-wren
    blue-breasted **18:** 60
    broad-billed **18:** 60
    emperor **18:** 60
    fairy-wren family 18: 60–61
    lovely **18:** 60
    orange-crowned **18:** 60
    splendid **18:** 60
    superb 18: 60, 62–63
    variegated **18:** 60, *61*
    Wallace's **18:** 60
falanouc **1:** 88, *91*
Falco **44:** 41
    araea **15:** (68)
    columbarius **15:** 8; **18:** 59
    mexicanus **15:** 8
    naumanni **15:** 8
    peregrinus **12:** 107; **15:** 8, 18–21, 33,

(42), 45, (48)
    punctatus **15:** 8
    rusticolus **15:** 8
    subbuteo **15:** 8; **17:** (13)
    tinnunculus **15:** 8, 22–23; **17:** (13); **18:** 59
falcon 11: 12, 84; **12:** 69; **15:** 8, (9), 10, 11–12, 50, 63, 91; **18:** 12
    barred forest- **15:** 8
    forest- **15:** 11–12
    peregrine 12: 107; **15:** 8, 11, 18–21, 33, (42), 45, (48)
    prairie **15:** 8, *12*
    pygmy **15:** 8
falconet, black-legged **15:** 8, *12*
Falconidae **15:** 8, 11
falconry **15:** (19)
false cleaner **40:** 90, 91
false heads **26:** (31), 82, 93, *97*
fanaloka **1:** 88
    Madagascan **1:** *91*, *91*
fanfish
    spotted **40:** 35
fangtooth 39: 8, 9, 16–21
    common **39:** 16, *16*, *17*
    shorthorn **39:** 16
fanray **33:** *29*
fantail *see* goldfish
fantail, yellow-bellied **17:** 66
Farancia abacura **48:** 109; **49:** 16
Farlowella **37:** 104
    knerii **37:** *111*
farmland, expanding **1:** 15–16
Fasciola hepatica **21:** *84*
fathead **39:** 80
feather stars 30: 92, *93*, 94–97
featherback **36:** 86
    giant **31:** *102*
featherfin
    African **31:** 104, 105
    false **31:** *104*, 105
feathers *see* plumage
feeding
    adaptations for **11:** 12–13
    courtship **16:** *28*, (29), (71); **17:** *18*, (76), 87
    sociable **17:** 77
    spinning **13:** 88
    stitching **13:** (55)
feet
    anisodactyl **18:** *18*, (18)
    of birds of prey **15:** 9, *14*, (42), 57
    bones of **11:** 10
    for gripping **19:** 36, 58
    heterodactyl **18:** (18)
    hypertrophied **13:** 93
    opposing toes **11:** (19)
    pamprodactyl **18:** (18)
    reversible toes **20:** (72)
    semizygodactyl **16:** 38; **17:** (22)
    syndactyl **18:** (18); **19:** (82)
    types **18:** *18*, (18)
    webbed **14:** 8; **18:** *18*, (18)
    zygodactyl **16:** 22; **17:** 20, (22);

18: 8, *18*, (18);
19: 58; **20:** 46
Fejervarya **43:** 82, 83, 85
Felderolia candescens **26:** *105*
Felis **2:** 10
    bengalensis **2:** 10
    caracal **2:** 10
    catus **2:** 10
    chaus **2:** 10
    concolor **2:** 10, *42–43*
    lynx **2:** 10, 40–41
    lynx canadensis **2:** 40, 41
    lynx lynx **2:** 40, 41
    lynx pardinus **2:** 40, 41
    margarita **2:** 10
    nigripes **2:** 10
    pardalis **2:** 10, 44–45
    rufus **2:** 10, 38–39
    serval **2:** 10, 46–47
    silvestris **2:** 10, 48–49
    temmincki **2:** 10
    tigrinus **2:** 10
    yaguarondi **2:** 10
Felovia vae **7:** 108
female choice **42:** 70
Fenestraja **33:** (27)
Fennecus zerda see *Vulpes zerda*
fer-de-lance (terciopelo) **48:** 109; **50:** (8),
    9, (52), 92–93, (111)
fermentation **5:** 11
ferox **35:** (69)
ferret 1: 45
    black-footed 1: 32, *34*, 35, 46–47
fertilization **37:** (12), *12*
    internal **42:** 14
    see also implantation; reproduction
Feylinia **46:** 8
Ficedula **17:** 66
    hypoleuca **17:** 66
Ficimia **49:** (63)
fieldfare 18: 44, 45, 58–59
fighting fish
    Siamese **38:** 76, **40:** 60, *60*, 61, 63,
        (63), *63*
filariasis **23:** (49)
file snakes 48: 40–41; **49:** 13, (82);
    50: (35), 37, 62
    acrochordid **49:** 13
    African **49:** 61
    Arafura 48: 17, 40, *41*, 42–43
    Asian **49:** 65
    Javan **48:** *41*
    little **48:** (41)
    marine **50:** 49
filefish 39: 11, 96, 97, 99, 100–105
    beaked **39:** 102, *103*
    black-saddled **39:** (102), 105
    harlequin **39:** 102, *103*
    long-nosed **39:** 102, *103*
    as mimic **39:** (102)
    scrawled **39:** *102*, 104
    tasseled **39:** *97*
Filosa **21:** 13
finch 18: 44, (81)

cactus **20:** 96, *96*
cardueline **16:** 77, 78–79, 81; **20:** 98
Cocos Island **20:** 96
finch family 16: 62, 76–77
fringilline **16:** 77
Galápagos 20: 96–97, 98
Gouldian 16: 90, 92–95
grosbeak **20:** *99*
large cactus ground **20:** 96, *97*
large ground **20:** 96, *96*
large tree **20:** 96, *96*
Laysan **20:** 98
mangrove **20:** 96
medium ground **20:** 96
rainbow (Gouldian) **16:** 90, 92–95
sharp-beaked ground **20:** 96, *96*
small ground **20:** 96, *97*
small tree **20:** 96
tree **20:** 96
vegetarian **20:** 96, *96*
warbler **20:** 96, *97*
white-winged snow **16:** 100
woodpecker **20:** 96, *96*
zebra **16:** 90
finfoot **14:** 82, 90
fingerfish **40:** 42
finnock **35:** 66, (68)
fins **31:** 16, (47), **38:** (96)
    cephalic **33:** 52, *53*
    of sharks **32:** 22, *22*, 63, (80)
fire brats (silverfish) **22:** 36–37
fire salamander 41: (17), 88, 90, 92,
    102–107; **42:** 26
    central Spanish **41:** 107
    Corsican **41:** (103)
    European **41:** 92
    Middle Eastern **41:** (103)
    North African **41:** (103)
    Pyrenean 41: 107
    spotted **41:** 104
    yellow-striped **41:** *104–105*
firecrown, green-backed **16:** 44, 46
fire-eye, white-backed **19:** 72, *75*
firefish 36: *22–23*, **40:** 99
fireflies 25: 36–37
    eastern **25:** *36–37*
fish
    as acrobats **31:** 92
    anatomy **31:** *14, 15, 22, 25, 27, 30*
    behavior **31:** 17
    biology **31:** 15
    bony **31:** (10), 15, **33:** 60–61
    breeding **31:** 19
    captive bred **38:** (41)
    cartilaginous 31: (10), *14*, 42, **32:**
        8–9, **33:** 8–15
    changing sex **40:** (16), (82), (86)
    characteristics **31:** (12)
        crossopterygian **41:** 13–14, *13*
    deepest living **36:** (27)
    definition 31: 8–21
    domesticated **38:** (98)
    evolution **31:** 13
    fleshy-finned **33:** 60

gadiform 36: 8–15, (14)
habitats **31:** 17
human (olms) **41:** 14, *26–27*, 27,
    48–49
and humans **31:** 20
as laboratory animals **36:** (59)
largest freshwater **31:** (56)
living groups **31:** 10–11
lobe-finned 31: 32–33, 42, 45, **33:**
    60
long-lived **31:** (61), **39:** 65
longest **35:** 82
mail-cheeked 39: 11, 52–53
    Mexican walking (axolotls) **41:** 18,
        27, *28*, 29, 56, 58, 59,
        60–63; **46:** (111)
oldest species **31:** 38
orders summary **31:** (10–11)
perchlike 40: 8–11
ray-finned 31: 42–43, **33:** 60
skeleton **31:** *14*, 15, *15*
smallest marine **40:** 94
spiny-finned 33: 106, **38:** 50, (51),
    39: 8–11
toxic **39:** (102), 109
warm-blooded **40:** 105, (106), (111)
fish and chips **32:** 47
"fish cat" (*poisson chat*) **37:** 14
fish farming **3:** 65; **31:** (21), **37:** (20),
    20, 42, (44)
    diseases **35:** (57)
    rainbow trout **35:** 76, 77
    salmon **35:** (57)
fish markets **33:** *15*
    eel fairs **33:** (73)
fish oil **32:** 22, 63, (80), **36:** 95, **37:** (46)
fisher **1:** 50–51; **8:** 20
fishflies **22:** 98
fishing **3:** 12, 15, 19, 37, 43, 105; **31:**
    20, *21*, **32:** 53, **36:** 24, 25, 91, **37:**
    33, 46–47, **40:** 11
    in Alaska **35:** (65)
    for arapaima **31:** *91*
    for arowana **31:** (95)
    bans **31:** (66)
    for capelin **35:** *28*
    for cod **36:** 38, 47, *47*, 49, 50
    cooperative, by dolphins **3:** (74)
    drift nets **36:** 107, 109
    for eels **33:** *72–73*
    for elephant fish **33:** 59
    game fish **35:** 13, (14), 18, *18–19*, 44,
        47, *54*, 66, 69, 70
    for hake **36:** 32, (35), (36)
    for herring **36:** 89, 107, *108–109*
    illegal **31:** (66), **32:** 39–41
    by Inuit **32:** 97, **35:** 20
    limits **36:** (47)
    as local industry **36:** *108*
    in Norway **36:** *108–109*
    overfishing **31:** 20, 21, **33:** 59, **36:**
        (30), 50, 51, 95, **40:** 107
    for piranhas **38:** 42, *43*
    quotas **35:** (65)

for salmon **35:** *54, 59*, (65)
for sardines **36:** *108*
for skate **33:** 31
for sprats **36:** *109*
for sturgeon **31:** 55, 56, *57*
for swordfish **40:** (110)
trawl net **36:** *109*
for trout **35:** *70–71*
for tuna **40:** 107
for whitebait **35:** (35)
fishing nets **3:** 22, 30, 50, *59*, 69, 71, 77, 79, 105
fishing techniques **14:** 20–22, (25), (106); **15:** 57
fishmeal **36:** 50, 95
Fistularia
   commersonii **39:** 49
   corneta **35:** 101, **39:** 49
   petimba **39:** 49
   tabacaria **39:** 49
Fistulariidae **39:** 11, 26, 48–49
Flabellifera **28:** 34
Flabellinopsis iodinea **30:** *41*
flagellates 21: 12, 13, 16–17
   commensal **21:** 17
   parasitic **21:** 16–17
   reproduction **21:** *14*
flagfish
   American **38:** 87
   Florida **38:** 87, 88
   orange **38:** 87
   Yucatán **38:** 87
flake **32:** 22, 47
flamefish **40:** 30, *30*
flamingo 11: 12; **19:** 36
   Andean **14:** 44, *45*
   Caribbean **14:** 44, 46
   Chilean **14:** 44
   flamingo family 14: 44–45
   greater 14: 44, 46–51
   James' **14:** 44
   lesser **14:** 44, 46; **20:** 26
flannelmouth 38: 18–19
flash markings **43:** 107
flashlight fish **35:** (88), **39:** 9, 16, 17, (18), 20
   Gulf **39:** 17
   splitfin **39:** 17
flatfish 32: 59, 67; **39:** 11, 84–87; **40:** 103
   American freshwater **39:** 92
   angler **39:** (90)
   as burrowers **39:** (86)
   "dextral" **39:** 85
   "sinistral" **39:** 86
flathead 39: 11, 53, 72–73
   armored **39:** 73
   bartail **39:** 72, 73
   crocodile **39:** 72, *72–73*
   deepwater **39:** 72, 73
   dusky **39:** 73
   fringelip **39:** *72*
   ghost **39:** 72, 73
Flatidae **24:** (74)

flatworms 21: 80–85
fleas 9: (18); **15:** (101); **22:** 110–113
   beach 28: 44–45
   cat **22:** 110, *112–113*
   and disease **22:** (113)
   dog **22:** *110*
   human **22:** 111
   jumping ability **22:** (111)
   rabbit **22:** *110–111,* 112–113, (113)
   rat **22:** *113*
   specific hosts **22:** 111
   water 28: *11,* 16–21
Flectonotus **43:** 45, (45)
flehmen **5:** (11), 62, 65
fleshy-finned fish **33:** 60
flicker **18:** 8
   Andean **18:** 8, (11)
   campo **18:** 8, (11)
flies 23: 36–41
   anatomy **23:** 36–39
   assassin (robber) **23:** 62–67
   banana **23:** (85)
   bee 23: 68–71
   black **23:** *52–53,* (53)
   black horsefly **23:** *60*
   "blinder" deerfly **23:** *58*
   blow 23: 108–111
   bluebottle (blow) **23:** *36–37,* 108–111
   bot 23: 96–97
   cactus **23:** (85)
   crane 23: *38,* 42–45
   dance 23: 72–75
   dark giant horsefly **23:** *60*
   deerflies 23: 58–61
   downlooker snipefly **23:** *59*
   drone **23:** *76, 78*
   dune bee **23:** *70*
   dung 23: 98–99
   elephant (horseflies) **23:** 58–61
   face (houseflies) **23:** 100–103
   families **23:** 36
   fever (March) **23:** 54–55
   flesh 23: 112–113
   flower (hover) **23:** 76–81
   fruit, large 23: 88–91
   fruit, small 23: 92–93
   gray (flesh) **23:** 112–113
   greenbottle (blow) **23:** 108, 109–110
   green colonel **23:** *57*
   hawthorn (March) **23:** 54–55
   horn (houseflies) **23:** 100–103
   hornet robber **23:** 66–67
   horseflies 23: *36–37,* 58–61
   houseflies and relatives 23: 100–103
   hover 23: 76–81
   jackal **23:** (106), *107*
   larvae **23:** 39–40
   life history **23:** 39–40
   long-horned general **23:** *57*
   long-legged **23:** (75)
   mantid **22:** 90, 92–95
   manure **23:** *98–99,* (99)
   March 23: 54–55

   marsh (snail) **23:** 94–95
   medflies **23:** (90)
   Mediterranean fruit **23:** (90)
   Mydas **23:** (40), (63)
   noonday **23:** *100–101*
   nostril (bot) **23:** 96–97
   parasite 23: 104–107
   petroleum **23:** (39)
   phantom crane **23:** (45)
   picture-winged **23:** (87)
   pomace (small fruit) **23:** 92–93
   robber 23: 62–67
   St. Mark's (March) **23:** 54–55
   snail 23: 94–95
   snipe **23:** (59)
   soldier 23: 56–57
   splayed deerfly **23:** *61*
   stable (houseflies) **23:** 100–103
   stalk-eyed 23: 86–87
   stiletto **23:** (65)
   stilt-legged 23: 84–85
   suborders **23:** 39
   tangle-veined **23:** (69)
   thick-headed (wasp) **23:** 82–83
   3-spot horsefly **23:** *58*
   tsetse **21:** (17); **23:** (103)
   vinegar (small fruit) **23:** 92–93
   walnut husk **23:** *88*
   warble 23: 96–97
   wasp 23: 82–83
flight **11:** 8, (13)
   insects **22:** (35)
   soaring **15:** (33)
flightless birds 11: 8, (10), 16–39; **12:** 8–27; **20:** 36, 42
flood water **4:** 80
flounder 39: 11, *84–85,* 88–91, 90; **40:** 103
   California **39:** 90
   eyed **39:** *88*
   lefteye **39:** 11, 84, 87, 88, 91
   panther **39:** *86–87*
   pelican **39:** 91
   righteye **39:** 11, 87, 88, 90, 91
   starry **39:** 85
flukes **21:** 80, 82–83, 83–84
   blood **21:** *83*
   liver **21:** *84*
Flustra foliacea **21:** 72
Fluviphylax pygmaeus **38:** 94
flycatcher 17: 60, 61; **18:** 72
   African paradise 17: 66, 67, 68–69
   African shrike **17:** 66
   African wattle-eyes **17:** 66
   Asiatic paradise **17:** 66, 67
   blue **17:** 66
   chinspot puffback *see* batis, chinspot
   fantail **17:** 66
   gray **17:** 66
   Mariqua **17:** 66
   monarch **17:** 66, 106
   Old World 17: 66–67
   olivaceous **17:** 30
   pale **17:** 66

pied **17:** 66
puffback **17:** 66
royal 17: 30, <u>34–35</u>, (37)
scissor-tailed **17:** *29*, 30
Seychelles black paradise **17:** 66, 67
spotted **17:** 66, *67*
spotted tody **17:** 30
Tickell's blue **17:** 66
tyrant 17: <u>28–31</u>, *29*, (37), (39), 108;
　19: 70, 76, 80
vermilion 17: 30, <u>36–41</u>
white-eyed slaty **17:** 66
white-tailed blue **17:** 66
flying fish 38: 50, <u>70–75</u>, 77
flying fox 9: 80, 86; **45:** (42)
　Indian 9: <u>88–91</u>
flying fox (fish) **34:** 54, *54*, 56
　Siamese (fish) **34:** 18, 56, 88
Fodiator **38:** 70
Foersichthys flavipinnis **38:** 81
foliage-gleaner **20:** 80
　chestnut-winged **20:** 80
　crested **20:** 80
folklore *see* myths and legends
food
　carrying **16:** (87)
　piracy *see* kleptoparasitism
　poisonous prey **15:** (105)
　poisons in **19:** (28), (36); **20:** 14,
　　17–18, (52), 70–72
　storing **17:** (79); **18:** 65, 66–67,
　　90–92, 97–98, 105, 110–111;
　　25: 71–72
food poisoning **7:** 74
food pouches **16:** (87)
food sharing **9:** (96)
foot trembling **13:** (24)
footballfish **36:** (14), *78–79*, 82
forams **21:** 20–21
Forcipomyia **23:** *52*
Fordonia leucobalia **49:** 15, (51)
forestry operations **5:** 26
forests
　in Brazil **4:** 90–91
　elephants in **5:** 22
　gallery forests **4:** 101
　gorillas in **4:** 26
　rain **20:** (78)
　see also deforestation
Forficula auricularia **22:** *58–59, 60–61,*
　61
Formica rufa **27:** *49*
Formicariidae **19:** 72, 75
Formicarius rufipectus **19:** 72
Formicidae **27:** <u>40–57</u>
fossa 1: 88, 90, *91*, <u>96–97</u>; **4:** 100
Fossa fossa **1:** 88
fossils **11:** (10); **12:** 8, 92; **13:** 8; **14:** 8;
　19: 42; **31:** *13*, 15, 34, (36), 38, 39,
　32: 12, 13, 14, **33:** (10), 62, 63, **35:**
　(17), **36:** (105), *105*
fossorial animals **7:** 18, 65
Fouchia **5:** 28
four-eyed fish 38: <u>90–93</u>

fovea **4:** 107
fox
　Arctic 2: 50, <u>70–73</u>, 87; **7:** (14)
　bat-eared 2: 50, <u>76–77</u>
　Blanford's **2:** 50, *53*
　blue Arctic **2:** 71, (72)
　Cape **2:** 50, *53*
　corsac **2:** 50, *53*
　"cross fox" **2:** 64, *65*
　fennec 2: 50, *52*, <u>74–75</u>
　gray **2:** 50, *52*
　Indian **2:** 50, *53*
　island gray **2:** 50
　kit (swift) **2:** 50, *52*, <u>68–69</u>
　red 1: 9; **2:** 50, (59), <u>64–67</u>, 70
　Rüppell's **2:** 50, *53*
　Samson **2:** 64
　swift 2: 50, *52*, <u>68–69</u>
　white Arctic **2:** 71, 72
fox, flying *see* flying fox
francolin **11:** 47
　crested **11:** 44
Francolinus sephaena **11:** 44
Frankliniella occidentalis **22:** *84*
Fratercula
　arctica **12:** 98, <u>104–107</u>; **17:** 51
　cirrhata **12:** 98
　corniculata **12:** 98
freeze branding **8:** (84)
freezing **15:** (80); **19:** 111
freezing tolerance **49:** (85)
Fregata **12:** 30; **15:** (26)
　andrewsi **12:** 44
　aquila **12:** 44
　ariel **12:** 44
　magnificens **12:** 44, 52, <u>62–65</u>
　minor **12:** 44
Fregatidae **12:** 44, 49
friarbird **20:** (91), 93
　noisy **20:** 88
frigatebird 12: 30, 44, 45, 49; **14:** (74);
　15: (26); **18:** (10)
　Ascension **12:** 44, 49
　Christmas Island **12:** 44, *49*
　great **12:** 44
　lesser **12:** 44
　magnificent 12: 44, 52, <u>62–65</u>
Fringilla **16:** 77
　coelebs **16:** 76, <u>78–79</u>
　montifringilla **16:** 76
　teydea **16:** 76
Fringillidae **16:** 76
fringillines **16:** 77
frogfish 36: (14), 55, <u>64–69</u>
　banded **36:** *55*
　bloody **36:** *14–15*
　brackish water **36:** 64
　flagpole **36:** *64*
　giant **36:** *66*
　longlure **36:** *64*
　roughbar **36:** 64
　sargassum *see* sargassum fish
frog-jumping contest **43:** *91*, (91)
frogmouth 15: <u>78–81</u>

　Bornean **15:** 78
　tawny **15:** 78, *81*
frogs 41: 12–13; **42:** <u>8–15</u>; **49:** 105
　adapting to environment **42:** 12
　African pig-snouted **42:** 92
　African rubber **42:** 105
　African sharp-snouted **42:** 98
　American marsupial **43:** (11)
　Archey's **42:** 19
　arum lily **43:** *18–19*
　Australian burrowing **42:** 92
　Australian gastric-brooding **42:** (85)
　Australian marsupial **43:** (11)
　Australian sandhill **43:** 16
　Australian water-holding 42: 40,
　　54; **43:** 34, <u>52–53</u>
　"backpack" **43:** 41
　baw baw **42:** 95
　big-toothed **42:** 78
　body forms **42:** 9–10
　brood **42:** 101
　Budgett's **42:** 76, 88, *88–89*; **43:**
　　34, 99
　burrowing **42:** 108, 109
　bush 43: 18, 19, 100, <u>106–107</u>
　bush squeakers 43: <u>12–15</u>
　cacos (dainty) **43:** 87
　Cape cacos **43:** 87
　Cape sand **43:** *84*
　casque-headed 42: (38); **43:** 37–38,
　　<u>40–41</u>, 86
　Caucasian parsley **42:** (21)
　Central American glass **43:** 101
　chirping **43:** 82, 87
　chorus **43:** 38
　clicking stream **43:** 83, *87*
　common 43: 83, <u>92–95</u>
　common argus reed **43:** (21)
　common painted **42:** 31
　coqui **42:** 81, 82, 84, 85
　Corsican painted **42:** 30–31
　crab-eating **42:** 55; **43:** (85)
　cricket **43:** 32, 38
　Cuban leaf litter **42:** 9
　dainty **43:** 87
　Darwin's 42: 14, 38; **43:** <u>8–9</u>, (11)
　Doria's **43:** 84, 85
　dumpy **43:** 54
　dwarf Budgett's 42: 40, <u>88–89</u>
　dwarf clawed **43:** (44)
　dwarf litter **42:** 34
　east Iberian painted **42:** 31
　edible 43: 83, <u>96–97</u>
　egg-eating **43:** (20)
　European common **42:** *13*, (18);
　　43: (85)
　extinct **41:** 17
　eyeshine **42:** (91)
　false tomato **42:** 109
　fertilization **41:** 12
　Fleay's barred **42:** (97)
　flying **43:** (62), 100, *101*; **44:** (45)
　foam-nesting **42:** 79, 90–91, 97;
　　43: (20)

food and feeding **42:** 12–13
forest **43:** 82, 85–86
Gardiner's **42:** 9; **43:** 10
gastric-brooding 42: 10, 14, 94, 95, 97, (97), 102–103
giant (Australian water-holding) **42:** 40, 54; **43:** 34, 52–53
giant banjo **42:** 93
giant barred **42:** (97)
giant waxy **42:** 11
gladiator **43:** 37, 38
glass 42: 10; **43:** 28–29, (35)
gliding **43:** 62–63, (62); **45:** (42)
golden **42:** 58, 75, (75)
golden bell **42:** (18)
gold-striped **43:** (73)
Goliath **41:** 17, (17); **42:** 8; **43:** 84, 90
Graf's hybrid **43:** 97
grass (common) **43:** 82, 83, 87, 92, 92–95
green **43:** 84–85, 91
greenhouse **42:** (80)
habitats **42:** 11, 12
hairy **42:** 11; **43:** 12, 15, (15)
Hamilton's **42:** 18
Hasselt's litter **42:** 35, 35
Hazara torrent **43:** 84
Himalayan spiny **43:** (85)
Hochstetter's **42:** 18, 18, 19
Hogsback **43:** 87
humming **42:** 96
Iberian parsley **42:** (21)
Italian hybrid **43:** 97
Lake Titicaca **41:** (12); **42:** 11, 76, 78, (78)
La Palma (Valerio's) glass **43:** 30–31
large-eyed litter **42:** 34, 35
laughing **43:** 96
leaf-folding **43:** 18
leaf-litter **42:** 76, 80; **43:** (73)
Lea's **42:** 96
life cycles **42:** 13–14, 13
litter 42: 10, 34–35, 40
live-bearing **42:** (85)
Loveridge's **42:** 94–95
Loveridge's snouted **42:** (60)
lowland-dwelling marsupial **43:** 44
Madagascan **42:** 10
Madagascan burrowing **42:** 104
Madagascan grass **43:** 87
mantella **44:** 104
marbled shovel-nosed 43: 16–17
marsh **42:** 92, 94, 97; **43:** 96, 97
marsupial **42:** 8, 10, 97, 97; **43:** 32, 42
Mascarene grass **43:** 10
Mexican burrowing 42: 8, 10, 22–23, 92, 98, 99; **43:** 16
micro **43:** 87
monkey (leaf) **42:** 8, 9–10, 10, (38); **43:** 32, 34, 36, 64–67, 107
montane forest **43:** 86
moss (chirping) **43:** 82, 87
mossy **43:** 105

mountain chicken (South American bullfrog) **42:** 90–91
mud **42:** 94, 97
narrow-mouthed 42: 10, 104–105
nest-building **42:** 76
New Zealand 42: 10, 16, 18–19
"pacman" **42:** 86, (86)
painted 42: 10, 25, 30–31
painted reed **43:** 21, (21), 22, 22–23
Palestinian painted **42:** 30
palm **43:** 10
paradoxical 42: 10; **43:** 26–27, 28
parsley 42: 10, 20–21
pig **43:** 91
pitcher breeders **43:** 107
pixie **43:** 82
poison arrow **43:** 78
pool **43:** 96, 97
puddle **43:** 87
pygmy **43:** 100
pygmy marsupial **43:** 45
rainbow burrowing **42:** 105, 105
red-legged **43:** 91, (91)
reed frogs and relatives 42: 10; **43:** 11, 18–23
Reinwardt's flying 43: 104–105
reproduction **42:** (12), 13–14
reticulated (Valerio's) glass **43:** 30–31
rhinoceros **43:** 84
rice-paddy **43:** 84–85
Riobamba marsupial 43: 41, 42–45
robber **42:** 76, 80
rocket **43:** 39, 70
Rocky Mountain tailed **42:** (17)
round-tongued **42:** 25
rubber **42:** 104, 105
running **43:** 18
sand **43:** 86–87
sandhill 42: 92, 95, 97, 98–99
screeching **43:** 12
sedge **43:** 18, 19
Seychelles 42: 10; **43:** 10–11
sharp-nosed grass **43:** 86, 87
sheep **42:** (111)
short-headed (rain) **42:** (38), 76–79, 80–85, 93, 104, 105, 106, (107)
shovel-nosed **42:** 10; **43:** (17)
shrinking (paradoxical) **43:** 26–27, 28
shrub **43:** 100
skittering **43:** 85
skunk **43:** 68, 72–73
slender litter **42:** 34
Smith **43:** 34–35
smoky mountain (South American bullfrog) **42:** 90–91
Solomon Islands palm **43:** 86
South American marsupial **42:** 14
southern 42: 10, 92–97
Spanish water **42:** (31)
Spencer's **42:** 95
sphagnum **42:** 95
splash **43:** 84
spotted litter **42:** 35

squeaker **43:** 12–13, 87
sticky **43:** 32, (35)
sticky-toed **43:** 86
strawberry (strawberry poison dart) **43:** 70, (71), 74–77, 80, 111
stream **42:** 80; **43:** 83
stump-toed **41:** (17)
survival **42:** 14
Table Mountain ghost **43:** 24
tailed 41: 16, 42–44, (45); **42:** 10, 16–17, 45
Thomasset's rock **43:** 10, 11, 87
or toads? **42:** (8)
tomato 42: 104, 105, 108–109
torrent **42:** 11, 94, 95, (97); **43:** 84
tortoise **42:** (108)
tree-hole breeders **43:** 107
tropical **42:** 76
Tungara **42:** 79
turtle **42:** 95, 98, 98–99, 99, (99)
tusked **42:** 96
Valerio's glass 43: 30–31
Wallace's flying **43:** 105
water 42: 10, 76; **43:** 82–87, 97
water loss **43:** (53), 57, (66)
waxy **42:** 12; **43:** 66, (66), 102
webbed **43:** 86
west Iberian painted **42:** 31
whipping **43:** 100
whistling **42:** 76, 81
white-lipped **42:** 76, 78; **43:** 83, 83
wood **43:** 83, 85, 92, 93, (93)
woodworker **42:** 94
see also bullfrog; ghost frogs; horned frogs; leaf frogs; poison dart frogs; rain frogs; treefrogs
fruitcrow **19:** 83
bare-necked **19:** 80, 83
fruiteater
band-tailed **19:** 84
barred 19: 80, 84–85
green-andblack **19:** 84
fry (salmon) **35:** 53, (54)
Fulcidax violacea **25:** 96–97
Fulgora laternaria **24:** 76
Fulgoridae **24:** 72–77
Fulica atra **14:** 82, 92
fulmar 12: 31, 83
northern 12: 28, 40–41
Fulmarus glacialis **12:** 28, 40–41
Funambulus pennantii **7:** 34
Fundulidae **38:** 84–85
Fundulopanchax **38:** 81
Fundulus 85
grandissimus **38:** 84
heteroclitus **38:** 84, 84, (88)
jenkinsii **38:** 84
julisia **38:** 84
zebrinus **38:** 84
fur farming **1:** 22, 35, 54, 55; **2:** (72); **8:** 46–47
fur trade **1:** 22, (23), 51, 54, 64, 68–69, 87, 93; **2:** 12–13, 35, 41, 44, 69, (72), 75; **3:** 12, 16;

4: 40, 85; **7:** 33, 41, 97;
8: (10), 36, 37, 46, 61, 90;
9: 43; **10:** 22, 65, (80)
see also skin trade
Furcifer **44:** 56
bifidus **44:** 57
labordi **44:** 61
lateralis **44:** 58, 59
minor **44:** 59
oustaleti **44:** 56, 57
pardalis **44:** 74–77
Furcula bifida **26:** *80*
Furipteridae **9:** 87
Furnariidae **20:** 80
Furnarius rufus **20:** 80, 84–87
fusilier **40:** 36

G

Gadidae **36:** 38–51, 52
Gadiformes **36:** 8–15
Gadomus longifilis **36:** 29
Gadus morhua **31:** 36, **36:** *8–9, 38, 38–39, 39*
Gagata cenia **37:** 48, *48*
galago
Demidoff's dwarf *see* bush baby, Demidoff's
Gabon **4:** 106
Garnett's **4:** 106
northern needle-clawed **4:** 106
Senegal **4:** 106
Somali **4:** 106
southern needle-clawed **4:** 106
thick-tailed **4:** 106, *107*
Thomas's **4:** 106
Zanzibar **4:** 106
Galago
gabonensis **4:** 106
gallarum **4:** 106
senegalensis **4:** 106
Galagoides
demidoff **4:** 106, 110–111
thomasi **4:** 106
zanzibaricus **4:** 106
galah **16:** 22, *24*
Galápagos Islands, giant tortoises **44:** 16; **47:** *85*
Galathea strigosa **28:** *86*
Galatheoidea **28:** 56, 86–89
galaxias **35:** 33

clarence **35:** 35
climbing **35:** *33*, 35
common **35:** *34*, 36
dwarf **35:** 32, 37
eastern little **35:** 37
marbled **35:** *37*
mountain **35:** *37*
Pedder **35:** 35, 37
Swan **35:** 33, 35
Galaxias
argenteus **35:** 32
brevipinnis **35:** *33*
divergens **35:** 32
fontanus **35:** 33, 35
globiceps **35:** 34
johnstoni **35:** 35
maculatus **35:** 33, *34*, (35), 36
occidentalis **35:** 33
olidus **35:** *37*
pedderensis **35:** 35, 37
postvectis **35:** 33
rostratus **35:** *32*, 33
truttaceus **35:** 33, 36
Galaxiella
nigrostriata **35:** 33
pusilla **35:** 37
galaxiid 35: 8, 32–37
Galaxiidae **35:** 32–37
subfamilies **35:** (34)
Galaxiinae **35:** (34)
Galbalcyrhynchus leucotis **17:** 20
Galbula
dea **17:** 20, 26–27
ruficauda **17:** 20, 27
Galbulidae **17:** 20, 21
Galbuliformes **17:** 22; **19:** 56
Galea musteloides **8:** 30
Galemys pyrenaicus **9:** 40, 52–53
Galeocerdo cuvier **31:** *12*, **32:** 54, 60–63
Galeomma turtoni **30:** *64*
Galeopithecidae **8:** 108
Galeorhinus galeus **32:** 22, 25
Galerida
cristata **18:** 22
modesta **18:** 22
Galictis
cuja **1:** 32
vittata **1:** 32
Galidia elegans **1:** 98
Galidictis
fasciata **1:** 98
grandidieri **1:** 98
gallery forests **4:** 101
Galliformes **11:** 44
Gallinago
gallinago **13:** 30, 50–51, 59; **18:** (10)
media **13:** 30
undulata **13:** 30
Gallinula
chloropus **14:** 82, 92–95
cachinmans **14:** 92
chloropus **14:** 92
guami **14:** 95
sandvicensis **14:** 95

nesiotis **14:** (94)
silvestris **14:** (94)
Gallirallus okinawae **14:** 82
galliwasps 45: 63; **46:** 52
giant 46: 66–67
Gallotia **45:** 58, (67)
gomerana **45:** (67)
simonyi **45:** 60–61, 66–67, (67)
Gallus gallus **11:** *9*, 44, 60–63
Gambusia
affinis **38:** (101)
affinis affinis **38:** (101)
affinis holbrooki **38:** (101)
holbrooki **38:** (101)
game birds 11: 44–49; **20:** (31)
game playing **19:** (62)
Gammaroidea **28:** 34
Gammarus locusta **28:** 44
Gangata schmidti **37:** *50–51*
gannet 12: 44, 45, (46), 47, 48
Australian **12:** 44
Cape **12:** 44
northern 12: 44, 47, 54–57, (94)
gape **16:** 91, 94–95
gar 31: 47, 72–75, (74), 80
alligator 31: 72, 74, 76–77, 79
Cuban **31:** *74–75*, 77
longnose 31: 72, 74, 77, 78–79
shortnose **31:** 74
spotted **31:** *72–73*, 74
tropical **31:** 74, 77
gar characin **38:** *24–25*, 25, 27, (27)
Garamba National Park **5:** 34
garfish *see* gar
Gargaphia solani **24:** (29)
Garibaldi **40:** *82*, 83
Garmanella pulchra **38:** 87
Garrulus glandarius **18:** 90, 97, 110–111
garter snake 48: 42; **49:** 12
African **50:** 14
Butler's **49:** (86)
California red-sided **49:** 88
checkered **49:** (89)
common 48: 109; **49:** (29), 84–89
eastern **49:** *84–85*
Hammond's **49:** *12*
northern red-sided **49:** 88
Oregon red-spotted **49:** 88
red-sided **48:** 17; **49:** 84, 85, *86–87*
red-spotted **41:** 108; **49:** *88*
San Francisco **49:** 88, *88–89*
two-striped **49:** *12*
Gasteracantha arcuata **29:** 109
Gasterochisma melampus **40:** 106, (107)
Gasteropelecidae **38:** 11, 28–29
Gasteropelecus
levis **38:** 29
maculatus **38:** 29
Gasterosteidae **39:** 10, 26, 28, 30–35
Gasterosteiformes **39:** 26–27
families summary **39:** (26)
Gasterosteus
aculeatus **39:** 26, 29, 33
aculeatus aculeatus **39:** 30, *30, 31,*

(32), *32*, 33, *33*
   aculeatus microcephalus **39:** 33
   aculeatus scantaeannae **39:** 33
   aculeatus williamsoni **39:** 33
   crenobiontus **39:** 33
   wheatlandi **39:** 33
Gasteruption assectator **27:** 31
Gastromyzon **34:** 108–109
Gastropholis **45:** 59
Gastrophryne
   carolinensis **42:** *110–111*, (111)
   olivacea **42:** 110–111
Gastrophysa viridula **25:** *13*, 99
Gastropoda **30:** 9, 10, 18–21
gastropods 30: 18–21
   anatomy **30:** 19–20
   coiling and torsion **30:** 19, 20–21
Gastrotheca **42:** 14, (51); **43:** (11), 32,
   41, 42, (45)
   cornuta **42:** (38); **43:** (44)
   marsupiata **43:** (44)
   monticola **43:** (44)
   ovifera **43:** *44*, (44)
   riobambae **43:** 41, 42–45
Gastrotricha **21:** 32, 69
gaucho
   fighting **38:** 82
   Turner's **38:** 82
gaur **6:** 62
Gavia
   adamsii **14:** 8
   arctica **14:** 8
   immer **14:** 8, 10–15
   stellata **14:** 8
Gavialinae **47:** 95, 98
Gavialis gangeticus **47:** 98–99
Gaviidae **14:** 8
Gazella
   dama **6:** 62
   leptoceros **6:** 62
   subguttarosa **6:** 62
   thomsoni **6:** 94–95
gazelle 5: 47
   dama **6:** *61*, 62
   goitered **6:** *61*, 62
   slender-horned **6:** *61*, 62
   Thomson's 6: 94–95, 97, 110
   Tibetan **6:** *61*, 62
Gecarcinus **28:** *109*
Gecarcoidea natalis **28:** 107
Geckolepis **45:** 9
geckos 44: 13, *13*, 25, 28, 29, 30;
   45: 8–13; **48:** 85
   Abbott's day **45:** *32–33*
   adhesion **45:** (9), 10
   Asian flying **44:** 30; **45:** (10)
   Australian velvet **45:** (10)
   banded **45:** (18), 63; **48:** (39)
   barking 44: 29; **45:** 11, 38–39
   cat **45:** 13
   common green **44:** 22–23; **45:** *37*
   common house **45:** (13)
   common wall (Moorish) **45:** 28–29

crocodile (Moorish) **45:** 28–29
day 45: 9–10, 11, 12, 32–37
Duvaucel's **45:** *11*
dwarf **45:** 10, *25–26*, (27), (36)
eyelid **44:** 25; **45:** 13
fat-tailed **45:** *10*
fish-scale **45:** 9
Florida reef **45:** 26
flying **43:** (62); **44:** 26, (45)
fringe-toed **45:** 12
fringe-toed velvet **45:** 12
frog-eyed **45:** *8–9*, 9
giant **45:** 9, *12*
giant ground **45:** 30, (39)
giant leaf-tailed 45: 20–21, 47
gold-dust day **45:** *35*
golden-tailed 45: 44–45
green-eyed **45:** (24), *25*
ground-dwelling **45:** 10–11
house **45:** 10, 11, (23)
on islands **45:** (13)
Jaragua dwarf **44:** 24
jeweled **45:** 12
knob-tailed **45:** (10), 12
Kuhl's flying 45: 40–43
Kuhl's parachute (Kuhl's flying)
   45: 40–43
leaf-tailed **44:** 28, 30, *30*, *30–31*; **45:**
   (10), 12
leopard 44: 22; **45:** (10), 14–17, 63
Madagascan day **44:** *8–9*
Moorish 45: 28–29
naked-toed **45:** (10)
New Caledonian **45:** 12
northern leaf-tailed **45:** 46–47
pad-tailed **45:** 12
palm **45:** *24–25*, (24)
parachute **45:** (10)
Rodrigues giant day **46:** (67)
senses **44:** 28
southern **44:** 25; **45:** 11–12
spiny-tailed **45:** 44, *45*
spotted sticky-toed **45:** 12
Standing's day **45:** *34*, 37
striped **45:** 11
striped day **45:** (27)
tails **45:** (10)
Thai bow-fingered **45:** *10*
thick-toed **45:** (39)
tokay 44: *26*, 29, 30; **45:** 9, 11,
   22–25
turnip-tailed **45:** 11
velvet **45:** 12
viper **45:** (10)
web-footed 44: 26, *28*; **45:** 11,
   30–31, (39)
western banded 45: 18–19
white-striped **45:** *24–25*, (24)
wonder **45:** (10)
yellow-headed **45:** (27)
Gehyra pilbara **48:** 85
geisha girl **38:** 65
Gekko **45:** (24)
   gecko **44:** *26*; **45:** 9, 11, 22–25

   smithii **45:** (24), *25*
   vittatus **45:** *24–25*, (24)
Gekkonidae **44:** (23), 25; **45:** 8, 61
Gekkoninae **45:** 8, 11
gelada baboon 4: 40, 42, 43, 62–63
Gelastocoridae **24:** 22–23
Gelastocoris **24:** *22*
   peruensis **24:** *23*
Gempylidae **35:** 101
gemsbok **6:** 62
Gemuendina **33:** (10)
genet 1: 18, 98
   aquatic **1:** 88, 91
   common 1: 88, 92–93
   European (common) **1:** 88, 92–93
   genet family 1: 88–91
   large-spotted **1:** 88
   small-spotted (common) **1:** 88, 92–93
genetic engineering **34:** 60
Genetta
   genetta **1:** 88, 92–93
   tigrina **1:** 88
gengorô-buna **34:** 44
Genicanthus
   personatus **40:** 50
   semifasciatus **40:** 51, *53*
Genyophryninae **42:** 104
Genypterus **36:** 24
   blacodes **36:** 24
   capensis **36:** 25
Geocapromys brownii **8:** 30
Geochelone **47:** 80, (81)
   carbonaria **47:** 82
   chilensis **47:** 82
   denticulata **47:** 82, *82–83*
   elegans **47:** 82
   elongata **47:** 82
   emys **47:** 82
   gigantea **47:** 30, *89*, (89)
   nigra **46:** (67); **47:** 84–89
   pardalis **47:** 80, 92–93
   platynota **47:** 82
   radiata **47:** 82, *82*
   sulcata **47:** 80
   yniphora **47:** 82
Geococcyx californianus **20:** 46, 56–61
Geocolaptes olivaceus **18:** 8
Geocrinia **42:** 92, 97
Geodipsas **49:** 14
Geogale aurita **9:** 24
Geometridae **26:** 74–77
Geomyda spengleri **47:** *79*
Geomyidae **7:** *12*
Geopelia
   cuneata **16:** 12
   striata **16:** 12
Geophagus **40:** 70
   brasiliensis **40:** 70, *74*
geophagus
   red-hump **40:** 72
   Suriname **40:** 72
Geopsittacus occidentalis **20:** 36
Georychus capensis **8:** 56
Geositta **20:** 83

cunicularia **20:** 80
Geospiza
　conirostris **20:** 96
　difficilis **20:** 96
　fortis **20:** 96
　fuliginosa **20:** 96
　magnirostris **20:** 96
　scandens **20:** 96
Geothlypis trichas **17:** 88, 94–97
gerbil 7: 13, 15
　bushveld **7:** *13*
　Mongolian 7: 88–89
gerenuk 6: 62, 98–99
Gergarina **21:** 13
Geronticus calvus **14:** 32
Gerreidae **40:** 36–37
Gerres maldivensis **40:** 37
Gerrhonotinae **46:** 50, 52
Gerrhonotus **44:** 27; **46:** 52, (69)
Gerrhosauridae **44:** 25, 28; **45:** 98, 100–101
Gerrhosaurus **45:** 98, 100, (111)
　validus **45:** *100–101*, 110–111
Gerridae **24:** 16–17
Gerris
　lacustris **24:** 16
　odontogaster **24:** 16–17
gharial 31: 79; **47:** 98–99
　false **44:** *8–9*; **47:** 94–95
ghost frogs 42: 10; **43:** 24–25
　African **42:** 11, 17
　Cape **43:** 25, *25*
　Natal **43:** 24
　Rose's **43:** *24–25*
　Table Mountain **43:** *24*, 25
ghoul **39:** 66
　bearded **39:** *62–63*, 67
　Chinese **39:** 67
giant salamanders 41: 14, 27, 36
　California **41:** 40, *40*, *42–43*, *44–45*
　Chinese **41:** (17), *30–31*, 31, (31), 32
　coastal **41:** 40, *40–41*
　Cope's **41:** 40, *40–41*, 45
　Idaho **41:** 40, (51)
　Japanese 41: (17), 30–31, 32
　Pacific 41: 27, 40–45, 51, (51); **42:** 17
Giardia lamblia **21:** 16–17
giardiasis **21:** 17
gibberfish **39:** 15
Gibberichthyidae **39:** 15
Gibberichthys pumilus **39:** 15
gibbon 4: *8*, 10, 12
　common (lar) **4:** 36, 38–39
　crested **4:** 37
　crested black **4:** 36
　gibbon family 4: 36–37
　kloss **4:** 36, 37, *37*
　lar 4: 36, 38–39
　moloch **4:** 36, 37
　Müller's **4:** 36, *37*
　white-handed (lar) **4:** 36, 38–39
Gibraltar, apes in **4:** 50
Gigantactinidae **36:** 74–83

Gigantactis **36:** *76*, 81
　vanhoeffeni **36:** *80–81*
Gigantocypris **28:** *33*
Gigantophis garstini **48:** (110)
Gigantopithecus **4:** 12
gigantura **35:** *92*
Gigantura
　chuni **35:** 92, *92*
　indica **35:** 92, *93*
Giganturidae **35:** 79, 92–93
gillaroo **35:** 66, (68), (69)
gills **31:** 15, *33*; (13)
gin-buna **34:** 44
Ginglymostoma
　brevicaudatum **32:** 35, (40)
　cirratum **32:** 16, 26, 34–35, (40)
Ginglymostomatidae **32:** (12), (30), 33, 36, (40)
Gir Forest Reserve **2:** (15)
Giraffa
　camelopardalis **6:** 52, 54–57
　camelopardalis angolensis **6:** 52
　camelopardalis antiquorum **6:** 52
　camelopardalis camelopardalis **6:** 52
　camelopardalis capensis **6:** 52
　camelopardalis peralta **6:** 52
　camelopardalis reticulata **6:** 52, 54
　camelopardalis rothschildi **6:** 52, 54
　camelopardalis thornicrofti **6:** 52
　camelopardalis tippelskirchi **6:** 52, 54
giraffe 5: 11, 12; **6:** 54–57, 60
　giraffe family 6: 52–53
　kordofan **6:** 52
　Masai **6:** 52, 54
　nubian **6:** 52
　reticulated **6:** 52, *53*, 54
　Rothschild's **6:** 52, 54, *56*
　southern African **6:** 52
　Thornicroft's **6:** 52, 53
　West African **6:** 52
giraffe-gazelle *see* gerenuk
Giraffidae **6:** 52–53
gladiators **22:** (79)
Glandulocaudinae **38:** 48–49
Glareola
　lactea **11:** 98
　maldivarum **11:** 98
　nordmanni **11:** 98
　nuchalis **11:** 98
　pratincola **11:** 98
Glareolidae **11:** 98; **13:** 90, 101
glaskilli
　Indian **38:** 68
glass schilbeid **37:** (34)
glassfish
　Asiatic 40: 20–21
　filament-finned **40:** 21
　giant **40:** 20
　highfin **40:** 20, *20*, 21
　Indian **40:** 20
　longspine **40:** 21
　transparent **40:** *21*
　Wolff's **40:** 21
Glaucidium

gnoma **15:** 50
　radiatum **15:** 50
Glaucomys
　sabrinus **7:** 61
　volans **7:** 34, 60–61
Glaucosoma scapulare **40:** 18
Glaucosomatidae **40:** 12–19
Glaucus atlanticus **30:** *38*
gleaning **9:** 84
glider
　feathertail (pygmy) **10:** 74, 77, 84–85
　greater **10:** 74
　mahogany **10:** 74, (77)
　pygmy 10: 74, 77, 84–85
　sugar 10: 74, 76, (76), 86–87, 88
gliding marsupials **10:** (76)
Glironia venusta **10:** 14
Glirulus japonicus **7:** 102
Glis glis **7:** 102, 104–105
glis *see* dormouse, edible
Globicephala melas **3:** 55, 66–67
Glomeris marginata **22:** 20–21
Glossamia aprion **48:** 42–43
Glossanodon
　melanomanus **35:** 23
　pseudolineatus **35:** 23
Glossina mortisans **23:** *103*
Glossolepis **38:** 54, 55, 57
　incisus **38:** *56*, 57
　wanamensis **38:** (56)
glowbelly **40:** 14, 15
glowworms **25:** (35)
Gloydius **50:** (89), (111)
glutton *see* wolverine
Glycimeridae **30:** 50, 53
Glyphis **32:** 25
　gangeticus **32:** 20
　glyphis **32:** 25
Glyphorynchus spirurus **17:** 28
Glypta **27:** *26*
Glyptauchen panduratus **39:** 67
Glyptocephalus zachirus **39:** 90
Glyptodon **9:** 66
　panochthus **9:** *64*
Glyptoperichthys **34:** 109, **37:** 108
Glyptosterninae **37:** (51)
Glyptosternon **37:** (50), 51
Glyptothorax **37:** 50
　coheni **37:** 50
Gnaphosidae **29:** (81)
gnatcatcher **17:** 60
Gnathanacanthus goetzeei **39:** 71
Gnathananthidae **39:** 68–71
Gnathanodon speciosus **40:** 34, *35*
Gnathiidea **28:** 34
Gnathobdellae **21:** 94
Gnathonemus **31:** 82
　curvirostris **31:** 106
　elephas **31:** *106–107*, 107
　petersii **31:** 106, *109*
Gnathophausia **28:** *36–37*
Gnathostomulida **21:** 32, 76, 77
gnats 23: 46–49
　buffalo **23:** 52

turkey **23:** (53)
gnawing **7:** 10, 16–17, 64
Gnophaela vermiculata **26:** *89*
gnu
    white-tailed **6:** 82
    see also wildebeest, blue
goat 6: 60–63
    domestic **6:** 63
    mountain 6: 62, 108–109
    wild **6:** 62
goatfish 35: 111, **40:** 38–39
    bicolor **40:** *38–39*
    blue-striped **40:** *38*
    finstripe **40:** 38
    half-and-half **40:** *38–39*
    mimic **40:** 39
go-away bird, white-bellied **16:** 38,
    40–41
Gobiidae **34:** 12, 16, 102, **38:** 50, **39:**
    (10), **40:** 9, 94–99
Gobio
    gobio **34:** 58–59
    gobio tungussicus **34:** 59
    hettitorum **34:** 59
Gobiodon citrinus **40:** 99
Gobioides broussonetii **40:** 94
Gobius niger **40:** 97
goblinfish **39:** 67
    leaf **39:** 67
goby 32: 67, **34:** 12, 16, 102, **38:** 50,
    39: (10), **40:** 84, 92, 94–99
    black **40:** 97
    black bumblebee **40:** 98
    black-rayed shrimp **40:** *97*
    carp **40:** 98
    citron **40:** *99*
    dwarf pygmy **40:** (10), 94
    fire **40:** 99
    gold bumblebee **40:** 98
    knight **40:** *95*
    loach **40:** 94, 99
    marble **40:** 97, 98
    peacock **40:** 98
    relationships **40:** (99)
    sand **40:** *94*, 96, 99
    sleeper **40:** 94, (96)
    sponge **40:** (99)
    violet **40:** 94
godwit 11: (15); **13:** 30
    bar-tailed 13: 30, 31, 34–39
    Hudsonian **13:** 30
goldeneye 12: 66; **14:** 54
    Barrow's **14:** 78
    bufflehead **14:** 78
    common 14: 52, 78–79; **18:** (57)
goldeye **31:** 84, (84)
goldfinch 16: 76
    American 16: 76, 80–81
    Eurasian **16:** 76, *76*
goldfish 31: 26, **34:** 8, 16, 31, 42–51,
    80
    bubble-eye **34:** *45*
    calico **34:** 50
    calico fantail **34:** *46*

common **34:** *42*, (44)
edible **34:** 42
fantail **34:** 49
hooded **34:** 50, (50), 51
matt **34:** 50
metallic **34:** 49
nacreous **34:** 50
Goliathus druryi **25:** *87*
Gonatodes **45:** (36)
    albogularis **45:** (27)
    ceciliae **45:** *26–27*
    vittatus **45:** 11, (27)
Gondwanaland **9:** 10; **10:** (11), 108
Gonepteryx rhamni **26:** *22–23*
Gongylophis **48:** 46, 75
Goniurosaurus **45:** 13
Gonocephalus chamaeleontinus **44:** 35
gonolek, crimson-breasted **15:** 104, *107*
Gonostoma elongatum **35:** *82–83*
goodea **38:** 106
goodeid 38: 50, 106–111
    ameca **38:** 109, 110
    butterfly **38:** *106–107*, 109
    as "cannibals" **38:** (110)
    crescent **38:** *111*
    gold sawfin **38:** *106*, 109, 110
    livebearing **38:** 110
    rainbow **38:** 110, (111)
    red-tailed **38:** *108–109*
Goodeidae **38:** 106–111
goose 14: 52, 53, 54, 55, 80; **15:** 34;
    18: (81)
    African pygmy **14:** 52
    Aleutian Canada **14:** (63)
    bar-headed **14:** 52, *52*, 55
    cackling **14:** 60, 63
    Canada 14: 52, 60–63
    Egyptian 14: 52, 64–65
    giant Canada **14:** 60
    greylag **14:** 52, 54
    Hawaiian **14:** 52, 53
    magpie **14:** 52, *52*
    pink-footed **14:** 52, *52*
    snow **14:** 52, *54*
    tundra-nesting **14:** 54
goosefish 36: 13, 60–63, 76
    American **36:** *60*, 61, 63
    European **36:** *60–61*, 63
gopher 7: 17, 18
    horned **7:** 12
    northern pocket 7: 26–27
    pocket **7:** *12*, 18
    western pocket (northern pocket)
    7: 26–27
Gopherus **47:** 80, 82, 90–91
    agassizii **47:** 90
    berlandieri **47:** 90, 90–91
    flavomarginatus **47:** 90, 91, (91)
    polyphemus **47:** *90*, 90–91
goral **6:** 62, 108
Gordius **21:** *77*
Gorgasia maculata **33:** *92*
Gorgonacea **21:** 43
Gorgonocephalus **30:** *101*

Gorgonorhynchus repens **21:** *87*
gorilla 4: *8*, 10, 12, 13
    Cross River **4:** 12, (21), 26
    eastern **4:** 12, (21)
    eastern lowland **4:** 12, *13*, (21)
    mountain 4: 12, 20–25
    silverback **4:** *13*, 22, *22–23*
    western **4:** 12, (21)
    western lowland 4: *8*, 12, (21),
    26–27
Gorilla
    beringei **4:** 12, (21)
    beringei beringei **4:** 12, 20–25
    beringei diehli **4:** 12, (21)
    gorilla **4:** 12, (21)
    gorilla diehli **4:** 12, (21), 26
    gorilla gorilla **4:** 12, (21), 26–27
Gorsachius goisagi **14:** 20
goshawk 15: 11, 41
    northern 15: 8, 38–39, (48), (60);
    18: (34)
Goura victoria **16:** 12, 14–15
gourami 37: (54), **40:** 57, 60–63
    chocolate **40:** 62, 63
    croaking **40:** 61, 63
    dwark **40:** 63
    elephant ear **40:** 62
    giant **40:** 61, 62
    giant redtail **40:** 62
    Indian **40:** 63
    kissing **40:** 61, *62*
    licorice **40:** 61, 63
    noble **40:** 62, 63
    ornate **40:** 63
    pointed-tail **40:** 63
    sevenstripe giant **40:** 62
    three-spot **40:** 63
Gracilinanus
    agilis **10:** 14
    dryas **10:** 14
grackle 18: 74, 75
    boat-tailed **18:** 74, *75*
    common 18: 74, 78–81
    slender-billed **18:** 75
Gracula religiosa **18:** 82, 88–89
Grallaria
    quitensis **19:** 72
    ruficapilla **19:** 72
Gramma loreto **40:** 22, *22*
gramma
    false **40:** 22, 24
    royal **40:** 22, *22*, 24
Grammatidae **40:** 22–25
Grammatorcynus
    bicarinatus **40:** 106
    bilineatus **40:** 106
Grammatostomias flagellibarba **35:** *80*
Grammicolepididae **39:** (25)
Grammicolepis branchiusculus **39:** (25)
Grand Banks **36:** 38
Grandisonia **41:** 21
    alternans **41:** (23)
    brevis **41:** (17)
Granuloreticulosa **21:** 13

Graphium antiphates **26:** *16–17*
Graphiurus ocularis **7:** 102
Graphocephala fennahi **24:** *86, 87*
Graspus graspus **28:** *103*
grass *see* sea grass
grass snake 42: 63, 71; **49:** <u>74–79</u>
   African 49: *60–61*
   big-headed **49:** (76)
   European **48:** *16, 17*; **49:** 55, 100
   olive **49:** *61*
grasshoppers 23: <u>8–11, 24–31</u>
   anatomy **22:** *11*
   bladder **23:** *29–30*
   eastern lubber **23:** *28–29*
   elegant **23:** *27*
   families **23:** 8
   feeding **23:** *25–27*
   gaudy **23:** *30–31*
   gold-horned lubber **23:** *28*
   horse-faced monkey **23:** *32–33*
   long-horned *see* katydids
   lubber **23:** 28–29
   mating **23:** *27–28*
   monkey 23: <u>32–33</u>
   nymphs **23:** *10*
   painted **23:** *24–25*
   pygmy 23: <u>34–35</u>
   short-horned **23:** 24
   "singing" **23:** *27–28*
   slender groundhopper **23:** *34, 34–35*
   stick **23:** (33)
   toad **23:** 29
grassquit, Cuban **16:** 62
grasswren
   striated **18:** 60
   white-throated **18:** 60
grayfish (dogfish) **32:** 47
grayling 35: 9, <u>42–45</u>
   Amur **35:** 44
   Arctic **35:** 44, (45), *45*
   aromatic flesh of **35:** (45)
   East Siberian **35:** 44
   European **35:** *42, 42, 43, 44, 44,* (45)
   Kosogol **35:** 45
   Mongolian **35:** 44
   southern **35:** *8–9*
"Grayling Zone" **35:** 42
grazing **5:** 12, 13, 30, 31; **6:** 67, 89
Great Gobi Strictly Protected Area **5:** 103
grebe 11: 11; **14:** 10, 44
   black-necked **14:** 16
   Clark's **14:** 16
   Colombian **14:** 16, 17
   giant pied-billed **14:** 16–17
   great **14:** 16
   great crested 14: 16, <u>18–19</u>, 93
   grebe family 14: <u>16–17</u>
   hoary-headed **14:** 16
   horned **14:** 16
   least **14:** 16
   little **14:** 16
   New Zealand **14:** 16
   pied-billed **14:** 16
   western **14:** 16, *17*

white-tufted **14:** 16
greenbul
   Appert's **16:** 56, 57
   yellow-whiskered **16:** 56, 57
greenfinch, western **16:** 76
greenlet **17:** 98
   gray-headed **17:** 98
   tawny-crowned **17:** 98
greenling 39: 11, 53, <u>74–75</u>
   kelp **39:** 75
   painted **39:** 75
   rock **39:** *74–75*
grenadier 36: 8, <u>28–31</u>
   blackspotted **36:** *30–31*
   deepwater **36:** (31)
   giant **36:** 29, (30)
   graceful **36:** 29
   purple **16:** 90, *90*
   rough-head **36:** *28*
   roundnose **36:** 30, (30)
   thorntooth **36:** *28–29*
Greta andromia **26:** *57*
gribbles **28:** 46, 49
griffon **20:** (11), 24, 26
   Ruppell's **20:** 8, 11
grilse (salmon) **35:** (54)
grison **1:** 32
   little **1:** 32, *34*
grizzly bear **35:** (64), *64*
grosbeak
   Kona **20:** 98
   pine **16:** 76, <u>82–87</u>
ground destabilization **7:** 49, 50, 59;
   8: 29, *57*, 66–67; **9:** 77;
   10: 99
ground puppies (hellbenders) **41:** (12),
   14, 30, <u>32–35</u>
groundfish **36:** 13
groundhog *see* woodchuck
ground-hornbill
   Abyssinian **18:** 48
   northern **18:** 48
   southern **11:** *12;* **18:** 48
ground-roller **15:** 86–87
   long-tailed **15:** 86, 87
grouper 32: 67, **39:** 109
   comet **40:** 24, 25
   giant **40:** (10), 15
   panther **40:** 16
   polka-dot **40:** 16
grouse 11: 48; **15:** 39; **19:** (91)
   black **11:** 44, *49*, 68
   grouse family **11:** 8
   red (willow) **11:** 44, <u>66–69</u>
   sage 11: 44, <u>70–73</u>
   willow 11: 44, <u>66–69</u>
Grues **14:** 82
Gruidae **14:** 82
Gruiformes **11:** 92; **14:** 82; **19:** 8
Gruinae **14:** 88
grunion **38:** 60, *61, 62*
grunt **40:** 36, 37
Grus
   americana **14:** 82, <u>84–87</u>

   antigone **14:** 82
   canadensis **14:** 82, 86
   carunculatus **14:** 82
   grus **14:** 82
Gryllacrididae **23:** 21
Gryllidae **23:** <u>16–19</u>
Gryllotalpa vinae **23:** *22*
Gryllotalpidae **23:** <u>22–23</u>
Gryllus bimaculatus **23:** 16
Guam, devastation by snakes **49:** 20–21,
   23
guan **11:** 48
   Andean **11:** 44
   common piping **11:** 44
   crested **11:** 44
   white-crested **11:** 44
guanaco 5: 92, <u>108–109</u>
   wild **5:** 93
guano **12:** (11), (49)
gudgeon 34: <u>58–59</u>, **40:** 94, 96
   blind **40:** 97
   carp **40:** 98
   cave **40:** 97
   Lena **34:** 59
   northern trout **40:** 98
   peacock **40:** 98
   purple-spotted **40:** 98
guenon **4:** *8*, 10, 40, 42, 43, 44
guiara **8:** 30
guillemot 12: 83, (98), 101
   black 12: 98, 101, <u>108–109</u>
guinea fowl **11:** 47, 49
   black **11:** 44, 49
   crested **11:** 44, 49
   helmeted **11:** 44, *48*, 49
   vulturine **11:** 44, *47*
guinea pig 8: 10, 30, <u>38–41</u>
   black **8:** 41
   domestic **8:** 38–39, *39*, 40
   wild **8:** 28, 39–40
guitarfish 33: <u>26–27</u>, 29
   common 33: <u>32–33</u>
   family summary **33:** (27)
   giant **33:** 27, 32
gular pouch **12:** 44, 46–47, 49;
   14: 32, 38
Gulf sierra **40:** 107
gull 11: 11; **12:** 64, 69, <u>74–77</u>, (94),
   107; **13:** 19, 71, 84; **14:** (62),
   (74); **18:** (81)
   black-headed **12:** 74–75, (77); **13:** 79
   Bonaparte's **12:** 74
   Franklin's **12:** 74
   great black-backed **12:** 74, 75, (77),
   93, 107
   herring 12: 74, 75, (77), <u>78–79</u>;
   13: 79
   ivory **12:** 74, *75*
   kelp **12:** 74, 76
   laughing **12:** 52, 74, (77)
   little **12:** 74, *75*
   mew **12:** 74, 81
   ring-billed **12:** 74
   Ross's **12:** 74, *75*

swallow-tailed **12:** 74
Gulo gulo **1:** 32, <u>56–57</u>
gundi 7: *12*, 13
  desert **7:** 108, 109
  felou **7:** 108, 109, *109*
  gundi family 7: <u>108–109</u>
  Lataste's **7:** *109*
  mzab **7:** 108, 109, *109*
  North African 7: 108, <u>110–111</u>
  Saharan **7:** 108
  Speke's **7:** 108, 109, *109*
guppy 31: 42, **38:** 50, <u>94–105</u>, 107
Gurgesiella **33:** (27)
gurnard 39: 11, 53, <u>54–57</u>, 66, 72
  armored **39:** 55, 56, 57
  flying **39:** 54, *54*, (55), 56, 57
  "footwalker" **39:** (57)
  grayish tub **39:** 57
  "handwalker" **39:** (57)
  helmet **39:** 53, 54, 57
  long-finned **39:** 56
  oriental flying **39:** *55*, 57
  red **39:** *56*
  red-bodied streaked **39:** 57
  saphirine **39:** 57
  spotwing flying **39:** 57
  yellow **39:** 57
gurnet **39:** 80
Guttera pucherani **11:** 44
gwyniad **35:** 40
Gyalopion **49:** (63)
Gygis alba **12:** 74
Gymnallabes typus **37:** 55
Gymnarchidae **31:** (43), (82), 85, (108), 110
Gymnarchus niloticus **31:** 82, (108), <u>110–111</u>
Gymnobelideus leadbeateri **10:** 74, <u>88–89</u>
Gymnobucco calvus **19:** 56
Gymnocephalus cernuus **40:** 16
Gymnochanda
  filamentosa **40:** 21
  flamea **40:** 20
  limi **40:** 20
Gymnocharcinus bergi **38:** 41
Gymnocorymbus ternetzi **38:** 41
Gymnocranius andleyi **40:** 41
Gymnodactylus **45:** 10
Gymnoderus foetidus **19:** 80
Gymnogeophagus
  balzanii **40:** 72
  steindachneri **40:** 72
  surinamensis **40:** 72
Gymnogyps **15:** 24
  californianus **15:** 8; **20:** 8, <u>16–21</u>
Gymnolaemata **21:** 69
Gymnomuraena zebra **33:** *80*
Gymnophiona **41:** 8, 20, 21
Gymnophthalmidae **44:** 25, (26); **45:** 82, (85)
Gymnophthalmus **45:** (85)
  speciosus **45:** *85*
  underwoodi **45:** 83, (85)

Gymnopleurus aenescens **25:** *80*
Gymnorhina tibicen **18:** 63; **20:** 93, 100, <u>110–111</u>
Gymnorhinus cyanocephalus **18:** 90
Gymnosomata **30:** 18
Gymnostinops montezuma **18:** 74
Gymnothorax
  bathyphilus **33:** 81
  javanicus **33:** 79, *79*
  meleagris **40:** 24
  moringua **33:** *82*
  nudivomer **33:** 81
  polyuranodon **33:** 81
  thyrsoideus **33:** 79
  undulatus **33:** *60*, *78*
Gymnotidae **33:** 100, (100)
Gymnotiformes **33:** <u>100–101</u>
  families summary **33:** (100)
Gymnura **33:** (36)
gymnure **9:** 12, 13
  Hainan **9:** 12, *13*
  short-tailed **9:** 12, *12*
  shrew **9:** 12, *12*
Gymnuridae **33:** (9), 36, 37
gynogenesis **45:** 90
Gypaetus barbatus **20:** 8, <u>22–23</u>
Gypohierax angolensis **20:** 8, <u>28–29</u>
Gyps **20:** 24
  africanus **20:** 8
  rueppellii **20:** 8
gyrfalcon **15:** 8, *12*
Gyrinidae **25:** <u>26–27</u>
Gyrinocheilidae **34:** 9, 10, 12, (88), 89
Gyrinocheilus **34:** 90
  aymonieri **32:** 107, **34:** 12, 88, <u>90–93</u>
  pennocki **34:** (92)
  pustulosus **34:** (92)
Gyrinomimus grahami **39:** 14
Gyrinophilus **41:** 68, 71
Gyrinus
  mexicanus **41:** 61
  minutus **25:** 26
Gyrodoras circularis **31:** 13

H

habitat
  destruction **1:** 62, 64; **2:** 35, 44, 79; **3:** 83; **4:** 24, 35, 87, 96, 101; **5:** 26, 63, 65, 91; **6:** 20, 47, 49, 51, 59, (66); **7:** 25, 63,

  107; **9:** 33, 62, 63, 85, 91; **10:** 27, (77), (95), **44:** 17, *35*, (99); **45:** 52–53
  see also deforestation
  preservation **4:** 51
habitats **31:** 17
habituation **4:** (23)
habu **50:** (8), 110
hacking **15:** (35)
hackleback **31:** 53
haddock 36: (10), 12, 25, 32, <u>38–51</u>
Haekel, Ernst **21:** 9
Haematopodidae **13:** 90, 91
Haematopus
  ater **13:** 90
  bachmani **13:** 90, <u>98–99</u>
  leucopodus **13:** 90
  longirostris **13:** 90
  moquini **13:** 90
  ostralegus **11:** *14–15*; **13:** 16, *36–37*, 90, <u>94–97</u>
  palliatus **13:** 90, 98
  unicolor **13:** 90
Haemopis sanguisuga **21:** *109*
Haemulidae **40:** <u>36–37</u>
hagfish 31: *14*, <u>26–31</u>, (31), 42
  Pacific **32:** 102
  skin of **31:** 29
Haideotriton **41:** 68, 71
hairstreaks (gossamer-winged butterflies) **26:** 28, 29
  American gray **26:** *31*
  green **26:** *28–29*
  martial **26:** *28*
hairyfish **39:** 15
hake 32: 83, **36:** 8, (10), 11, 12, 13, (14), <u>32–37</u>, (36), 52
  Atlantic **36:** 32, *33*, 34
  black **36:** 36
  Boston **36:** 36
  Cape **36:** 34, (36)
  Carolina **36:** 36
  Gulf **36:** 36
  luminous **36:** 32, *32*, 37
  Peruvian **36:** 34
  phycine **36:** 32, 36
  red **36:** 36
  silver **36:** 33
  southern **36:** 32, *34–35*, 37, (37)
  squirrel **36:** 36
  true **36:** 32, 33
  white **36:** 36
Halcyon **14:** 102
  cyanoventris **14:** 100
  senegaloides **14:** 100
Halesus radiatus **22:** *102–103*
halfbeak 38: 50, <u>76–77</u>
  Beaufort's **38:** 77
  Celebes **38:** 77, *77*
  threadjaw **38:** *76*, 77
  wrestling **38:** *76–77*, 77
Haliaeetus **15:** 30
  albicilla **15:** 30
  leucocephalus **15:** 8, (21), <u>30–35</u>

pelagicus **15:** 8, 30
vocifer **20:** 28
halibut **39:** 11, 91, 93
  Atlantic **39:** 88, 89
  bastard **40:** 103
  Pacific **39:** 88
Halichoerus grypus **3:** <u>42–43</u>
Halictidae **27:** (95)
Halieutaea retifera **36:** *72–73*
Halieutichthys aculeatus **36:** *70*
Halieutopsis **36:** 70
Haliichthys taeniophorus **39:** (42)
Halimochirurgus
  alcocki **39:** 99
  centriscoides **39:** 98
Haliotis rufescens **30:** *23*
Halobates **24:** (17)
Halocyprida **28:** 9
Halophryne diemensis **36:** *55*
halosaur **33:** 96
  Gilbert's **33:** *96–97*
Halosauridae **33:** (62), <u>96–97</u>
Halosaurus **33:** *65*
  ovenii **33:** *96*
hamadryad (king cobra) **50:** (8), 9,
  12–13, <u>34–35</u>
hamanishiki **34:** 49, 51
hamerkop **14:** 32, 65
hammer stones **1:** (74); **4:** 31–32, (31)
hammerjaw **35:** 101
hamster 7: 11, 15, 18, 19
  golden 7: <u>84–85</u>
  Syrian (golden) **7:** <u>84–85</u>
handfish **36:** (14), 67
  red **36:** *64–65*
hangingflies 22: <u>104–109</u>
Hapalemur
  aureus **4:** 96
  griseus **4:** 96
  simus **4:** 96
Hapalochlaena lunulata **30:** *84*, 88–89
Hapalogenys analis **40:** 37
Hapaloptila **19:** 57
  castanea **19:** 56
Haplochromis **40:** 78
Haplophryne triregium **36:** *76*
haplorhines *see* primates, higher
Haplotaxida **21:** 94
Haptenchelys texis **33:** 85
Hara **37:** 50
  filamentosa **37:** 48
  hara **37:** 48, *48–49*
  horai **37:** 48
  jerdoni **37:** 48
hardhead **35:** 73
hardun **44:** 36
hardyhead **38:** 63
  Murray **38:** (63)
hare 8: 61
  Arctic 8: 74, <u>82–85</u>
  brown 8: 62, <u>86–89</u>
  calling *see* pika, American
  Cape **8:** 80
  European **8:** 64

greater red rockhare **8:** *63*, 64
Greenland (Arctic) **8:** 74, <u>82–85</u>
hare family 8: <u>64–67</u>
hispid **8:** *63*, 64, 66
hunting **8:** (89)
Jameson's red rockhare **8:** 64
mouse *see* pika, American
Patagonian *see* mara
polar (Arctic) **8:** 74, <u>82–85</u>
Smith's red rockhare **8:** 64
snowshoe 8: 62, 64, <u>74–79</u>
harlequin
  glass **34:** 64
  Hengel's **34:** 64
  slim **34:** 64
  see also rasbora
Harmothoe inbricata **21**: 98
Harpa articularis **30:** *34*
Harpactes **19:** 34
  ardens **19:** 34
  duvaucelii **19:** 34
  erythrocephalus **19:** 34
  wardi **19:** 34
Harpacticoida **28:** 9
Harpadon **35:** 94
  nehereus **35:** (96)
Harpia harpyja **15:** 8, <u>40–43</u>
Harpobittacus **22:** *108–109*
harrier **15:** (9), 10–11, 12
  hen **13:** 14; **15:** 8, 10, *12*
hartebeest **6:** 62
  Lichtenstein's **6:** 62
harvestfly, dogday **24:** *81*
harvesting **3:** 28; **6:** 18
  controlled **3:** 12, 16
  sustainable **3:** 15
Hasemania nana **38:** 8
hatchetfish 35: 78
  Asian **34:** 19; **38:** 29
  diaphanous **35:** 90
  elongate **38:** 29
  freshwater 38: <u>28–29</u>
  giant **38:** 29
  half-naked **38:** 29
  Indian **38:** 29
  lovely **38:** 29
  marbled **38:** *28*, 29
  marine 35: <u>90–91</u>
  Pacific **35:** *80–81*, *90*, *91*
  silver **38:** *29*
  spotted **38:** 29
Hawaiian Islands National Wildlife
Refuge **3:** 31
hawfinch 16: 76, *76*, 86, <u>88–89</u>
hawk **11:** 12, 13; **15:** 8, (9), 10, 12–13,
  39, (48), 50, 63
  bat **9:** 84; **15:** 8, 13
  sharp-shinned **15:** 8, 12, 38; **18:** 39
hawkfish 40: <u>66–67</u>
  dwarf **40:** 66
  falco **40:** 66
  giant **40:** 66
  longnose **40:** 66, *67*
  scarlet **40:** *66*

headfish **39:** 111
headlight fish **35:** *102–103*
headstander 38: <u>20–21</u>
  black line **38:** *21*
  glass **38:** 35
  high-backed **38:** 21
  spotted **38:** *20*, 21
  striped **38:** *20*, 21
hearing
  in birds **11:** 13; **15:** 52
  in fish **38:** (10)
heart urchins **30:** 93, 104, 108–109
  purple **30:** *104*
hedgehog 1: *9*, *10*, 14; **8:** 12;
  9: 8, 9, 11
  African **9:** 12, 13
  African pygmy 9: 12, <u>20–21</u>
  Asian **9:** 12
  collared **9:** 12
  Daurian **9:** 12
  desert **9:** 12, *13*
  dwarf (African pygmy) **9:** 12, <u>20–21</u>
  eastern European **9:** 12
  four-toed (African pygmy) **9:** 12,
    <u>20–21</u>
  hairy **9:** 12, 22
  hedgehog family 9: <u>12–13</u>
  Hugh's **9:** 12, 13
  long-eared **9:** 12, *12–13*
  Madagascan **9:** 25
  North African **9:** 12, *13*
  western European 9: 12, <u>14–19</u>
  white-bellied (African pygmy) **9:** 12,
    <u>20–21</u>
Helaemyia petrolei **23:** (39)
Helarctos malayanus **2:** 82
Heleioporus **42:** 97
Heleophryne **42:** 11, 17; **43:** <u>24–25</u>
  natalensis **43:** 24
  purcelli **43:** 25, *25*
  rosei **43:** *24*, *24–25*, 25
Heleophrynidae **42:** 10
Helicolenus
  dactylopterus dactylopterus **39:** (67)
  percoides **39:** (67)
Helicomitus **22:** 96
Heliconiidae **26:** <u>52–55</u>
Heliconius
  erato **26:** *53*, *54–55*
  isabella **22:** *34*
  sara **26:** 55
Helicophagus **37:** 42
Heliobolus **45:** 58, (63)
  lugubris **44:** 30; **45:** 60, <u>62–63</u>
Heliophobius **7:** 9
  argenteocinereus **8:** 56
Heliothryx **16:** (45)
  aurita **16:** 44
Heliozoa **21:** 13
Heliozoans **21:** 21
Helix
  aspersa **30:** *45*; **49:** (93)
  pomatia **30:** *46–47*
hellbender 41: (12), 14, 30, <u>32–35</u>

Ozark **41:** 35
Hellmayrea gularis **20:** 80
helmetcrest, bearded **16:** 44, *44*
Helminthophis **48:** 18
Helobdella **21:** *106–107*
Heloderma **46:** 74
　horridum **44:** 28, 30; **46:** 74, *75*, 77, 80–81
　suspectum **44:** 27–28, 30; **46:** 74, 76–79
　texanum **46:** 74
Helodermatidae **44:** 25; **46:** 74
Helogale parvula **1:** 98, 106–107
Helostoma temminckii **40:** 61, *62*
Helostomatidae **40:** 60–63
Hemachatus haemachatus **43:** 99; **48:** 17; **49:** 100; **50:** 9, 14, (30), (39)
Hemerobiidae **22:** 92
Hemibelideus lemuroides **10:** 74
Hemicentetes semispinosus **9:** 24
Hemichordata **21:** 32, 77, 79
Hemidactyliini **41:** 70–71
Hemidactylium **41:** 68, 71
　scutatum **41:** 70
Hemidactylus **45:** 10, 11, (23)
　frenatus **45:** (13)
Hemiechinus
　aethiopicus **9:** 12
　auritus **9:** 12, *12–13*
　collaris **9:** 12
Hemigaleidae **32:** (12), (42)
Hemigalus derbyanus **1:** 88
Hemignathus
　lucidus **20:** 98
　wilsoni **20:** 98
Hemigrammopetersius caudalis **38:** 31
Hemimerina **22:** (59)
hemiodids 38: 16–17
Hemiodontidae **38:** 16–17
Hemiodus
　argenteus **38:** *16*
　gracilis **38:** 17
　immaculatus **38:** 17
　microlepis **38:** 17
　quadrimaculatus **38:** 17
　semitaeniatus **38:** 17, *17*
　unimaculatus **38:** 17
hemiodus
　barred **38:** 17
　feather **38:** 17
　four-banded **38:** 17
　half-lined **38:** 17, *17*
　one-spot **38:** 17
　red-tailed **38:** 17
　silver **38:** 17
　slender **38:** 17
　yellow-tailed **38:** 17
Hemiphractinae **43:** 32, 37–38, (45)
Hemiphractus **42:** (38); **43:** 32, 40–41, (45), 86
hemipode, Andalusian **11:** 92, *92*, 93
Hemiprocne
　comata **15:** 70
　longipennis **15:** 70

mystacea **15:** 70
Hemiprocnidae **15:** 70, 71
Hemiptera **22:** 30
　classification **24:** 8, 10
　life cycle and development **24:** 13–14
Hemiramphidae **38:** 73, 76–77
Hemiramphus **38:** 77
Hemirhamphodon pogonognathus **38:** *76*, 77
Hemiscylliidae **32:** (12), (30), 33
Hemisorubim platyrhynchos **37:** 87
Hemisotidae **42:** 10
Hemisquilla ensigera californiensis **28:** *38–39*
Hemisus **42:** 92, 98; **43:** (17)
　marmoratus **43:** 16–17
Hemisynodontis **37:** 71
Hemitheconyx **45:** 13
　caudicinctus **45:** *10*
Hemitragus jemlahicus **6:** 62
Hemitrakis leucoperiptera **32:** 25
Hemitremia flammea **34:** 74
Hemitripteridae **39:** 76–81
Hemitripterus
　americanus **39:** 80
　villosus **39:** 80
Hemmigrammus pulcher **38:** *9*
hemocoel **27:** 24–25
hemocyanin **29:** 11, 38
hemocysts **27:** 24–25
Heosemys spinosa **47:** (31)
hepatitis B virus **24:** 35
Hepsetidae **38:** 24–27
Hepsetus odoe **38:** *24*, 27
Hepteronotus reticulatus **24:** 94
Heptranchias **32:** 98
　perlo **32:** 99
herding, predator avoidance **5:** 10
herling **35:** 66, (68)
hermaphrodites, protandrous **28:** (68); **30:** 26
Hermissenda **30:** *21*
　crassicornis **30:** *10*, *41*
hermit **16:** (45)
　great-billed **16:** 44
　long-tailed **16:** 44, *46*
　reddish **16:** 44
Hermodice carunculata **21:** *99*
heron 12: 45; **16:** (26); **18:** (81)
　black **14:** 20
　capped **14:** 23
　day herons **14:** 20, 22–23
　goliath **14:** 20, 65
　gray 14: 20, 24–27
　great blue **14:** 20, 22; **18:** 80
　green-backed **14:** 20, (22)
　heron family 14: 20–23
　Japanese night **14:** 20
　lineated tiger **14:** 20, *20*
　little blue **14:** 20, 22, 23
　night herons **14:** 20, 22–23
　purple **14:** 20, *20*
　tiger **14:** 20
　yellow-crowned night **14:** 20, *20*

Herpestes
　edwardsii **1:** 108–109
　ichneumon **1:** 98
　naso **1:** 98
Herpestidae **1:** 88
herpetology **21:** (33)
Herpyllus blackwalli **29:** *81*
herring 32: 83, **36:** 33, 50, 84–89, 97, 98–111
　Atlantic **36:** (88), *98–99*, 105
　"Battle of the Herring" **36:** (111)
　blackfin wolf **36:** 96, *96*
　"deciduous" scales **36:** 100
　denticled **36:** 84, 88
　distribution of **36:** (88)
　freshwater **36:** 87, 98, (104)
　Hilsa **34:** 94
　Pacific **36:** *89*, 105
　"red herrings" **36:** (111)
　river **36:** (101)
　smoking of **36:** 111
　trapped by whales **36:** *102–103*
　whitebait **36:** 111
　whitefin wolf **36:** 96
　Who's Who **36:** (85)
　wolf 36: 87, 96–97
herring smelt **35:** 22
Hersilia
　bicornutus **29:** *65*
　savignyi **29:** *65*
Hersiliidae **29:** 64–65
Hesperiidae **26:** 62–65
Heteractis magnifica **21:** 61
Heteralocha acutirostris **20:** 100
Heterandria formosa **38:** 95, 97
Heterenchelyidae **33:** (62)
Heterixalus **43:** 18, *19*
　betsileo **42:** 14–15
　madagascariensis **43:** *19*
Heterocentrotus **30:** 105
Heterocephalus glaber **8:** 56, 58–59
heterodactylism **18:** (18)
Heterodon **48:** 17; **49:** 13, 16
　nasicus **49:** 100–103
　platyrhinos **49:** (102)
　simus **48:** *16*; **49:** (102)
Heterodontidae **32:** (12), (26)
Heterodontiformes **32:** 26–27
Heterodontus **32:** 18, 26
　portusjacksoni **32:** 28–29
Heterohyrax **8:** 102
　antineae **8:** 103
　brucei **8:** 103
　chapini **8:** 103
Heteromirafra ruddi **18:** 22
Heteromyidae **7:** *12*
Heteronarce **33:** (20)
Heteronetta atricapilla **14:** 54
Heteropneustes
　fossilis **37:** 10, 56–57
　microps **37:** 57
Heteropneustidae **37:** 11, 30, (32)
Heteroptera **24:** 8, *10*, 11–12, 13
Heteroscelus incanus **13:** 30

Heterotidinae **31:** (82), 86, 88
Heterotis **31:** 82, 87
  niloticus **31:** 83, 86–87, 105
Heterotrichea **21:** 13
heterotrophs **21:** 9
Hexabranchus sanguineus **30:** *40,* 41–42
Hexacontinium **21:** 21
Hexacorallia **21:** 43
Hexagenia **22:** 40
Hexagrammidae **39:** 11, 53, 74–75
Hexagrammos
  decagrammus **39:** 75
  lagocephalus **39:** *74–75*
  otakii **39:** 74
Hexanchidae **32:** (12), (98)
Hexanchiformes **32:** 98–99
Hexanchus **32:** 98
  griseus **32:** 20, 101, *102*
  nakamurai **32:** (103)
Hexapoda **22:** 9
hexapods **22:** 26–27
Hexaprotodon liberiensis **5:** 66
Hexatrygon **33:** (34)
Hexatrygonidae **33:** (9), (34)
Hexodon latissimum **25:** *76–77*
hibernation **2:** 87–88, 93, 97, 100;
  7: 19, 51, 54–55, 107; **9:** 13, 18, 27,
  82, 104, 105, 111; **10:** 111; **15:** (75),
  78, 95; **16:** (51); **30:** 47; **44:** (67);
  49: (86)
hierarchy **20:** (27)
hiker's diarrhea **21:** 17
hillstar **16:** (45)
  Andean **16:** 44
Himalaya Mountains **1:** 30
Himantolophidae **36:** (14), 74–83
Himantolophus **36:** *74–75*
  groenlandicus **36:** *78–79*
Himantopus
  himantopus **13:** 72, 79, 82–85
  leucocephalus **13:** 72, (85)
  melanurus **13:** 72, (85)
  mexicanus **13:** 72, (85)
  novaezelandiae **13:** 72
Himantura **33:** (34)
Himatione sanguinea **16:** 76; **20:** 98
Hiodon
  alosoides **31:** 84, (84)
  tergisus **31:** 82, (84)
Hiodontidae **31:** (43), (82), (84)
hippo *see* hippopotamus
Hippocamelus
  antisensis **6:** 10
  bisculus **6:** 10
Hippocampus **39:** 46, (46)
  abdominalis **39:** 38
  bargibanti **39:** *27*
  breviceps **39:** *47*
  capensis **39:** *40,* (46)
  denise **39:** (40)
  guttulatus **39:** *40–41*
  reidi **39:** *39*
Hippodamia convergens **25:** *58–59*
Hippoglossus **39:** 93

hippoglossus **39:** 88
  stenolepis **39:** 89
Hippoidea **28:** 56, 90–93
Hippolais **17:** 60, 61
  polyglotta **17:** 60
hippopotamus 5: *8,* 9, 10; **8:** 48
  common 5: 66, *66,* 67, 68–73
  hippopotamus family 5: 66–67
  pygmy **5:** 66, 66–67, *67*
Hippopotamus amphibius **5:** 66, 68–73
hippotigres **5:** 52
Hippotragus
  equinus **6:** 62
  leucophaeus **6:** 63
  niger **6:** 62
Hiranetis braconiformis **24:** *40–41*
hirling **35:** 66, (68)
hirola **6:** 62
Hirudinea **21:** 77, 94, 106–111
Hirudo medicinalis **21:** *106,* (108),
  108–109
Hirundapus
  caudacuta **15:** 70
  cochinchinensis **15:** 70
Hirundinidae **15:** 94; **20:** 87
Hirundo rustica **15:** 94, *96–99*
Hirundopyrrhonota **15:** 94
  ariel **15:** 94
  rupestris **15:** 94
Hispidoberycidae **39:** 15
Hispidoberyx ambagiosus **39:** 15
Histiobranchus bathybius **33:** *84*
Histrio histrio **36:** 64, (68), *68–69*
Histrionicus histrionicus **12:** 66
hoatzin 20: 46–47, 64–67
hobby **17:** (13)
  northern **15:** 8, 11
Hofmannophila pseudospretella **26:** *111*
hog
  giant forest 5: 74, 75, 84–85
  pygmy **5:** 74
  red river **5:** 74
  see also warthog
hogchoker **39:** 92
hognose snake 41: 98–99; **49:** (78);
  50: 57
  American **48:** 17; **49:** 13, 16
  dusty **49:** (102)
  eastern **49:** (102)
  Madagascan **49:** 13
  Mexican **49:** (102)
  plains **49:** (102)
  southern **48:** *16;* **49:** (102)
  western 49: 100–103
hoki **36:** *36–37*
Holacanthus **40:** 52
  passer **32:** 68
Holaspis **45:** 58
  guentheri **45:** 40, 58–59, 60
Holbrookia texanus **44:** 82
Holconia immanis **29:** *66–67*
Hollardia hollardi **39:** 98
Holocentridae **39:** 9, 16–21
Holocentrus adscensionis **39:** 21

holocephalids **33:** 54
Holodactylus **45:** 13
Holopneustes inflatus **30:** *107*
Holothuria forskali **30:** *113*
Holothuroidea **30:** 91, 110–113
Homalopsinae **48:** 33; **49:** 8, 15–16,
  64, (65)
Homaloptera orthogoniata **34:** 15,
  109, *109*
Homalopteridae **34:** 9, 10, 89
Homalopteryx laminata **22:** *68*
Homarus
  americanus **28:** 70–71, (71), *74*
  gammarus **28:** *70,* (71)
homeothermy **1:** 9–10, 14
homing instinct **12:** (30); **16:** (17), 18
Hominidae **4:** 10
Homo sapiens **1:** 14; **4:** 12; **21:** 33
Homopus **47:** 80
  signatus **47:** 81
Homoroselaps **49:** 106
honey guide, African **1:** 83
honeybees 7: 13; **27:** *12,* 110–113
  honeybee dance **27:** (113)
  honeybees and relatives
    27: 102–113
  nests **27:** 110–111
honeycreeper
  crested **20:** 98, *99*
  Hawaiian 20: 98–99
honeydew **27:** (48)
honeyeater 18: 72
  banded **20:** 88, *91*
  blue-faced 20: 88, 92–93
  cardinal **20:** 88, *88*
  honeyeater family 20: 88–91
  New Holland **20:** 88, *90,* 95
  regent **20:** 88, (91)
  scarlet **20:** 88
  singing **20:** 88
  strong-billed **20:** 88, 90–91
  yellow-plumed **20:** 88, *89*
  yellow-streaked **20:** 88
honeyguide 17: 20–23; **19:** 56
  black-throated 17: 20, *21,* 24–25
  greater (black-throated) **17:** 20, *21,*
    24–25
  green-backed **17:** 20
  Indian **17:** 20, *20*
  lesser **17:** 20
  lyre-tailed **17:** 20, *20*
  Zenker's **17:** 20
hoofed mammals 5: 8–13
hoopoe 17: 8–9, 14–19; **19:** 97
Hoplerythrinus unitaeniatus **38:** 25
Hoplias
  macrophthalmus **38:** 25
  malabaricus **38:** 25, *25*
Hoplichthis haswelli **39:** 73
Hoplichthyidae **39:** 53, 72–73
hoplo **37:** 101, 103
  cascudo **37:** 101, 103
  dwarf **37:** *103*
  spotted **37:** *103*

Hoplobatrachus **43:** 84
  occipitalis **43:** 84
  tigerinus **43:** 84
Hoplocarida **28:** 9, 34
Hoplocercinae **44:** 80
Hoplodactylus **44:** (23); **45:** 12
  duvaucelii **45:** *11*
  maculatus **45:** 12
Hoplomys gymnurus **8:** 30
Hoplophryne **42:** 105
Hoplosternum **37:** 101, 103
  littorale **37:** 101
Hoplostethus atlanticus **39:** 21
Horaglanis krishnai **37:** 55
Horaichthys setnai **38:** 65
Hormiphora plumosa **21:** 45
hornbill 1: 107; **17:** (109); **19:** 48–51
  Abyssinian ground **19:** 48
  African pied **19:** 48
  eastern yellow-billed **19:** 48, *51*
  great (great Indian) **19:** 48, 49, (49),
    52–55
  great Indian 19: 48, 49, (49), 52–55
    great pied (great Indian) **19:** 48, 49,
      (49), 52–55
  helmeted **19:** 48, 49, *49*, (49)
  Indian pied **19:** 48
  knobbed **19:** 48, *48*
  long-tailed **19:** 48
  northern ground **19:** 48
  red-billed **19:** 48, *50*
  red-billed dwarf **19:** 48, *49*
  rhinoceros **19:** 48
  rufous **19:** 48
  rufous-necked **19:** 48, *49*
  southern ground **11:** *12*; **19:** 48
  Sulawesi tarictic **19:** 48
  Sulu **19:** 48, (50)
  wreathed **19:** 48, 50
horned frogs 41: 18, 19; **42:** 34, (38),
  76; **43:** 86, 99
  Argentine (Bell's) **42:** 86–87
  Bell's 42: 86–87
  Chacoan **42:** 87
  horned marsupial **42:** (38); **43:** (44)
  South American **42:** 36; **43:** 52
  Surinam **42:** *76–77*
hornero 20: 80
  rufous 20: 80, 84–87
hornets, giant **27:** 63
horns **5:** 29, 31, 36–37, (37), 40, 41; **6:**
  9, 56, 60, 111
  on snakes **49:** (73)
horntails (sawflies) **27:** 14–21
  giant **27:** *15*
  larvae **27:** 19
hornwrack **21:** 72
horse 1: 15; **5:** *8*, 9, 10, 11, *11*, 12, 62
  ancestral **1:** *8*
  Camargue **5:** *60–61*
  dawn **5:** 42
  domestic **5:** (43)
  draft **5:** (43), 58
  feral *see* mustang

horse family 5: 42–45
  Mongolian wild 5: 42, 45, 54–55
  Przewalski's (Mongolian wild) **5:** 42,
    45, 54–55
  racehorses **5:** (43)
  wild (Mongolian wild) **5:** 42, 45,
    54–55
  wild (mustang) *see* mustang
horsefish **39:** 11, 68
  smooth **39:** 71
  spinenose **39:** 71
  spiny **39:** 71
horse's friend **40:** 36
Hospitalotermes **22:** *66–67*
hot springs **4:** 48
hound (fish) **32:** 46
houndfish **38:** 73
houting **35:** 38, *39*, 40, 41
huchen 35: 48–51
  Japanese **35:** (50)
Hucho
  bleekeri **35:** (50)
  hucho **35:** 48–51
  ishikawae **35:** (50)
  perryi **35:** (50)
  taimen **35:** (50)
huemul
  Chilean **6:** 10
  Peruvian **6:** 10, *12–13*
huia **20:** 100
hujeta **38:** 25, 26
human **4:** 10–11, 12
humans, indifference to **16:** (86)
humbug **40:** 80
hummingbird 11: 11; **18:** (80); **19:** 43,
  80, 94; **20:** 88
  Allen's **16:** 44
  bee **11:** (9); **16:** 44
  black-chinned **16:** 44, *46*
  black-eared fairy **16:** 44
  blue-tailed **18:** (56)
  calliope **16:** 44
  cinnamon **16:** 44
  fairy **16:** (45)
  giant **16:** 44, *44*
  hummingbird family 16: 44–47;
    19: 43; **20:** (73)
  ruby-throated 16: 44, 47, 52–55
  ruby-topaz **16:** 44, *44*
  rufous **16:** 44, *45*, 46
  steely-vented **16:** 44, *47*
  sword-billed 16: 44, 48–51
  volcano **16:** 44
hunchen *see* huchen
hung mei ue **34:** (65)
hunting
  partnerships **2:** (60)
  techniques **14:** 100–102; **15:** 10,
    12–13, 15–16, 18–19, 65; **19:** (65)
Huso huso **31:** 52, (56), (57), 64–67
huss **32:** 22, 47
hutia 7: *12*; **8:** 11, 31, *31*
  Brown's **8:** 30
  Cuban 8: 30, 52–53

  Desmarest's Cuban (Cuban) **8:** 30,
    52–53
  eared **8:** 30
  Hispanolan **8:** 30
  prehensile-tailed **8:** 30
  West Indian **8:** 11
Hyaena
  brunnea **2:** 102
  hyaena **2:** 102, 104–107
Hyalinobatrachium **43:** 28
  colymbiphyllum **43:** (31)
  fleischmanni **43:** 29
  valerioi **43:** 30–31
hybridization **2:** 59
hybrids **14:** (69)
Hydatina amplustrum **30:** *37*
hydras **21:** 46–47
  freshwater **21:** 46
  green freshwater **21:** *47*
Hydrelaps darwiniensis **50:** 44, (45)
Hydrobates pelagicus **12:** 28
Hydrobatidae **12:** 28, 31; **20:** (14)
Hydrobia ulvae **30:** 29
Hydrochaeridae **7:** 12
Hydrochaeris hydrochaeris **8:** 30, 48–51
hydrocorals **21:** 46
Hydrocynus goliath **38:** 30, *30*
Hydrocyrius columbiae **24:** 20–21
Hydrodamalis gigas **3:** 47
Hydrodynastes gigas **49:** 16
Hydroida **21:** 43
hydroids **21:** 46, 47–48
  stalked **21:** 48
Hydrolagus
  colliei **33:** *54–55*
  purpurescens **33:** 54
Hydromantes **41:** 68, 70, 73
Hydrometra stagnorum **24:** (19)
Hydrometridae **24:** (19)
Hydromys chrysogaster **7:** 9
Hydrophasianus chirurgus **14:** 96
Hydrophiidae **50:** 12
Hydrophiinae **50:** 12, 14–15, (39)
Hydrophilidae **25:** (26)
Hydrophis **50:** (45), 47, *47*
  semperi **50:** (47)
Hydropodura aquatica **22:** *29*
Hydropotes inermis **6:** 10
Hydrosaurus **44:** 32, 34, 35
  pustulatus **44:** *35*
Hydrozoa **21:** 43, 46–49
Hydrozoans **21:** 46–49
  life cycles **21:** (48)
Hydrurga leptonyx **3:** 9, 38–39
Hyemoschus aquaticus **6:** 10
hyena
  brown **2:** 102, 103, *103*
  hyena family 2: 102–103
  spotted 2: 102, *102–103*, 103,
    108–109
  striped 2: 102, 103, 104–107
Hyla **43:** 32, 36, (49), (59)
  andersonii **43:** 35
  arborea **43:** 46–47

boans **43:** 38
caerulea **43:** (55)
chrysoscelis **43:** 36, 107
cinerea **43:** 48–49, 51
colymba **43:** (35), 38
ebraccata **49:** 105
faber **43:** *34–35*
geographica **43:** 37
intermedia **43:** (47)
japonica **43:** (47)
lindae **43:** *33*
meridionalis **43:** 46, *46–47*, (47)
picadoi **43:** (76)
pseudopuma **43:** 35
rosenbergi **43:** 37, 38
squirella **43:** 51
versicolor **43:** 36, 107
zeteki **43:** (76)
Hylephila phyleus **26:** *65*
Hyles lineata **26:** *69*
Hylidae **42:** 8, 10, (22), (38), 92; **43:** 28, 32, *33*, 37, *64–65*
Hylinae **43:** 32, 36, 38–39
Hyllus diardi **29:** *41*
Hylobates
  concolor **4:** 36
  klossii **4:** 36
  lar **4:** 36, 38–39
  moloch **4:** 36
  muelleri **4:** 36
  syndactylus **4:** 36
Hylochoerus meinertzhageni **5:** 74, 84–85
Hylocichla mustelina **18:** 44
Hylodes **42:** 78
Hylodinae **42:** 78
Hylomanes momotoula **19:** 42
Hylomantis **43:** 67
Hylomys
  hainanensis **9:** 12, *13*
  sinensis **9:** 12, *12*
  suillus **9:** 12, *12*
Hylopetes
  lepidus **7:** 36
  spadiceus **7:** 34, 36
Hylophilus
  ochraceiceps **17:** 98
  pectoralis **17:** 98
Hymenocephalus gracilis **36:** 29
Hymenocera picta **28:** 35
Hymenochirus **42:** 46, 48–49, (49)
  boettgeri **42:** 46, 49; **43:** (44)
  boulengeri **42:** 46
  curtipes **42:** 46, *48*
  feae **42:** 46
Hymenoptera **22:** 30; **27:** 8–13
  anatomy **27:** 12–13
  classification **27:** 8, 9–10
  sex determination **27:** 13
  sociability **27:** 11–12
Hymenoptera neurotica **27:** 58
Hynobiidae **41:** *26–27*, 27, 36–37
Hynobius **41:** 36, (37)
  amjiensis **41:** 36

chinensis **41:** 37
Hypancistrus zebra **37:** 107
Hypentelium **34:** 99
  roanokense **34:** 99
Hyperiidae **28:** 34
Hyperoliidae **42:** 10; **43:** 11, (17), 18–23
  predators **43:** (22)
Hyperolius **43:** 18, 19, (20)
  acutirostris **43:** 19
  argus **43:** (21)
  horstocki **43:** *18–19*
  marmoratus **43:** *21*, (21), 22, *22–23*
  mosaicus **43:** 19
Hyperoodon ampullatus **3:** 55, 90–91
hyperparasites **27:** (27)
Hyphessobrycon
  erythrostigma **38:** *38–39*, 41
  herbertaxelrodi **38:** 40, *40*
Hypnidae **33:** (9), (20)
Hypnos **33:** (20)
  monopterygius **33:** (22)
Hypocryptadius cinnamoomeus **18:** 68
Hypoderma
  bovis **23:** 96
  lineatum **23:** *96–97*
Hypogeophis **41:** 21
  rostratus **41:** 22, *23*, (23)
Hypomesus
  chishimaensis **35:** 29
  nipponensis **35:** 26
  olidus **35:** 27
  pretiosus **35:** 26, 27
  transpacificus **35:** *27*, 29
Hypopachus variolosus **42:** (111)
Hypophthalmichthys
  molitrix **34:** 18, 88
Hypopomidae **33:** (100), 101
Hypoptychidae **39:** 26, 28–29
Hypoptychus dybowskii **39:** 26, 28, 29
Hyporhamphus **38:** 77
Hypostomus **34:** 109, **37:** 107, **38:** (40)
  plecostomus **37:** 108
  punctatus **37:** *104*
Hypseleotris compressa **40:** 98
Hypsibarbus vernayi **34:** *12–13*
Hypsilurus **44:** 32, 34
  boydii **44:** 34
  dilophus **44:** *34–35*
  spinipes **44:** 34
Hypsipetes philippinus **16:** 56
Hypsiprymnodon moschatus **10:** 48, 72
Hypsiprymnodontidae **10:** 48
Hypsypops rubicundus **40:** *82*, 83
Hyptiotes paradoxus **29:** *56*
Hyracoidea **1:** *10*; **5:** (12), 14
Hyracotherium **5:** 42
hyrax 1: *10*; **5:** (10), (12), 14; **8:** 68, 102–105
  Ahaggar **8:** 103
  Bruce's yellow-spotted **8:** 103, *104–105*
  Cape rock (rock) **8:** 103, *104–105*, 105, 106–107
  eastern tree **8:** 103

  Matadi **8:** 103
  rock 8: 105, 106–107
  southern tree **8:** *102–103*, 103
  tree **8:** 104
  western tree **8:** 103
  yellow-spotted **8:** 105
Hysterocarpus traski **40:** (17)
Hystrichopsylla schefferi **22:** 111
Hystricidae **7:** *12*; **8:** 12
Hystricognathi **7:** (8), *12*; **8:** 8–11, 28, 55
Hystrix
  africaeaustralis **8:** 12
  brachyura **8:** 12
  cristata **8:** 12, 16–19

I

i'iwi **20:** 98, *99*
Ibacus peronii **28:** *12*
ibex 6: 62, 106–107
  alpine **6:** 106, 107
  nubian **6:** 106
  Siberian **6:** 106, 107
  walia **6:** 106, 106–107
Ibidorhyncha struthersii **13:** 90, 104–105
Ibidorhynchidae **13:** 90
ibis 13: 104; **14:** 22, 28, 32
  bald **14:** 32
  glossy 14: 32, 40–41
  Hadada **14:** 32, *33*
  white **14:** 22
ibisbill 13: 90, 93, 104–105
icefish **35:** 8, 31
  clearhead **35:** *31*
  Japanese **35:** *30*
Icerya purchasi **24:** *106*; **25:** (56)
Ichneumia albicauda **1:** 98
Ichneumon suspiciosus **27:** *31*
Ichneumonidae **27:** 22–31
Ichneumonoidea **27:** (23)
ichneumons
  mating **27:** 29–30
  penetrating wood **27:** (24)
Ichnotropis **45:** 61
Ichthyophis **41:** 9, 21
  kohtaoensis **41:** 21
Ichthyopiidae **41:** 21
Ichthyostega **41:** *13*
Ictaluridae **37:** 14–21, (44)
Ictalurus **37:** 14, (19), (21)

Jacamaralcyon tridactyla **17**: 20
Jacamerops aurea **17**: 20
jacana 14: <u>96–97</u>
   African **14**: 96
   American 14: 96, <u>98–99</u>
   northern (American) **14**: 96, <u>98–99</u>
   pheasant-tailed **14**: 96
   wattled **14**: *99*
Jacana
   jacana **14**: *99*
   spinosa **14**: 96, <u>98–99</u>
Jacanidae **14**: 96
jack 32: 67; **36**: *94*; **40**: <u>34–35</u>
   crevalle **40**: *34*
   with ray **33**: *47*
jackal, **black-backed 1**: 83; **2**: 50,
   <u>62–63</u>
jackdaw, western **18**: 90, 93, 106
jackrabbit
   antelope **8**: *62*, 64, 66, *66*
   black-tailed **8**: 64, <u>80–81</u>
jacksmelt **38**: 63
Jacobson's organ **2**: 12; **5**: (11), 65
Jadera obscura **24**: *58–59*
jaeger **12**: 76, 88, 92, (94); **14**: (74)
   long-tailed **12**: 74, 76; **13**: (36)
   parasitic **12**: 74, 76
   pomarine **12**: 74, 76, *77*
jaguar 2: 10, <u>36–37</u>
   black **2**: 37
jaguarundi **2**: 10, *12*
Janthina **30**: *29*
Japalura **44**: 35
javelina *see* peccary, collared
javelinfish **36**: *28–29*
jawfish **40**: 22, 25
   bartail **40**: 25
   fine-spotted **40**: *25*
jay 18: 90, 92
   blue 16: 71; **17**: 103; **18**: 39, 90,
   <u>94–99</u>
   Eurasian 18: 90, 93, 97, <u>110–111</u>
   Florida scrub **18**: 90, 91–92
   gray **18**: 90, 91
   Pander's ground **18**: 90
   pinyon **18**: 90
   Steller's **18**: 90, (97), (98)
jeju **38**: 25
jellied eels **33**: (73)
jelly animals 21: <u>42–43</u>
jellyfish 21: *34–35, 43,* <u>50–55</u>
   Australian box **21**: *52*, (54)
   freshwater **21**: *54*
   and humans **21**: 54
   jelly **21**: (52)
   lion's mane **21**: *50–51*
   moon **21**: *50*
   reproduction **21**: 53–54
   structure **21**: 51–52
   swimming **21**: 52–53
   upside-down **21**: *53*
jellynose fish **35**: 78
Jenynsia **39**: 84
   lineata **38**: 92

multidentata **38**: 92
jerboa **7**: *12*, 17
Jezebels (whites) **26**: <u>22–27</u>
jird *see* gerbil
jizz **17**: (96)
John Dory *see* dory
jollytail
   common **35**: 36
   Murray **35**: *32*, 33
jonasfish
   Antarctic **35**: *98, 98–99*, 99
Jordanella floridae **38**: 87, *88*
Julida **22**: *17*
Julidochromis
   regani **40**: *72–73*
   transcriptus **40**: 72
julie **40**: 70
   Clemie **40**: *72*
   striped **40**: *72–73*
jungle fowl 11: *9*
   red 11: 44, <u>60–63</u>
Junonia coenia **26**: *41*
Jynginae **18**: 8
Jynx torquilla **18**: 8, <u>12–13</u>

K

kagu 11: 92, <u>96–97</u>; **14**: 90; **19**: 8
kaka **20**: 36, *37*, 38
kakapo 16: 22; **20**: 36, <u>42–45</u>
kakariki
   red-fronted **16**: 22, *23*
   yellow-fronted **16**: 22, *23*
Kalophryne **42**: 105
Kaloula **42**: 105
   pulchra **42**: 104
kaluta, little red **10**: *25*, 27
Kalyptatherina helodes **38**: 59
Kammerer, Paul **42**: (33)
kangaroo 8: 62; **10**: 8, (10), <u>48–53</u>
   Bennett's tree **10**: 48
   eastern gray (gray) **10**: 48, *53*, <u>60–63</u>
   Goodfellow's tree 10: 48, <u>66–67</u>
   gray 10: 48, *53*, <u>60–63</u>
   red 10: 11, 48, <u>54–59</u>, 60, 63
   tree (Goodfellow's tree) **10**: 48, 51,
   52, <u>66–67</u>
   western gray **10**: 60, (62)
kangaroo rat 7: 13, 17
   bannertail **7**: *18–19*
   Ord's 7: <u>24–25</u>

Kannabateomys amblyonyx **8**: 30
Karroo desert **2**: 77
Karyorelicta **21**: 13
Kasidoridae **39**: 15
Kasidoron edom **39**: 14, 15
Kassina **43**: 18, 22
   senegalensis **43**: 27
kassinas, African spotted **43**: 27
katrana **38**: 56
Katsuwonus pelamis **40**: 106
katydids 23: 8, 10, <u>12–15</u>; **29**: *41, 76*
   deception **23**: 15
   defense **23**: 15
   feeding **23**: 12–13
   mating **23**: 14
   rhinoceros **23**: *11, 13,* 14
   singing **23**: 14
Kaupichthys
   japonicus **33**: 77
   nuchalis **33**: 77
kea 16: 22, 23; **20**: 36, <u>38–41</u>
kelpfish **40**: (93)
kelt (salmon) **35**: (54)
Kennyi Mbuna **40**: 69
Kentosaurus **44**: *10–11*
Kentrocapros aculeatus **39**: 106
Kentropyx **45**: 82, 83
   pelviceps **45**: (87)
keratin **5**: 10, 29, (37); **6**: 60; **8**: 20;
   25: 53
Kerilia jedoni **50**: (45)
Kerodon rupestris **8**: 30
kestrel 11: 13; **17**: (13); **18**: 59; **44**: 41
   common 15: 8, 12, <u>22–23</u>
   Eurasian (common) **15**: 8, 12, <u>22–23</u>
   lesser **15**: 8, 10
   Mauritius **15**: 8, (11)
   Seychelles **15**: (68)
Ketupa **15**: 56
keystone species **5**: 26; **6**: (68); **7**: 32, 93
khur *see* ass, Asian wild
kiang *see* ass, Asian wild
kickininee **35**: (61)
killdeer **13**: 8, *8*
killifish 34: 72, **38**: 50, <u>84–85</u>, 103,
   (111)
   bluefin **38**: *84–85*, 85
   brown-banded clown **38**: 81
   chocolate-brown-banded clown **38**:
   81
   common **38**: 84
   Cuban **38**: (89)
   diamond **38**: 84
   Gardner's **38**: 80, *82–83*
   giant **38**: 84
   Jamaican **38**: (89)
   Mediterranean **38**: 89
   Nigerian **38**: 80
   Pahrump **38**: 110
   plains **38**: 84
   pygmy **38**: 84
   scaleless **38**: 89
   snakeskin **38**: 87
   spotted **38**: 85

starhead **38:** 81
Tanganyika pearl **38:** 103, *104–105*, 105
kin-buna **34:** 44
Kinetoplastida **21:** 13, 17
king snake 49: (54), 59
black **49:** 48, 50
California **49:** 48, 50, (51)
California mountain **49:** (54); **50:** 26
common 49: 48–51, (54)
desert **49:** 49
gray-banded **49:** (54)
Mexican **49:** (54)
prairie **49:** (54)
Querétaro **49:** (54)
scarlet **49:** (53), 56
Sonoran mountain **49:** *54*, (54)
southern Florida **49:** *50–51*
speckled **49:** 50
variable **49:** *49*
kingdoms 21: 8–11
kingfish
butterfly **40:** 106, (107)
kingfisher 17: 22; **18:** 13; **19:** 42, 43, 48
African dwarf **14:** 100
belted 14: 100, 103, 104–107
common **14:** 100, *102*
common paradise- **14:** 100, 102
Javan **14:** 100, *101*
kingfisher family 14: 100–103
little **14:** 100
mangrove **14:** 100, 103
pied **14:** 100, *100*, 102
red-backed **14:** 100
sacred **14:** 100, 102
shovel-billed **14:** 100, 102
Tahiti **14:** 100, 102
"king-of-the-herring" **35:** 101, *108*, 109
"king-of-the-salmon" **35:** 107
kingklip
great **36:** 25
Kinixys **47:** 80
belliana **47:** 80
erosa **47:** 80
homeana **47:** 80, *81*
kinkajou **1:** 20, *21*
Kinorhyncha **21:** 32, 77, 79
Kinosternidae **47:** 9, 28, (31)
Kinosternon
flavescens **47:** 64–65
scorpoides **47:** 64–65
subrubrum **47:** 31
kippers **36:** *110*, 111
kiskadee, great **17:** *29*, 30
kite 15: 10–11, 12, 50
black **15:** 8, 11, 13; **17:** (13); **20:** 23
black-shouldered **44:** 41
Everglade 15: 8, 13, 28–29
red **15:** 8, 11
snail (Everglade) **15:** 8, 13, 28–29
swallow-tailed **15:** 8, *12*
kittiwake 12: 74, 80–85
(black-legged) **12:** 74, 80–85

red-legged **12:** 74
kiunga **38:** 59
Kiunga ballochi **38:** (56), 59
kiwi 11: 16, 18; **20:** (14), 42
brown **11:** 16, 36–39
great spotted **11:** 16, *19*
little spotted **11:** 16
kiyi **35:** 38, 40, 41
Kleidocerys resedae **24:** 46–47
kleptoparasitism (food piracy) **12:** 52, 63–64, 93, (94); **13:** 16, 109; **14:** 72, (74); **15:** (26), 32; **23:** 97, 112
klipspringer **5:** *8*; **6:** *60*, 62
knifefish 31: 85, (108)
African 31: 82, 104–105
arowana **31:** 105
banded **33:** 100
black ghost 33: 102–103
clown 31: 102–103, 104
electric **33:** (100), 104
featherfin **31:** 102
ghost **31:** (108), **33:** 100, (100)
glass **33:** (100), *101*
mottled **33:** (100), 101
naked-back **31:** (108), **33:** (100)
new world 33: 100–101, 104
Old World **31:** 82, 102
sand **31:** (108), **33:** (100)
knight fish **39:** 18, 20
Knightia (fossil) **36:** (105), *105*
knot 13: 30, 55, 64–65
koala 10: (10), 77, (77), 92–97
koaro **35:** *33*, 35
kob **6:** 62
Kobus
ellipsiprymnus **5:** *75*; **6:** 62, 92–93
ellipsiprymnus defassa **6:** 92–93
ellipsiprymnus ellipsyprymnus **6:** 92–93
kob **6:** 62
leche **6:** 92
vardonii **6:** 62
Kogia
breviceps **3:** 55
simus **3:** 55
koi **31:** 63, **34:** 8, *10–11*, 32, 34, 38, 39, 40, *40*
Gangetic **40:** 58
gold ghost **34:** *40–41*
ornamental **34:** *38–39*
kokako 20: 100, 102–103
kokanee *see* salmon
kokopu
giant **35:** 32
shortjaw **35:** 33
Kondokavia longimana **12:** 34
kookaburra **11:** 109; **14:** 100–102
blue-winged **14:** 100, (103)
laughing **14:** 100, *103*, (103); **18:** 63
korhaan, black **11:** 84
korora *see* penguin, little
korrigum **6:** 88
Kosswigichthys asquamatus **38:** 89
krait 50: 14, (35)

blue-banded sea **50:** 37
red-headed **50:** 21
Rennel Island sea **50:** 37
sea **50:** *15*, 44, 49
yellow-lipped sea 50: 9, 36–37
Krefft, Gerard **47:** 38
Kribia uellensis **40:** 97
krill 28: 52–55
antarctic **28:** *54–55*
feeding **28:** 54
fisheries **28:** (54)
Kristensen, Reinhardt **21:** (28)
kroki **39:** 67
Kruger National Park **2:** 31
Kryptopterus **37:** *36–37*
bicirrhis **37:** *31*, (34), 40
cryptopterus **37:** (34)
macrocephalus **37:** (34)
minor **37:** (34)
Kryptopterus bicirrhis **37:** 30
kudu, greater 6: 78–79
Kuhl, Dr Heinrich **45:** (41)
kulan *see* ass, Asian wild
kultarr **10:** *25*, 27
kurper **40:** 58
Cape **40:** 59
Eastern Province rocky **40:** 59
Kyarranus
loveridgei **42:** 94
sphagnicola **42:** 95

L

Labeo **34:** 54–57
chrysophekadion **34:** 56
congoro **34:** 55
cyclorhynchus **34:** 56
forskalii **34:** 56
labeo
black **34:** 56
Labichthys **33:** 87
labido
blue-white **40:** *68*
Labidochromis
caeruleus **40:** *68*
Labidura riparia **22:** *58*, 60
laboratory animals **4:** 40, 87; **7:** 15, 66, (75), 83, 86; **8:** (41); **42:** 55, (55)
see also medical research
Labridae **39:** (10), **40:** 9, 12, 53, 84–87, 89, 101

Labroides **33:** 51, (82)
 bicolor **40:** 84
 dimidiatus **40:** *86*, 90
 rubrolabiatus **40:** 84
Lacerta **45:** 58, (73), (77)
 agilis **45:** *70–71*, (71), (73)
 lepida **45:** 60, 64–67, (73)
 monticola **45:** 60, (73)
 perspicillata **45:** (60)
 saxicola **45:** 89
 schreiberi **45:** *65*, (65), *72–73*
 vivipara **44:** *29*; **45:** 61, 68–73
lacertas, jeweled (eyed lizards) **45:** 64–67
Lacertidae **44:** 25, 28, 84, (105); **45:** 58–61
lacewings
 green **22:** 90, 92
 larvae, defense **22:** (92)
 and relatives 22: 90–97
Lachesis **50:** (8), 63, 65, 94–95
 melanocephala **50:** 94
 muta **50:** 50, 54, 94, *94*
 stenophrys **50:** 94, *95*
Lactoria cornuta **39:** *106*, 107, *107*
Ladigesia roloffi **38:** 30
lady beetles (ladybugs) **25:** 54–59
ladybirds (ladybugs) **25:** 54–59
ladybugs 25: 54–59
 convergent **25:** *58–59*
 7-spot **25:** *54*, **27:** *29*
Lagenodelphis hosei **3:** 71
Lagenorhynchus
 acutus **3:** 71
 albirostris **3:** 71
 cruciger **3:** 71
 obliquidens **3:** 55, 70–71
 obscurus **3:** 71
Lagidium peruanum **8:** 30
Lagoa crispata **26:** *108*
Lagocephalus laevigatus **39:** 109
Lagochila lacera **34:** 96, 99
lagomorphs **1:** *10*; **8:** 61–63
Lagopus **15:** 34
 lagopus **11:** 44, 66–69
Lagostomus maximus **8:** 30
Lagostrophus fasciatus **10:** 48
Lagothrix
 flavicauda **4:** 72
 lagotricha **4:** 72, 82–83
Laguvia shawi **37:** 48
Laliostoma **43:** 100
Lama
 glama **5:** 92, 104–107
 guanicoe **5:** 92, 108–109
 pacos **5:** 92, (106)
Lamarckiana **23:** 29
lamellae **14:** 54
Laminiceps **24:** *52–53*
Lammellibranchiida **21:** 77
lammergeier 20: 8, 22–23
Lamna nasus **32:** 22, 25
Lamnidae **32:** (12), (74)
Lamniformes **32:** 74–75
Lampetra fluviatilis **31:** *12*

lampeye **38:** 94–105
 banded **38:** 103
 blue-green **38:** 105
 Brichard's **38:** 103
 filamentosus **38:** *104*
 large-finned **38:** 105
 Rancurel's **38:** *104*
 red stripe **38:** 104
 variable **38:** 105
 yellow-finned **38:** 81, 104
lamprey 31: *14*, 25, 26–31, (31), 42, (108)
 brook **31:** 30
 dwarf **31:** 30
 parasitic damage **31:** (30)
 river **31:** *12*
 sea **31:** *28*, *28–29*
Lamprichthys tanganicanus **38:** 103, *104–105*
Lamprididae **35:** 82, 105
Lampridiformes **35:** 82
 families summary **35:** (79)
Lampropeltis
 alterna **49:** (54)
 arabicus **49:** 68
 calligaster **49:** (54)
 fuscus **49:** (69)
 getula **49:** 48–51, (54), 59
 lineatus **49:** 68
 mentalis **49:** 68
 mexicana **49:** (54)
 mexicana thayeri **49:** *49*
 pyromelana **49:** *54*, (54)
 ruthveni **49:** (54)
 triangulum **48:** *9*; **49:** (29), 52–57; **50:** *24*, 26, 88
 zonata **49:** (54); **50:** 26
Lamprophiinae **49:** 8, 12–13
Lamprophis **49:** 12, (69)
 aurora **49:** 12, 69
 fiskii **49:** 13, (69)
 fuliginosus **49:** 12, 66–69; **50:** 62
 geometricus **49:** 13
 inornatus **49:** *68*
lampshells 21: 70–71
Lampyridae **25:** 36–37
Lampyris noctiluca **25:** *36*
lancehead (terciopelo) **50:** (8), 9, (52), 92–93, (111)
 common **50:** (8), *11*, *52–53*, 92
 Patagonian **50:** 50
lancelet 31: 24–25, 31, 42
lancer
 black **37:** *26–27*, 27
 harlequin **37:** 27
lancetfish 35: 80, 100–101
 longnose **35:** 80, 100, *100*
 shortnose **35:** 100, *101*
Langaha **49:** 14, (71)
 alluaudi **49:** 73
 madagascariensis **49:** 14, 70–73
 pseudoalluaudi **49:** 73
Langorchestes
 conspicillatus **10:** 48

 hirsutus **10:** 48
langur 4: 42
 Hanuman 1: *12–13*; **4:** 40, 41, 64–67
 Malabar **4:** 40
Laniarius
 atrococcineus **15:** 104
 ferrugineus **15:** 104
Lanice conchilega **21:** *97*
Laniidae **15:** 104; **19:** (74)
Lanioturdus torquatus **15:** 104
Lanius **15:** 104, 105, 106
 collaris **15:** 104
 collurio **15:** 104, 108–111; **20:** (48)
 excubitor **15:** 104; **18:** 59
 ludovicianus **15:** 104
 senator **15:** 104
lantern-belly **40:** 12, 14, 15
lanterneye fish **35:** (88), **39:** 9, 16
lanternfish 35: 81, 102–103
 blue **35:** 81, 102
 horned **36:** 83
 large-scaled **35:** 103
 metallic **35:** *102*
lanternflies 24: *12*, 72–77
Lanthanotidae **44:** 25; **46:** 82
Lanthanotus borneensis **45:** (99); **46:** 72, 100–101
Lapemis **50:** (45)
 hardwickii **50:** 46
lapwing 13: 8, 22–25
 gray-headed **13:** 8
 red-wattled **13:** 8
largenose **39:** 15
Laridae **12:** 74
Lariscus insignis **7:** 36
lark 15: 19, 94; **20:** (31)
 ashy-crowned sparrow **18:** 22
 Australasian bush **18:** 22
 black **18:** 22, *22*
 black-crowned sparrow **18:** 22
 calandra **18:** 22
 crested **18:** 22, *22*
 desert **18:** 22, *22*
 greater hoopoe **18:** 22, 23
 greater short-toed **18:** 22
 horned 18: 22, 28–29
 Karoo **18:** 22
 lark family 18: 22–23
 Razo **18:** 22, 23
 red-winged **18:** 22, *23*
 Rudd's **18:** 22, 23
 rufous-naped **18:** 22
 rufous-winged bush **18:** 22
 sand **18:** 22, 23
 shore (horned) **18:** 22, 28–29
 sparrow **18:** 22, 23
 Stark's **18:** 22, 23
 sun **18:** 22
Larosterna inca **12:** 74
Larus
 argentatus **12:** 74, 78–79; **13:** 79
 atricilla **12:** 52, 74
 canus **12:** 74, 81
 delawarensis **12:** 74

dominicanus **12:** 74
marinus **12:** 74, 93, 107
minutus **12:** 74
philadelphia **12:** 74
pipixcan **12:** 74
ridibundus **12:** 74; **13:** 79
Larvacea **31:** 22–23
larvacean **31:** 23, 25
larvae
  eel *see* leptocephali
  oarfish **35:** *109*
Lasiocampidae **26:** *84–87*
Lasioglossum calceatum **27:** *94–95*
Lasiognathus **36:** *76–77*, 80
Lasiorhinus
  krefftii **10:** 74, (101)
  latifrons **10:** 74, (101)
Lasius fuliginousus **27:** *47*
lassa fever **7:** 14
latchet **39:** 56
Laternaria laternaria **24:** *76*
Lates
  calcarifer **40:** 14
  niloticus **40:** 11, 13, *13*, (79)
Lathamus discolor **16:** 22; **19:** 12
Laticauda **50:** *15*, 37, 44, 45
  colubrina **33:** 81; **50:** 9, 36–37
  crockeri **50:** (36), (47)
Latidae **40:** 11, 12–19
Latimeria **31:** 35
  chalumnae **31:** 15, 32, *34*, *35*, 36,
    32: 101, **38:** (110)
  menadoensis **31:** *34*, 35
Latimeriidae **31:** 34–37
Latrodectus bishopi **29:** 100
Laudakia **44:** 32, 36, (40)
  stellio **44:** 32, 36
Laurasia **9:** 10
Lauriea siagiani **28:** *88–89*
lavaret **35:** 40
leaf frogs 42: 8, 9–10, 10, (38); **43:** 32,
    34, 36, 64–67, 107
  Australian red-eyed **42:** *9*
  flap-heeled **43:** *60*, 62
  lesser red-eyed **43:** 58
  Malayan (Asian horned toads) **42:** 9,
    10, 34–35, 36–39, 40, (89);
    43: 86
  orange-sided **43:** *64–65*
  red-eyed 42: 35; **43:** 54, 58–63,
    65, 67
  related species **43:** 67
  Solomon Islands **43:** 86
  Trinidad **43:** *37*, 65
  Venus **43:** 64
leaf insects 22: 52–57
leaffish 40: 56–57
  Amazon **40:** *56*, 57
  common **40:** 57
  Gangetic **40:** 57
  Guyana **40:** 57
  Indonesian **40:** 57
  Malabar **40:** 57
leafhoppers 24: 86–89

feeding habits **24:** 87–88
plant damage **24:** 87–88
rhododendron **24:** 86, 87
"songs" **24:** (89)
leatherjacket **39:** 100, 102
  diamond **39:** 104
Lebiasina
  astrigata **38:** 23
  panamensis **38:** 23
Lebiasinidae **34:** 102, **38:** 11, 22–23
lechwe **6:** 92
leeches 21: 106–111
  horse **21:** *109*
  leaf **21:** *110–111*
  medicinal **21:** *106*, (108), *108–109*
leerfish **40:** 34
legskate *see* skate
Leimadophis epinephelus **43:** 80
Leiognathidae **40:** 34–35
Leiognathus
  elongatus **40:** 35
  equulus **40:** 35
Leioheterodon **49:** 13
  madagascariensis **49:** *15*
Leiolepidinae **44:** 36
Leiolepis **44:** 32, 36
  guentherpetersi **44:** 37
  triploida **44:** 37
Leiolopisma **46:** 12–13
  laterale **46:** (11)
  telfairi **48:** 77
Leiopelma **42:** 18–19
  archeyi **42:** 19
  hamiltoni **42:** 18, *19*
  hochstetteri **42:** 18, *18*
  pakeka **42:** 19
Leiopelmatidae **42:** 10
Leiopython albertisii **48:** 82
Leipoa ocellata **11:** 44, 82–83
leks **11:** 48; **13:** 33; **15:** 85; **16:** 47, 57;
    19: 82, (91); **20:** (44)
lemming 2: 72; **7:** 13, 17, 65
  collared **7:** 9
  Norway 7: 66, 90–91
Lemmus lemmus **7:** *90–91*
lemur 1: 96; **4:** 96–97
  bamboo **4:** 96, 97
  black **4:** 96, *96*
  black-and-white ruffed **4:** 104, *105*
  brown **4:** 97
  brown mouse **4:** 96
  Coquerel's dwarf **4:** 96
  crowned **4:** 96
  dwarf **4:** 97, *97*
  eastern woolly **4:** 96
  fat-tailed dwarf **4:** 96
  flying **8:** 108; **45:** (42)
  fork-marked **4:** 96
  giant sloth **4:** 96
  golden bamboo **4:** 96
  gray mouse **4:** 96
  greater bamboo **4:** 96
  greater dwarf **4:** 96
  hairy-eared dwarf **4:** 96

indri **4:** 96, 97
Milne-Edwards's sportive **4:** 96, *97*
mongoose **4:** 96, *96*
mouse **4:** 97, *97*
pygmy mouse **4:** 8, 96, 97
red ruffed **4:** 104, *105*
ringtailed 4: 9, 96, 97, 98–101
ruffed 4: 96, 104–105
sportive **4:** 97
weasel sportive **4:** 96
western woolly **4:** 96
Lemur catta **4:** 96, 98–101
Leontopithecus
  caissara **4:** 88
  chrysomelas **4:** 88
  chrysopygus **4:** 86, 88
  rosalia **4:** 86, 88–91
leopard 2: 9, 10, 13, 30–33
  black **2:** 30, *31*
  clouded **2:** 9, 10
  melanistic **2:** 30, *31*
  snow 2: 10, 13, 34–35
Lepas **28:** 27
  anatifera **28:** *24–25*
Lepidarchus adonis **38:** 30
Lepidobatrachus **42:** 76, 87, 88; **43:** 99
  asper **42:** 88
  laevis **42:** 88, *88–89*
  llanensis **42:** 40, 88–89
Lepidochelys
  kempi **47:** 12, (15)
  olivacea **47:** *13*
Lepidocolaptes
  affinis **17:** 28
  albolineatus **17:** 28
  lacrymiger **17:** 28
Lepidogalaxias salamandroides
    35: 8, (36)
Lepidogalaxiidae **35:** (36)
Lepidophyma **45:** 54
  flavimaculatum **45:** 55
  pajapanensis **45:** *54–55*
Lepidopsetta bilineata **39:** 90
Lepidoptera **22:** 30, *30–31*
  classification **26:** 8, 10–11
Lepidorhynchus denticulatus **36:** *28–29*
Lepidosauria **44:** 18
Lepidosiren **31:** 41
  paradoxa **31:** 38, *38*, 41, *41*; **43:** 27
Lepidosirenidae **31:** (33), 38–41, **33:** 63
Lepidotidae **31:** (72), 73
Lepidotrigla argus **39:** 56
Lepilemur
  edwardsi **4:** 96
  mustelinus **4:** 96
Lepisosteidae **31:** (43), (72), 73, 76, 78
Lepisosteus **31:** 72, 74
  (Atractosteus) spatula **31:** 72
  gavial **31:** 79
  (lepisosteus) osseus **31:** 72
  oculatus **31:** *72–73*, 74
  osseus **31:** 72, 74, 77, 78–79
  platostomus **31:** 74
Lepomis **40:** 26, 27

cyanellus **40**: *26*
gibbosus **40**: 26, *29*
macrochirus **37**: 18, **40**: *26–27*, 27
megalotis **40**: 26
Leporidae (leporids) **8**: 60, 64, 67
leporin **38**: 21
　black-lined **38**: 21
　striped **38**: 21
Leporinus **38**: 21
　nigrotaeniatus **38**: 21
　striatus **38**: 21
leprosy **9**: (76)
Leptacanthichthys **36**: 82
Lepticidium **1**: *8*
Leptinotarsa decemlineata **25**: *103*
Leptobrachella **42**: 34
Leptobrachium **42**: 34, 35
　hasselti **42**: 35, *35*
　hendricksoni **42**: 35
Leptocelis centralis **24**: *53*
leptocephali (eel larvae) **33**: (64), *64*, 68,
　(72), 85, *85*, *90–91*
Leptochariidae **32**: (12), (42)
Leptocoma
　sericea **19**: 94
　zeylonica **19**: 94
Leptocottus armatus **39**: *78*
Leptodactylidae **42**: 8, 10, 76, 87, 92;
　43: (11), 34, 52, (73)
Leptodactylinae **42**: 78–79
Leptodactylodon **43**: 12
Leptodactylus **42**: 76, 78–79
　knudseni **42**: *76–77*
　macrosternum **43**: 27
　pentadactylus **42**: 90–91
Leptodeira **49**: 16
　septentrionalis **43**: 61
Leptolalax **42**: 34
Leptolebias minimus **38**: 80
Leptolucania ommata **38**: 84
Leptopelis **43**: 18, 23
　brevirostris **43**: 23
　flavomaculatus **43**: *23*
　palmatus **43**: 18
Leptophis **49**: 26
Leptophlebia marginata **22**: *38*
Leptoptilos
　crumeniferus **14**: 32, 36–39
　dubius **14**: 36
Leptosomidae **15**: 86
Leptosomus discolor **15**: 86
leptospirosis **1**: 87; **7**: 14
Leptostraca **28**: 34, 36
Leptosynanceia asteroblepa **39**: 52
Leptotarsus ducalis **23**: *43*
Leptotyphlopidae **44**: 15; **48**: 9, 18, 19,
　(35)
Leptotyphlops **48**: 19; **50**: (25)
　blandfordi **48**: 20
　dulcis **48**: 20, 22–23
　humilis **48**: 23
　occidentalis **48**: *19*
Lepus
　alleni **8**: 64

americanus **8**: 64, 74–79
arcticus **8**: 82–85
californicus **8**: 64, 80–81
europaeus **8**: 64, 86–89
Lerista **44**: (26); **46**: 8, 12
　apoda **46**: 12
　viduata **46**: 12
Lestidiops
　mirabilis **35**: *99*
　ringens **35**: 98
Lestodelphys halli **10**: 14
Lestoros inca **10**: 14
Lethoplosternum **37**: 103
　pectorale **37**: *103*
Lethotremus awae **39**: 82
Lethrinidae **40**: 40–41
Lethrinus
　olivaceus **40**: 40, *40–41*
　varietatus **40**: 41
Leucage nigrovittata **29**: 103
Leucichthys **35**: 38, 40
Leuciscinae **34**: 72–79, 84–87
Leuciscus **34**: 77
　aphipsi **34**: 78
　borysthenicus **34**: 78
　carolitertii **34**: 78
　cephalus **34**: 68, 73, 78, 79
　danilevskii **34**: 78
　idus **34**: 68, 73, *76–77*, 77, 80
　illyricus **34**: 78
　keadicus **34**: 78
　lehmani **34**: 78
　leuciscus **34**: 72, 73, 78, 79
　microlepis **34**: 78
　polylepis **34**: 78
　souffia **34**: 78
　squaliusculus **34**: 78
　svallize **34**: 78
　turskyi **34**: 78
　ukliva **34**: 78
　waleckii waleckii **34**: 77
Leucopsar rothschildi **18**: 82
Leucoraja **33**: (27)
Leuresthes tenuis **38**: 60, 61
leverets **8**: 88
Lialis burtoni **44**: 29; **45**: *48–49*
Lialisinae **45**: 8
Liasis **48**: 82, (84)
Libelloides
　coccajus **22**: *90*
　longicornis **22**: 96
Libellula
　cyanea **22**: *26–27*
　quadrimaculata **22**: *50–51*
　saturata **22**: *42–43*
Liberiictis kuhni **1**: 98
Libyaspis coccinelloides **24**: *63*
lice 22: 88–89
　body **22**: (89)
　crab **22**: 88–89
　cymothoid fish **28**: *30*
　dog **22**: 88
　head **22**: 88–89
　on humans **22**: (89)

jumping plant 24: 96–97
marine fish **28**: *30*
whale **3**: *57*, 92, 102, 108
Lichanura **48**: 72
Lichenostomus ornatus **20**: 88
Lichia amia **40**: 34
lifestyles **31**: 17
lightfish
　port and starboard **39**: 20
light-producing fish **35**: 78, *80*, *80–81*,
　81, *82–83*, *84–85*, 87, (88), *88–89*,
　89, 90, 102, *102–103*, **36**: 29, (57),
　59, 79, **39**: (18)
Ligia oceanica **28**: *46, 49*
Limacodidae **26**: 106–109
Limanda limanda **39**: 90, *90–91*
Limax maximus **30**: *48–49*
Limidae **30**: 59
Limnephilus flavicornis **22**: *103*
Limnochromis
　auritus **40**: 74
　staneri **40**: 74
limnochromis
　Staner's **40**: 74
Limnodromus
　griseus **13**: 30, 58–61
　sclopaceus **13**: 58
Limnodynastes **42**: 92, 93, 94, 97
　interioris **42**: *93*
　spenceri **42**: *95*
Limnodynastidae **42**: 92
Limnogale mergulus **9**: 24
Limnonectes **43**: 82, 84, 85
　doriae **43**: 84
　plicatellus **43**: 84
Limosa
　haemastica **13**: 30
　lapponica **13**: 30, 34–39
limpets 30: 22–25
　blue **30**: *25*
　common **30**: *22*
　giant keyhole **30**: *24*
　keyhole **30**: 22
　shimmering **30**: *22–23*
　slipper **30**: *26, 30–31*
limpkin 14: 82–83, 90–91
Limulus polyphemus **29**: *10, 10–11*
linalool **27**: 90
Lineatriton **41**: 68
Lineus **21**: *86–87*
　longissimus **21**: *86*
ling **39**: 75
　Atlantic **36**: *48–49*
　pink **36**: 24
lingcod **32**: 102, **39**: 74, *74*, 75
Lingula anatina **21**: *70*
Linn (Linnaeus), Carolus (Carl) **21**: 9
Linophryne **36**: 77, 79, *82–83*
Linophrynidae **36**: 74–83
linsang **1**: 89, 90, 91
　African **1**: 88, *90*
　banded **1**: 88
　spotted **1**: 88
Linyphia triangularis **29**: *112, 113*

Linyphiidae **29**: <u>112–113</u>
Liochlorophis vernalis **49**: (59), (86)
Liolaemus **44**: 81, 85
lion 1: *15*; **2**: *8–9*, 9, 10, *13*, <u>14–19</u>;
  6: 82; **8**: *18–19*
  Asian **2**: (15)
  Barbary **2**: 17
  mountain *see* puma
lionfish **39**: 53, 60, 61, (61), (62), 64
  red **39**: *59*
lionhead **34**: *42*, 49, 51
  Chinese **34**: 51
  Japanese **34**: 51
  red-eyed **34**: *47*
Liophis **48**: (77)
Liosomadoras oncinus **37**: 77
Liothyrella uva **21**: *70–71*
Liotyphlops **48**: 18
Liparidae **39**: 53, <u>82–83</u>
Liparis florae **39**: 83
Lipaugus vociferans **19**: 80
Lipogenys gilli **33**: 97
Lipogramma
  flavescens **40**: 24
  robinsoni **40**: 24
Lipophrys
  nigriceps **40**: 93
  pholis **40**: *90*
Liposarcus **34**: 109, **37**: 108
  anisitsi **37**: *106–107*
Liposcelis terricolis **22**: *86*
Lipotes vexillifer **3**: 55, (61)
Lipotyphla **9**: 10
Lirimiris **26**: *82*
Lissocarcinus **28**: *112*
Lissocarpa vespiformis **24**: *86–87*
Lithobius forficatus **22**: *22–23*
Lithodidae **28**: (98)
Lithodytes **42**: 76
  lineatus **43**: (73)
Lithognathus lithognathus **40**: 40
Litocranius walleri **6**: 62, <u>98–99</u>
Litoria **43**: 32, (55), 57
  aurea **42**: (18)
  caerulea **43**: 32, <u>54–57</u>
  chloris **42**: *9*; **43**: 57, *57*, (59)
  ewingii **42**: (18)
  gracilenta **43**: 57
  infrafrenata **43**: 54, *54–55*, 57
  nasuta **43**: 39
  raniformis **42**: (18)
  splendida **43**: 54, 57
Litostomatea **21**: 13
Littorina
  obtusata **30**: *26*
  peruviana **30**: *28–29*
  saxatilis **30**: *28*
"littorinid zone" **30**: (28)
Liua **41**: 36, (37)
livebearer **38**: 50, 94, 106, 107, 109
  dwarf **38**: 95, 96, *97*
  Mexican **38**: 106
  one-sided **38**: 92, 93, **39**: 84
  piketop **38**: 96

porthole **38**: 96
Rio de la Plata one-sided **38**: 92
Liza abu **38**: 53
lizardfish 35: 79, <u>94–97</u>
  deep-sea **35**: 96, 97
  gracile **35**: *94*
  highfin **35**: 96, 97
  orangemouth **35**: *94*
  suspicious **35**: 96
  variegated **35**: *96–97*
lizards 44: *13*, <u>24–31</u>
  African blue-tailed tree **45**: 40, 58–59,
    60
  African desert 45: <u>74–75</u>
  African flat **44**: 30
  African girdled **44**: 28
  African keel-bellied **45**: 59
  African sand 45: 59, <u>74–75</u>
  alligator 44: 25, (26), 27, 28, (105);
    46: <u>50–55</u>
  American horned **44**: 15, 28, 30, 34,
    (49)
  angle-headed **44**: 32, 34, 34–35
  armadillo 45: <u>104–105</u>
  Australian snake **44**: 30
  Aztec (Gila monster) **44**: 27–28, 30;
    46: 74, 75, <u>76–79</u>
  Baja California legless **46**: 64, 64–65
  beaded 44: 25, 29; **46**: <u>74–75</u>, (79)
  bearded dragon **44**: 32, 34, 51, (51)
  beauty **44**: 35
  big water (hellbenders) **41**: (12), 14,
    30, <u>32–35</u>
  black girdle-tailed 45: <u>102–103</u>
  black-headed scaly-foot **45**: *51*
  blind **44**: 25, (26), 28, 82; **45**: 13
  bob-tailed (stump-tailed skinks) **46**: 9,
    10, 14, 15, <u>44–47</u>
  Borneo earless monster **45**: (99)
  Broadley's flat 45: <u>106–107</u>
  bronzeback **45**: (49), 50
  Burton's snake **44**: 29; **45**: *48–49*
  bushveld 44: 30; **45**: 60, <u>62–63</u>
  butterfly **44**: 32, 36–37
  caiman 45: 83–84, <u>92–93</u>
  California legless **46**: (55), 64–65,
    64–65
  Cape crag 45: <u>108–109</u>
  Caribbean ground **1**: 109
  Central American green spiny **44**: 85
  central bearded dragon 44: 30,
    <u>50–51</u>
  changeable (garden) **44**: 32, 35, (37),
    <u>46–47</u>
  Chinese crocodile 44: 30; **45**: 93;
    46: *70–71*, <u>72–73</u>, 101
  chisel-toothed **44**: *13*, 25, 32
  coast horned 44: <u>102–105</u>
  collared 44: 25, 81, 84, <u>88–89</u>, 108
  common flying 44: <u>44–45</u>
  common fringe-toed **45**: (79)
  common garden **44**: 35
  common green forest 44: *46–47*
  common scaly-foot **45**: *49*, 50

common side-blotched (side-blotched)
  44: 24, 82, 84, 105, <u>108–109</u>;
  45: 56–57; **50**: 105
common wall 45: *59*, <u>76–77</u>
crag **45**: 100, (101), (109)
crevice spiny **44**: 85
crocodile **44**: 25
dab **44**: 32, 33, 34, 36, 37; **50**: 70
decorative features **44**: 28
defense **44**: 29–30
desert **45**: 74–75
desert horned **50**: 105
desert night **45**: *55*, (57)
Dickerson's collared **44**: 88
dragon 44: 25, 32, <u>32–37</u>
dwarf crag **45**: (109)
dwarf plated **45**: 100
earless dragon **44**: 34
eastern bearded **44**: 50
eastern glass 44: *26*; **46**: <u>60–61</u>
El Hierro giant **45**: *60–61*, *66–67*, (67)
Erhard's wall **45**: 61, 77
European common (viviparous) **44**: *29*;
  45: 61, <u>68–73</u>
European glass 46: 51, <u>62–63</u>
European sand **45**: *70–71*, (71), (73)
evolution **44**: *10*
eyed 45: 60, <u>64–67</u>, (73)
feeding on python eggs **48**: 92
fence **44**: 10, 82
flap-footed 44: 25; **45**: <u>48–53</u>
flat **45**: 99, (101), (107)
Florida (eastern) glass **44**: *26*; **46**:
  <u>60–61</u>
flying **43**: (62); **44**: 30, 32, 33, 44
flying dragon (common flying) **44**:
  <u>44–45</u>
food and feeding **44**: 29
as food for pythons **48**: 86
forest dragon **44**: 32
four-eyed **44**: 80
frilled 44: 30, 32, 34, <u>42–43</u>
fringe-toed **44**: *80–81*, 82; **50**: 105
Galápagos lava 44: <u>110–111</u>
garden 44: 32, 35, (37), <u>46–47</u>
giant **45**: *66–67*, (67)
giant plated 45: *100–101*, <u>110–111</u>
Gila monster 44: 27–28, 30; **46**: 74,
  75, <u>76–79</u>
girdled **44**: 25, (26)
girdle-tailed 44: 27; **45**: <u>98–101</u>,
  (103)
glass 44: 25, (26), 30; **46**: <u>50–55</u>
golden spectacled **45**: 85
granite night 45: <u>56–57</u>, (107)
grass **45**: 59, (81), 98
green **44**: 25; **45**: (65), (73)
green crested **44**: *33*
green spiny **44**: *82–83*
horned **44**: 34, 84, 85, 106
hump-nosed **44**: *37*, (37)
Iberian rock **45**: 60, (73)
island night **45**: (57)
"Jesus Christ" (plumed basilisks)

44: 25, 26, 80, 81, 86–87
jeweled (eyed) **44:** 25; **45:** 60, 64–67, (73)
jungle racers 45: 82, 86–87
knob-scaled **46:** 70
knob-tailed **44:** 25
Komodo dragon **44:** 24, 24–25
La Gomera giant **45:** (67)
lava **44:** 25, 81
leaf-nosed **44:** (37)
legless **44:** (26); **45:** 64; **46:** (61)
Lilford's wall **45:** 60–61, 77
limb reduction/absence **44:** (26)
locomotion **44:** 25–27
Malaysian armored spiny dragon **44:** 35
Mexican beaded 44: 28, 30; **46:** 74, *75*, 77, 80–81
Mexican night **45:** *54–55*
Milos wall **45:** 61
mimic glass **46:** 61
mole (ajolotes) **46:** 110–111
Moroccan rock **45:** (60)
mountain **44:** 35
night 44: 25, 28; **45:** 54–55
North African sandfish **44:** 27
North American alligator **46:** 52
North American legless 46: 64–65
northern alligator **46:** 50, 69
northern fence **44:** 85
ocellated (eyed) **45:** 60, 64–67, (73)
ornate sandveld **45:** *57–58*
Pallas's (European) glass **46:** 51, 62–63
Palmer's side-blotched **44:** (109)
Philippine sail-fin **44:** *35*
pine-cone (stump-tailed skinks) **46:** 9, *10*, 14, 15, 44–47
plated 44: 25, 28; **45:** 98–101, (111)
plated snake **45:** 101
pricklenape **44:** 35
prickly **44:** 32
rainbow (*Cnemidophorus deppei*) **45:** *90–91*
rainbow (red-headed rock agamas) **44:** 38–41
red-headed (garden) **44:** 32, 35, (37), 46–47
rough-scaled **45:** 61
sail-fin **44:** 32, 34, 35
sand **45:** 59, 74–75
sandfish **44:** 84
sand racers **45:** (67), (79)
sandveld **45:** (63)
scales **44:** 27–28
scaly-footed **45:** 48, (49)
scheltopusik (European glass) **46:** 51, 62–63
Schreiber's **45:** *65*, (65), *72–73*
scorpion **46:** *51*
senses **44:** 28–29
shingleback (stump-tailed skinks) **46:** 9, *10*, 14, 15, 44–47
short-horned **44:** *103*, *104–105*
shovel-snouted **44:** 84; **45:** 60, *74–75*

side-blotched 44: 24, 82, 84, 105, 108–109; **45:** 56–57; **50:** 105
six-lined grass 45: 80–81
sizes **44:** 24–25
Skyros wall **45:** 61
sleepy (stump-tailed skinks) **46:** 9, *10*, 14, 15, 44–47
snake **44:** (26), 28, 29; **45:** 48, 51
snake-eyed **45:** (60)
southern alligator 46: 68–69
Spanish eyed **45:** (65)
spectacled **44:** 25; **45:** 82, 83, (85)
spinifex snake **45:** *52–53*
spiny **44:** 85
spiny-tailed **44:** *9, 84–85*
spiny-tailed dab 44: 52–55
spotted sand **45:** *74–75*
sungazer **45:** 99
swollen-nosed side-blotched **44:** (109)
tails discarded **44:** 30
Texas earless **44:** 82
Texas horned **44:** *104*
Texas spiny **44:** *27*
thorny devils 44: 15, 29, 32, 34, 48–49
viviparous 44: *29*; **45:** 61, 68–73
wall 44: 25, 28, 30, (105); **45:** 58–61, 76–77
water dragon **44:** 32, 34
wedge-snouted **44:** 84
wedge-snouted sand **45:** *74*
worm **41:** 20; **44:** *8, 10, 11*
Yarrow's spiny **44:** 85
yellow-spotted night **45:** 55
zebra-tailed **44:** 82
see also agamas; anole; chameleons; chuckwallas; galliwasps; geckos; iguanas; monitor lizards; racerunners; slow worm; tegu; whiptails; worm lizards
llama 5: 12, 92, 93, *93*, 104–107
loach 34: 11, 13, 14, 88–89
banded **34:** (104)
Bengal **34:** *105*
Borneo **34:** *100–101*, 101
Botia **34:** (104), 106, 108
chain **34:** (104)
Chinese fine-scaled weather **34:** 107
Chinese weather **34:** 107
clown 34: 14, 102–105
common **34:** 89
coolie **34:** 100, 101
dwarf **34:** (104)
eel **34:** 101
European weather **34:** 106, 107
flat **34:** 108, 109
half-banded kuhli **34:** 101
horse-faced **34:** 100
Indian kuhli **34:** 101
Italian **34:** 89
Japanese weather **34:** 107
Java **34:** 101
kuhli 34: 9, 14, 88, 100–101, 102, 108

long-nosed **34:** 100
Myer's **34:** *14–15*, 101
Myer's hill-stream **34:** 89, 109
Pakistan **34:** (104)
pond **34:** 106
red-finned **34:** *104–105*
redtail **34:** 14
river 34: 11, 14, 100, 108–109
saddled hill-stream **34:** 15, 109, *109*
slimy **34:** *14–15*, 101
spined **34:** *88–89*, 89, 100, 101, 102
spiny **34:** 101
stone 34: 14, 89, 108, 109, 110–111
sucking **34:** 12, 89, 90
torrent 34: 108–109
weather 34: 14, 100, 102, 106–107, 108
zebra **34:** (104)
see also botia
lobe-finned fish 31: 32–33, 42, 45, **33:** 60
Who's Who **31:** (33)
Lobodon carcinophagus **3:** 9, 36–37
Lobotes surinamensis **40:** 36
Lobotidae **40:** 36–37
Loboza **21:** 13
lobsters 28: 70–79
American **28:** *70–71*, (71)
Atlantic squat **28:** *86–87*
Caribbean spiny **28:** *82, 84–85*
common **28:** 70
as human food **28:** 78
migration **28:** 77–78
overfishing **28:** 83
pink squat **28:** *88–89*
pistol **28:** 76
"red whalefeed" **28:** 87
reef **28:** *58–59*
ridgeback slipper **28:** *83*
sense of gravity **28:** (77)
slipper 28: 82–85
spiny 28: 82–85
spiny squat **22:***8*; **28:** 86
squat 28: *14–15*, 86–89
traps for **28:** (78), *79*
lobtailing **3:** 96, 109
locomotion
bipedal **44:** 26, 81, 87
boas **48:** 51
caecilians **41:** 22–23
lizards **44:** 25–27
plantigrade **9:** 8, 12, 22, 68
snakes **48:** 10–12
Locustella **17:** 61
naevia **17:** 60
locusts **23:** 24, (26)
Loddigesia mirabilis **16:** 44
logging **1:** 51, 77; **2:** 21; **6:** 20
Loliginidae **30:** 72
Loligo **30:** 76
opalescens **30:** *83*
Lonchothrix emiliae **8:** 30
Lonchura **16:** 90
cucullata **17:** (109)

punctulata **16:** 90
long tom **38:** 73
longclaw **17:** 44
  yellow-throated **17:** 44, *45*
longfin **40:** 25
longwings 26: <u>52–55</u>
Lontra
  canadensis **1:** 32, <u>64–67</u>
  felina **1:** 32
lookdown **40:** 35
loon
  Arctic **14:** 8, *9*
  common 14: 8, <u>10–15</u>
  loon family 14: <u>8–9</u>
  red-throated **14:** 8
  yellow-billed **14:** 8
loosejaw **35:** (88), 89
  black **35:** 89
  stoplight **35:** *84*, 89
Lopha
  cristagalli **30:** *71*
  folium **30:** *56–57*
Lophiidae **36:** <u>60–63</u>, 76
Lophiiformes **36:** <u>8–15</u>
Lophiomys imhausi **7:** 66
Lophius
  americanus **36:** *60*, 61
  budegassa **32:** 107
  piscatorius **32:** 107, **36:** *60–61*, 63
Lophocebus
  albigena **4:** 40
  aterrimus **4:** 40
Lophodes sinistraria **26:** 74
Lophogastrida **28:** 34, 37
Lopholithodes mandtii **28:** *98*
lophophorates **21:** 68
Lophornis
  adorabilis **16:** 44
  magnifica **16:** 44
  pavoninus **16:** 44
lophotid fish
  Schlegel's **35:** 104
Lophotidae **35:** 82, <u>104–105</u>
Lophotrochozoa **21:** 32, 69
Lophotus
  capellei **35:** 104
  lacepede **35:** 104, *104*, *105*
Lophozosterops dohertyi **18:** 68
Lophura nycthemera **11:** 44
Loricariichthys **37:** (110)
Loricariidae **34:** 109, **37:** 11, <u>104–111</u>
Loricella angasi **30:** *14*
Loricifera **21:** 32, 69
Loriculus
  philippensis **16:** 22
  vernalis **20:** 36
lorikeet 16: (25)
  ornate **16:** 22
  rainbow 19: 12, <u>16–19</u>, 21
Lorinae **16:** (25)
loris 4: 106–107
  pygmy **4:** 106
  slender **4:** 106, *106*
  slow 4: 106, <u>108–109</u>

Loris tardigradus **4:** 106
Lorius lory **19:** 12, <u>20–21</u>
lory 16: (25)
  black **20:** 36
  black-capped 19: 12, <u>20–21</u>
  violet-eared **19:** 12, *14–15*
Lota **36:** 39
  lota **36:** (51)
lotus-bird **14:** 96
louse *see* lice
louse-flies **15:** (74)
love charms **3:** 61
lovebugs (March flies) **23:** <u>54–55</u>
Loveridgea ionidesi **46:** 104
Lovettia sealii **35:** 33, (34), (35)
Lovettinae **35:** (34)
Loxia
  curvirostra **16:** 76, (84); **18:** (34)
  pytopsittacus **16:** 76
Loxocemidae **48:** 9, 28
Loxocemus bicolor **44:** 101; **48:** 31,
  <u>38–39</u>
Loxodonta
  africana **5:** 14, <u>16–21</u>
  cyclotis **5:** 14
Loxops
  coccinea **20:** 98
  maculata **20:** 98
  parva **20:** 98
  virens **20:** 98
Loxosceles rufescens **29:** *58–59*
Loxoscelidae **29:** (59)
Lucania goodei **38:** *84–85*, 85
Lucanidae **25:** <u>74–75</u>
Lucanus cervus **22:** *32;* **25:** *74*
  Lucifuga
    dentatus **36:** 27
    subterranea **36:** 27
Lucigadus nigromaculatus **36:** *30–31*
lucines **30:** 62, 63
Lucinidae **30:** 50, 63
Luciocephalus pulcher **40:** 57, 63
Luciosoma **34:** <u>54–57</u>
  bleekeri **34:** 57
  setigerum **34:** *56–57*, 57
  spilopleura **34:** 57
lucky charms **8:** 67; **9:** 79
Lumbriculida **21:** 94
Lumbricus terrestris **21:** *102, 104–105*
Lumiconger **33:** (91)
luminous crustaceans **28:** 29, 53
luminous insects **25:** (35), 36–37,
  43, (44)
lumpfish 39: 53, <u>82–83</u>
lumphead **40:** 68
lumpsucker **39:** 82, *82*, *83*
lungfish 31: 32, 33, <u>38–41</u>, 42, 45,
  (47), 80, 87; **33:** 63
  African **31:** 38, *38*, 40, 41, 46, 48
  Australian **31:** *32–33*, 38, *38*, 39, 40,
    41
  Ethiopian **31:** *39*, 40
  Queensland **31:** *32–33*
  South American **31:** 38, 39, 41, *41*,

  46, 48; **43:** 27
  spotted **31:** 40
lungs **11:** *13*, (13)
Luscinia
  calliope **18:** 44, (50)
  megarhynchos **18:** (27), 38, 44, (50)
  svecica **18:** 44, (50), (56)
Lutjanidae **39:** 109, **40:** <u>36–37</u>, 39
Lutjanus
  fuscescens **40:** 36
  kasmira **40:** 39
  maxweberi **40:** 36
  sebae **40:** *37*
Lutra
  lutra **1:** 32, <u>58–63</u>
  maculicollis **1:** 32
  sumatrana **1:** 32
Lutraria **30:** 70–71
  lutraria **30:** *71*
Lutrariidae **30:** 50
Lutreolina crassicaudata **10:** 14
Lutrogale perspicillata **1:** 32
Luxilus **34:** <u>68–71</u>
  cardinalis **34:** *70–71*
Lybius **19:** (58)
  bidentatus **19:** 56
Lycaena phlaeas **26:** 28
Lycaenidae **26:** <u>28–33</u>
Lycaeninae **26:** 29
Lycaon pictus **2:** 50, <u>78–79</u>
Lycidae **25:** <u>38–39</u>
Lycocorax pyrhopterus **19:** 106
Lyconodes argentus **36:** 37
Lycophidion **49:** 13
Lycosa **29:** 84
  narbonensis **29:** *82–83*
Lycosidae **29:** <u>82–85</u>
Lycus
  constrictus **25:** *11*
  vittatus **25:** 38–39
Lygaeidae **24:** <u>44–47</u>
Lygaeus kalmii **24:** 44
Lygocoris pabulinus **24:** *30–31*
Lygodactylus **45:** 10, (36)
Lygosoma travancorium **46:** (11)
Lygus rugulipennis **24:** 30
Lymantria
  dispar **26:** (101)
  monacha **26:** 98
Lymantriidae **26:** <u>98–101</u>
Lyme disease **29:** (32)
Lymnaea
  peregra **30:** 45
  stagnalis **30:** *44*
Lyncodon patagonicus **1:** 32
lynx 2: 10, 12, 38, <u>40–41</u>; **8:** *76–77*
  Canadian **2:** 40, 41
  Eurasian 2.40 **2:** 41
  Iberian **2:** 40, 41
Lyothyrella uva **21:** *70–71*
Lyramorpha **24:** *64–65*
lyrebird 11: <u>104–105</u>
  Albert's **11:** 104, *104*, 105
  superb 11: 104, *104*, <u>106–109</u>;

18: (41)
lyretail
red **38:** *78*
Lyriocephalus scutatus **44:** *13, 37,* (37)
Lyrognathus robustus **29:** *47*
Lysandra bellargus **26:** *29, 30*
Lysapsus **43:** 27
Lysiosquilla **28:** *41*
Lysmata **33:** (82), *82*
Lythrurus **34:** <u>68–71</u>
snelsoni **34:** 70

M

Mabuya **46:** 8, 9, 10, (11), 14
capensis **46:** <u>30–31</u>
carinata **46:** 14
maculilabris **46:** *11*
multifasciata **46:** 14
striata wahlbergi **46:** *12*
wrightii **46:** 14
Macaca
fuscata **4:** 40, <u>48–49</u>
nigra **4:** 40, <u>52–53</u>
silenus **4:** 40
sylvanus **4:** 40, <u>50–51</u>
macacos d'agua **31:** 92
macaque 4: *8,* 40, 42, 43, 66
Barbary 4: 40, 42, <u>50–51</u>
black 4: 40, <u>52–53</u>
Celebes (black) **4:** 40, <u>52–53</u>
Japanese 4: 40, 42, <u>48–49</u>
lion-tailed **4:** 40, *41*
Sulawesi crested (black) **4:** 40, <u>52–53</u>
macaw 19: (14)
blue-and-yellow **19:** 12
hyacinth **19:** 12, *12*
red-and-green **19:** 28
scarlet 16: 22; **19:** 12, <u>24–29</u>
Maccullochella
peelii peelii **40:** *13,* 14
Macgregoria pulchra **19:** 106
Machaerhamphus alcinus **15:** 8
Machimus atricapillus **23:** 62
Machtima crucigera **24:** *52–53*
mackerel 31: (47), **32:** 59, 83, **36:** 33,
49, **38:** 50, **39:** (10), **40:** 11,
<u>104–107</u>, 108
Atka **39:** 75
Atlantic **40:** *104,* 106, 107
double-lined **40:** 106

horse **40:** 34
Monterey Spanish **40:** 107
Okhostk Atka **39:** 74
Pacific **40:** *104–105*
shark **40:** 106
snake **35:** 101
Spanish **40:** 106
Macramphosidae **39:** 11
Macraspis lucida **25:** *80*
Macrelaps **49:** 106
Macrobrachium **28:** *62, 64*
macrocephaly **47:** 39
Macrocheira kaempferi **28:** 104
Macrochirichthys **34:** 19
Macroclemys
schmidti **47:** (50)
temminckii **47:** 30, <u>46–51</u>
Macrodasyoidea **21:** 69
Macrodipteryx longipennis **15:** 78,
<u>84–85</u>
Macrogalidia musschenbroekii **1:** 88
Macrognathus **33:** (106), 110
aculeatus **33:** *110*
siamensis **33:** *107*
Macronectes **12:** 31
giganteus **12:** 17, 28
halli **12:** 28
Macronyx **17:** 44
croceus **17:** 44
Macropanesthia rhinoceros **22:** *72*
Macropodidae **10:** 48, 50
Macropodus **40:** 61, 63
opercularis **40:** 61, *61,* 63
Macropoma **31:** 34
mantelli **31:** 35
Macroprotodon cucullatus **50:** 15
Macropus
fuliginosus **10:** (62)
giganteus **10:** 48, <u>60–63</u>
parryi **10:** 48
robustus **10:** 48
rufogriseus **10:** 48, <u>64–65</u>
rufus **10:** 48, <u>54–59</u>
Macroramphosus **39:** 50
gracilis **39:** 50
scolopax **39:** 51
Macrorhamphosodes platycheilus **39:** 98
Macroscelidea **1:** *10;* **9:** 58
Macroscelides proboscideus **9:** 59
Macroscincus coctei **46:** (67)
Macrosiphum
albifrons **24:** *14*
cholodkovskyi **24:** *103*
Macrostylus **9:** 86
Macrotema **33:** (106)
Macrotermes **22:** 67
Macrothylacia rubi **26:** *84–85*
Macrotis
lagotis **10:** 27, <u>44–45</u>
leucura **10:** 27
Macroumis berglax **36:** 28
Macrouridae **36:** <u>28–31</u>
Macrovipera schweizeri **50:** 79
Macrurocyttidae **39:** (25)

Macrurocyttus acanthopodus **39:** (25)
Macruronidae **36:** <u>32–37</u>
Macruronus **36:** 37
novaezelandiae **36:** *36–37*
Maculinea arion **26:** 28
Maculolachnus submacula **24:** *103*
Madagascar, carnivores in **1:** 90, 96–97
Madame X **32:** 35
Madoqua
kirkii **6:** 62
saltiana **6:** 62
madtom **37:** 10, 15, 16, 17, (19), 20, 21
Ozark **37:** *17*
Madtsoia bai **48:** (110)
maggots **23:** (110)
magnetic pull (navigation) **33:** (70)
magpie 14: (39)
Asiatic **18:** 90
Australian 18: 63; **20:** 93, 100,
<u>110–111</u>
black-billed **18:** 90, 104, (107)
Eurasian 18: 90, <u>104–107</u>
green **18:** 90
yellow-billed **18:** 90; **19:** 93
magpie-robin, Seychelles **18:** 44, 45
mahseer 34: *20,* <u>20–21</u>
Deccan **34:** 21
golden **34:** 8, 20, 21
high-backed **34:** 21
putitor **34:** 21
Thai **34:** *20–21,* 21
mail-cheeked fish 39: 11, <u>52–53</u>
maize **38:** 17
Makaira
indica **40:** 108
mazara **40:** (10), 110
nigricans **40:** (10), 108, *108*
Makalata armata **8:** 30
Malacochersus **47:** 80
tornieri **47:** 81
Malaconotus
blanchoti **15:** 104
cruentus **15:** 104
Malacoptila
panamensis **19:** 56
rufa **19:** 56
Malacoraja **33:** (27)
Malacosoma
californicum **26:** *86*
neustria **26:** *84, 86*
Malacosteus niger **35:** *84,* 89
Malacostraca **28:** 9, 34
malacostracans 28: <u>34–37</u>
Malapteruridae **37:** <u>60–63</u>
Malapterurus
cavalliensis **37:** 62
electricus **31:** (108), **37:** *60,* 61, 62,
62–63, 63
microstoma **31:** (108), **37:** *60–61,* 62
minjiriya **37:** 62
oguensis **37:** 62
malaria 21: <u>26–27</u>, **23:** (49); **43:** 18, 21
life cycles **21:** (27)
malaxation **27:** 70

Malaza empyreus **26:** *63*
male's milk **43:** 9
malimbe, Cassin's **16:** 100, (104)
Malimbus cassini **16:** 100
malkoha, red-faced **20:** 46
mallard 14: 52, 66–69
  banded **14:** 68
mallee fowl 11: 44, 48, 82–83
Mallotus villosus **35:** 26, *26–27*, *28*
Malpolon **49:** (14)
  monspessulanus **49:** 15, 61
Malpulutta **40:** 61
  kretseri **40:** 63
Malthopsis **36:** 70
Maluridae **18:** 60
Malurus
  amabilis **18:** 60
  cyaneus **18:** 60, 62–63
  cyanocephalus **18:** 60
  grayi **18:** 60
  lamberti **18:** 60
  pulcherrimus **18:** 60
  splendens **18:** 60
mamba 50: (8), 9, 12, 14, 16–19
  black **50:** 9, 14, 16, 17, *18–19*, 95
  eastern green **50:** 16, *16*, 19
  green **50:** 16, 17
  Jameson's **50:** 16
  Jameson's green **50:** 19
  meaning of name **50:** (17)
  western green **50:** 16, *16–17*, 19
mammalogy **21:** (33)
mammals 1: 8–17
  changing species **1:** 15–16
  diversity of **1:** (11), 14–15
  evolution **1:** *10*; **44:** *10*
  major groups **1:** 11
mammoth **5:** 8
Mammuthus **5:** 8
mamo **20:** 99
Manacus manacus **19:** 80
manakin 19: 80–83, (83), (91)
  blue **19:** 80
  blue-crowned **19:** 80
  golden-crowned **19:** 80
  golden-headed **19:** 80
  green **19:** 80
  long-tailed **19:** 80
  red-capped **19:** 80, *82–83*
  tiny tyrant **19:** 80
  white-bearded **19:** 80
  wing-barred **19:** 80
  wire-tailed **19:** 80
manatee 1: *10*; **3:** 46–47; **5:** (10), (12)
  Amazonian **3:** *47*
  Caribbean (West Indian) **3:** *46*, *47*, 48–51
  West African **3:** 47
  West Indian 3: *46*, *47*, 48–51
mandrill 4: 40, 42, 60–61
Mandrillus
  leucophaeus **4:** 40
  sphinx **4:** 40, 60–61
maneater **32:** 84

mangabey **4:** 40, 42, 43
  agile **4:** 40, 42
  black **4:** 40, 42
  gray-cheeked **4:** 40, *40*, 42
  white **4:** 40, 42
mangrove swamps **4:** 71
Manis
  gigantea **9:** 65
  temminckii **9:** 65
  tricuspis **9:** 65
mannikin **16:** 90
  bronze **17:** (109)
Mannophryne **43:** 68, 70
Manomera tenuescens **22:** *52–53*
Manorina **20:** 93
Manta **33:** (36)
  birostris **32:** 9, **33:** 12, 34, 50–51, 52
Mantella **42:** 58; **43:** 100, 101, 108–111
mantellas 42: 58; **43:** 101, 108–111
  arboreal **43:** 110
  Baron's **43:** 110
  beautiful **43:** *108–109*
  black-eared **43:** 110
  blue-legged **43:** 110
  brown **43:** 109
  Cowan's **43:** 110
  golden **43:** *109*, 110
  green **43:** 110
  green-backed **43:** 110
Mantellidae **42:** 10; **43:** 100, 101; **44:** 104
mantid flies **22:** 90, 92–95
Mantidactylus **43:** 100, 101, *110–111*, (111)
mantids 22: 74–79
Mantis religiosa **22:** *74*; **48:** (66)
mantis, praying (mantids) **22:** 9, 74–79
Mantispidae **22:** 92
mantling **15:** *20*
Mantodea **22:** 30, 74–79
Mantophasmatodea **22:** (79)
manucode
  curl-crested **19:** 106, 108
  trumpet **19:** 106, 108
Manucodia
  comrii **19:** 106
  keraudrenii **19:** 106
maomao
  pink **40:** 15
mara 8: 8, 30, 32–35
Maratecoara lacortei **38:** 80
Margaritiferidae **30:** 50
Margarops **18:** 36
Margulis, Lynn **21:** 10
Marine Stewardship Council **35:** (65)
marlin 38: 50, **39:** (10), **40:** 11, 108–111
  Atlantic blue **40:** (10), 108, *108*
  Atlantic white **40:** 110
  black **40:** 108, 109
  Indo-Pacific blue **40:** 10, 110
  striped **40:** (110), *111*
Marmosa
  mexicana **10:** 14

  murina **10:** 14
marmoset
  common 4: 86, 92–93
  dwarf **4:** 86
  Geoffroy's **4:** 86, *87*
  marmoset family 4: 86–87
  pygmy **4:** 86
  silvery **4:** 86
Marmosops
  dorothea **10:** 14
  fuscatus **10:** 14
marmot 7: *16*, 35, 36
  alpine (European) **7:** 34, 52–53
  European 7: 34, 52–53
Marmota **7:** 34
  marmota **7:** 34, 52–53
  monax **7:** 34, 50–51
Marpesia
  berania **26:** 15
  petreus **26:** *42–43*
Marphysa sanguinea **21:** 98
Marpissa muscosa **29:** *74–75*
marsupials 1: *10*; **10:** 8–13
  Australian carnivorous 10: 24–27
  other plant-eating 10: 74–77
marten 7: 36
  American 1: 48–49
  American pine (American) **1:** 48–49
  pine **1:** 32, *35*
  yellow-throated **1:** 32
Martes
  americana **1:** 48–49
  flavigula **1:** 32
  martes **1:** 32
  pennanti **1:** 50–51
martin **15:** 94–95
  African river **15:** 94
  crag **15:** 94
  fairy **15:** 94, *94–95*
  house **15:** 94, 95
  purple **15:** 94, 95
  sand *see* swallow, bank
  white-eyed river **15:** 94
Marukawichthys ambulator **39:** 80
massasauga 48: 17; **50:** 9, 54, 106–107
  desert **50:** 107
masseter muscles **7:** 16–17, 64; **8:** 12, *12*
Massoutiera mzabi **7:** 108
Mastacembelidae **33:** (106), 107, 110–111
Mastacembeliformes **33:** 106–107
Mastacembelus **33:** (106), 110
  armatus **33:** 110
  circumcinctus **33:** 110
  erythrotaenia **33:** *110–111*
  plagiostomus **33:** 110
Mastagias **21:** *43*
Masticophis **49:** 10
Mastigophora **21:** 13, 16–17
Mastigoproctus giganteus **29:** *28*
mastigures **44:** 32, 33, 37
Mastodonsaurus **41:** *13*

Masturus lanceolatus **39:** 111
matabueys (bushmasters) **50:** (8), 50, 54, 63, 65, <u>94–95</u>
Maticora **50:** 14, (25), (35)
  bivirgata **49:** 16; **50:** 9, <u>20–21</u>
  intestinalis **49:** 16; **50:** 20
mating
  with incubating females **14:** 69
  see also courtship
Matsubarichthys inusitatus **39:** 69, (70)
Maurolicus muelleri **35:** 90
Maxillopoda **28:** 9
mayflies 22: <u>38–41</u>
  dark olive **22:** *39*
  green drake **22:** *39, 41*
Mazama americana **6:** 10
meadowlark **17:** 44; **18:** 74, 75
  eastern **18:** 74
mealybugs 24: <u>112–113</u>
  long-tailed **24:** *112*
meat trade *see* bushmeat trade
Mechanitis lysimnia **26:** *56*
meconium **27:** 172
Mecoptera **22:** 30, <u>104–109</u>
Mecopus torquis **25:** *107*
medaka **34:** 61, **38:** 50, 64, 65, (68), 69, *69*
  Celebes **38:** (68)
  dwarf **38:** (68)
  golden **38:** 65
  Japanese **38:** *64*, 65, 66, (68)
  marmorated **38:** (68)
  matano **38:** (68)
  yellow-finned **38:** (68)
medical applications, cantharidin
  25: (63)
medical research **4:** 13, 32, 63, 78, 93; **7:** 15, (75); **8:** (41); **9:** 77, 97
  see also laboratory animals; surgery
medicine **6:** 51; **7:** (31); **46:** (85), 99
  body parts for **2:** 21, 33, (97), 100; **6:** 107; **7:** 63; **8:** 41; **9:** 91
  Chinese **5:** 37
meerkat 1: 19, 98, 99, <u>100–105</u>
  gray (meerkat) **1:** 19, 98, 99, <u>100–105</u>
  slender-tailed (meerkat) **1:** 19, 98, 99, <u>100–105</u>
Megaceryle alcyon **14:** 100, <u>104–107</u>
Megachasma pelagios **32:** 20, <u>76–77</u>, 93
Megachasmidae **32:** (12), (74)
Megachile
  centuncularis **27:** *84–85*
  willughbiella **27:** *86, 87*
Megachilidae **27:** <u>84–91</u>
Megachiroptera **9:** 80, 86
Megaderma lyra **9:** <u>98–99</u>
Megadermatidae **9:** 87, 98
Megadyptes antipodes **12:** 8
Megaelosia **42:** 78
Megalaima
  asiatica **19:** 56
  rafflesii **19:** 56
  virens **19:** 56
Megalamphaidae **39:** 13

Megalamphodus megalopterus **38:** *41*
Megalania **46:** (83)
Megalechis **37:** 103
Megalodoras irwini **37:** (78)
Megalomycteridae **39:** 15
Megalopidae **33:** (62), **36:** 86
Megalops atlanticus **33:** <u>98–99</u>
Megaloptera **22:** 30, <u>98–99</u>
Megalopygidae **26:** 108
megamouth *see* shark
Megapodiidae **11:** 44, 48–49
Megapodius freycinet **11:** 44
Megaptera novaeangliae **3:** 55, <u>102–105</u>
Megascolides australis **21:** (105)
Megasoma elephas **25:** *88–89*
Megatherium **9:** *64*
Megathura crenulata **30:** *24*
Megistolotis lignarius **42:** 94
Megophryidae **42:** 9, 10, 34, 38, 40
Megophrys **42:** 34, 35, 38, (38)
  nasuta **42:** 34, <u>36–39</u>, (89); **43:** 86
Mehelya **49:** 13, 61; **50:** (35), 62
Meiacanthus nigrolineatus **40:** 91, *91*
meiolaniids **47:** 83
Melaeornis **17:** 66
  fischeri **17:** 66
  mariquensis **17:** 66
  microrhynchus **17:** 66
  pallidus **17:** 66
Melamphaes
  danae **39:** 13
  simus **39:** *13*
Melamphaidae **39:** <u>12–15</u>
melamphid
  highsnout **39:** 13
Melamprosops phaeosoma **20:** 98
Melanargia galathea **26:** *47*
Melanerpes uropygialis **18:** 8
melanin **14:** (50); **17:** (38)
melanism **17:** (38); **49:** (29), 47, 89; **50:** (53), (63), 82
  acquired **47:** (71)
Melanitta
  fusca **12:** 66; **14:** 52
  nigra **12:** 66
  perspicillata **12:** 66
Melanobatrachinae **42:** 104
Melanocetidae **36:** <u>74–83</u>
Melanocetus **36:** 80, 82
  johnsonii **36:** *74*
Melanochlora sultanea **17:** 70
Melanocorypha
  calandra **18:** 22
  yeltoniensis **18:** 22
Melanogrammus **36:** (40)
  aeglefinus **36:** 38, 39, *42–43*, 51
Melanonidae **36:** <u>52–53</u>
Melanonus
  gracilis **36:** 52
  zugmayeri **36:** 52
Melanophidium **48:** 28
melanophores **48:** (37)
Melanophryniscus **42:** 56, 57
  stelzneri **42:** *57*

Melanoptila glabrirostris **18:** 36
Melanosuchus niger **47:** <u>106–107</u>
Melanotaenia **38:** 54, (56), 57
  boesemani **38:** (56)
  goldiei **38:** *54*
  nigrans **38:** *55*
  splendida inornata **38:** 57
Melanotaeniidae **38:** 50, 52, <u>54–59</u>
Melanotis
  caerulescens **18:** 36
  hypoleucus **18:** 36
Melaphaes lugubris **39:** 13
Meleagrididae **11:** 44, 49
Meleagris gallopavo **11:** 44, <u>76–81</u>
Meles meles **1:** 32, <u>78–81</u>
Melichineutes robustus **17:** 20
Melichthys niger **39:** 103
Melignomon zenkeri **17:** 20
Meliphaga
  macleayana **20:** 88
  virescens **20:** 88
Meliphagidae **20:** 88
Meliponinae **27:** 108
Melithreptus validirostris **20:** 88
Melittidae **27:** 90–91
Mellisuga helenae **11:** (9); **16:** 44
Mellivora capensis **1:** 32, <u>82–83</u>
Meloe proscarabaeus **25:** *62*
Melogale personata **1:** 32
Meloidae **25:** <u>62–67</u>
Melolontha melolontha **22:** *35*; **25:** *11, 83*
Melopsittacus undulatus **16:** 22, <u>26–31</u>, (35)
Melursus ursinus **2:** 82
Membracidae **24:** <u>90–95</u>
Membracis foliata **24:** *15*
Membranipora **21:** <u>72–73</u>
menarana **49:** 15
Mene maculata **40:** 35
menhaden **36:** 98, 102
Menidae **40:** <u>34–35</u>
Menotyphla **9:** 10, 58
Menura
  alberti **11:** 104
  novaehollandiae **11:** 104, <u>106–109</u>; **18:** (41)
Menuridae **11:** 104
Mephitidae **1:** 32, 84
Mephitis
  macroura **1:** 32
  mephitis **1:** 32, <u>84–87</u>
Mercenaria mercenaria **30:** *68*
merganser **12:** 66, 68; **14:** 54, 55
  Brazilian **14:** 55
  red-breasted **12:** 66, *66*, 69
Mergini **12:** 66
Mergus **14:** 54
  octosetaceus **14:** 55
  serrator **12:** 66
Meriones unguiculatus **7:** <u>88–89</u>
Merlangius merlangius **36:** *46–47*
merlin **15:** 8, 9; **18:** 59
Merlucciidae **36:** <u>32–37</u>

Merluccius
   albidus **36:** (35)
   angustimanus **36:** (35)
   australis **36:** (35)
   capensis **36:** 34, (35), (36)
   gayi **36:** 34, (35)
   merluccius **36:** *32, 33,* 34, (35)
   productus **36:** (35)
mermaid fish **32:** 105
mermaids **3:** 53
mermaid's purse **33:** *27, 30*
Meroles **45:** 58, 74–75
   anchietae **45:** 60, *74–75*
   cuneirostris **45:** *74*
Meropidae **17:** 8
Meropogon forsteni **17:** 8
Merops
   albicollis **17:** 8
   apiaster **17:** 8, 10–13
   bullockoides **17:** 8
   hirundineus **17:** 8
   nubicus **11:** *84;* **17:** 8
   pusillus **17:** 8
Merostomata **29:** 8, 10–11
merry widow **38:** 96
Mertensiella **41:** 88, 92, (103); **43:** 45
   caucasica **41:** *92–93*
Mertensophryne **42:** 56
   micranotis **42:** (60)
Mesaspis **46:** 52
Mesechinus
   dauricus **9:** 12
   hughi **9:** 12
Mesembrina meridiana **23:** *100–101*
mesites **14:** 82
Mesocapromys auritus **8:** 30
Mesocricetus auratus **7:** 86–87
Mesogastropoda **30:** 18, 26–31
Mesomys hispidus **8:** 30
mesonychids **3:** 56
mesopredators **36:** (34)
Mesozoa **21:** 32, 34, 35
Messelobunodon **1:** *8*
Messor **27:** *40–41*
Meta segmentata **29:** *105*
metabolic endothermy **48:** 102
Metachirus nudicaudatus **10:** 14
metalmarks 26: 34–37
   blue doctor **26:** *35*
Metaphrynella **42:** 104
   pollicaris **42:** (111)
Metasyrphus luniger **23:** *80–81*
Metatheria **10:** (10)
metazoans **21:** 30–31
Metellina segmentata **29:** *105*
methyl palmitate **27:** 67
Metriaclima lombardoi **40:** *69*
Metridium senile **21:** *56*
Metynnis argenteus **38:** 45
metynnis
   redhook **38:** 45
miacid **1:** *9*
Miacoidea **1:** 88, 98
Miagrammopes **29:** 57

mice *see* mouse
Mico
   argentata **4:** 86
   humilis **4:** 86
Micoureus
   alstoni **10:** 14
   constantiae **10:** 14
Micralestes
   acutidens **34:** 72
   occidentalis **38:** 31
   stormsi **38:** 31
Micrastur ruficollis **15:** 8
Micrathena sagittata **29:** *109*
Micrathene whitneyi **15:** 50
Micrelaps **49:** 106
   bicoloratus **50:** (21)
Micrixalus **43:** 100
Microbatrachella **43:** 82
   capensis **43:** 87
Microcaecilia **41:** 21
   albiceps **41:** 21
Microcavia australis **8:** 30
Microcebus
   coquereli see Mirza coquereli
   murinus **4:** 96
   myoxinus **4:** 96
   rufus **4:** 96
Microcerberidea **28:** 34
Microchera albocoronata **16:** 44
Microchiroptera **9:** 80, 86
Microctenopoma **40:** 58, 59
   fasciolatum **40:** 59
Microgadus tomcod **36:** 39, (51)
Microgale
   melanorrachis **9:** 24
   parvula **9:** 24
Microglanis **37:** 88, 89
   iheringi **37:** *88–89*
   poecilus **37:** 88
Microhierax fringillarius **15:** 8
Microhylidae **42:** 10, 95, 104, 105,
   (108), 109, (111); **43:** (17)
Microhylinae **42:** 104
Microlophus **44:** 80, 81, 110–111
   albemarlensis **44:** 111
   delanonis **44:** *111*
   grayi **44:** *110*
Micromesistius **36:** 33
Micromischodus sugillatus **38:** 16
Micrommata virescens **29:** 66
Microperoryctes
   longicauda **10:** 27
   murina **10:** 27
Micropeza corriziolata **23:** *84*
Micropezidae **23:** 84–85
Micropotamogale
   lamottei **9:** 24
   ruwenzorii **9:** 24
Micropsitta meeki **16:** 22
Micropterus **40:** 26
   dolomieu **31:** 79
   salmoides **34:** 97, **40:** 26, *28–29*
Microsaura **44:** 62
microscopes **21:** (12)

Microspora **21:** 13
Microstigmus comes **27:** *77*
Microstomatidae **35:** *8–9*
Microstomus
   kitt **39:** 89
   pacificus **39:** 89, 92
Microstylum **23:** *64–65*
Microsynodontis **37:** 71
microteiids **44:** (26)
Microtus agrestis **7:** 92–93
Micruroides **49:** 62
   euryxanthus **49:** 25; **50:** 12, 22, *22,*
    25, (25)
Micrurus **41:** 21; **48:** 34; **49:** 62; **50:** 9,
   12, 12–13, 22–27
Mictacea **28:** 34, 37
Mictyris longicarpus **28:** *109*
midges
   biting **23:** (52)
   nonbiting 23: 50–53
   seashore **23:** 50–51
midshipman **36:** 54, 55, 57, (57), 59
   plainfin **36:** (56), *57*
migration **3:** 82, 85, 87, 93–94, 103,
   (105), 109; **5:** 18, 109; **6:** 17, 23, 37,
   84–85, 96, 101; **7:** 91; **9:** (83), 102,
   (103), 106–107; **11:** 15; **12:** (30),
   (87), **14:** 54–55; **15:** (98), (103); **16:**
   (54); **19:** (14); **20:** (13); **35:** 39, 40,
   36: 34, 36, 55, 106
   eels **33:** 71, (72), 73, 88, 89, (93)
   fat buildup for **13:** (32)
   lampreys **31:** 30, 31
   monarch butterflies **26:** (61)
   noctuids **26:** 94
   of irruptive species **16:** (84); **18:** (34)
   salmon **35:** 52, 53, 54, 59, 63
   seesaw **15:** 92–93
   skippers **26:** 63–64
   sturgeons **31:** 54, 58, 62, 65
   trout **35:** 69
Mikrogeophagus ramirezi **40:** *74–75*
Milesia crabroniformis **23:** *76*
Milichiidae **23:** (106)
milksnake 44: *14;* **49:** 52–57; **50:** 26,
   88
   black **49:** 57
   eastern **49:** (53), 55, 56, *56–57*
   Ecuadorian **49:** (53)
   Honduran **49:** 57
   Mexican **49:** 57
   Nelson's **50:** *24*
   Pueblan **49:** *55,* 57
   Sinaloan **48:** *9;* **49:** (53), 57
Milleporina **21:** 43
miller's thumb **39:** 76, *77,* (79)
millions fish **38:** 98
millipedes 22: *14–15,* 16–21
   breeding **22:** 18–20
   cylindrical **22:** *17*
   defense **22:** (21)
   flat-backed **22:** *17,* 21
   giant **22:** *16, 18–19, 19*
   pill **22:** *20–21*

sound production **22:** 18
walking movement **22:** (17)
milu *see* deer, Père David's
Milvus
  migrans **15:** 8; **17:** (13); **20:** 23
  milvus **15:** 8
Milyeringa veritas **40:** 97
Mimagoniates microlepis **38:** 35
Mimallonidae **26:** (86)
mimicry **22:** 34; **50:** 20–21, *24,*
  25–26, (25)
  Batesian **41:** 86; **42:** 82; **43:** (73), 110;
    44: 12; **48:** 35; **50:** 21, (23), 26
  by birds **11:** 104, 109; **18:** 39–40, (41),
    89, (99); **20:** (91)
  by bugs **24:** 31, 37, *40–41, 56,*
    86–87, 95
  by butterflies **22:** 34; **26:** 19–21, 44
  by cockroaches **22:** *68*
  color **50:** 24
  egg-eating snakes **49:** 33–34
  by flies **23:** 79–80, 84, 88
  by frogs/toads **42:** (38), 56–57; **43:**
    (73)
  of fruits and flowers by vipers **50:** 91
  by insects **22:** 33–34
  by long-horned beetles **25:** 95
  by lizards **44:** 30; **45:** (51), 60, 62–63
  by mantid flies **22:** *93*
  by mantids **22:** *79*
  by moths **26:** 80–82
  Müllerian **22:** 34; **41:** 86; **43:** (73),
    110; **50:** 21, 25–26
  by octopuses **30:** *87*
  by salamanders **41:** 72–73, 91
  by zebra flatworms **21:** *81*
Mimidae **18:** 36
Mimodes graysoni **18:** 36
Mimophis mahfalensis **49:** 13
Mimus
  gilvus **18:** 36
  gundlachii **18:** 36, 38
  polyglottos **18:** 36, 38–41
  saturninus **18:** 36
miner **20:** 83, 93
  common **20:** 80
miner's cat *see* raccoon, ringtail
mink 1: 35
  American 1: 32, 35, *35*, 52–55, 62;
    7: 99; **9:** 53
  European **1:** 54, (55)
minnow 34: 10, 16, 16–19, 72–79, 80,
  35: 32, **40:** (96)
  Amur **34:** 73
  Bankok **34:** 72
  black Persian **38:** 89
  black-stripe **35:** 33
  bluntnose **34:** 75, (79)
  bullhead **34:** (79)
  Chinese **34:** 73
  coppernose **34:** *64–65*
  Corfu **38:** (88)
  elongate poso **38:** 65
  Eurasian **34:** 73, 74, (75)

European **34:** 72, *72*, 73
fathead **34:** 68, (71), *75*, (79)
lake **34:** 74
oriental white **34:** 19
poso **38:** 65, *66–67*
Sarasin's **38:** 65, 67
sheepshead **34:** 72, **38:** 87
silver **34:** 72
slim **34:** (79)
Spanish **38:** (88)
spotted *see* inanga
swamp **34:** 74
trout **35:** 36
Valencia **38:** (88)
White Cloud Mountain **34:** 62,
  62–63, (65), 72
minor invertebrate groups 21: 68–69
Minous **39:** 66
  monodactylus **39:** 66
Minytrema melanops **34:** *96–97,* 99
Miopithecus talapoin **4:** 40
Mirafra
  africana **18:** 22
  assamica **18:** 22
  hypermetra **18:** 22
  javanica **18:** 22
Mirapinna esau **39:** 15
Mirapinnidae **39:** 15
Miridae **24:** 30–33
Miris striatus **24:** *31*
Mirounga
  angustirostris **3:** 9, 32–35
  leonina **3:** 32
Mirperus jaculus **24:** *56–57*
mirrorbelly **35:** 24, *24,* 25
Mirza coquereli **4:** 96
Mischocyttarus immarginatus **27:** *67*
Misgurnus **34:** 14, 100, 102, 106
  anguillicaudatus **34:** 107
  fossilis **34:** 106–107
  mizolepis **34:** 107
Misophrioida **28:** 9
Mistichthys luzonensis **40:** 94
Misumena vatia **29:** *68, 72–73*
mites 29: 30–33
  animal hosts **29:** 33
  diseases **29:** (32)
  house-dust **29:** *30–31,* (32)
  scabies **29:**
  size **29:** 32
  velvet **29:** *31*
Mitsukurina owstoni **32:** 10, 90–91
Mitsukurinidae **32:** (12), (74)
Mitu
  tomentosa **11:** 44
  tuberosa **11:** 44
Mixophytes **42:** 92, (97)
Mnemiopsis
  leidyi **36:** 95
  mccradyi **21:** *42*
Mniotilta varia **17:** 88, (91)
moa, giant **11:** (9)
mobbing **15:** (67); **17:** 24
Mobula **33:** (36), 52

japonica **31:** *21*, **33:** 52–53
mobula
  spinetail **33:** 52
Mobulidae **33:** (9), 10, 36
mochokid **37:** 73
Mochokidae **31:** (108), **37:** 8, 11, 70–75
Mochokiella **37:** 71
  paynei **37:** 71
Mochokus **37:** 71
mockingbird 18: 36–37
  Bahama **18:** 36, 38
  blue **18:** 36, *37*
  blue-and-white **18:** 36, *37*
  chalk-browed **18:** 36
  Galápagos **18:** 36, *36*
  northern 18: 36, 38–41
  Socorro **18:** 36, 37
  tropical **18:** 36
Moducia typicalis **28:** 12
Mogurnda mogurnda **40:** 98
Moho braccatus **20:** 90
mojarra **40:** 36, 37
  flagfin **40:** 37
  striped **40:** 37
mola 39: 11, 96, 110–111
Mola mola **39:** 110, *110, 111*
moldewarp *see* mole, European
mole 1: *10*; **9:** 9, (10), 11
  coast **9:** 40, *41*
  desert (Grant's) golden **9:** 56–57
  European 9: 40, 42, 44–47
  giant golden **9:** 40
  golden **5:** (10); **9:** 9, 10–11, *11*,
    40, 41, 42, (42)
  golden mole family 9: 40–43
  Grant's desert golden **9:** 40
  Grant's golden 9: 56–57
  hairy-tailed **9:** 40, *42*
  Japanese **9:** 54
  Juliana's golden **9:** 40, *43*
  marsupial 10: (10), 26, 27, 42–43
  mole family 9: 40–43
  northern marsupial **10:** 43
  northwestern marsupial **10:** 27
  Persian **9:** 40, 43
  small-toothed **9:** 40, 43
  star-nosed 9: 40, 42, 48–51
  see also shrew mole
mole rat 7: 15, 18, 65; **8:** 9
  African **7:** *12*; **8:** 56
  Balkan blind (lesser blind) **7:** 100–101
  blind **7:** 12–13, 15, 18; **8:** 57
  Cape **7:** *10*; **8:** 56
  Cape dune **8:** 56
  common **8:** 56, 57
  Damara **8:** 56, *57*
  dune **8:** 57
  Ehrenberg's **7:** *18*
  giant **8:** 57
  giant Angolan **8:** 56, 57
  lesser blind 7: 100–101
  Mechow's **8:** 56, 57
  mole rat family 8: 56–57
  naked 1: (11), 14; **7:** 13; **8:** 10,

56, 57, 58–59
Namaqua dune **8:** 56
silvery **7:** 9; **8:** 56
southern dune **8:** 56
molehills **9:** 43
Molidae **39:** 11, 96, 110–111
Mollusca **21:** 32
mollusks 3: 25, *25*; **30:** 8–11
anatomy **30:** 8
shell **30:** 9, (10)
molly **38:** 96, 100, 101
black **38:** *102–103*
sailfin **38:** *100*, 101, 102
sphenops **38:** 101, 102
Yucatán **38:** 101
Moloch **44:** 32
horridus **44:** 15, 29, 34, 48–49
Molossidae **9:** 87
Molothrus **17:** 93, 103, 105
ater **16:** 71; **18:** 74, 79
bonariensis **18:** 74; **20:** 86
molting **11:** 11
delayed **12:** (89)
wing feathers **14:** 19, 53, 59
Molva **36:** 39
molva **36:** *48–49*
Momotidae **19:** 42
Momotus
aequatorialis **19:** 42
mexicanus **19:** 42
momota **19:** 42, 44–45
Monacanthidae **39:** 11, 96, 100–105,
(102)
Monachus schauinslandi **3:** 9, 30–31
monarch, black **17:** 66
Monarcha axillaris **17:** 66
Monarchidae **17:** 66, 106
Monasa **19:** 57
morphoeus **19:** 56
mongoose
Alexander's **1:** 98
Angolan **1:** 98
banded 1: *18–19*, 98, 103–104,
110–111
broad-striped **1:** 98
brown **1:** 98
bushy-tailed **1:** 98, *99*
common Bengal (Indian gray)
1: 108–109
common gray (Indian gray)
1: 108–109
common Indian (Indian gray)
1: 108–109
dwarf 1: 98, 99, *99*, 106–107, 111
Egyptian **1:** 98, *99*
Gambian **1:** 98
giant-striped **1:** 98
Indian (Indian gray) **1:** 108–109
Indian gray 1: 108–109
Jackson's **1:** 98
Liberian **1:** 98
long-nosed **1:** 98
Madagascan **1:** 98
marsh **1:** 98, *99*

Meller's **1:** 98
mongoose family 1: 98–99
narrow-striped **1:** 98, *99*
Pousargues' **1:** 98
ringtailed **1:** 98, *99*
Selous' **1:** 98, *99*
slender **1:** 98
white-tailed **1:** 98, *99*
yellow **1:** 98, 101
monito del monte **10:** 11, 16, (16)
monitor lizards 44: 25, 29; **45:** (95);
46: 54, 82–85; **50:** 70
Bengal 46: 88–91; **50:** 31
body form **46:** 83–84
Borneo earless 46: 72, 100–101
crocodile tree **46:** *84*, (84), 85, (85),
94
defense **46:** 84–85
desert **46:** 39, 83
Dumeril's **46:** (84)
feeding **46:** 84, (84)
goannas **46:** 82
Gould's (sand) **46:** 82, 92–93
Gray's **46:** (84)
green tree **46:** 82
habitats **46:** 82–83
Indian 46: 88–91
King's rock **46:** 82
Komodo dragon 46: 82, 94–97
lace **46:** (85)
mangrove **46:** 82, (85)
Merten's water **46:** 82
Nile 46: 83, (83), (85), 98–99
Perentie **46:** 84
pygmy **46:** 82
pygmy stripe-tailed **46:** (84)
"racehorse goanna" (sand) **46:** 82,
92–93
reproduction **46:** 85
ridge-tailed 46: 86–87
Salvadori's **44:** 24
sand 46: 82, 92–93
savanna **46:** *82–83*
senses **46:** 84
short-tailed **46:** 82, 85
spiny-tailed (ridge-tailed) **46:** 86–87
water **46:** 82, 83, (85), *89*, (89), (90)
white-throated **46:** 82, 83, (84), *85*
monkey
Allen's swamp **4:** 40, *41*
black-handed spider 4: 72, 76–77
Bolivian squirrel **4:** 72
brown howler 4: 72, 74–75
Central American spider (black-
handed spider) **4:** 72, 76–77
cheek-pouch **4:** 40, 42
cloaked *see* colugo
common squirrel **4:** 72, 78
common woolly (Humboldt's woolly)
4: 72, 82–83
De Brazza's **4:** 40, *42–43*
dusky-leaf **4:** 40
golden leaf **4:** 40
golden snub-nosed **4:** 40

green (vervet) **4:** 40, 42, 44–47
grivet (vervet) **4:** 40, 42, 44–47
guenon (vervet) **4:** 40, 42, 44–47
Hanuman langur **6:** *13*
howler **4:** 10, 72, 83
Humboldt's woolly 4: 72, 82–83
leaf **4:** 40, 40–42
leapers **4:** 72
long-haired spider **4:** 72
mantled howler **4:** 72
mustached **4:** 40, *41*
New World monkey family
4: 72–73
night (northern night) **4:** 72, *73*,
84–85
northern (northern night) **4:** 72, *73*,
84–85
northern night 4: 72, *73*, 84–85
Old World monkey family 4: 40–43,
72
owl (northern night) **4:** 72, *73*, 84–85
patas **4:** 40, *41*, 42, 43
proboscis 4: 40, 41, 70–71
red howler **4:** 72
rhesus **4:** 42
savanna (vervet) **4:** 40, 42, 44–47
snow *see* macaque, Japanese
southern night **4:** 72
spider **4:** 8, 72, 75
squirrel 4: 72, 78–79
swingers **4:** 72
thumbless **4:** 40
vervet 4: 40, 42, 44–47
woolly **4:** 72
yellow-tailed woolly **4:** 72
monkfish **32:** 106, 107, **36:** 13, 60, 63
mono 40: 42–43
African **40:** 42
silver **40:** 42, *42*
Monocentridae **39:** 9, 16–21
Monocentris
japonica **39:** *17–18*
reedi **39:** 20
Monocirrhus polyacanthus **40:** 56, *56*
Monodactylidae **40:** 42–43
Monodactylus
argenteus **40:** *42*
falciformis **40:** 42
kottelati **40:** 42
sebae **40:** 42
Monodelphis
domestica **10:** 14
kunsi **10:** 14
Monodon monoceros **3:** 55, 84–85
Monogenea **21:** 77, 81, 82
Monognathidae **33:** (62), 94–95
Monogononta **21:** 69
Monopeltis **46:** 102, 105
capensis **46:** 104, 105
Monoplacophora **30:** 9, 12–13
Monopterus **33:** (106)
albus **33:** 108–109
indicus **33:** 106
Monotremata **1:** *10*; **10:** 104

monotremes, spiny **8:** 12
Monstrilioida **28:** 9
Montatheris hindii **50:** 58
Montifringilla nivalis **16:** 100
moon fish **38:** 12, *12–13*, 13, 14
mooneye **31:** 82, 84, (84)
moonfish **40:** 34, 35, 42
moonrat 9: 9, 11, 12, 13
    Dinagat **9:** 12
    greater 9: 12, 22–23
    lesser **9:** 12
    Mindanao **9:** 12, *13*
moor **34:** 49
    black **34:** *48*
moorhen
    common 14: 82, 92–95
    San Christobal **14:** (94)
    Tristan **14:** (94)
moose 6: 10, 12, 14–19, 21–22
    Alaskan **6:** 14–15, *17*
    disease **6:** 18
    eastern **6:** 15
    northwestern **6:** 15
    shiras **6:** 15
mora **36:** 52
Morelia **48:** 82
    amethistina **48:** 88–89
    bredli **48:** 90
    clastolepis **48:** 88
    kinghorni **48:** 88
    nauta **48:** 88
    oenpelliensis **48:** 79
    spilota **48:** 80, 82, 86, 90–93, 103;
      49: 55
    tracyae **48:** 88
    viridis **44:** *8–9*; **48:** (58), 82, 94–97;
      50: 91
morid cod **36:** 52
Moridae **36:** 52–53
Moringua **33:** 74
    edwardsii **33:** 74, *74*, 74–75, *75*
Moringuidae **33:** (62), 74–75
Mormoopidae **9:** 87
mormyrid **31:** (109)
    African **33:** 101
Mormyridae **31:** (43), (82), 85, 106–109,
    33: 101, **37:** 60
Morone saxatilis **37:** 18, **40:** 14
Moronidae **39:** (10), **40:** 12–19
Morphidae **26:** 50–51
Morpho
    menelaus **26:** *50, 51*
    peleides **26:** *50–51*
morphos 26: 50–51
morrillo **8:** 51
Morus
    bassanus **12:** 44, 54–57, (94)
    capensis **12:** 44
    serrator **12:** 44
Moschidae **6:** 10
Moschiola meminna **6:** 10
Moschus
    berezovskii **6:** 10
    chrysogaster **6:** 10, 50–51

fuscus **6:** 10
moschiferus **6:** 10
mosquito fish **38:** 100, (101)
    eastern **38:** (101)
    Gambusian **38:** (101)
    western **38:** (101)
mosquitoes 6: (22); **21:** (27), 91;
    23: 46–49
    blood feeding **23:** 48, (49)
    disease and **23:** (49)
    egg-laying **23:** 46–48
    feeding **23:** 48, 49
    head **23:** *37*
    ring-legged **23:** *46, 47, 49*
moss animals 21: 72–73
Motacilla
    alba **17:** 44, 46–49; **20:** (48)
    alba alba **17:** 46
    alba yarrelli **17:** 46
    capensis **17:** 44
    cinerea **17:** 44
    clara **17:** 44
    flava **17:** 44
    flaviventris **17:** 44
Motacillidae **17:** 44
moths 26: 8–15
    ailanthus webworm **26:** *112*
    anatomy **26:** *10*, 11–12
    angle-shades **22:** *32–33*
    atlas **26:** *70*
    bagworm 26: 110–111
    black arches **26:** *98*
    black-waved flannel **26:** *108*
    borer (clearwinged) **26:** 104–105
    brown house **26:** *111*
    carpenter **26:** (105)
    Chinese oak silk **26:** 8–9
    clearwinged 26: *104–105*
    eggar (tent caterpillar) **26:** 84–87
    eggs **26:** 12–13, (13)
    emperor (giant silkworm) **26:** 70–73
    ermine 26: 112–113
    European fox **26:** 84–85
    European silver Y **26:** 95
    fairy **26:** *112–113*, (113)
    flannel **26:** 108
    flower **26:** *94*
    garden tiger (great tiger) **26:** *88, 90*
    geometer (measuringworm)
      26: 74–77
    giant agrippa **26:** *93*
    giant saturniid **22:** *11*
    giant silkworm 26: 70–73
    great tiger **26:** 88
    gypsy **26:** (101)
    hawk (sphinx) **26:** 66–69
    hieroglyphic **26:** *94–95*
    hornet **26:** *104*
    inchworm (measuringworm)
      26: 74–77
    lackey **26:** *84*
    lappet (tent caterpillar) **26:** 84–87
    looper (measuringworm) **26:** 74–77
    luna **26:** *71*

Madagascan hawk **26:** *66*
magpie **26:** *14*
measuringworm 26: 74–77
micro **26:** 111
oak beauty **26:** *74*
owlet 26: 92–97
pepper **26:** (75)
plume 26: 102–103
poplar kitten **26:** *80*
processionary **26:** (83)
puddling **26:** (15)
pupae **26:** 14–15
royal (giant silkworm) **26:** 70–73
sack-bearers **26:** (86)
silkworm 26: 78–79
slug-caterpillar 26: 106–109
smoky **26:** 108–109
sphinx 26: 66–69; **27:** *30*
sweetheart underwing **26:** *92*
tent caterpillar 26: 84–87
tiger 26: 88–91
tussock 26: 98–101
white plume **26:** *102, 102–103*
yucca **26:** (113)
see also caterpillars
motmot **19:** *42–43*, 48
    blue-crowned 19: 42, 44–45
    blue-throated **19:** 42
    broad-billed **19:** 42, *43*
    highland **19:** 42
    keel-billed **19:** 42
    rufous **19:** 42
    rufous-capped **19:** 42
    russet-crowned **19:** 42
    tody **19:** 42
    turquoise-browed **19:** 42
mouflon **6:** 62, 63
mouse 7: *10*, 12
    African climbing **7:** 64
    birch **7:** 17
    coarse-haired pocket (desert-pocket)
      7: 22–23
    Costa Rican harvest **7:** 80
    Cozumel Island harvest **7:** 80
    deer 7: *64*, 82–83
    desert **7:** *65*
    desert pocket 7: 22–23
    field (wood) **7:** 13, 78–79
    hairy harvest **7:** 80
    harvest **7:** 64
    house 7: 13, 14–15, 65–66, 68–71
    jumping **7:** 17, 19
    kangaroo **7:** 17
    long-clawed marsupial **10:** 27
    long-tailed field (wood) **7:** 13, 78–79
    marsupial **10:** (25), 27, 40
    meadow jumping **7:** *16*
    mole **7:** 65
    mouse family 7: 64–67
    New World **7:** 14, *64*, 65
    Nicaraguan harvest **7:** 80
    Old World **7:** 14, 65, *65*
    pencil-tailed tree **7:** *65*
    pig mouse **8:** 38

plains **7:** *65*
pocket **7:** *12*, 18
pygmy **7:** *64*
shaker **7:** (69)
singing **7:** (69)
spiny **7:** *65*; **8:** 11, 12
three-striped marsupial **10:** *25*, 27
waltzing **7:** (69)
western harvest 7: 80–81
West Indian key **8:** 11
white-footed (deer) **7:** *64*, 82–83
wood 7: 13, 78–79
mousebird 18: (18)
blue-naped **20:** 68, *68*, 72
mousebird family 16: (18);
20: 68–69
red-backed **20:** 68
red-faced **20:** 68, *68*
speckled 20: 68, 70–73
white-backed **20:** 68
white-headed **20:** 68, *69*
mouse-hare *see* pika
mouselike rodents 7: 16–19
mouthbrooders **40:** (77)
Javan **40:** 62
Mozambique **40:** 77
peacock **40:** 61
mouths **39:** (15)
swallower eel **33:** 94, *95*
Moxostoma **34:** 99
lacerum **34:** 99
mud devils (hellbenders) **41:** (12), 14,
30, 32–35
muddler **39:** 80
mudfish **35:** 33, **38:** 84
brown **35:** 36
Northland **35:** 36
Tasmanian **35:** 33, 36
mudminnow 35: 8, 20–21
central **35:** 21
eastern **35:** 21
European **35:** 21
Olympic **35:** 20
western **35:** 33
mudpuppy 41: *26–27*, 27, 29, 46–47,
49
mudskipper **40:** 9, 95, 96, *96*
Mugil cephalus **38:** 52, *52*
Mugilidae **38:** 50, 52–53, **40:** 39
muktuk **3:** 85
mulgara **10:** 27
mullet 38: 50, 52–53, **40:** 38–39
abu **38:** 53
goldie river **38:** 53
gray **38:** 52, *52*, **40:** 39
longarm **38:** 53
mountain **38:** 53
red **35:** 111, **40:** 38
rock **40:** 38
thicklip gray **38:** 53
warty-lipped **38:** *53*
Mullidae **35:** 111, **40:** 38–39
Mulloidichthys mimicus **40:** 39
Mullus surmuletus **40:** 38

multituberculates **7:** 10
mummichog **38:** 84, *84*, (88)
Mungos
gambianus **1:** 98
mungo **1:** *18–19*, 98, 110–111
Mungotictis decemlineata **1:** 98
munia, spotted **16:** 90
Munida
gregaria **28:** *14–15*, *87*
rugosa **28:** *86–87*
Muntiacus
crinifrons **6:** 10
muntjak **6:** 10
reevesi **6:** 46–47
muntjac 6: 12, 46–47
Chinese **6:** 46–47
hairy-fronted **6:** 10
Indian **6:** 10
Reeves's **6:** 46–47
Muraena **33:** 64, (83)
pardalis **33:** 83, *83*
Muraenesocidae **33:** (62)
Muraenidae **33:** (62), 78–83, **39:** 109
Muraenolepis **36:** 53
Muranolepididae **36:** 52–53
Murexia
longicaudata **10:** 27
rothschildi **10:** 27
Muricidae **30:** 34–35
Muridae **7:** *12*, 65
Murinae **7:** 14
muriqui **4:** 72
murre **12:** (94), (98), 100–101
common **12:** 98, *101*, 110
thick-billed **12:** 98, 101
murrelet **12:** 101
ancient **12:** 98, (98)
Kittlitz's **12:** 101
marbled **12:** 101
Mus
musculus **7:** 68–71
musculus brevirostris **7:** 71
musculus domesticus **7:** 71
musculus musculus **7:** 71
musculus wagneri **7:** 71
porcellus **8:** 38
Musca domesticus **23:** *100*, 102
Muscardinus avellanarius **7:** 102,
106–107
Muscicapa striata **17:** 66
Muscicapidae **17:** 66
Muscidae **23:** 100–103
music, skylark-inspired **18:** (27)
musk **1:** 85; **6:** 51
muskellunge **35:** *10*
see also muskie
muskie **35:** (14), 17, 18
tiger **35:** (14)
muskox 6: 62, 104–105
muskrat 7: 13, 65, 96–97
common 7: 96–97
Musophaga rossae **16:** 38
Musophagidae **16:** 38
mussels 30: 54–55

brown **30:** *54*
common **30:** *55*
date **30:** 54
edible **30:** 54
fan **30:** 54, 58, 59
freshwater 30: 60–61
horse **30:** *54–55*
marine **30:** 54
orb **30:** 61
southern rainbow **30:** *60–61*
swan **30:** 60
mustang 5: 42, 58–61
Mustela
erminea **1:** 32, 36, 40–43
frenata **1:** 32, 36
lutreola **1:** 54, (55)
nigripes **1:** 32, 46–47
nivalis **1:** 32, 36–39
putorius **1:** 32, 44–45
vison **1:** 32, 52–55
mustelids **1:** 32–35
Mutillidae **27:** 38–39
mutton birds **50:** (40)
mutualism **16:** (50)
Mya arenaria **30:** *62*
Myadestes townsendi **18:** 44
Mycetophagidae **25:** (52)
mycoplasma microbes **47:** (91)
Mycteria americana **14:** 32, 34–35
Myctophidae **35:** 81, 102–103
Myctophiformes **35:** 81
families summary **35:** (79)
Myctophum affine **35:** *102*
Mydaidae **23:** (63)
Mydas **23:** (63)
fulvifrons **23:** *63*
Mydaus
javanensis **1:** 32
marchei **1:** 32
Mygalomorphae **29:** 38, 41
Myiarchus tuberculifer **17:** 30
myiasis **23:** *108*
Myidae **30:** 70
Myiopsitta monachus **20:** 36
Myiornis ecaudatus **17:** 30
Mylabris tiflensis **25:** *64*
Myleus **38:** 47
rubripinnis **38:** 45
Myliobatidae **33:** (9), 36, 46
Myliobatis **33:** (36)
californica **33:** 14, (38), *48–49*, (49)
Myliobatoidei **33:** (34–36), 34–39
Mylossoma **38:** 47
duriventre **38:** 45
myna 18: (41)
bank **18:** 82
brahminy (pagoda) **18:** 82, 83
common (house) **18:** 82, 83, 88
crested **18:** 82
hill 18: 82, 88–89
Myobatrachidae **42:** 10, 92, (94); **43:**
(11)
Myobatrachus **42:** 92
gouldii **42:** 98, *98–99*, (99)

Myocastor coypus **8:** 30, 44–47
Myocastoridae **7:** *12*; **8:** 31
Myodocopa **28:** 9
myoglobin **3:** 11, 87
Myoictis melas **10:** 27
Myomimus
   personatus **7:** 102
   roachi **7:** 102
   setzeri **7:** 102
Myomorpha **7:** (8)
Myopa testacea **23:** *82–83*
Myoprocta exilis **8:** 30
Myosciurus pumilio **7:** 34
Myosorex varius **9:** 28
Myotis lucifugus **9:** 104–105
Myoxidae **7:** *12*
Myoxocephalus scorpius **39:** 76
Myriapoda **22:** 9
myriapods 22: 14–15
Myrichthys colubrinus **33:** 81
Myripristis berndti **39:** *21*
Myrmaridae **22:** (86)
Myrmeciza exsul **19:** 72
Myrmecobiidae **10:** 24
Myrmecobius fasciatus **10:** 27, 34–35
Myrmecophaga tridactyla **9:** 65, 68–71
Myrmotherula
   axiliaris **19:** 72
   obscura **19:** 72
   surinamensis **19:** 72
Myrocongridae **33:** (62)
Mysateles prehensilis **8:** 30
Mysida **28:** 34
Mysidacea **28:** 9, 42–43
Mysidia **24:** *76–77*
Mysis relicta **28:** *42*
Mystacinidae **9:** 87
Mysticeti **3:** 54
Mystus
   gulio **37:** 26, 27
   keletius **37:** 28
   micracanthus **37:** *22*
   numurus **37:** 28, *28–29*
   tengara **37:** *24*, 27
   vittatus **37:** 28
myths and legends **11:** (32); **12:** (80); **14:** (14), (39), (87), (102); **18:** (93), (102); **20:** (86)
Mytilidae **30:** 50
Mytilus edulis **30:** *55*
Myxine **31:** *26*
Myxinidae **31:** 26–31
Myxocyprinus **34:** 95
   asiaticus **34:** 12, 88, 94–95, 95, 99
myxomatosis **8:** 72, 93; **22:** 110, (113)
Myzomela
   cardinalis **20:** 88
   sanguinolenta **20:** 88
Myzopodidae **9:** 87
Myzostomaria **21:** 77, 94, 96
Myzus persicae **24:** *100*

N

Nabidae **24:** 36–37
Nabis feras **24:** *36*
Nacerdes melanura **25:** (61)
naga-buna **34:** 44
nagana **23:** (103)
Naja **49:** (71); **50:** 14, (29)
   kaouthia **50:** 28, (29)
   naja **48:** *16*; **50:** (8), 9, 12, 28–31, 42
   nigricollis **44:** 41
   nigricollis nigricollis **50:** *31*
   nigricollis woodi **50:** 32
   nivea **50:** 9, 12, 32–33
   oxiana **42:** 71; **50:** (29)
   pallida **44:** 41
Namib Desert **25:** 68–70, 71; **29:** 67; **45:** (31)
nandid
   African **40:** 57
   four-spined **40:** 57
   Malaysian tiger **40:** 57
   tiger **40:** 57
Nandidae **40:** 56–57
Nandinia binotata **1:** 88
Nandus nandus **40:** 57
Nannaethiops
   unifasciatus **38:** 15
   unitaeniatus **38:** 15, *15*
Nannocharax elongatus **38:** 14
Nannosciuris exilis **7:** 36
Nannospalax leucodon **7:** 100–101
Nannostomus
   eques **38:** *10*
   espei **38:** 23
   trifasciatus **38:** *22*
Nanoloricus mysticus **21:** *69*
Nanorana **43:** 84
Nanseria **35:** 101
Naprepa **26:** *82*
Narcine **33:** (20)
   brasiliensis **33:** 22
   entemedor **33:** *22–23*
Narcinidae **33:** (9), (20)
Narke **33:** (20)
Narkidae **33:** (9), (20)
Narnia inornata **24:** 52
narwhal 3: 55, 84–85
Nasalis
   concolor **4:** 40
   larvatus **4:** 40, 70–71
Nasica longirostris **17:** 28
Naso
   annulatus **40:** 101

   vlamingii **40:** *101*
Nassophorea **21:** 13
Nasua
   narica **1:** 20
   nasua **1:** 20, 28–29
Nasuella olivacea **1:** 20
Nasutitermes **22:** 62
   corniger **22:** *66*
   ephratae **22:** *65*
Natalichthys **40:** 22
Natalidae **9:** 87
Natantia **28:** 56
Natator depressus **47:** *14–15*
national parks/nature reserves **2:** (15), 16, 31; **5:** 34, (102), 103
Natricinae **49:** 8, 12, 77
Natriciteres **49:** 12
Natrix **49:** 12, (76); **50:** 15
   maura **42:** (31); **49:** (76)
   megalocephala **49:** (76)
   natrix **42:** 71; **48:** *16*, 17; **49:** 55, 74–79, 100
   tessellata **49:** (76)
natural selection **32:** (70), **40:** (77)
Naucrates ductor **33:** 50, **39:** *111*, **40:** 34
Naultinus **44:** (23); **45:** 12, (36)
   elegans **44:** *22–23*; **45:** *37*
Nautichthys oculofasciatus **39:** 80, *81*
Nautilidae **30:** 72
Nautiloidea **30:** 9, 72
Nautilus pompilus **30:** *74, 75*
nautiluses 30: 74–75
   eyes **30:** (86)
   paper **30:** (89)
   pearly **30:** 74
navigation **15:** 76–77; **33:** (70)
   homing **12:** (30); **16:** (17), 18
Neacoryphus bicrucis **24:** *44–45*
Neamblysomus julianae **9:** 40
Nebaliopsis **28:** 36
Nebrius ferrugineus **32:** 24, 35, (40)
Necrosia **22:** *32*
Necrosyrtes monachus **20:** 8, 24
nectar **4:** 105
nectar-feeders **16:** (25), 44; **19:** 17,18
Nectarinia
   afra **19:** 94
   famosa **19:** 94, 96–97
   johnstoni **19:** 94, 96
Nectariniidae **19:** 94
Nectocaecilia **41:** (24)
Nectogale elegans **9:** 28
Nectoliparis pelagicus **39:** 83
Nectophrynoides **42:** 56, 60, (85)
   liberiensis **42:** 60, (85)
   malcolmi **42:** 60
   occidentalis **42:** 60, (85)
   tornieri **42:** 60
   viviparus **42:** 60
Necturus
   alabamensis **41:** (46)
   beyeri **41:** (46)
   lewisi **41:** (46)

maculosus **41**: *26–27*, 46–47, 49
punctatus **41**: (46)
needlefish 38: 50, 70–75
European **38**: 73
gaping **38**: 73
Hawaiian crocodile **38**: 73
zigzagging **38**: *73*
Negaprion brevirostris **32**: 16, (18), 55
nelma **35**: 39
Nemadoras humeralis **37**: *80–81*
Nemaster rubiginosa **30**: *96*
Nemateleotris magnifica **40**: 99
Nematocera **23**: 36, 38
nematocysts **21**: 43, 58, 60
Nematoda **21**: 32, 77, 88–91
Nematogenyidae **37**: 11
Nematomorpha **21**: 32, 77–78
Nematopogon swanmerdamella
26: *112–113*
Nembrotha rutilans **30**: *39*
Nemertea **21**: 32, 77, 86–87
Nemestrinidae **23**: (69)
Nemichthyidae **33**: (62), 64, *65*, 86–87
Nemichthys **33**: *64*, 86–87, 87
Nemipteridae **40**: 40–41
Nemorhaedus goral **6**: 62, 108
Neoaploactis tridorsalis **39**: 69
Neobatrachia **42**: 10
Neobatrachus pelobatoides **42**: 95, *96*
Neobisium muscorum **29**: *20*
Neoceratias spinifer **36**: 79, 80, 82
Neoceratiidae **36**: 74–83
Neoceratodus forsteri **31**: *32–33*, 38, *38*
Neochanna **35**: 33
apoda **35**: 36
cleaveri **35**: 33
diversus **35**: 36
heleios **35**: 36
Neocirrhites armatus **40**: *66*
Neoconger **33**: 74
Neocottus werestschagini **39**: 77
Neocyttus acanthorhynchus **39**: 24
Neodrepanis **20**: 74
coruscans **20**: 74
hypoxantha **20**: 74
Neofelis nebulosa **2**: 10
Neogastropoda **30**: 18, 32–35
Neolamprologus **40**: 69
neolebias
Ansorge's **38**: *13*, 15
Axelrod's **38**: 14
banded **38**: 14
Neolebias
ansorgii **38**: *13*, 15
axelrodi **38**: 14
lozii **38**: 14
trilineatus **38**: 15
Neomorphinae **20**: 47
Neomys fodiens **9**: 28
Neopetrolisthes maculatus **28**: 88–89
Neophascogale lorentzi **10**: 27
Neophema chrysogaster **19**: 12
Neophoca cinerea **3**: 9
Neophron percnopterus **11**: (25); **20**: 8

Neopilina **30**: 12–13
galatheae **30**: 12–13
Neoptataecus waterhousii **39**: 71
Neoraja **33**: (27)
Neoscopelidae **35**: 103
Neoscopelus macrolepidotus **35**: 103
Neosebastes
pandus **39**: 66
thetidis **39**: 66
Neoseps **46**: 8
reynoldsi **46**: 12, 21
Neosilurus ater **37**: *66–67*
Neotanaidomorpha **28**: 34
neoteny **41**: 28–29, 40, 49, 56, 60, 67, 91
facultative neotenics **41**: 57
obligate neotenics **41**: 56
Neothyonidium magnum **30**: *92–93*
Neotis nuba **11**: 84
Neotoma lepida **7**: 84–85
Neotragus
batesi **6**: 62
pygmaeus **6**: 62
Neotrypaea californiensis **28**: 80–81
Nepa cinerea **24**: *20*
Nepenthes **43**: 107
Nephelobates **43**: 68, 70
Nephila **42**: 82
maculata **23**: *52*
Nephrotoma **23**: *44*
Nephrurus **45**: (10), 12
Nephtys caeca **21**: 97
Nepidae **24**: 20–21
Neptunides polychromus **25**: 86–87
Nereis
diversicolor **21**: *97*
virens **21**: *95*
Neriidae **23**: (85)
nerites **30**: 26–27
Nerodia **49**: 12, (76), (83); **50**: 15
clarki **49**: (81)
cyclopion **48**: 109; **49**: (83)
cyclopion floridana **49**: *82–83*
fasciata **49**: (51), 80–83
sipedon **49**: 83, (83)
taxispilota **49**: *82–83*, (83)
Nerthra **24**: *22*
Nesionixalus **43**: 18
Nesolagus
netscheri **8**: 64
timminsi **8**: 64
Nesomantis thomasseti **43**: 10, 87
Nesomimus parvulus **18**: 36
Nessia **46**: 8, 14
nest parasitism *see* brood/nest parasitism
nestboxes **18**: (57)
Nestor
meridionalis **20**: 36, 38
notabilis **16**: 22; **20**: 36, 38–41
nests **11**: 14
"apartment block" **16**: (104)
edible **15**: 77
fortified mud "oven" **20**: 86, *86*,
87, *87*

mud-building **20**: (105)
weaving **16**: 104, (104), (105)
net devil **36**: 79
Nettapus auritus **14**: 52
Nettastomatidae **33**: (62)
Neurergus **41**: 88, 92
Neuroptera **22**: 30, 90–97
Neuroterus
numismalis **27**: *33*
quercus-baccarum **27**: *32*
Neurotrichus gibbsii **9**: 54–55
New Zealand, mammals introduced into
1: 43; **10**: (80)
New Zealand, reptiles in **44**: (23)
newts 41: 9–12, 27, (29), 88–93
alpine **41**: *89*
American **41**: 88
American rough-skinned **41**: 91
American western **41**: (92)
Bosca's **41**: (111)
California **41**: 88, *90–91*, 108
Chinese fire-bellied **41**: (95)
Chinese spiny **41**: 91, 101
common (smooth) **41**: *29*, 89, 110–111
crested **41**: (92), (111)
crocodile **41**: 88
eastern 41: 86, *88–89*, 91, 98–99
fire-bellied **41**: 88, 91
Italian **41**: (111)
Japanese fire-bellied 41: 94–95
Japanese spiny **41**: 91, 101
Japanese sword-tailed **41**: (95)
knobby **41**: 88, 91
Kunming Lake fire-bellied **41**: (95)
life cycle **41**: *28*
mandarin **41**: 88, *91*
marbled **41**: (111)
North African sharp-ribbed **41**: (27)
paddle-tailed **41**: 88
palmate **41**: 89, (111)
red-bellied **41**: *89*, 92, 108
red-spotted (eastern) **41**: 86, *88–89*,
91, 98–99
rough-skinned 41: 44, 88, 108–109
sharp-ribbed 41: (27), 91, 100–101
skin toxins **41**: 91
smooth 41: *29*, 89, 110–111
Spanish sharp-ribbed (sharp-ribbed)
41: (27), 91, 100–101
spiny **41**: 88, *92*
spotted **41**: 92
stout **41**: 88
warty **41**: 88, 91
Nicator chloris **16**: 56
nicator, common **16**: 56
Nicrophorus **25**: 28, 30
vespillo **25**: *29*
nictitating membrane **7**: 28
nighthawk
common **15**: 78–79
Nacuda **15**: 78, *79*
nightingale **18**: (27)
European **18**: 38, 44, *44*, (50)

nightjar 15: 78–81, 80, 82, 94; **20:** 74
  American common **15:** 78
  European **15:** 78; **18:** 12
  satanic **15:** 78
  standard-winged 15: 78, (80),
    84–85
Nigma puella **29:** *53*
nigoro-buna **34:** 44
Nilaus afer **15:** 104
Nile Perch disaster **40:** (79)
nilgai **6:** 62
Nilio testaceus **25:** *70*
Niltava
  grandis **17:** 66
  tickelliae **17:** 66
niltava, large **17:** 66
ningaui **10:** (24)
  Pilbara **10:** *25*, 27
  southern **10:** 27
Ningaui
  timealeyi **10:** 27
  yvonneae **10:** 27
Ninia **49:** 16
Ninox novaeseelandiae **15:** 50
niquim **36:** 55
nishikigoi (koi) **34:** 38
Nisitrus **23:** *19*
nkupe **38:** 14
Noctilio
  albiventris **9:** 108
  leporinus **9:** 108–109
Noctilionidae **9:** 87
Noctuidae **26:** 92–97
  feeding **26:** (96)
noddy
  black **12:** 74
  brown **12:** 74
  lesser **12:** 74, *77*
Noemacheilus
  barbatulus **34:** 14, 89, 110–111
  (Nemacheilus) barbatulus **34:** 108
noise pollution **3:** 88, 95
nok (African arowana) **31:** 86
Nometigonus crysoleucas **34:** (87)
Nomorhamphus liemi **38:** 77, *77*
Nonnula rubecula **19:** 56
noodlefish 35: 8, 30–31
  dwarf **35:** 31
  Sundaland **35:** 31
noolbenger *see* possum, honey
Noroma nigrolunata **26:** *99*
nostrils **11:** (37); **12:** 28, *30*, 44;
    19: 62, 94
notacanth 33: *65*, 96–97, 107
Notacanthidae **33:** (62), 96–97
Notacanthus chemnitzii **33:** 96
Notaden **42:** 92, 93, 95
Notechis
  ater **50:** 12, 38–41
  scutatus **50:** 38–41
Notemigonus **34:** 68–71
  crysoleucas **34:** 68, (71), 85
Notesthes robusta **39:** 67
Notharchus tectus **19:** 56

nothobranch
  black-spotted **38:** 81
Nothobranchius **38:** (79), 81, 83
  melanospilus **38:** 81
Nothoprocta
  bonapartei **11:** 40
  ornata **11:** 40
  pentlandii **11:** 40
Nothopsis rugosus **49:** 10
Notocheiridae **38:** 55, (59)
Notocheirus **38:** (59)
Notodontidae **26:** 80–83
Notodoris gardineri **30:** 39
Notograptidae **40:** 22–25
Notograptus **40:** 25
Notolepis coatsi **35:** *98*, *98–99*, *99*
Notonecta glauca **24:** *24*, *24–25*, *25*, *26*
Notonectidae **24:** 24–27
Notophthalmus **41:** 88, 91
  viridescens **41:** 86, *88–89*, 98–99
Notopogon **39:** 50
Notopteridae **31:** (43), (82), 102, 104,
    36: 86
Notopteroidei
  families summary **31:** (82)
Notoraja **33:** (26)
Notorus
  albater **37:** *17*
  flavus **37:** 16
Notoryctemorphia **10:** 24
Notoryctes
  caurinus **10:** 27, 43
  typhlops **10:** 27, 42–43
Notoryctidae **10:** 24, 26
Notorynchus cepedianus **32:** *99*
Notostraca **28:** 18
Nototriton **41:** 68, (77)
  richardi **41:** (77)
  tapanti **41:** (77)
Notropis **34:** 68–71
  amblops **34:** (71)
  harperi **34:** (71)
  lineopunctatus **34:** (71)
  moralesi **34:** 70
  orca **34:** 70
Noturus **37:** 15, (19)
Novumbra hubbsi **35:** 20
Nucella lapillus **30:** *32*, 34–35
Nucifraga
  caryocatactes **18:** 90
  columbiana **18:** 90
Nucras **45:** 58, (63)
  ornata **45:** *57–58*
Nuculidae **30:** 50
Nuda **21:** 43
nudibranch
  aeolid **30:** *41*
  black-lined **30:** *20–21*
  defense **30:** (41)
Nudibranchia **30:** 18, 38–43
nukupu'u **20:** 98
numbat 10: 13, 24, 25, 26, 34–35
numbfish **33:** (20)
Numenius

  arquata **13:** 30, 40–43
  borealis **13:** 30
  phaeopus **13:** (15), 16, 30, (36)
  tenuirostris **13:** 30
Numida meleagris **11:** 44
Numididae **11:** 44, 49
nunbird **19:** 57
  white-faced **19:** 56
  white-fronted **19:** 56, *57*
nunlet **19:** 57
  rusty-breasted **19:** 56
nursehound **32:** 57
nutcracker **11:** 15
  Clark's **18:** 90, *92*
  spotted **18:** 90, 92, *93*
nuthatch 17: 77, (91); **20:** 80
  Algerian **18:** 64, 65
  brown-headed **18:** 64, 65
  Eurasian **18:** 64, *64*, *65*
  giant **18:** 64
  nuthatch family 18: 64–65
  pygmy **18:** 64, 65, 67
  red-breasted 18: 64, 66–67
  rock- **18:** 64, *64*
  white-breasted **18:** 64
  white-browed **18:** 64, 65
nutria *see* coypu
nyala, mountain **6:** 62
Nyctanassa violacea **14:** 20
Nyctanolis **41:** 68
Nyctea scandiaca **12:** 73; **15:** 50, 58–61
Nyctereutes procyonoides **2:** 50
Nycteridae **9:** 87
Nyctibates **43:** 12
Nyctibiidae **15:** 78, 80
Nyctibius
  grandis **15:** 78
  griseus **15:** 78
Nycticebus
  coucang **4:** 106, 108–109
  pygmaeus **4:** 106
Nycticryphes semicollaris **14:** 96
Nyctixalus **43:** 100
Nyctyornis athertoni **17:** 8
Nymphalidae **26:** 11, 38–45
Nymphalinae **26:** 40–43
Nymphicus hollandicus **16:** 22, (35),
    36–37
Nystalus chacu

O

o'o **20:** 90
  Kauai **20:** 90
o'u **20:** 98
oarfish 35: _78–83_, 105, _108–109_
  crested **35:** 104, _104, 105_
  larva of **35:** _109_
Obaichthys **31:** _72_
Obelia geniculata **21:** _46_
Occella impi **39:** 80
Oceanites oceanicus **12:** 28
Oceanodroma
  furcata **12:** 28
  homochroa **12:** 28
  leucorhoa **12:** 28, _42–43_
  melania **12:** 28
  monorhis **12:** 28
ocelot 1: _17_; **2:** 10, _12_, _44–45_
Ochlodes venata **26:** _62_
Ochotona
  alpina **8:** 94
  collaris **8:** 94, 98
  himalayana **8:** 94
  princeps **8:** 94, _98–101_
  pusilla **8:** 94
Ochotonidae **8:** 60
Octocorallia **21:** 43
Octodon bridgesi **8:** 30
Octodontidae (octodonts) **7:** _12_;
  8: 29–31
Octodontomys gliroides **8:** 30
octodonts **7:** _12_; **8:** 29–31
Octomys mimax **8:** 30
Octopoda **30:** 72, _84–89_
Octopodidae **30:** 72
Octopus
  bimaculoides **30:** _88_
  cyanea **30:** _73_
  maorum **30:** _84–85_
octopuses 30: _84–89_
  blue-ringed **30:** _84_
  day **30:** _73_
  eyes **30:** (86)
  lesser **30:** _85_
  Maori **30:** _84–85_
  mimic **30:** _87_
  poison **30:** 88–89
  in shells **30:** (89)
  two-spotted **30:** _88_
Ocypode quadrata **28:** _56–57_
Ocyurus chrysurus **40:** _36_
Odatria **46:** _82_
Odobenidae **3:** 8
Odobenus rosmarus **3:** 9, _24–29_
Odocoileus virginianus clavium **49:** 97
Odocoileus
  hemionus **6:** 10, _34–37_
  virginianus **6:** 10, (36)
Odonata **22:** 30, _42–51_

Odontaspididae **32:** (12), (74)
Odontoceti **3:** 54
Odontochila **25:** _22_
Odontodactylus scyllarus **28:** _38, 40_
Odontomyia viridula **23:** _57_
Odontophrynus **42:** 76
Odontotaenius disjunctus **25:** _75_
Odontotermes obesus **22:** _62–63_
Odonus niger **39:** 103
Oecanthus quadripunctatus **23:** _16–17_
Oecophylla
  longinoda **27:** _40–41_
  smaragdina **27:** _42, 48–49, 52–53,_
  _54–55_
Oedemera nobilis **25:** _61_
Oedemeridae **25:** (61)
Oedipina **41:** 68, (77)
  poelzi **41:** 69
Oedipoda miniata **23:** _24_
Oedura **45:** (10), _12_
  filicipoda **45:** _12_
Oenanthe oenanthe **18:** 44
Oestridae **23:** _96–97_
Ogcocephalidae **36:** _70–73_, 76
Ogcocephalus **36:** 70
  darwini **36:** _12–13_
  nasutus **36:** 70, _72–73_
Ogdoecosta **25:** _101_
Oiketicus elongatus **26:** _111_
oil **3:** 22, 34, 52, 58, 85, 89, 91, 101
oilbird **15:** 78, _80_, 81
oilfish **35:** (28), **39:** 78
  Baikal **39:** 53, 78, 79, (80)
  big Baikal **39:** 79
  little Baikal **39:** 79
Okamejei **33:** (27)
okapi 6: 52, _52–53_, _58–59_
Okapia johnstoni **6:** 52, _58–59_
Olallamys edax **8:** 30
old wife 40: _54–55_
oldsquaw _see_ duck, long-tailed
Oligobrachia ivanovi **21:** _92_
Oligochaeta **21:** 77, 94, _102–105_
Oligodon **48:** (39); **49:** 11
Oligohymenophorea **21:** 13
Oligosoma **44:** (23)
  suteri **44:** (23)
olingo **1:** 20, 21
olm 41: 14, _26–27_, 27, _48–49_
  European **41:** 70
Ololygon **43:** 36
  rubra **43:** _36_
Olyras crathis **26:** _56–57_
omega-3 oil **36:** 87
Ommatopia pictifolia **23:** _12_
Ommotokotia elongata **32:** 96
Ompok
  bimaculatus **37:** (34)
  congica **37:** (34)
  eugeniatus **37:** (34), _34–35_
Omusudis lowei **35:** 101
onager _see_ ass, Asian wild
Oncea **28:** _31_
Oncomeris flavicornis **24:** _64_

Oncorhynchus
  aquabonita **35:** (75)
  aquabonita aquabonita **35:** (75)
  aquabonita gilberti **35:** (75), _75_
  gorbuscha **35:** _64–65_, (65)
  keta **35:** (65)
  kisutch **35:** (65)
  mykiss **35:** _72–77_
  mykiss aquabonita **35:** (75)
  nerka **35:** 9, _58–65_, (61), 73
  tschawytscha **35:** (65)
Ondatra zibethicus **7:** _96–97_
Oneirodidae **36:** _74–83_
Oniscoidea **28:** 34
Onophas columbaria **26:** _62–63_
Onuxodon **36:** 22
Onychodactylus **41:** 36, (37)
  japonicus **41:** _26–27_
Onychogalea
  fraenata **10:** 48
  unguifera **10:** 48
Onychognathus walleri **18:** 82
Onychophora **21:** 32; **22:** 13
Onychorhynchus coronatus **17:** 30,
  _34–35_, (37)
Onymacris rugatipennis **25:** _69–70, 71_
Oonopidae **29:** 38
opah **35:** 82, 105
Opalinata **21:** 13
open bill, African **14:** 32, _33_
Opheodrys aestivus **49:** _58–59_, 73
Ophiarachnella incrassata **30:** _98_
Ophichthidae **33:** (62), (66)
Ophichthus
  bonaparti **33:** _85_
  cruentifer **33:** (66)
Ophidiidae **36:** _24–27_
Ophidiocephalus, taeniatus **45:** (49), 50
Ophioderma wahlbergi **30:** _92_
Ophiodes **46:** 52
  yacupoi **46:** _54–55_
Ophiodon elongatus **32:** 102, **39:** 74, _74_
Ophiomorus punctatissimus **44:** (26)
Ophiophagus hannah **50:** (8), 9, _12–13_,
  _34–35_
Ophioscincus **46:** (11)
Ophiotrix fragilis **30:** _98–99_
Ophisaurus **44:** (26); **46:** 51–52, (55)
  apodus **45:** 64; **46:** 51, _62–63_
  mimicus **46:** 61
  ventralis **44:** 26; **46:** _60–61_
Ophisops **45:** 58
  elegans **45:** (60)
Ophisternon **33:** (106)
Ophiuroidea **30:** 91, 98
Ophryophryne **42:** 34
Ophthalmotilapia ventralis **40:** 73
Opiliones **29:** _22–25_
Opisthobranchia **30:** 9, 10, 18, _36–37_
Opisthocomidae **20:** 46, 47
Opisthocomus hoazin **20:** 46, _64–67_
Opisthoproctidae **35:** _24–25_
Opisthoproctus
  grimaldii **35:** 24, _24_

soleatus **35:** 25, *25*
Opisthothylax immaculatus **43:** 22
Opistognathidae **40:** 22–25
Opistognathus
  cuvieri **40:** 25
  punctatus **40:** *25*
Oplomus dichrous **24:** *62*
Oplurinae **44:** 80
Oplurus **44:** 80
opossum 1: 87
  agile gracile mouse **10:** 14
  Alston's woolly mouse **10:** 14
  American 10: 14–17
  bare-tailed woolly **10:** 14
  black four-eyed **10:** 14
  black-shouldered **10:** 14, 16, *17*
  brown four-eyed **10:** 14
  bushy-tailed **10:** 14
  Central American woolly **10:** 14, *17*
  Chilean shrew **10:** 14
  common (Virginia) **10:** *8*, 13, 14,
    15, 16, 17, 18–23
  Dorothy's slender mouse **10:** 14
  elegant fat-tailed **10:** 14
  gray-bellied shrew **10:** 14
  gray-bellied slender mouse **10:** 14, *15*
  gray four-eyed **10:** 14, *17*
  gray short-tailed **10:** 14
  Incan shrew **10:** 14
  lutrine **10:** 14
  Mexican mouse **10:** 14, *17*
  murine mouse **10:** 14
  pale-bellied woolly mouse **10:** 14
  pallid fat-tailed **10:** 14
  Patagonian **10:** 14
  pygmy short-tailed **10:** 14
  shrew **10:** 16
  silky shrew **10:** 14
  Virginia 10: *8*, 13, 14, 15, 16, 17,
    18–23
  water **10:** 13, 14, 16, *17*
  white-eared **10:** 14
  wood spirit gracile mouse **10:** 14
  woolly **10:** 16
Opsanus tau **36:** 54, *54*, (59)
Opsaridium **34:** 65
  christyi **34:** *64–65*
Opsariichthys **34:** 65
oranda **34:** 49, 50, 51
  chocolate pompon **34:** 51
orange fin **35:** 66, (68)
orange-tips (whites) **26:** 22–27
orangutan 4: *8*, 10, 12, 13, 14–19
  Bornean **4:** 12, 14–15, 18, *18–19*
  Sumatran **4:** 12, 14–15, 18
orca **3:** 55, (57), 62–65
Orcinus orca **3:** 55, 62–65
Orconectes limosus **28:** 75
Oreamnos americanus **6:** 62, 108–109
Orectolobidae **32:** 10, (12), (30), 33
Orectolobiformes **32:** 30–33
Orectolobus
  japonicus **32:** 37
  maculatus **32:** 37

ornatus **32:** 37
  wardi **32:** 37
oreo **39:** 22, 24, 25
  black **39:** 24, 25
  ox-eyed **39:** 24
  smooth **39:** 24, 25
Oreocharis arfaki **18:** 68
Oreochromis mossambicus **40:** 77
Oreolalax **42:** 34
Oreophryne **42:** 104–105
Oreophrynella **42:** 56, 60
Oreosoma atlanticum **39:** 24
Oreosomatidae **39:** 10, 22–25
Oreotragus oreotragus **6:** 62
Oreotrochilus **16:** (45)
  estella **16:** 44
Orestias **38:** 88
  luteus **38:** 89
  mulleri **38:** 89
  tschudii **38:** 89
orestias
  Muller's **38:** 89
  Tschudi's **38:** 89
  yellow **38:** 89
orfe **34:** 68, 73, 75, *76–77*
  golden **34:** 79
Orgyia vetusta **26:** *100*
oribi **5:** *11*; **6:** *61*, 62
Oriestias **38:** (89)
origin **1:** 8
  reproduction **1:** 12–14
oriole 17: 108; **18:** 74, 75
  Altamira **18:** 74, 76
  Baltimore 18: 74, 76–77
  black-backed **18:** 74, 76
  Bullock's **18:** 74, 76, 77
  Montserrat **18:** 74, 75
  New World *see* blackbird, American
    blackbird family
ornithology **21:** (33)
Ornithoptera alexandrae **26:** 16, *16*
Ornithorhynchus anatinus **10:** 106–109
Oroaetus isidori **15:** 8
oropel **50:** 91
oropendola **18:** 74, 75
  black **18:** 74
  chestnut-headed **18:** 74, *75*
  crested **18:** 74
  Montezuma **18:** 74, *74*
  russet-backed **18:** 74
Ortalis vetula **11:** 44
Orthonectida **21:** 32, 35
Orthoptera **22:** 30; **23:** 8–11
  anatomy **23:** 8–10
  life cycle **23:** 10–11
Ortyxelos meiffrenii **11:** 92
Orycteropus afer **9:** 65, 78–79
Oryctolagus cuniculus **8:** 64, 68–73
oryx
  Arabian 6: 62, 90–91
  scimitar-horned **6:** 62
  white (Arabian) **6:** 62, 90–91
Oryx
  dammah **6:** 62

  gazella **6:** 62
  leucoryx **6:** 62, 90–91
Oryzias **38:** 67
  celebensis **38:** (68)
  dancena **38:** 65
  javanicus **38:** (68), 69
  latipes **34:** 61, **38:** *64*, 65, *65*
  latipes sinensis **38:** (68)
  marmoratus **38:** (68)
  matanensis **38:** (68)
  minutillus **38:** (68)
  nigrimas **38:** (68)
  orthognathus **38:** (68)
  profundicola **38:** (68)
Oryzorictes tetradactylus **9:** 24
Osbornictis piscivora **1:** 88
osetra **31:** 66
Osmeridae **35:** 22, 26–29
Osmeriformes **35:** 8, (9)
Osmerus
  eperlanus **35:** 27, (28)
  mordax **35:** 26
  mordax dentex **35:** 26
  mordax mordax **35:** 26
  spectrum **35:** 29
osmeteria **26:** *18–19*, (19), *20*
Osmia rufa **27:** *85*, 88
osmoconformers **28:** (105)
osmotic stress **21:** 14
Osornophryne **42:** 56
Osphronemidae **40:** 60–63
Osphronemus **40:** 61
  exodon **40:** 62
  goramy **40:** 61
  laticlavus **40:** 62
  septemfasciatus **40:** 62
osprey 12: 64; **15:** 8, *8*, 14–17, 21,
  (21), 32, 35, (42), 56; **17:** (22);
  18: (18), 80, (81)
Osteichthyes **33:** 8, 60, (60)
Osteocephalus **43:** 32, 38
  oophagus **43:** (76)
osteoderms **45:** (99)
Osteoglossidae **31:** (43), (82), 83, 86,
  88, (90), 92, 96, 98
Osteoglossiformes **31:** 82–85
  families summary **31:** (82)
Osteoglossinae **31:** (82), 92, 96, 98
Osteoglossoidei
  families summary **31:** (82)
Osteoglossum **31:** 82, 84, 92–95, 99
  bicirrhosum **31:** *84–85*, 92, 93, *93*
  fereira **31:** 93
Osteolaemus tetraspis **47:** *94–95*, 96
Osteopilus **43:** (32)
  brunneus **43:** 38
  septentrionalis **43:** (49), 50–51
Ostraciidae **39:** 11, 106–107, 110
Ostracion
  cubicus **39:** 107
  meleagris **39:** *106–107*, 107
Ostracoda **28:** 9, 32–33
Ostracontidae **39:** 96
Ostreidae **30:** 50

Ostreiformes **30:** 9, 50, 56–57
ostrich 11: 8, (9), 10, 16–19, 20–25, (30), 34, 40, (109); **12:** 8; **20:** 10–11, 31
Otariidae **3:** 8
Otididae **11:** 84
Otiorhynchus singularis **25:** 110
Otis tarda **11:** 84, 88–91
oto **37:** 110
  dwarf otocinclus **37:** 110
Otocinclus **37:** 106
  affinis **37:** 110
otocinclus
  redfin **37:** 104
Otocyon megalotis **2:** 50, 76–77
Otolemur
  crassicaudatus **4:** 106
  garnettii **4:** 106
Otophryne **42:** 104, 105
Otophryninae **42:** 104
otter 1: 19, 35, 54; **8:** 48
  Cape clawless **1:** 32
  Congo clawless **1:** 32
  European 1: 58–63
  European river **1:** 60
  giant **1:** 18, 32
  giant river 1: 68–69
  hairy-nosed **1:** 32
  Indian smooth-coated **1:** 35
  marine **1:** 32
  North American river 1: 32, 64–67
  northern river (North American river) **1:** 32, 64–67
  sea 1: 19, 32, 72–75
  short-clawed 1: 32, 70–71
  smooth-coated **1:** 32
  spot-necked **1:** 32, 35
otter shrew **9:** 11, 24, 25
  giant **9:** 24, 25
  Ruwenzori **9:** 24, 25
Otus
  asio **15:** 50; **18:** 39; **48:** (23)
  scops **15:** 50
ounce *see* leopard, snow
Ourebia ourebi **6:** 62
ouzel, ring **18:** 44
ovenbird family 20: 80–81
overfishing *see* fishing
Ovibos moschatus **6:** 62, 104–105
oviparity **27:** 13; **46:** 14
Ovis
  aries **6:** 62
  canadensis **6:** 100–103
  musimon **6:** 62
Ovophis **50:** 111
ovoviviparity **25:** 19, 99; **42:** 60, (85); **45:** 72–73; **46:** 14, (22)
owl 7: (37); **9:** 33; **11:** 10, 13; **12:** 69; **15:** 12, 39 50–53, 94; **17:** (22), (109); **18:** (10)
  barn 15: 50, 53, 64–69; **18:** (57)
  bay **15:** 53, 64
  boobook **15:** 50
  burrowing **15:** 50, 51, 53

Congo bay **15:** 50, 53
  eagle **11:** 13; **15:** 56, (60), 62
  eastern screech **15:** 50; **48:** (23)
  elf **15:** 50, 50
  great gray **11:** 13, (68)
  great horned 15: 34, 50, 56, 62–63
  hawk **15:** 50
  little **15:** 50
  long-eared **15:** 50, 52–53
  Malaysian eagle **15:** 50, 50
  northern eagle **15:** 50, 53
  northern pygmy **15:** 50
  northern spotted **41:** (45)
  oriental bay **15:** 50, 50, 53
  Pel's fishing 15: 50, 56–57
  scops **15:** 50
  snowy 7: (14); **12:** 73; **15:** 50, 58–61
  spectacled **15:** 50, 50
  spotted **15:** 50, 53
  spotted wood **15:** 50, 50
  tawny 15: 50, 54–55
owlet, jungle **15:** 50
owlet-nightjar **15:** 81
  Archbold's **15:** 78
  Australian **15:** 78, 80
owlflies **22:** 90, 96–97
oxpecker **5:** 38; **6:** (73); **18:** 82
  red-billed **18:** 82, 83
  yellow-billed **18:** 82
Oxybelis **49:** (18), (73)
  aeneus **49:** 52
  fulgidus **49:** (18)
Oxycirrhites typus **40:** 66, 67
Oxycomanthus bennetti **30:** 95
Oxyeleotris marmorata **40:** 97
Oxylebius pictus **39:** 75
Oxymonacanthus longirostris **39:** 102, 103
Oxynotidae **32:** 47
Oxyopes
  heterophthalmus **29:** 78
  schenkeli **29:** 79, 80
  superbus **29:** 78–79
Oxyopidae **29:** 78–81
Oxypogon guirinii **16:** 44
Oxyporhamphus **38:** 77
Oxyrrhachis versicolor **24:** 93
Oxythyrea funesta **25:** 85
Oxyura jamaicensis **14:** 52
Oxyuranus **50:** (8), 9
  microlepidotus **50:** 42–43
  scutellatus **50:** 9, 42–43
Oxyzygonectes dovii **38:** 93
oyster beds **33:** (38), (49)
oyster cracker
  American **36:** 54, (59)
oystercatcher 13: 16, 90–93; **14:** 98
  African black **13:** 90, 90–91, 92
  American **13:** 90, 92–93, 98, 99
  American black 13: 90, 92, 98–99
  Australian pied **13:** 90, 92, (92)
  black (American black) **13:** 90, 92, 98–99
  blackish **13:** 90, 92
  Eurasian 11: 14–15; **13:** 36–37, 90,

(92), 94–97
  Magellanic **13:** 90, (92)
  variable **13:** 90
oystercrusher **32:** 28
oysters 30: 56–57
  eastern **30:** 56
  Pacific **30:** 52–53
  pearls **30:** 56–57, 61
  saddle **30:** 58, 59
  spiny **30:** 52
  wing **30:** 58, 59
Ozotocerus bezoarticus **6:** 10

P

Paa **43:** 84
  hazarensis **43:** 84
paca **7:** 12; **8:** 11, 28, 30, 30
  mountain **8:** 30
pacarana **7:** 12; **8:** 28, 31
Pachycalamus brevis **46:** 105
Pachycerianthus multiplicatus **21:** 57
Pachycondyla commutata **27:** 43
Pachydactylus **45:** 10, (39)
Pachyhynobius **41:** 36, (37)
Pachymedusa **43:** 67
Pachypanchax **38:** 81
  playfairii **38:** 81
Pachypoda guatemalensis **24:** 32–33
Pachyptila **12:** 31
  vittata **12:** 28
Pachytriton **41:** 88, 92
  labiatus **41:** 92
Pacifastacus lenuisculus **28:** 72–73
pacu 31: 91, **38:** 8, 35, 42–47
  black **38:** 47
  black-finned **38:** 45
  redhook **38:** 45
  silver **38:** 45
Padda oryzivora **16:** 90, 98–99
paddlefish 31: 47, 52–57, 74
  American 31: 53, 54–55, 70–71, **32:** 90
  Chinese **31:** 53, **32:** 90
pademelon
  red-legged **10:** 48, 51
  red-necked **10:** 48
Pagarus prideauxi **28:** 76–77
Pagophilus groenlandica **3:** 44–45
Pagrus pagrus **40:** 40

Paguma larvata **1:** 88
Paguroidea **28:** 56, <u>94–101</u>
Pagurus bernhardus **28:** *94*
painted snipe 14: <u>96–97</u>
   American **14:** 96, 97
   greater **14:** 96, 97, *97*
pair-bonds **11:** (49); **12:** 14, *56*, 79,
   88–89; **14:** 57, 68, 99; **15:** (16); **16:**
   (29), 60, (67), 90–91;**17:** (76); **18:** 26,
   89, 93; **19:** 19, *26–27*, 53, 62; **20:** 86
Palaeacanthocephala **21:** 77
Paleosuchus palpebrosus **47:** *94–95*
paleozoology **21:** (33)
palila **20:** 98
Palinura **28:** 56, <u>82–85</u>
Palmatogecko **45:** 11
   rangei **44:** 26, *28*; **45:** <u>30–31</u>, (39)
Palmatorappia solomonis **43:** 86
palmchat **18:** 30; **19:** 43
Palmeria dolei **20:** 98
Palonia castelnaui **36:** 98
Palpares **22:** 95, *94–95*
Palpigradi **29:** (29)
pamprodactylism **18:** (18)
Pan
   paniscus **4:** 12, <u>34–35</u>
   troglodytes **4:** 12, <u>28–33</u>
panaque **37:** 107
Panaque suttoni **37:** 107
panchax
   playfair's **38:** 81
   striped **38:** *79*
panda bear *see* panda, giant
panda
   giant 2: 82, <u>98–101</u>
   lesser (red) **1:** 20, 21, <u>30–31</u>; **2:** (99)
   red 1: 20, 21, <u>30–31</u>; **2:** (99)
Pandaka pygmaea **40:** (10), 94
Pandalus
   borealis **28:** *60, 68*
   platyceros **28:** *60–61*
Pandinus imperator **29:** 16
Pandion haliaetus **12:** 64; **15:** 8, <u>14–17</u>,
   (21), 32, (42), 56; **17:** (22); **18:** (18),
   80
Pandionidae **15:** 8
Pangasianodon **37:** 46
Pangasiidae **37:** 38, <u>42–47</u>
Pangasius **37:** 42, 46
   djambal **37:** 44
   gigas **37:** 32, <u>45–47</u>; **37:** 46, 47
   hypophthalmus **37:** 41, 42, *42–43*, 43
   sanitwongsei **37:** 42, 44, *44–45*
   sutchi **37:** 43
pangasius
   giant **37:** *44–45*
Pangio **34:** 9, 100, <u>100–101</u>, 102
   anguillaris **34:** 101
   goaensis **34:** 101
   kuhlii **34:** 88, *100*, 101
   myersi **34:** *14–15*, 101
   oblonga **34:** 101
   semicincta **34:** 101
   shelfordii **34:** *100–101*, 101

pangolin 1: *10*; **9:** <u>64–67</u>
   African **9:** 66
   armored **9:** *64*
   Asian **9:** 66
   giant **9:** 65, 66
   ground **9:** *64–65*, 65
   tree **9:** 65
Panorpa
   communis **22:** *104–105, 106–107*
   nuptialis **22:** *104*
panther
   black **2:** 30, *31*
   see also leopard; puma
Panthera
   leo **2:** 10, <u>14–19</u>
   leo persica **2:** (15)
   onca **2:** 10, <u>36–37</u>
   pardus **2:** 10, <u>30–33</u>
   tigris **2:** 10, <u>20–25</u>
   uncia **2:** 10, <u>34–35</u>
Pantherophis **49:** 10
Pantholops hodgsoni **6:** 62
Pantodon buchholzi **31:** 82, <u>100–101</u>
Pantodontidae **31:** (43), (82), 100
Pantophthalmus tabaninus **23:** *40–41*
pantotheres **7:** 10, 11
Panulirus
   argus **28:** *82, 84–85*
   marginatus **28:** *83*
Papasula abbotti **12:** 44
Papilio **22:** 31
   aegeus **26:** *18–19*
   glaucus **26:** 21
   machaon **26:** *16–17*
Papilionidae **26:** <u>16–21</u>
Papilioninae **26:** 17–18
Papio
   cynocephalus **4:** 40, <u>54–57</u>
   hamadryas **4:** 40, <u>58–59</u>
Papyrocranus **31:** <u>104–105</u>
   afer **31:** 82, 104
   congoensis **31:** 104, 105
Parablennius gattorugine **40:** *92–93*, 93
Parabrotulidae **36:** 26, 27
Parabuthus **29:** *18–19*
   capensis **29:** *16–17*
Paracanthopterygyii **36:** <u>8–15</u>
Paracentropogon **39:** 60
Parachanna **40:** 64
   africana **40:** 65
   insignis **40:** 65
   obscura **40:** 65
Paracheilognathus **34:** 66
Paracheirodon
   axelrodi **38:** 8, 35, 37, *37*
   innesi **38:** 8, 35, 39
   simulans **38:** 40
Paracynictis selousi **1:** 98
Paracyprichromis brieni **40:** 73
Paradisaea
   apoda **19:** 106
   guilielmi **19:** 106
   raggiana **19:** 106, <u>110–111</u>
   rudolphi **19:** 106

Paradisaeidae **19:** 106
Paradisaeinae **19:** 106
paradise fish **40:** 36, 61, *61*, 63
   threadfin **40:** 37
paradox fish **39:** 10, 26
Paradoxurus
   hermaphroditus **1:** 88, <u>94–95</u>
   jerdoni **1:** 88
   zeylonensis **1:** 88
Paragnathobdellae **21:** 94
Parahydrophis mertoni **50:** 44, (45)
Parailia
   congica **37:** *40–41*
   occidentalis **37:** (34), 40
   (Parailia) congica **37:** 40
   (Parailia) occidentalis **37:** 40
   pellucida **37:** (34)
   spiniserratus **37:** 40, (40)
Parajalysus nigrescens **24:** *49*
parakeet **18:** (81)
   Australian king **16:** 22, *22*
   Carolina **16:** 23
   crimson-winged **16:** 22, *22*
   monk **20:** 36
   mulga **16:** 22, *23*
   painted **19:** 12
   rose-ringed **16:** 22
   sun *see* conure, sun
Paralepididae **35:** 80, <u>98–99</u>
Paralichthyidae **39:** 90
Paralichthys
   californicus **39:** 90
   olivaceus **40:** 103
Paraliparis **39:** 83
Paraluteres prionurus **39:** (102)
Paramastax nigra **23:** 32
Parambassis
   baculis **40:** 21
   gulliveri **40:** 20
   lala **40:** 20, *20*
   ranga **40:** 20
   wolfii **40:** 21
Paramecium **21:** *22, 22–23*
Paramesopodopsis rufa **28:** *43*
Paramesotriton **41:** 88, 91
Paramythia montium **18:** 68, <u>72–73</u>
Paramythiidae **18:** 68, 69
Parantechinus
   aplicalis **10:** 27
   bilarni **10:** 27
Parapercis
   nebulosus **40:** 19
   schauinslandi **40:** *18–19*
Paraphrynus **29:** *26–27*
Paraplagusia **39:** 94
Paraploactis obbesi **39:** *70*
Paraponera clavata **27:** *41, 56–57*
parapox virus **7:** 44
Parascalops breweri **9:** 40
Parascolopsis boesemani **40:** 41
Parascyllidae **32:** (12), (30), 33
Parasitellus fucorum **29:** *33*
parasites **9:** 84; **21:** 17, (25), 26–27
   host-parasite relationship **21:** (85)

see also tapeworms
Parasitica **27:** 8, 10, 23
parasitoids **27:** 22–31
  finding hosts **27:** 25–26
parasitology **21:** (33)
Parasphendale agrionina **22:** *75*
Parataeniophorus gulosus **39:** 15
Paratherina cyanea **38:** 59
Paratrachichthys **39:** 21
Paratrygon **33:** (34)
Parauchenipterus **37:** 83
Parawixia bistriata **29:** *43*
parazen **39:** (25)
Parazen pacificus **39:** (25)
Parazenidae **39:** (25)
Parazoa **21:** 32, 34
Parcoblatta **22:** *71*
Pardosa
  amentata **29:** *82*
  nigriceps **29:** *84–85*
Pareas **49:** 8, 16, 90–93
  hamptoni **49:** 90
  margaritophorus **49:** *90*, 91
  vertebralis **49:** 16, 90–91, *91*, *92–93*
Pareatinae **49:** 8, 16, 90
Pareutropius
  debauwi **37:** (34), *38–39*, 40
  longifilis **37:** *41*
  vanderweyeri **37:** (34), 40
Paridae **17:** 70; **18:** 64
Paristiopterus
  gallipavo **40:** 55
  labiosus **40:** 55
Parmops coruscans **39:** 17
Parnasiinae **26:** 18
Parodontidae **38:** 17
Paroliogolophus agrestis **29:** *22*
Paroodectes **1:** 9
Parophrys vetulus **39:** 90
Parosphromenus **40:** 61, 63
  ornaticauda **40:** 61
parota, Lawes' **19:** 106
Parotia **19:** (108)
  lawesii **19:** 106
Parotocinclus maculicauda **37:** 104
parr (salmon) **35:** 53, (54)
parrot 11: 12; **16:** 22–25; **18:** 8, (18), (41), (81)
  eclectus 19: 12, 22–23
  forest 19: 12–33
  gray **16:** 22, 23, (35); **19:** 12; **20:** 36
  Meek's pygmy **16:** 22
  night **20:** 36
  orange-bellied **19:** 12, (14)
  owl *see* kakapo
  Pesquet's **16:** 22, 23; **20:** 36
  Philippine hanging **16:** 22
  pygmy **16:** 22
  swift **16:** 22; **19:** 12, (14)
  unusual 20: 36–45
  vernal hanging **20:** 36
parrotbill, Maui **20:** 98, *99*
parrotfinch 16: 90
  blue-faced 16: 90, (92), 96–97

parrotfish 34: 102, **40:** 9, 88–89
  bumpheaded **40:** 88
  chameleon **40:** *89*
  green humphead **40:** 88, *88*
  rusty **40:** *88*
parthenogenesis **44:** 37; **45:** (13), 61, 82, 83, 88–90, (89), (91); **48:** (25)
  in beetles **25:** 97, 107
  in bugs **24:** 101, 108, 112
  in crustaceans **28:** 20, 33
  in insects **22:** 41, 55, 81, 87
  in scorpions **29:** 19
partridge 11: 40, 45, 47, (47)
  gray 11: 44, 47, 64–65
  red-legged **11:** 44, 47, 64
Parula americana **17:** 88, 93
Parulidae **17:** 88; **19:** (74)
Parupeneus barberinoides **40:** *38–39*
Parus
  ater **17:** 70
  atricapillus **17:** 70, 74–79
  bicolor **17:** 70
  caeruleus **17:** 70
  carolinensis **17:** 70, 74, (78)
  cristatus **17:** 70
  gambeli **17:** 70, (78); **18:** 67
  hudsonicus **17:** 70, (78)
  major **17:** 70; **18:** 69
  montanus **17:** 70, 76
  palustris **17:** 70, 77
  rufescens **17:** 70, (78)
Parvimolge **41:** 68
Passalidae **25:** (75)
Passer
  domesticus **16:** 62, 100, 108–111; **18:** 42, 57; **20:** 87
  hispaniolensis **16:** 100
  luteus **16:** 100
  montanus **16:** 100; **18:** 13
  simplex **16:** 100
Passeriformes **16:** 90
Passerina
  ciris **16:** 62, 72–75
  cyanea **16:** 62
passerines **14:** 94; **16:** 77; **17:** 76; **18:** (18), 57, 75; **19:** 93; **20:** 80
Pasteurella tularense **8:** 81
Pastinachus **33:** (34)
Pataecidae **39:** 68–71
Pataecus fronto **39:** 70
patagium **8:** 108; **10:** (76), 84, 86
Patagona gigas **16:** 44
Patagonia **5:** 108
Patella
  coerulea **30:** *25*
  vulgata **30:** 22, *22–23*
pathology **21:** (33)
Pauropoda **22:** 14
pauropods **22:** (14), *15*
Pavo cristatus **11:** 44, 52–55
Pavoraja **33:** (26)
peafowl 11: (49)
  blue (Indian) **11:** 44, 45–46, (49),

52–55
  Indian 11: 44, 45–46, (49), 52–55
peal **35:** 66, (68)
pearlfish 36: 8, 22–23, 24, 25, 26
  banded **38:** 82
  blue sailfin **38:** 80
  Bruce's **38:** 82
  golden-striped **38:** 82
  high-head **34:** 49, 51
  least **38:** 80
  preserved in pearl **36:** (23)
  silver **36:** 23
  spotted **38:** 82
pearls **30:** 56–57, 61
pearlscale **34:** 49
  high-head **34:** 49, 51
pearlside **35:** 90
Pecari **5:** 88
  tajacu see Tayassu tajacu
peccary 5: *8*, 12
  Chacoan **5:** 88, 89, *89*
  collared 5: 88, 89, 90–91
  peccary family 5: 88–89
  white-lipped **5:** 88, 89, *89*
Peckoltia **37:** 107
  pulcher **37:** 107
peckoltia
  striped **37:** 107
  zebra **37:** 107
Pecten maximus **30:** *58*
Pectinator spekei **7:** 108
Pectinidae **30:** 50
Pedetes capensis **7:** 20–21
Pedetidae **7:** *12*
Pedicillina **21:** *68*
Pediculus
  humanus **22:** (89)
  humanus capitis **22:** 89
Pedioplanis **45:** 59, 74–75
  lineocellata **45:** *74–75*
pedogenesis **41:** 28–29
pedomorphosis **41:** 28–29
Pedostibes **42:** 56, 72, (73)
  hosii **42:** 58, 72–73
Pedum spondyloidum **30:** *67*
Pegasidae **39:** 10, 26, 36–37
Pegasus
  lancifer **39:** 36
  laternarius **39:** 36
  volitans **39:** 36, *37*
Pelagodroma marina **12:** 28
Pelamis **49:** (82); **50:** 44–49
  platurus **48:** 25; **50:** 45, (45), 47, (48), 49, 80
Pelangia mbutaensis **38:** 57
Pelatachina tibialis **23:** *105*
Pelea capreolus **6:** 62
Pelecanidae **12:** 44, 46
Pelecaniformes **12:** 44, 48
Pelecanoides
  garnotii **12:** 28
  georgicus **12:** 28
  megallani **12:** 28
  urinatrix **12:** 28

Pelecanoididae **12:** 28, 31
Pelecanus **15:** 26
    occidentalis **12:** 44, 50–53
    thagus **12:** 44, 50
pelican 12: 44–49, 64; **14:** 22, 25;
    15: 26
    brown 12: 44, 50–53
    Peruvian **12:** 44, 50, 51
pellets, owl's **15:** (66)
Pelobates **42:** 40
    cultripes **42:** 40, *41*
    fuscus **42:** 42–43
Pelobatidae **42:** 10, 34, 40, 76, 92;
    43: 34, 86
Pelodryadidae **43:** 39
Pelodryadinae **43:** 32, 39
Pelodytes
    caucasicus **42:** 20, (21)
    ibericus **42:** 20, (21)
    punctatus **42:** 20–21
Pelodytidae **42:** 10, (21)
Pelomedusa subrufa **47:** 41, (42)
Pelomedusidae **47:** 9, 28
Pelophryne **42:** 56, 60; **48:** 79
    misera **42:** 58
Pelteobagrus
    brashnikowi **37:** 29
    fluvidraco **37:** 27
Peltocheirus **24:** *86*
Peltops
    blainvillii **20:** 100
    montanus **20:** 100
peltops
    lowland **20:** 100
    mountain **20:** 100
Pelusios **47:** (42)
    castanoides **47:** 41, 42
    niger **47:** *41*
    seychellensis **47:** 42
    sinuatus **47:** *43*
    subniger **47:** 40–43
Penaeidea **28:** 56, 60–69
Penaeus meruguiensis **28:** *63*
pencilfish 34: 102, **38:** 22–23
    cross-banded **38:** 23
    Panama **38:** 23
    three-lined **38:** *22*
    three-striped **38:** *10*
Penelope
    montagnii **11:** 44
    pileata **11:** 44
    purpurascens **11:** 44
Penelopides exarhatus **19:** 48
penguin 3: 38–39; **11:** 8; **12:** 28, 45,
    98, 103; **13:** 93, 110, 111
    Adélie **12:** 8, *8*, 9, *10*, (10), 20, 21,
        22, (23); **13:** 109
    African **12:** 8, (10)
    Antarctic (chinstrap) **12:** 8, (11),
        20–23, 102
    bearded (chinstrap) **12:** 8, (11), 20–23,
        102
    chinstrap 12: 8, (11), 20–23, 102
    crested (rockhopper) **12:** 8, 10, 26–27

    emperor 12: 8, 10, (10), 12–17
    erect-crested **12:** 8
    fairy (little) **12:** 8, 10, (10), 24–25
    Fiordland **12:** 8
    Galápagos 12: 8, 10, 18–19
    gentoo **12:** 8, 10, (10), 21–22, (23)
    Humboldt **12:** 8, (10)
    jackass **12:** 10
    king **12:** 8, 10, (10), *11*, 12; **13:** 109
    little 12: 8, 10, (10), 24–25
    little blue (little) **12:** 8, 10, (10), 24–25
    macaroni **12:** 8, *9*, 10, 20; **13:** 109,
        110–111
    Magellanic **12:** 8, *8*
    penguin family 12: 8–11
    ringed (chinstrap) **12:** 8, (11), 20–23,
        102
    rockhopper 12: 8, 10, 26–27
    southern blue (little) **12:** 8, 10, (10),
        24–25
    Victoria (rockhopper) **12:** 8, 10, 26–27
    yellow-eyed **12:** 8, 10
Pennatulacea **21:** 43
Pentaceropsis recurvirostris **40:** 55, *55*
Pentaceros decacanthus **40:** 55
Pentacerotidae **40:** 54–55
Pentalagus furnessi **8:** 64
pentamerism **30:** 90, 110
Pentapodus caninus **40:** 41
Pentatomidae **24:** 60–69
peppershrike **17:** 98
    rufous-browed **17:** 98
Peracarida **28:** 9, 34
Perameles
    bougainville **10:** 27
    nasuta **10:** 27
Peramelidae **10:** 24
Perca **36:** 16
    flavescens **40:** *12*, 16, 26
    fluviatilis **40:** *14*, 16, 26
Perccottus
    glenii **40:** 99
perch 36: 16, **37:** 18, **38:** 50, **39:** (10),
    28, **40:** 12–19
    climbing 40: 9, 57, 58, 58–59, 60
    common **40:** 16
    Eurasian **35:** 35, **40:** *14*, 16, 26
    freshwater **40:** 12
    giant **40:** 12, 13
    gurnard **39:** 64, 66
    high-bodied climbing **40:** 58
    livebearing **40:** (17)
    Nile **40:** 11, 13, *13*
    ocean **39:** *58*, 64
    orange sea **40:** *16*
    pearl **40:** 12, 18
    pirate 36: 8, 16, 20–21
    red gurnard **39:** (67)
    rough gurnard **39:** 66
    rubberlip sea **40:** (17)
    Sacramento **40:** 26
    sea **39:** 64
    temperate **40:** 12

    Tule **40:** (17)
    western pygmy **40:** 14
    Westralian pygmy **40:** 14
    Yarra pygmy **40:** 14
    yellow **40:** *12*, 16, 17, 26
perchlet
    Commerson's glassy **40:** 20, 21
    dusky-fin glassy **40:** 21
    glassy **40:** 20
    Himalayan glassy **40:** 21
perchlike fish 40: 8–11
    families summary **40:** (8)
    midgets to giants **40:** (10)
Percichthyidae **40:** 12–19
Percidae **35:** (12), **39:** (10), **40:** 12–19
Perciformes **40:** 8–11
    families summary **40:** (8)
Percis japonica **39:** 80
Percopsidae **36:** 16–17
Percopsiformes **36:** 8–15
Percopsis
    omiscomaycus **36:** 16, *16*, 17
    transmontana **36:** 16
Perdix perdix **11:** 44, 64–65
peregrine *see* falcon, peregrine
perfume industry **1:** (91); **7:** (31)
Perga affinis **27:** *19*
Periclemenes **28:** *67*, 69
    colemani **28:** 65
    imperator **28:** *57*
Peripatus acacioi **22:** *12–13*
Periplaneta americana **22:** *68, 69*
Perisoreus canadensis **18:** 90
Perissocephalus tricolor **19:** 80
Perissodactyla **1:** *10*; **5:** 10, 12, 43
Perissodus **40:** 74
Peristedion
    cataphractum **39:** 57
    miniatum **39:** 57
Perithemis tenera **22:** *47*
periwinkles **30:** 26, 27, (28)
    flat **30:** *26*
    rough **30:** (28)
Perla bipunctata **22:** 80
Perna perna **30:** *54*
Pernis apivorous **15:** 8
Perodicticus potto **4:** 106
Peromatus **24:** *60–61, 68–69*
Peromyscus
    leucopus **7:** 83
    maniculatus **7:** 82–83
Peroryctes
    broadbenti **10:** 27
    raffrayana **10:** 27
Peroryctidae **10:** 24
pest control (biological control)
    by ants **24:** 54; **27:** 39
    by blow flies **23:** 111
    by bugs **24:** 36–37, 45–46, (49),
        62–64, (75)
    by ladybugs **25:** (56)
    by moths **26:** (103)
    by parasitoids **27:** 30–31
    by parasitic flies **23:** 106–107

by weevils **25:** 110
pests, birds as **18:** (81), (87)
Petauridae **10:** (76)
Petaurista
  elegans **7:** 36
  petaurista **7:** 36
Petauroides volans **10:** 74
Petaurus
  breviceps **10:** 74, <u>86–87</u>
  gracilis **10:** 74
Petinomys crinitus **7:** 34
petrel 11: 13; **12:** 29, 31, 64
  ashy storm- **12:** 28
  black storm- **12:** 28
  Bulwer's **12:** 28, *31*
  common diving- **12:** 28, *31*
  diving- **12:** 29, 31
  European storm- **12:** 28, *31*
  fork-tailed storm- **12:** 28
  gray **12:** 28
  Hawaiian **12:** 28
  Leach's storm- 12: 28, <u>42–43</u>
  northern giant **12:** 28, *30*
  southern giant **12:** 17, 28, *28*
  South Georgia diving- **12:** 28
  storm- **12:** 29, 31, 93; **20:** (14)
  Swinhoe's storm- **12:** 28
  Tahiti **12:** 28
  white-faced storm- **12:** 28
  Wilson's storm- **12:** 28, 31, *31*
Petrobius maritimus **22:** *37*
Petrocephalus
  catostoma **31:** 106
  simus **31:** 107
Petrodomus tetradactylus **9:** 59
Petrogale
  persephone **10:** 48
  xanthopus **10:** 48, <u>70–71</u>
Petromuridae **7:** *12*; **8:** 31
Petromus typicus **8:** 30, <u>54–55</u>
Petromyzon marinus **31:** 28, *28–29*
Petromyzontidae **31:** <u>26–31</u>, (108),
  33: 63
Petropedetinae **43:** 82, 87
Petropsaro **34:** 31
Petropseudes dahli **10:** 74
pets **1:** 22, 29, 35, 45, 95, 109; **2:** 75;
  4: 53, 78, 81, 83, 85, 87, 88,
  101; **7:** 15, (69), 83, 86; **8:** 39,
  42, (72); **9:** 13, 21
  see also cat, domestic; dog, domestic
Peucetia viridans **29:** *80–81*
pewee, tropical **17:** 30
Phacochoerus
  aethiopicus **5:** 74
  africanus **5:** 74, <u>80–83</u>
Phaenicophaeus pyrrhocephalus **20:** 46
Phaeodaria **21:** 13
Phaeognathus **41:** 68
  hubrichti **41:** 68
Phaethon
  aethereus **12:** 44, 59
  lepturus **12:** 44, <u>58–59</u>
  rubricauda **12:** 44

Phaethontidae **12:** 44, 47–48
Phaethornis **16:** (45)
  malaris **16:** 44
  ruber **16:** 44
  superciliosus **16:** 44
Phago loricatus **38:** 12, *12*
Phalacrocoracidae **12:** 44, 48
Phalacrocorax
  aristotelis **12:** 44
  atriceps **12:** 44
  auritus **12:** 44
  bougainvillii **12:** 44
  carbo **12:** 44, <u>60–61</u>
  harris **12:** 44
  punctatus **12:** 44
  pygmaeus **12:** 44
  urile **12:** 44
Phalaenoptilus nuttallii **15:** 78
Phalanger **10:** 82
  carmelitae **10:** 74
  gymnotis **10:** 74
Phalangeridae **10:** 76
phalarope 11: 12; **13:** <u>72–75</u>
  gray (red) **13:** 72, 75, <u>86–87</u>
  red 13: 72, 75, <u>86–87</u>
  red-necked 13: 72, 75, <u>88–89</u>
  Wilson's **13:** 72, 75, *75*
Phalaropodidae **13:** 72
Phalaropus
  fulicarius **13:** 72, <u>86–87</u>
  lobatus **13:** 72, <u>88–89</u>
Phalera sundana **26:** *81*
Phallichthys amates **38:** 96
Phallostethidae **38:** 55, (59)
Phaner furcifer **4:** 96
Pharomachrus
  antisianus **19:** 34
  auriceps **19:** 34
  mocinno **19:** 34, <u>38–39</u>
Phasanius colchicus **11:** 44, (54), <u>56–59</u>
phascogale **10:** (25)
  brush-tailed **10:** *26*, 27
  red-tailed **10:** *25*, 27
Phascogale
  calura **10:** 27
  tapoatafa **10:** 27
Phascolion strombi **21:** 78
Phascolorarctos cinereus **10:** 74, <u>92–97</u>
Phascolosorex
  doriae **10:** 27
  dorsalis **10:** 27
Phasianidae **11:** 44, 45–47
phasma, great brown **22:** *52*
Phasmahyla **43:** 67
Phasmatodea **22:** 30, <u>52–57</u>
Phasmida **21:** 77
pheasant 11: 45–47; **15:** 39
  blood **11:** 44, 46
  blue eared- **11:** 44
  common 11: 44, 46, (54), <u>56–59</u>
  golden **11:** 44, 46, 46, 49, 56
  Lady Amherst's **11:** 44, 46, 56
  ring-necked (common) **11:** 44, 46,
  (54), <u>56–59</u>

silver **11:** 44
Phelsuma **44:** 25; **45:** 9–10, 11, <u>32–37</u>
  abbotti **45:** *32–33*
  gigas **46:** (67)
  laticauda **44:** *8–9*; **45:** *35*
  madagascariensis **45:** *33,* 34
  standingi **45:** *34,* 37
Phelypera distigma **25:** *108–109*
Phenacogrammus
  altus **38:** 31
  interruptus **38:** 30, *30–31*
Phenacostethus smithi **34:** 72
Phenax variegata **24:** *72*
Phengodidae **25:** (35)
pheromones **7:** 66, 70; **22:** 11; **27:** 43,
  (45), (65), 69, 73, 75, 111–112
Phiale tristis **29:** *75*
Phibalura flavirostris **19:** 80
Philaenus spumarius **24:** 78, *78, 78–79*
Philander
  andersoni **10:** 14
  opossum **10:** 14
Philautus **43:** (76), 100, <u>106–107</u>
  hosii **43:** 107
  variabilis **43:** 107
  vermiculatus **43:** *106–107*
Philemon **20:** (91), 93
  corniculatus **20:** 88
Philepitta **20:** 74
  castanea **20:** 74
  schlegeli **20:** 74
Philetairus socius **11:** 8; **16:** 100, (104)
Philipomyia **23:** *58–59*
Philomachus pugnax **13:** 30
Philoria frosti **42:** 95, 97
Philoscia muscorum **28:** *46–47, 48–49*
Philothamnus **49:** 11; **50:** 17
Philydor erythropterus **20:** 80
Phlaeothripidae **22:** 85
Phlegopsis nigromaculata **19:** 72
Phlogophora meticulosa **22:** *32–33*
Phlyctenanthus australis **21:** *60*
Phobetron **26:** 106
Phoca
  groenlandica **3:** 9, <u>44–45</u>
  sibirica see *Pusa sibirica*
  vitulina **3:** 9, <u>40–41</u>
Phocarctos hookeri **3:** 9
Phocidae **3:** 8
Phocoena phocoena **3:** 55, <u>78–79</u>
Phodilus **15:** 64
  badius **15:** 50
  prigoginei **15:** 50
Phoebastria immutabilis **12:** 28
Phoebetria
  fusca **12:** 28
  palpebrata **12:** 28
Phoebis sennae **26:** *24–25*
Phoebodus **32:** 101
Phoeniconaias minor **14:** 44, 46; **20:** 26
Phoenicoparrus
  andinus **14:** 44
  jamesi **14:** 44
Phoenicopteridae **14:** 44; **19:** 36

Phoenicopteriformes **14:** 44
Phoenicopterus
  chilensis **14:** 44
  ruber **14:** 44, 46–51
Phoenicurus
  ochruros **18:** 44
  phoenicurus **18:** 44
Phoenix (mythical bird) **14:** (51)
Pholadidae **30:** 71
Pholcidae **29:** 60–63
Pholcus phalangioides **29:** 60, 61, 62–63
Pholidichthyidae **40:** 23
Pholidichthys leucotaenia **40:** 23
Pholidocercus **1:** 9
Pholidota **1:** 10; **9:** 64
Phoneutria **29:** 87
phoresy **29:** (21), 33
Phoronida **21:** 32, 68, 69, 74–75
Phoronis **21:** 75
Phoronopsis viridis **21:** 74
phrororhachids **11:** (10)
Photobacterium **36:** (79)
  phosphoreum **36:** 29
Photoblepharon palpebratum **39:** 18
photophores **35:** 88–89, 90, 91, 102
photosynthesis **21:** 9, 60, (65), (66), 93
Phoxinus **34:** 16, 73, 74, 75
  cumberlandensis **34:** 73, (77)
  eos **34:** 73
  erythrogaster **34:** 73, 74, 75
  lagowskii **34:** 73
  neogaeus **34:** 73
  oreas **34:** 74
  oxycephalus **34:** 73
  pecnurus **34:** 74
  perenurus **34:** 74
  phoxinus **34:** 72, 72
  tennesseensis **34:** 74
Phractocephalus hemioliopterus **37:** 29, 84, 87
Phreatoicidea **28:** 34
Phrictus quinquepartilus **24:** 12
Phromnia rosea **24:** 74–75
Phryganea grandis **22:** 102
Phrygilus dorsalis **16:** 62
Phrynarachne tuberosa **29:** 70
Phrynobatrachus **43:** 87
Phrynocephalus **44:** 32, 33–34, 36
  helioscopus **44:** 36
  mystaceus **44:** 36, 36
Phrynohyas **43:** 32
  venulosa **43:** (35), 36–37
Phrynomantis **42:** 104, 105
Phrynomedusa **43:** 67
Phrynomerinae **42:** 104
Phrynomerus **42:** 104, 105
Phrynosoma **44:** 15, 25, 28, 30, 34, (49), 84, 85, 102, 106
  cornutum **44:** 104
  coronatum **44:** 80, 102–105
  douglassi **44:** 103
  hernandesi **44:** 104–105
  platyrhinos **50:** 104
Phrynosomatinae **44:** 80

Phthanophaneron harveyi **39:** 17
Phthiraptera **22:** 30, 88–89
Phthirus pubis **22:** 88–89
Phycidae **36:** 32–37
Phycis **36:** 36
Phycodurus eques **31:** 9, **39:** (42), 44
Phylidonyris novaehollandiae **20:** 88, 95
Phyllastrephus apperti **16:** 56
Phyllium **22:** 54–55
Phyllobates **43:** 68, (71), 72, 80, 81, (81)
  aurotaenia **43:** 78
  lugubris **42:** 82; **43:** (73)
  terribilis **42:** 9; **43:** 72, 78–81
Phyllocarida **28:** 9, 34
Phyllodactylus **45:** 10
Phyllomedusa **43:** 32, 36, 64–67, 107; **49:** 16
  bicolor **42:** 11; **43:** 66–67
  boliviana **43:** (66)
  hypochondrialis **43:** (66), 67
  hypochondrialis azurea **43:** 34–35
  iheringi **43:** 66
  lemur **43:** 65
  marginata **43:** 39
  sauvagei **42:** 12; **43:** 66, (66), 102
  tarsius **43:** 66, 67
  tomopterna **43:** 64–65, 67
  trinitatus **43:** 37, 64–65, 65, 67
  vaillanti **43:** 66
  venustus **43:** 64
Phyllomedusinae **43:** 32, 39
Phyllomorpha laciniata **24:** 55, 55–56
Phyllophaga vandinei **42:** 64
Phyllopharyngea **21:** 13
Phyllopteryx **39:** 41
  taeniolatus **39:** 10–11, (42)
Phyllorhynchus **48:** (39)
Phylloscartes nigrifrons **17:** 30
Phylloscopus **17:** 60, 64
  borealis **17:** 60
  collybita **17:** 60, 62
  trochilus **17:** 52, 60, 62–65
Phyllostomidae **9:** 87
Phyllurus **44:** 25, 28, 30; **45:** (10), 12, (47)
  cornutus **45:** 46
Phylodryas **49:** (39)
Phylolaemata **21:** 69
Phymateus **23:** 30–31
Phyrinus **29:** 26
Physalaemus **42:** 76, 79, 79
Physeter catodon **3:** 55, 86–89
Physiculus **35:** 101
Physignathus **44:** 32, 34
  cocincinus **44:** 34; **48:** (58)
  lesueurii **44:** 34
Physonota alutacea **25:** 14–15
Phytomastigophora **21:** 13, 16
Phytonomus nigrirostris **25:** 104
Pica
  hudsonia **18:** 90, 104, (107)
  nuttalli **18:** 90, (107)
  pica **18:** 90, 104–107
Picassofish

Arabian **39:** 103
Picidae **18:** 8, 64
Piciformes **17:** 20; **19:** 56, 70
Picinae **18:** 8
pickerel 35: 8, 10–19, **38:** 27
  chain **35:** 14–15, 18
  grass **35:** 16, 16–17
  redfin **35:** 16
Picoides tridactylus **18:** 8
piculet **18:** 8
  white-barred **18:** 8
Picumninae **18:** 8
Picumnus cirratus **18:** 8
Picus viridis **18:** 8, 20–21
piddocks **30:** 62, 71
pie
  gray tree **18:** 90
  tree **18:** 91
Pieridae **26:** 22–27
Pieris
  brassicae **26:** 24–25
  rapae **26:** (24)
pig 5: 8, 10, 12
  bearded **5:** 74, 75
  bushpig **5:** 74, 75
  lard pig **5:** (78)
  pig family 5: 74–75
pig mouse **8:** 38
pigeon 11: 13; **15:** 19, (21); **18:** (81)
  African green **16:** 12
  feral (rock dove) **16:** 12, 16–19; **18:** (81)
  green imperial **16:** 12, 13
  passenger **13:** 15
  pigeon family 16: 8, 12–13
  rock *see* dove, rock
  town *see* dove, rock
  Victoria crowned 16: 12, 14–15
  wood **18:** (10)
pigfish **3:** 78; **32:** 28, **39:** 11, 68, 71, **40:** 36
piglet **38:** 17
piha, screaming **19:** 80
pika 8: 60, 62
  Alpine **8:** 94
  American 8: 67, 94, 96, 98–101
  Asian **8:** 97
  collared **8:** 94, 97, 98
  common (American) **8:** 94, 96, 98–101
  Eurasian **8:** 98, 100
  Himalayan **8:** 94, 96
  pika family 8: 94–97
  Rocky Mountain (American) **8:** 94, 96, 98–101
  Russian steppe **8:** 94, 97
  Sardinian **8:** (96)
pike 35: 8, 10–19, **36:** 33, **38:** 27
  African **38:** 24, 27
  Amur **35:** 18
  blue **35:** (12)
  characin *see* pike characin
  cichlid *see* pike cichlid
  emperor's **35:** (17)

kafue **38:** *24*, 27, (27)
northern 31: 78, **35:** *10–11*, 11, *12–13*, (14), 17, (17), *18–19*, **37:** 18, **38:** 27, (27)
northern, habitat **35:** *14*
pike characin **38:** 12, *12*, 13
Cuvier's **38:** 25
golden **38:** 26
spotted **38:** (26), *27*
striped **38:** 24, 26
pike characoids 38: 24–27
pike cichlid **37:** (108), **38:** (40), **40:** 70, (71)
pikehead 40: 56–57, 57, 63
pike-perch **40:** *9*, 16
pilchard **36:** 50, *86–87*, 98, *98*, 99, 100, 101, 105, 106, 107, 111
Pilherodius pileatus **14:** 23
pilot fish **33:** 50, 51, **39:** *111*, **40:** 34
pim **37:** 10, 85, 86
angelicus **37:** 86, 87
"blind" **37:** (89)
bumblebee **37:** *88–89*, 89
graceful **37:** 86
porthole shovelnose **37:** 87
shovelnosed **37:** 87
spotted shovelnose **37:** 87
Pimelodella **37:** 85, 87
gracilis **37:** 86
kronei **37:** (89)
lateristriga **37:** (89)
pictus **37:** 86
Pimelodidae **37:** 84–89, (87), 104
Pimelodus **37:** 86, 87
pictus **37:** 86
Pimephales **34:** 68, (71)
notatus **34:** 75, (79)
promelas **34:** (71), *75*, (79)
tenellus **34:** (79)
vigilax **34:** (79)
Pinaroloxias inornata **20:** 96
pineal organ (third eye) **36:** (31)
pineapple fish **39:** 9, 16, *17–18*, 18, 20
pinecone fish **39:** 9, 16, 18, 20
luminescent **39:** 20
pingers **3:** 79
Pinguinus impennis **12:** 101
Pinguipedidae **40:** 12–19
Pinicola enucleator **16:** 76, 82–87
Pinnidae **30:** 59
Pinnipedia **1:** *10*; **3:** 8–13
Pinnotheres ostreum **28:** 111–112
Pinnotheridae **28:** 111–112
pintadinho **37:** 84, (86), 91
pintail **14:** 52, *53*
pinto **5:** 59
Pipa **42:** 46, 48, 49; **43:** (11)
arrabali **42:** 47, (51)
carvalhoi **42:** 47, (51)
myersi **42:** 47
parva **42:** 47, *49*, (51)
pipa **42:** 46, 47, *47*, 48, 50–51
pipefish 39: 26, 38–47
armored **39:** 42

banded **39:** *45*
ghost **39:** 26, 38, 42, 43
ornate ghost **39:** *42–43*
river **39:** (46)
pipehorse **39:** 38, 40, 41, 42
pipi **30:** *63*
Pipidae **42:** 10, 11, 46
pipistrelle **9:** 87
pipit 17: (39)
buff-bellied **17:** 44, 45
meadow **17:** 44, 45, 50, 51; **20:** (48)
plain-backed **17:** 44, 45
Richard's **17:** 44, *44–45*, 45
rock 17: 44, 50–51
Sprague's **17:** 44, 45
tawny **17:** 44
tree **17:** 44, 45
wagtail and pipit family 17: 44–45
water **17:** 44, 50
Pipra
coronata **19:** 80
erythrocephala **19:** 80
filicauda **19:** 80
mentalis **19:** 80
vilasboasi **19:** 80
Pipreola
arcuata **19:** 80, 84–85
intermedia **19:** 84
riefferii **19:** 84
Pipridae **19:** 80
Piprites chloris **19:** 80
piracatinga **37:** 84, (86), 91
piracy *see* kleptoparasitism
piraíba **37:** 87
piranha 31: 91, **37:** 84, **38:** 35, 42–47, (44), (45), **40:** 102
black **38:** 44
black-spot **38:** 46–47
blacktail **38:** 44
diet **38:** (45)
gold **38:** 46
red-bellied **38:** 8, *42*, 43, *43*, 47
San Francisco **38:** 44
wimple **38:** *44–45*
pirarucu **31:** 82, 88
Pirata piraticus **29:** *83*
Piroplasmea **21:** 13
Pisaura mirabilis **29:** *42*, 88, (91), *92–93*
Pisauridae **29:** 88–93
Pisilus tipuliformis **24:** 42
pit vipers 42: 82; **48:** (97), (105); **49:** 48; **50:** 9, 50–55
arboreal **50:** (111)
bamboo **50:** 59
brown **50:** 111
Central American palm **50:** (111)
eyelash (eyelash viper) **48:** (97); **49:** (51), 105; **50:** 9, *10–11*, 59, 90–91
Himalayan **50:** 50
Japanese habu **50:** 110
Malaysian 50: 9, 96–97
palm **50:** 59
Pope's 50: 108–111

shore **50:** 111
Sumatran **50:** *110–111*
Wagler's **50:** *9*, 111
white-lipped **50:** *54*, 110
see also copperhead
Pitangus sulphuratus **17:** 30
pitcher plants **43:** 107
Pithecia
albicans **4:** 72
irrorata **4:** 72
monachus **4:** 72
pithecia **4:** 72
Pithys albifrons **19:** 72
Pitohui dichrous **43:** (81)
pitohui, hooded **43:** (81)
pitta 17: 28–31, (30); **19:** (74)
African **17:** 30, *30*
Bengal (Indian) **17:** 30, 42–43
blue **17:** 30
blue-tailed **17:** 30, *31*
blue-winged (Indian) **17:** 30, 42–43
Gurney's **17:** 30, *31*
Indian 17: 30, 42–43
noisy **17:** 30, *30*
Pitta
angolensis **17:** 30
brachyura **17:** 30, 42–43
cyanea **17:** 30
guajana **17:** 30
gurneyi **17:** 30
versicolor **17:** 30
Pittidae **17:** 28, 31; **19:** 74
Pituophis **49:** 11
catenifer annectans **49:** *8–9*
Pityriasis gymnocephala **20:** 100
placental mammals **10:** 8, 9–11, 13
Placozoa **21:** 32, 35
Plagiodontia aedium **8:** 30
Plagiopylea **21:** 13
Plagiostoma giganteum **30:** *53*
Plagiotremus
rhinorhynchos **40:** 91
tapeinosoma **40:** *90*
Plagiotryptus hippiscus **23:** *32–33*
Plagopterus argentissimus **34:** 53, 71
plague **7:** 14, 76–77
bubonic **22:** (113)
plaice **39:** 11, 84
European **39:** *88*, 89, *89*, 90, 91, 93
Planaria **21:** 80–81, 81–82
planigale **10:** (24)
common **10:** *25*, 27
Papuan **10:** 27
Planigale
maculata **10:** 27
novaeguineae **10:** 27
plant control **24:** 54–55, 91
plantain-eater, eastern gray **16:** 38
planthoppers
delphacid **24:** (75)
flatid **24:** (74)
fulgorid (lanternflies) **24:** *12*, 72–77
plants
and ants **27:** (46)

Hymenoptera and **27:** 8–9
Plasmodium **21:** *26, 26–27*
Platalea
    ajaja **14:** 32, *42–43*; **19:** 36
    leucorodia **14:** 32
    minor **14:** 32
Platanista
    gangetica **3:** 55, (61)
    minor **3:** 55, (61)
Plataplochilus
    miltotaenia **38:** 104
    mimus **38:** 104
Plataspidae **24:** (63)
Platichthys stellatus **39:** 85
platy **38:** 96, 100, 103
    blood-red **38:** *51*
    hybrid **38:** (100)
    maculatus **38:** 109
    southern **38:** 100
    variatus **38:** 100
Platycephalidae **39:** 11, 53, *72–73*
Platycephalus
    fuscus **39:** 73
    indicus **39:** 72, 73
Platycpoida **28:** 9
Platydesmida **22:** *14–15*
Platydoras
    costatus **37:** *78*
    siamensis **37:** 41
Platyhelminthes **21:** 32, 77, 80–85
Platymantinae **43:** 82, 85–86
Platymantis **43:** 82, 85–86
Platypelis **42:** 104, (108)
    milloti **42:** 105
Platyplectrurus **48:** 28
Platypoecilus **38:** (100)
Platyptilia gouodactyla **26:** *102*
platypus 1: 14
    duck-billed 10: 105, 106–109
Platyrhina **33:** (27)
    sinensis **33:** 29
Platyrhinidae **33:** (9), (27)
Platyrhinoidis **33:** (27)
    triseriata **33:** *29*
platyrrhines **4:** 11
Platysaurus **44:** 30; **45:** 98, 99–100
    broadleyi **45:** 106–107
Platysilurus
    malarmo **37:** 87
Platyspizia crassirostris **20:** 96
Platystacus **37:** 92
Platysteiridae **17:** 66
Platysternidae **47:** 9, 28
Platysternon megacephalum **47:** 56–57
Platystomatichthys sturio **37:** 87
play **18:** (103); **19:** (62); **20:** (40)
"playing dead", fish **32:** *18*
Plebeia **27:** *109*
pleco **34:** 109, **37:** 26, 101, 104, 106, 107, (108), 110
    blue-eyed **37:** 107
    butterfly **34:** 109
    Hong Kong **34:** 108, 109
    red sailfin **37:** *111*

snowking **37:** *106–107*
spiny **37:** 107
spotted **37:** *104*
Plecoglossidae **35:** 26–29
Plecoglossus
    altivelis altivelis **35:** *26,* 29, *29*
    altivelis ryukyuensis **35:** 29
Plecoptera **22:** 30, 80–81
Plecotus auritus **9:** 110–111
Plectorhinchus
    chaetodonoides **40:** 37
    harrawayi **40:** 37
    orientalis **40:** *10–11,* 37
Plectrogenium
    barsukovi **39:** 65
    nanum **39:** 65
Plectrophenax
    hyperboreus **16:** 62
    nivalis **16:** 62, 64–65
Plectrurus **48:** 28
Plegadis falcinellus **14:** 32, 40–41
Pleocyemata **28:** 56, 58
Plesiobatidae **33:** (9), (34)
Plesiobatis **33:** (34)
Plesiopidae **40:** 22–25
Plesiotrygon **33:** (34)
    iwamae **33:** *35*
Plethodon **41:** 68
    aureolus **41:** 85
    cinereus **41:** 87
    glutinosus **41:** 84–85
    jordani **41:** *71,* 72, *72–73*
    kentucki **41:** 85
Plethodontidae **41:** (12), 27, 29, 68, 93, 96
Plethodontinae **41:** 68, 70
Plethodontini **41:** 71
Pleurobrachia **21:** *44–45*
    pileus **21:** 44
Pleurobranchomorpha **30:** 37
Pleurodeles **41:** 88, 91
    poireti **41:** (27)
    waltl **41:** (27), 100–101
Pleurodema **42:** 76
Pleurodira **47:** 9, 9–10, *10,* 38
Pleurogrammus
    azonus **39:** 75
    monopterygius **39:** 75
Pleuronectes
    flesus **39:** 90
    platessa **39:** 84, *88,* 89, *89,* 93
Pleuronectidae **39:** 11, *84–85,* 87, 88–91, 92
Pleuronectiformes **39:** 84–87
    families summary **39:** (84)
Pleuronectoidei **33:** 11
Plexippus paykulli **29:** *76*
Pliocercus **50:** 26
Pliohippus **5:** 42
Ploceidae **16:** 62, 90, 100; **18:** 42
Ploceus cucullatus **16:** 100, 102–105
Plotosidae **37:** 66–69
Plotosus lineatus **37:** *12,* 66, *66,* 67,

68–69, **40:** 24
plover 12: 74; **20:** (31)
    American golden 13: 8, 10–15
    Arctic **13:** 9
    black-bellied 13: 8, 10, 16–17
    blacksmith 13: 8, 20–21
    crab 13: 76, 90, 93, (93), 100–103
    double-banded **13:** 8, 9, 27
    Egyptian **11:** 98, 99, (103)
    Eurasian golden **13:** 8, 10, 55
    gray (black-bellied) **13:** 8, 10, 16–17
    gray-headed **13:** 8
    Pacific golden **13:** 8, 9, 10
    plover family 13: 8–9, 30
    quail **11:** 92
    ringed 13: 8, 18–19
    spur-winged **13:** 8
    wattled **13:** 8, *8*
plumage
    aigrettes **14:** *21,* 29
    cleaning **14:** (22)
    countershading **11:** (102)
    courtship **14:** 22–23, 29
    dimorphic **14:** (22); **17:** (37)
    eating **14:** 18
    elongated feathers **15:** 84, 85, *85,* 86, (99); **19:** (108)
    flight feathers **14:** 59
    form and function **11:** 11, *11*
    iridescence **18:** (80)
    juvenile **11:** 31–33; **12:** (77); **14:** 23
    morphs **12:** 76
    saving heat **13:** (111)
    tail streamers **15:** (86), (99); **19:** 38
    waterproofing **12:** 8, 29; **14:** 53
Pluvialis **13:** 9
    apricaria **13:** 8, 10, 55
    dominica **13:** 8, 10–15
    fulva **13:** 8, 10
    squatarola **13:** 8, 10, 16–17
Pluvianus aegyptius **11:** 98, (103)
poacher 39: 76–81
    dragon **39:** 80
    pixie **39:** 80
    sturgeon **39:** 80
poaching **4:** 24, 27; **5:** 39, (102)
Poblana **38:** (63)
pochard **12:** 66; **14:** 52, 53
Podager **15:** 78
Podarcis **45:** 58, 76–77, (77)
    erhardii **45:** 61, 77
    gaigeae **45:** 61
    lilfordi **45:** 60–61, 77
    milensis **45:** 61
    muralis **45:** *59,* 76–77
Podargidae **15:** 78, 79
Podargus strigoides **15:** 78
Podiceps
    andinus **14:** 16
    auritus **14:** 16
    cristatus **14:** 16, 18–19, 93
    major **14:** 16
    nigricollis **14:** 16
Podilymbus podiceps **14:** 16

Podoces panderi **18**: 90
Podocnemis
    expansa **47**: *30–31*, 45
    unifilis **47**: <u>44–45</u>
Podogymnura
    aureospinula **9**: 12
    truei **9**: 12, *13*
Podothecus
    accipenserinus **39**: 80
Poecilia **38**: 96
    formosa **38**: 101
    latipinna **38**: *100*, 101, 102
    reticulata **38**: 94, *94*, *94–95*, 107
    sphenops **38**: 101, 102
    velifera **38**: 101, 102
Poecilictis libyca **1**: 32
Poeciliidae **38**: 50, 68, <u>94–105</u>
poeciliids **38**: 50
Poeciliopsis gracilis **38**: 96
Poecilocharax **38**: 33
    bovallii **38**: 32
    weitzmani **38**: 32, *32*
Poecilogale albinucha **1**: 32
Poecilostomatoida **28**: 9
Poelagus marjorita **8**: 64
Poephila **16**: 90
    guttata **16**: 90
poetry, bird-inspired **18**: (27)
Pofadder **50**: (61)
pogge **39**: *79*
Pogona **44**: 32, 34, 51
    barbata **44**: 51
    vitticeps **44**: 30, <u>50–51</u>
Pogonomyrmex **27**: 52
    occidentalis **27**: *52*
Pogonophora **21**: 32, 77, <u>92–93</u>
Poiana richardsoni **1**: 88
pointer
    blue **32**: 84
poison dart frogs 41: *18*; **42**: 9, 10,
    13, 58, 82, 84, (89);
    43: (11), 38–39, <u>68–73</u>, (81), 108;
    44: 104
    black-and-yellow **43**: *68–69*, 73
    blue poison **43**: 71, (71), *77*
    buzzing **43**: 71–72
    dyeing **43**: *70–71*, (71), 73
    granular **43**: (76)
    green-and-black **43**: 70, *70*, 77
    harlequin **43**: (76)
    Kokoe **43**: 78
    Lehmann's **43**: (71), (76)
    mimic **43**: *73*
    orange 43: <u>78–81</u>
    red **43**: (76)
    sky-blue **43**: 72
    splendid **43**: (71)
    strawberry 43: 70, (71), <u>74–77</u>, 80,
    111
    terrible (orange) **43**: <u>78–81</u>
    three-colored **43**: 73, (80)
poisons, in diet **19**: (28), (36); **20**: 14,
    17–18, (52), 70–72
poker

down **31**: *106*, *108–109*
Poladryas minuta **26**: *44–45*
polecat 1: <u>44–45</u>
    European **1**: 32, *34*, 35, *35*
    marbled **1**: 32, 34, *34*
Polemaetus bellicosus **15**: 8
Polemon **49**: 106
    notatus **49**: 108
Poliocephalus
    poliocephalus **14**: 16
    rufopectus **14**: 16
Polioptilinae **17**: 60
Polistes
    nest organization **27**: 70–72
    cinerascens **27**: *73*
    fastidiosus **27**: *68–69*
    instabilis **27**: *62–63*, *70–71*
Polistotrema stouti **32**: 102
Pollachius
    pollachius **36**: *10*, (40), *40*
    virens **36**: 39, (40)
pollack **31**: 42, **36**: *10*, 38, 39, (40), *40*,
    (42), 43, 49, 51
    walleye **36**: 50, 51
pollan **35**: 40
Pollenia rudis **23**: *111*
pollination **16**: (50)
pollock **36**: 38, (40)
pollution **1**: 61, 62, 64, 69, 71, 75;
    2: (88); **3**: 12, 41, 59, 61, 65,
    67, 74, 79, 83; **12**: 57, 111;
    14: 15, 17, 29, (107); **15**: 17;
    35: 49, 50; **42**: 14, 20, (21);
    43: 65
    chemicals **12**: 53; **15**: 11, 21, (21),
    35, 49, 68
    noise pollution **3**: 88
polyandry **11**: 35; **14**: 94, 96, 98–99
    successive **11**: (30); **14**: 97
Polybia occidentalis **27**: *66–67*
Polyborus plancus **15**: 8, <u>24–27</u>
Polycentrus schomburgkii **40**: 57
Polychaeta **21**: 77, 94, <u>98–101</u>
Polychrotinae **44**: 80
Polycirrus caliendrum **21**: *28*
Polycystina **21**: 13
Polydactylus indicus **40**: 39
polyembryony **27**: 23–24
polygyny **11**: (30), 35
Polymixia
    berndti **35**: *111*
    japonica **35**: 110
    lowei **35**: 111
    nobilis **35**: 110, *110*
    salagomeziensis **35**: 111
    yuni **35**: 111
Polymixiidae **35**: 82, <u>110–111</u>
Polymixiiformes **35**: (79)
polymorphism **22**: 33; **43**: (21); **49**: 38,
    (51), (53)
Polynemidae **38**: 52, **40**: <u>36–37</u>
Polynemus **40**: 37
Polyodon spathula **31**: 53, *54–55*,
    <u>70–71</u>, **32**: 90

Polyodontidae **31**: (43), (52), 70
Polyommatinae **26**: 29
Polypedates **43**: 100, (105)
    leucomystax **43**: (105)
    otilophis **43**: *101*
polyphenism **22**: 33
Polyphylla fullo **25**: *82*
Polyplacophora **30**: 9, <u>14–15</u>
Polypteridae **31**: (43), <u>44–51</u>
Polypterus **31**: 47, 48, 49, (51)
    bichir bichir **31**: 51
    delhezi **31**: *48–49*
    ornatapinnis **31**: *44–45*, 50
    palmas **31**: *44*
    senegalus **31**: 50
    senegalus senegalus **31**: *46–47*
Polyspilota aeruginosa **22**: *74–75*, 77
Polysticta **12**: 70; **14**: 52
    stelleri **12**: 66
polyvalents **50**: (11)
Pomacanthidae **39**: (10), **40**: 23, (47),
    <u>50–53</u>, 54, 101
Pomacanthus **40**: 52
    imperator **40**: *52*
Pomacentridae **40**: 9, <u>80–83</u>
Pomatoschistus minutus **40**: *94*, 96
pomfret **40**: 34, 35
    Atlantic **40**: 35
    eastern **40**: 43
    Woodward's **40**: 43
pompano 32: 67, **40**: <u>34–35</u>
Pompilidae **27**: <u>58–61</u>
pompon **34**: 49, 51
    orange **34**: 51
pondskaters (water striders) **24**: <u>16–17</u>
Pongo
    abelii **4**: 12, <u>14–19</u>
    pygmaeus **4**: 12, <u>14–19</u>
Pontinus kuhlii **39**: 61
Pontoporia blainvillei **3**: 55, (61)
pony
    Falabella **5**: (43)
    feral *see* mustang
    Welsh **5**: *42–43*
    wild *see* mustang
ponyfish **40**: 34
    common **40**: 35
    Indo-west Pacific slender **40**: 35
poolfish **38**: 110, (111)
poor-cod **36**: 38
poorwill **15**: 78
Poospiza torquata **16**: 62
Popicipedidae **14**: 16
Popricopida **28**: 9
porbeagle **32**: 22, 25
Porcellanidae **28**: 86
Porcellio scaber **28**: *48–49*
porcupine 1: 50–51; **7**: 8; **8**: 10, <u>12–15</u>
    African 8: 10, 12, 12–13, 14, <u>16–19</u>
    African brush-tailed **8**: 12
    American **8**: 10
    American tree **8**: 9
    Asian brush-tailed **8**: 12
    bahia hairy dwarf **8**: 12

bicolored tree **8**: 27
Brazilian tree **8**: 12, 13
brown hairy dwarf **8**: 12
brush-tailed **8**: 14, 16
Cape **8**: 12, *15*
crested (African) **8**: 10, 12, 12–13, 14, 16–19
in Europe **8**: (19)
hairy dwarf **8**: 12
long-tailed **8**: 12, 14, 16
Malayan **8**: 12, *12*, 14
Mexican tree (tree) **8**: 12, 13, 14, 26–27
New World 7: *12*; **8**: 12–15
North African (African) **8**: 10, 12, 12–13, 14, 6–19
North American 7: (8); **8**: 10, 12, 13, 14, 20–25
Old World 7: *12*; **8**: 12–15
South African **8**: 19
tree 8: 12, 13, 14, 26–27
upper Amazon **8**: 12
porcupinefish 39: 11, 96, 97, 108–109
blotched **39**: *108–109*
longspine **39**: 109
porcupinelike rodents 8: 8–11
Porcus piscus **3**: 78
porgy 40: 40–41
Porichthyinae **36**: 55
Porichthys **36**: (57), 59
notatus **36**: (56), *57*
Porifera **21**: 32, 34, 36–41
Poroderma
africanum **32**: 56–57
marleyi **32**: 56
pantherinum **32**: 56
Poromitra
crassiceps **39**: 13
megalops **39**: 13
oscitans **39**: 13
Poropuntius malcolmi **34**: *27*
Porotergus **33**: 101
porpoise
common (harbor) **3**: 55, 78–79
harbor 3: 55, 78–79
porpoising **3**: 69
Portia labiata **29**: (77)
Portuguese man-of-war **21**: 46, *48–49*, 49
Portunus **28**: *104*
pelagicus **28**: *113*
possum 10: (10), 75–77
Arnhemland **10**: 80
brush-tipped ringtail **10**: 74
common brushtail 10: *10*, 74, 76, 78–81
common ringtail **10**: 74, *76*
copper ringtail 10: 74, 90–91
Daintree River ringtail **10**: 74
eastern pygmy **10**: 74
feathertail **10**: 74
green ringtail **10**: 74
honey 10: 8, 74, 75–76, 102–103
Leadbeater's 10: 74, *76*, 77, 88–89

marsupial gliding **7**: (37)
mountain brushtail **10**: 74
mountain pygmy **10**: 74, 76, *77*, (77)
pygmy **42**: *66–67*
ringtail **10**: (77)
rock ringtail **10**: 74
scaly-tailed **10**: 74
striped **10**: 74, *76*
western pygmy **10**: 74
Weyland ringtail **10**: 74
see also opossum, Virginia
Potamalosa **36**: 87
Potamochoerus
larvatus **5**: 74
porcus **5**: 74
Potamogale velox **9**: 24
Potamogalidae **9**: 11
Potamon fluviatilis **28**: *105*
Potamotrygon **33**: (34), 43
motoro **33**: 42–43
Potamotrygonidae **33**: (9), (34)
Potomotyphlus **41**: (24)
potoo **15**: 80-81
common **15**: *78*, *80*
giant **15**: 78
potoroo 10: 48, 50, 51, 72–73
Gilbert's **10**: 73
long-footed **10**: 48
long-nosed (potoroo) **10**: 48, 50, 51, 72–73
Potorous
longipes **10**: 48
tridactylus **10**: 48, 72–73
Potos flavus **1**: 20
potto **4**: 106, 106–107
golden **4**: 106
Martin's false **4**: 106
pouches **10**: (10)
pout **36**: 38
pouting **36**: *11*, *44–45*
powan **35**: 38, 40, *41*
prahoc (Apollo shark paste) **34**: (57)
prairie chicken (greater) **11**: 44, 74–75
prairie dog 1: 46–47; **7**: 13, 15, 18, 36
black-tailed 7: 34, 56–59
plains (black-tailed) **7**: 34, 56–59
Utah **7**: 58
white-tailed **7**: 58
Prasinohaema virens **46**: 9
pratincole 11: (103); **13**: 90, 93, 100–101
Australian **11**: 98, *98*
black-winged **11**: 98
collared **11**: 98, *98*
little **11**: 98
oriental **11**: 98
pratincole family 11: 98–99
red-winged (collared) **11**: 98, *98*
rock **11**: 98, 99
prawns 28: 60–69
hinge-beak **28**: *66–67*
or shrimps **28**: (60)
spotted Pacific **28**: *60–61*
tiger **28**: *62*

praying mantis **22**: 9, 74–79; **48**: (66)
preen glands **14**: 109
preen oil **19**: 52
preening 11: 11; **14**: *59*
mutual **14**: 41; **19**: *26–27*, 62
pregnancy testing **42**: (55), (69)
Premnas **40**: 82
biaculeatus **40**: 81
Prepona antimache **26**: *40*
Presbytis **4**: 41
comata **4**: 40
femoralis **4**: 40
prey
impaling **15**: 105–106, 108
poisonous **15**: (105)
priapium fish (priapiumfish) **38**: (59)
Smith's **34**: 72
Priapulida **21**: 32, 77, 78
Priapulus caudatus **21**: *78*
pricklefish 39: 9, 12–15
prickly eye
Shelford's **34**: *100–101*, 101
Prietella **37**: 15, (19)
lundbergi **37**: 21
phreatophila **37**: 16
primates 1: *10*; **4**: 8–11
higher **4**: 11
lower 4: 11, 106–107
Prinia subflava **17**: 60
prinia, tawny-flanked **17**: 60
Priodontes maximus **9**: 65
prion **12**: 31
broad-billed **12**: 28, *28*
Prionodon
linsang **1**: 88
pardicolor **1**: 88
Prionodura newtoniana **19**: 100
Prionotus
carolinus **39**: 56, 57
evolans **39**: 56
Prionyx kirbyi **27**: *81*
Priotelus temnurus **19**: 34
Pristidae **33**: (9), 10
family summary **33**: (16)
Pristigasteridae **36**: 88
Pristiophoridae **32**: (12), (108)
Pristiophoriformes **32**: 108–109
Pristiophorus **32**: 108
cirratus **32**: 110
japonicus **32**: *10*
Pristiopsis
leichhardti **33**: 18
Pristis **33**: 16, (16)
microdon **32**: 108, 110, **33**: 18–19
nudipinnus **32**: 111
pectinata **32**: 108, 110, **33**: *16–17*
perotteti **33**: 16
pristis **32**: 110, **33**: 16
Pristobrycon **38**: (45)
calmoni **38**: 44
Pristoidei **33**: 16–17
Pristolepis
fasciata **40**: 57
grootii **40**: 57

marginata **40:** 57
Proatheris superciliaris **49:** 33; **50:** 58
Proboscidea **1:** *10*; **5:** 14
Prosciger aterrimus **19:** 12
Procambarus clarki **28:** *8–9*
Procapra picticaudata **6:** 62
Procatopus
  aberrans **38:** 105
  nototaenia **38:** 105
  similis **38:** 105
Procavia capensis **8:** 103, 106–107
Procaviidae **8:** 102
Procellaria cinerea **12:** 28
Procellariidae **12:** 28, 31; **20:** (14)
Procellariiformes **12:** 28
Proceratophrys **42:** 87
Procetichthys kreffti **39:** 14, (15)
Prochilodontidae **38:** 19
prochilodus
  silver **38:** *19*
Procolobus **4:** 41–42
  badius **4:** 40
Proconia marmorata **24:** *88–89*
Proconias tricarunculata **19:** 80
Procottus
  gurwicii **39:** 77
  jeittelesii **39:** 77
Proctotrupoidea **27:** (23)
Procyon
  cancrivorus **1:** 20
  gloverellani **1:** 26
  lotor **1:** 20, 22–27
  pygmaeus **1:** 26
Procyonidae **1:** 20–21
Prodotiscus **17:** 20–21
  zambesiae **17:** 20
Proechimys semispinosus **8:** 30
Profundilidae 85
Profundulus punctatus **38:** 85
Prognathodes guyanensis **40:** 46
Progne subis **15:** 94
prokaryotes **21:** 9
Prolagus **8:** (96)
Promethichthys prometheus **35:** 101
prominents 26: 80–83
  coxcomb **26:** *80–81*
  defense **26:** 82–83
pronghorn 6: *60*, 62, (63), 110–111
  American **2:** 26; **6:** 63
pronking **6:** 97
Pronolagus
  crassicaudatus **8:** 64
  randensis **8:** 64
  rupestris **8:** 64
Propaleotherium **1:** *8*
Propithecus
  diadema **4:** 96
  tattersalli **4:** 96
  verreauxi **4:** 96
Proscylliidae **32:** (12), (42)
Prosobonia
  cancellata **13:** 30
  lelucoptera **13:** 30
Prosobranchia **30:** 9, 10, 18

Prosopium **35:** 38–41, (41)
  abyssicola **35:** 39
  coulteri **35:** 39
  cylindraceum **35:** 40
  gemmifer **35:** 39, 40
  spilonotus **35:** 39
  williamsoni **35:** 39, *39*
prostaglandin E2 **42:** 103
Prostheceraeus vittatus **21:** *80*
Prostomatea **21:** 13
Prosymna **48:** (39)
protection, legal **1:** 35, 47, 51, 62, 69,
  74; **2:** 21, 28, 33, 35, 39, 44,
  49, 55, (97), 100; **3:** 12, 19,
  59, 74, 107; **5:** 41, 60; **9:** 85;
  10: 28, 32, 37, 43, 71, (95);
  41: 83, (83); **42:** 108; **44:** (16);
  48: (73), (108)
Protective Oceanic Device (POD) **32:** (25)
Proteidae **41:** *26–27*, 27, 29
Proteles cristata **2:** 102, 110–111
Proteus
  anguinus **41:** 14, *26–27*, 48–49, 70
  anguinus parkelj **41:** 48
Protista **21:** 12, 13
Protoavis **11:** (10)
Protobranchia **30:** 50
Protomelas **40:** *78–79*
Protonotaria citra **17:** 88
Protophormia **23:** *36–37*
protoplasm **21:** 13–14
Protopteridae **31:** (33), 38–41
Protopterus **31:** 39, 40, 41
  aethiopicus **31:** *39*, 40
  amphibius **31:** 40
  annectens **31:** *38*, 40
  dolloi **31:** 40
Protoreaster nodosus **30:** *91*
Protosalanx hyalocranius **35:** *31*
protostomes **21:** 31
Protostomia **21:** 32, 69
Prototheria **10:** 104
Prototroctes oxyrhynchus **35:** *8–9*
protozoans **21:** 12–15
  reproduction **21:** 14
Protula magnifica **21:** *100–101*
Protura **22:** 26, (26–27)
provisioning
  mass **27:** 66, 79
  progressive **27:** 66, 79
prowfish **39:** 70, 71
  Australian **39:** 68
  warty **39:** *71*
  whiskered **39:** 71
Prunella
  collaris **18:** 36
  himalayana **18:** 36
  immaculata **18:** 36
  modularis **18:** 36, *42–43*; **20:** (48)
  montanella **18:** 36
  ocularis **18:** 36
Prunellidae **18:** 36, 37
Psalidoprocne obscura **15:** 94
Psaltiparus minimus **17:** 70

Psaltria exilis **17:** 70
Psammobates **47:** 80
Psammobatis **33:** (26)
Psammodromus **45:** 58, (67), (79)
  algirus **45:** 78–79
Psammophinae **49:** 8, 12–13, 13, 15
Psammophis **44:** 41; **49:** 8, 13, (14), 15,
  26, 60–61; **50:** 17
  condenarus **48:** *16*
  leightoni **49:** *60–61*
  mossambicus **49:** 60
  phillipsii **49:** *61*
  schokari **49:** *14–15*, 61
  sibilans **49:** 15, 60
  subtaeniatus subtaeniatus **49:** *60*
Psammophylax **49:** 15, 61; **50:** 33
  variabilis **49:** 15
Psaracolius
  angustifrons **18:** 74
  decumanus **18:** 74
  guatimozinus **18:** 74
  wagleri **18:** 74
Pselaphacus giganteus **25:** *50–51*
Psephotus varius **16:** 22
Psephurus gladius **31:** 53, **32:** 90
Psettodidae **39:** 86
Pseudacanthicus
  hystrix **37:** 107
  spinosus **37:** 107
Pseudacris **43:** 32, 38
pseudantechinus
  fat-tailed **10:** *25*, 27
  Woolley's **10:** 27
Pseudantechinus
  macdonnellensis **10:** 27
  woolleyae **10:** 27
Pseudaspis cana **48:** 109; **49:** 13; **50:** 32
pseudautotomy **41:** (79)
Pseudecheneis **37:** 50
  sulcatus **37:** 50
Pseudemys **47:** 10
  alabamensis **44:** *8*
  nelsoni **47:** 29
Pseudeutropius atherinoides **37:** 41
Pseudhymenochirus **42:** 46
  merlini **42:** 46
Pseudidae **42:** 10; **43:** 28
Pseudis **43:** 27
  minuta **43:** 27
  paradoxa **43:** 26–27
  paradoxa platensis **43:** 27
Pseudobalistes naufragium **39:** 104
Pseudobranchus
  axanthus **41:** (54)
  striatus **41:** *54*, (54)
  striatus axanthus **41:** (54)
Pseudobufo **42:** 56
  subasper **42:** 58
Pseudocalotes **44:** 35
Pseudocarchariidae **32:** (12), (74)
Pseudoceros zebra **21:** *81*
Pseudocetopsis gobioides **37:** 90
Pseudocheiridae **10:** (76)
Pseudocheirus peregrinus **10:** 74

Pseudochelidon
  eurystomina **15**: 94
  sirintarae **15**: 94
Pseudochirops
  archeri **10**: 74
  cupreus **10**: 74, 90–91
Pseudochirulus
  caroli **10**: 74
  cinereus **10**: 74
Pseudochromidae **40**: 22–25
Pseudochromis
  bitaeniatus **40**: 23
  moorei **40**: *23*
  paccagnellae **40**: 22
  paranox **40**: 23
Pseudococcidae **24**: 112–113
Pseudococcus
  adonidum **24**: *112*
  affinis **24**: *113*
Pseudocolochirus axiologus **30**: *110*
Pseudocordylus **45**: 98, 100
  microlepidotus **45**: 108–109
  nebulosus **45**: (109)
Pseudocreobotra ocellata **22**: *78–79*
Pseudocuma cercaria **28**: *50*
Pseudocyttus maculatus **39**: 24
Pseudodoras niger **37**: *76*, 77
Pseudoeurycea **41**: 68
Pseudoficimia **49**: (63)
Pseudogastromyzon myersi **34**: 89, 108, 109
pseudogastromyzon
  ornate **34**: 109
Pseudoginglymostoma brevicaudatum
  32: 35, (40)
Pseudohaje **50**: 14
Pseudohemiodon **37**: (110)
Pseudois nayaur **6**: 62
Pseudolamellibranchia **30**: 9, 50, 58–59
Pseudoliparis belyaevi **39**: 83
Pseudomeloe collegialis **25**: *64*
Pseudomops **22**: *70–71*
Pseudomugil **38**: 55, *58*
  furcatus **38**: 59
  majusculus **38**: 59
  mellis **38**: 56
Pseudomugilidae **38**: 54–59
Pseudomyrmex ferruginea **27**: *46*
Pseudonaja **50**: 14
Pseudonestor xanthophrys **20**: 98
Pseudopallene ambigua **29**: *12–13*
Pseudopentaceros richardsoni **40**: 55
pseudophrynamine **42**: (101)
Pseudophryne **42**: 92, 93, 97, 100–101
  australis **42**: 100, 101
  bibroni **42**: 97
  coriacea **42**: 101
  corroboree **42**: 93, 100, *100*, *100–101*
  covacevichae **42**: 101
  pengilleyi **42**: 100
Pseudopimelodus **37**: 85, 88, 89
Pseudoplatystoma fasciatum **37**: *87*
Pseudoplesiops

rosae **40**: 23
typus **40**: 23
pseudopods **21**: 18–19
Pseudopotto martini **4**: 106
Pseudoraja **33**: (26)
pseudoruminants **5**: 70
Pseudoryx nghetinhensis **6**: 62
Pseudoscaphirhynchus
  fedtshchenkoi **31**: 56
  kaufmanni **31**: *43*
Pseudoscorpiones **29**: 20–21
pseudoscorpions 29: 20–21
Pseudosphromenus **40**: 61, 63
Pseudothecadactylus australis **45**: 12
Pseudotriacanthus strigilifer **39**: 99
Pseudotriakidae **32**: (12), (42)
Pseudotriton **41**: 68, 71
  montanus **41**: 86
  ruber **41**: 86–87, 91
Pseudotyphlops philippinus **48**: 28, (31)
Pseudoxyrhophiinae **49**: 13
Psilopa petrolei **23**: (39)
Psittacidae **16**: 22; **18**: (41); **19**: 12; **20**: 36
Psittacula krameri **16**: 22
Psittacus erithacus **16**: 22, (35); **19**: 12; **20**: 36
Psittirostra
  bailleui **20**: 98
  cantans **20**: 98
  psittacea **20**: 98
Psittrichas fulgidus **16**: 22; **20**: 36
Psocoptera **22**: 30, 86–87
Psolus chitonoides **30**: *111*
Psophia
  crepitans **19**: 8, 10–11
  leucoptera **19**: 8
  viridis **19**: 8
Psophiidae **19**: 8
Psychidae **26**: 110–111
Psychrolutes phrictus **39**: 80
Psychrolutidae **39**: 76–81
Psylla alni **24**: 96–97
Psyllidae **24**: 96–97
Psyllophryne didactyla **41**: (17); **42**: (79)
ptarmigan **13**: (110); **15**: 34
  willow *see* grouse, willow
Ptarmus jubatus **39**: 70
Ptenopus **44**: 29; **45**: 11, (39)
  garrulus **45**: 38–39
Pteraclis velifera **40**: 35
Pterapogon kauderni **40**: 31, *31*
Pteridophora alberti **19**: 106
Pteriidae **30**: 59
Pterinochilus junodi **29**: *36–37*
Pternohyla **43**: 33, 38
Pterobrycon myrnae **38**: 48
Pterocles **16**: 8
  alchata **16**: 8
  burchelli **16**: 8
  lichtensteinii **16**: 8
  namaqua **16**: 8
Pteroclididae **16**: 8
Pterocnemia pennata **11**: 16, 34

Pterodroma **12**: 31
  cahow **12**: 28
  mollis **12**: 28
  rostrata **12**: 28
  sandwichensis **12**: 28
Pteroglossus
  frantzii **19**: 56
  inscriptus **19**: 56
  viridis **19**: 56, 66–67
Pteroidichthys amboinensis **39**: *66*
Pterois **39**: 60
  volitans **39**: 59
Pteromylaeus **33**: (36)
Pteronarcyidae **22**: *80–81*
Pteronotropis **34**: 68–71
  hubbsi **34**: 69
Pteronura brasiliensis **1**: 32, 68–69
Pterophoridae **26**: 102–103
Pterophorus pentadactyla **26**: *102*, *102–103*
Pterophyllum **38**: (40), **40**: 68
  altum **40**: 78
  leopoldi **40**: 78
  scalare **37**: (108), **40**: *76*, 78
Pteroplatus **25**: *90–91*
Pteroplatytrygon **33**: (34)
  violacea **33**: 34
Pteropodidae **9**: 86; **45**: (42)
Pteropus **9**: 86
  giganteus **9**: 88–91
pterosaur **44**: *10–11*
Pterostichus madidus **25**: *17*
Pterygoplichthys gibbiceps **37**: *111*
Pterygota **22**: 30
Pterygotrigla polyommata **39**: 56
Ptilinopus **16**: 13
  magnificus **16**: 12
  perousii **16**: 12
  pulchellus **16**: 12
Ptilocercus lowii **9**: 59
Ptilodon capucina **26**: *80–81*
Ptiloglossa guinnae, nests **27**: 90
Ptilonorhynchidae **19**: 100
Ptilonorhynchus **19**: 102
  violaceus **19**: 100, 104–105
Ptiloris
  magnificus **19**: 106
  paradiseus **19**: 106
  victoriae **19**: 106
Ptilosphen insignis **23**: *84–85*
Ptomaphila lacrymosa **25**: *31*
Ptyas mucosus **50**: 31
Ptychadena **43**: 82, 87
  madagascariensis **43**: 87
  mascareniensis **43**: 10
  oxyrhynchus **43**: *86*, 87
Ptychadeninae **43**: 82, 87
Ptychocheilus **34**: 16
  lucius **34**: 19
Ptychoptera contaminata **23**: *45*
Ptychopteridae **23**: (45)
Ptychoramphus aleluticus **12**: 98
Ptychozoon **43**: (62); **44**: (45); **45**: (10), (41), 42

kuhli **44:** 26, 30; **45:** 40–43
puddling **26:** (15), *16–17*
pudu **6:** 10, 12
  northern **6:** 10
  southern **6:** 10, *12*
Pudu
  mephistophiles **6:** 10
  pudu **6:** 10
puff adder 48: 109; **50:** (8), 9, 14, 58, 60–63
  Somali **50:** 62
  western hognose snake **49:** (67), 100–103
puffback **15:** 104, 105
  black-backed **15:** 104
puff-belly **39:** 80
puffbird 17: 22; **19:** 56–59
  pied **19:** 56, *56*
  rufous-necked **19:** 56
  swallow-winged **19:** 56, *57*, (59)
  white-eared **19:** 56, *56*
  white-whiskered **19:** 56
puffer 31: 43, **32:** 58, **33:** 83, **39:** 11, 96–97, 108–109, 110
  black-saddled **39:** (102)
  black-spotted **39:** 109
  dangerous cuisine **39:** 108
  dogface **39:** 109
  eyespot **39:** 109
  figure-of-eight **39:** 109
  freshwater **39:** 109
  Fugu **39:** *109*
  giant **39:** 109
  green **39:** 109
  guineafowl **39:** 109
  Malabar **39:** 109
  mosaic **39:** 109
  ocellated **39:** 109
  red-bellied **39:** 109
  redeye **39:** 109
  sharpnose **39:** 109
  smooth **39:** 109
  spotted Congo **39:** 109
  starry **39:** 109
  three-toothed **39:** 108, 109
  tiger **39:** 109
  Valentinni's sharpnose **39:** (102), *108*
  venomous **36:** 55
  white-spotted **39:** 109
pufferfish *see* puffer
puffin 11: 12; **12:** 88, 93, 101–102; **17:** 51
  Atlantic 12: 98, (98), 101, 104–107, 110
  horned **12:** 98, 101
  tufted **12:** 98, 99, 101
Puffinus **12:** 25
  gravis **12:** 28
  griseus **12:** 28, 38–39
  lherminieri **12:** 28
  puffinus **12:** 28, 106
  tenuirostris **50:** (40)
puku **6:** 62
Pulex irritans **22:** 111

Pulmonata **30:** 9, 10, 18, 44–49
Pulsatrix perspicillata **15:** 50
Pulvinaria regalis **24:** *107*
puma 2: 10, 13, 42–43
pumpkinseed **40:** 26, (27), *29*
punare **8:** 30
Pungitius
  hellenicus **39:** 26, (35)
  laevis **39:** 34
  platygaster **39:** 34
  platygaster aralensis **39:** 34
  pungitius **39:** 30, (32), 33, *34*
  pungitius pungitius **39:** *30–31*, 33, 34
  pungitius tymensis **39:** 33
  sinensis kaibarae **39:** 34
  sinensis sinensis **39:** 34
punkies **23:** (52)
Puntius **34:** 24, 25, (26), 28
  tetrazonia **34:** 24, 25
  see also Barbus
pupfish 38: 50, 86–89, 103
  desert **38:** *87*
  Devil's Hole **38:** 86, 87, *87*
  La Trinidad **38:** 87
  Owens **38:** *89*
  Salt Creek **38:** 87
purpletuft **19:** 83
  dusky **19:** 80
purpurin **30:** 35
Pusa sibirica **3:** 9
putitor **34:** 20
Pycnogonida **22:** 9
Pycnogonum littorale **29:** *12*
Pycnonotidae **16:** 56; **18:** 69
Pycnonotus
  barbatus **16:** 56, 58–61
  cafer **16:** 56
  erythropthalmos **16:** 56, (61)
  jocosus **16:** 56
  latirostris **16:** 56
  nigricans **16:** 56
  xanthopygos **16:** 56
Pycodorus **39:** 41
Pygarrhichas albogularis **20:** 80
Pygathrix roxellana **4:** 40
Pygocentrus **38:** (45)
  cariba **38:** *46–47*
  nattereri **38:** 8, *42*, 43, *43*
  piraya **38:** 44
  rhombeus **38:** 44
Pygoplites diacanthus **31:** *12*, **40:** *50*
Pygopodidae **44:** 25, (26); **45:** 8, 48–53
Pygopodinae **45:** 8
Pygopus **45:** 48, (49)
  lepidopodus **45:** *49*, 50
  nigriceps **45:** *51*
Pygoscelis **12:** 10
  adeliae **12:** 8, 20; **13:** 109
  antarctica **12:** 8, 20–23
  papua **12:** 8, 22
Pylodictis **37:** 15
  olivaris **37:** 16
Pyralidae **26:** (103)
Pyramodon **36:** 23

Pyriglena leuconota **19:** 72
Pyrocephalus
  rubinus **17:** 30, 36–41
  cocachacrae **17:** (38)
  obscurus **17:** (38)
Pyrochroa
  coccinea **25:** 60
  serraticornis **25:** *60–61*
Pyrochroidae **25:** 60–61
Pyrops **24:** *72–73*
Pyrrhocorax graculus **18:** 90
Pyrrhocoridae **24:** 48–49
Pyrrhocoris apterus **24:** *48*
Pyrrhula
  pyrrhula **16:** 76, (87)
  picta **19:** 12
Python
  anchietae **48:** 81
  curtus **48:** 81, 98–99
  molurus **48:** *82–83*, 83, 100–103, (108), 109
  regius **48:** 81, 104–105
  reticulatus **48:** 106–111
  sebae **48:** *80*, (108), 109
Pythonidae **48:** 9, 80
Pythonodipsas carinata **49:** 10
pythons 48: 80–83
  African **48:** *80*
  African rock **48:** (108), 109
  Ambon **48:** 88
  amethystine 48: 88–89
  Angolan **48:** 81
  anthill **48:** 80, (84), 85
  Australian Oenpelli **48:** 79
  ball (royal) **48:** 81, 104–105
  Bismarck ringed **48:** 80, 82
  black-headed 48: 80, 86–87, (105); **50:** (35)
  blood (short-tailed) **48:** 81, 98–99
  Borneo blood **48:** *99*
  Bredl's carpet **48:** 90
  breeding **48:** 82–83
  Burmese 48: *82–83*, 100–103
  burrowing (American sunbeam snakes) **44:** 101; **48:** 38–39
  carpet 48: 82, 86, 90–93, 103; **49:** 55
  Children's 48: 84–85
  D'Alberti's (white-lipped) **48:** 82
  diamond **48:** 90, 103
  egg brooding **48:** (83)
  in folklore **48:** 83
  giant **48:** 81
  golden **48:** *101*
  green tree 44: *8–9*; **48:** 56, (58), 82, 94–97; **50:** 91
  Halmahera **48:** 88
  Indian 48: 80, 83, 100–103, (108), 109
  Indian rock **48:** 100
  Irian Jaya carpet **48:** *92–93*
  jungle carpet **48:** *93*
  Kinghorn's **48:** 88
  Papuan **48:** 82

reproduction **48:** 17
reticulated 48: 106–111
royal 48: 81, 104–105
scrub (amethystine) **48:** 88–89
short-tailed 48: 81, 98–99
skin trade **48:** 106–107
spurs **48:** (49)
Stimson's **48:** (84)
Tanimbar **48:** 88
water **48:** 82
white-lipped (D'Alberti's) **48:** 82
woma **48:** 80, *81*, 86, (105)
Pyxicephalinae **43:** 82, 87
Pyxicephalus **43:** 82, 87
adspersus **42:** (89); **43:** 52, 98–99, 103
edulis **43:** (99)
Pyxis **47:** 80

Q

quagga **5:** 45, 48
quail **11:** 45, 46–47
button *see* button quail
common **11:** 44, 47
Gambel's **11:** 44, 47
Montezuma **11:** 44, *46*
New World **11:** 46, 47, 51
Old World **11:** 46–47
Quelea quelea **16:** 100, 106–107
quelea, red-billed 16: 100, 106–107
quetzal 19: 36, 37
crested **19:** 34
eared **19:** 34
golden-headed **19:** 34
resplendent 19: 34, 38–39
quillback **34:** 95, 99
quillpig *see* porcupine, North American
quills **8:** 12, (14), 16–17, (21)
see also spines
Quinkana fortirostrum **47:** 95
quinones **25:** 73
Quiscalus
major **18:** 74
palustris **18:** 75
quiscula **18:** 74, 78–81
quokka 10: 48, 52, 68–69
quoll 10: (25), 27
New Guinea **10:** *25*, 27
northern 10: 27, 32–33

R

rabbit 1: 43; **8:** 61, 62
Amami **8:** *62*, 64
American swamp **8:** 66
annamite **8:** 64
brush **8:** 64
bunyoro **8:** *63*, 64
bush *see* hare, snowshoe
chocolate Dutch **8:** *72–73*
cottontail **1:** 87
desert **8:** 66
domestic (European) **8:** *60–61*, 62, 64, 68–73
European 8: *60–61*, 62, 64, 68–73
forest **8:** 66
marsh **8:** 65
Mexican volcano **8:** 64
Old World (European) **8:** *60–61*, 62, 64, 68–73
pygmy **8:** 64, (93)
rabbit family 8: 64–67
riverine **8:** *62*, 64
rock *see* pika
snowshoe *see* hare, snowshoe
Sumatran **8:** *63*, 64
Sumatran short-eared **8:** 64–66
swamp **8:** 62
volcano **8:** *63*, 64
see also cottontail
rabbit hemorrhagic disease **8:** 72
rabbit warrens **8:** 70–71
rabbitfish **33:** 55, *56–57*
rabies **1:** 26, 87; **2:** (67), 77, 79; **7:** 14, 74; **9:** 84, 97, 103
raccoon
Barbados **1:** 26
common 1: 20, 21, 22–27
Cozumel Island **1:** 26
crab-eating **1:** 20
raccoon family 1: 20–21
ringtail **1:** 20, *20*, 21, *21*
racehorse **39:** 11
racerunners 44: 25, (26), 30; **45:** 82–85
breeding **45:** 84
conservation **45:** 84–85
food and feeding **45:** 84
Rachovia **38:** (79)

Rachycentridae **40:** 32–33
Rachycentron canadum **40:** 33
racing pigeons **16:** (17), 18
Racochilus toxotes **40:** (17)
Raconda russeliana **36:** 89
Radiata **21:** 30, 32
Radiicephalidae **35:** 105
Radiicephalus elongatus **35:** 105
radiolarians **21:** *14–15*
ragworms 21: *97*
and allies 21: 98–101
rail 11: 92; **14:** 82–83
Okinawa **14:** 82
water **14:** 82
Zapata **14:** 82
rain frogs 42: 8, 9, 10, (38), 80–85, 93, 104, 105, (107); **43:** 27
American green treefrogs **43:** 48–49, 51
bushveld 42: 106–107
common (bushveld) **42:** 106–107
Namaqua **42:** *107*, (107)
rain frog family 42: 76–79
southern African **42:** 95
strawberry **42:** (107)
rainbowfish 38: 50, 52, 54–59
Antonia's Celebes **38:** 59
black-banded **38:** *55*
blue Celebes **38:** 59
Boeseman's **38:** (56)
Cairns **38:** 57
Celebes **38:** 59
checkered **38:** 57
forktail **38:** 59
golden arrow **38:** *58*
Lake Wanam **38:** (56)
Madagascan **38:** 55, 56, *57*
Mbuta **38:** 57
New Guinea **38:** (56), 57
ornate **38:** 57
relatives of **38:** (59)
Sentani **38:** (56)
threadfin **38:** 57, *59*
Raja **33:** (27)
batis **33:** 30
clavata **33:** 28–29
inornata **33:** 26
Rajella **33:** (27)
Rajidae **31:** (108); **33:** (9), 15, 26, (26–27)
Rajiformes **33:** 26
families summary **33:** (9)
Rajoidea **33:** 26, (26–27)
Rajoidei **33:** 26–27
families summary **33:** (26–27)
Rallidae **14:** 82; **19:** (74)
Rallus aquaticus **14:** 82
Ralpharia magnifica **21:** 48
Ramphastidae **19:** 56, 58
Ramphastos **19:** 60, (61), 62
ambiguus **19:** 61
sulfuratus **19:** 56, 60–65
toco **19:** 56
Ramphotyphlops

angusticeps **48:** 19
braminus **48:** 19, 20, 24–25
nigrescens **48:** 20
suluensis **48:** 20
Rana **41:** 8; **42:** 78; **43:** 82, 83
aquensis **41:** *13*
aurora **43:** 91, (91)
caerulea **43:** (55)
catesbeiana **41:** (65); **42:** 9, (89);
43: 83, *83*, (85), 88–91
chalconata **43:** 83, *83*
clamitans **43:** *84–85*, 91
crancivora **42:** 55; **43:** (85)
finchi **43:** 83
grylio **43:** 91
klepton esculenta **43:** 83, 96–97
klepton grafi **43:** 97
klepton hispanica **43:** 97
perezi **42:** (31)
ridibunda **43:** 96
spinosa **43:** (85)
sylvatica **43:** 83, (85), 92, 93, (93)
temporaria **42:** *13*, (18); **43:** 83,
(85), 92–95
Ranatra linearis **24:** *20*
ranchu **34:** 51
black **34:** *51*
Yokohama **34:** (50), 51
Rancipitidae **36:** 52–53
Rangifer tarandus **6:** 10, 20–25
Raniceps raninus **36:** 53, *53*
Ranidae **42:** 10, (38); **43:** (11), (17), 39,
52, 82
Raninae **43:** 82, 83–84, 86
Ranixalinae **43:** 82, 87
Ranodon **41:** 36, (37)
Ranzania laevis **39:** 110, 111
Ranzovius **24:** (33)
raphael
spotted **37:** *78–79*
striped **37:** (78), *78*
Raphicerus campestris **6:** 62
Raphidioptera **22:** 30, 100–101
Raphus cucullatus **15:** (11)
rasbora 34: 60–65
Espe's **34:** 64
fire **34:** *62*, 64
glass harlequin **34:** 64
harlequin **34:** *60–61*, 64
Hengel's harlequin **34:** 64
slim harlequin **34:** 64
winged **34:** 19
Rasbora
heteromorpha **34:** 64
vaterifloris **34:** *62*, 64
Rasborinae **34:** 60–65
rat 1: 15; **7:** *12*
African marsh **7:** 65
Amazon bamboo **8:** 30
armored **8:** 30
armored spiny **8:** 30
Asian climbing **7:** 64
Atlantic bamboo **8:** 30
Australasian water **7:** 65

Australian water **7:** 9, 17, *65*
bamboo **8:** 31
black (ship) **7:** *11*, 13, 14–15, 72,
75, 76–77
bristle-spined **8:** 30
broad-headed spiny **8:** 30
brown 7: 14–15, 72–75, 77;
8: 10; **10:** 11
brush-furred **7:** *65*
cane **7:** *12*; **8:** 31
Central American climbing **7:** *64*
Central American vesper **7:** *64*
Chilean rock **8:** 30
chinchilla **7:** *12*
common (brown) **7:** 14–15, 72–75,
77; **8:** 10; **10:** 11
dassie 7: *12*; **8:** 31, 54–55
desert wood 7: 84–85
golden-backed tree **7:** 67
greater cane **8:** 30
greedy olalla **8:** 30
house (ship) **7:** *11*, 13, 14–15, 72,
75, 76–77
Indonesian key-footed **7:** 64
Kenyan crested **7:** 66
lesser cane **8:** 30
Natal multimammate **7:** *65*
New World **7:** *64*
Norway (brown) **7:** 14–15, 72–75,
77; **8:** 10; **10:** 11
Old World **7:** 14, *65*
Owl's spiny **8:** 30
pack (desert wood) **7:** 84–85
painted tree **8:** 30
Panama spiny **8:** 30, *31*
plague (ship) **7:** *11*, 13, 14–15,
72, 75, 76–77; **50:** 43
plain brush-tailed **8:** 30
plains viscacha **8:** 30
pouched **7:** 18
rat family 7: 64–67
rock **8:** 29
roof (ship) **7:** *11*, 13, 14–15, 72, 75,
76–77
rufous tree **8:** 30
ship 7: *11*, 13, 14–15, 72, 75, 76–77
smooth-tailed giant **7:** *65*
South American climbing **7:** *64*
spiny **7:** *12*; **8:** 31
spiny tree **8:** 30
trade (desert wood) **7:** 84–85
tuft-tailed spiny tree **8:** 30
viscacha rat **8:** 29, 30
vlei **7:** *65*
water *see* vole, water
see also chinchilla rat; kangaroo rat;
mole rat; viscacha
rat-bite fever **7:** 74
ratel *see* badger, honey
ratfish **33:** 55
Atlantic **33:** *56–57*
Pacific **33:** *54–55*
spotted **33:** *54–55*
ratites 11: 16–19

rat-kangaroo **10:** 51, 52
desert **10:** 48
musky **10:** 48, 72
rufous **10:** 48, *51*
see also potoroo
ratsnake 49: 10, (39)
American 49: 10, 40–43
Baird's **49:** (43)
Baja **49:** 10, (43)
black **48:** *17*; **49:** 40, 41, 42, (43);
50: 88
Central American **49:** (43)
European **49:** 45
Everglades **49:** 40, *40–41*, 42, (43)
gray **49:** 40, 42, (43)
Great Plains **49:** 47
green **49:** 10, (43)
Indian **50:** 31
North American **48:** 58, (97)
red (corn snake) **49:** 10, (43), 46–47
Texas **49:** 40, 42, *42–43*, (43)
transcaucasian **49:** 45
trans-pecos **49:** 10, (43)
yellow **49:** 40, *41*, 42, (43)
rattail **36:** 28, 29, 30, (30), 31
long-finned Atlantic **36:** 29
luminous **36:** 29
rattlesnake 50: (8), 9, 10, *50*, 54–55,
58, (111)
banded rock **49:** (71); **50:** *99*
eastern diamondback **50:** (8), (55),
65, 103
horned (sidewinders) **48:** 11–12,
(58); **50:** 9, 54, 55, 104–105
Mojave **50:** 99, 103
pigmy **50:** 101
rattle **44:** *13*; **50:** 100–103
red diamond **50:** (102), *103*
rock **50:** 99–100
roundups **50:** (100)
speckled **50:** 99
tiger **50:** 99
timber **50:** 88, (100)
Tortuga Island **50:** (102)
western diamondback 50: *8*, (8),
9, 42, 98–103
see also massasauga; sidewinder
Rattus
norvegicus **7:** 72–75
rattus **7:** 76–77
villosissimus **50:** 43
ratufa *see* squirrel, Indian giant
Ratufa
affinisi **7:** 36
bicolor **7:** 36
indica **7:** 34, 62–63
raven 13: (36); **14:** (39); **18:** 63, 93,
(93); **20:** 23
common 18: 90, 92, 100–103
ray 31: *14*, 42, 46, **32:** 9, 59, 86, 104,
108, 110, **33:** 8–15, **40:** 103
bat **33:** 14, (38), *48*, (49)
butterfly **33:** 36, 37
camouflage **33:** 22–23

coffin **33:** (22)
Cortez electric **33:** *22–23*
cownose **32:** (18)
deep-sea blind **33:** 22
devil **31:** *21*, **33:** 10, 11, 36
eagle **33:** 36
electric 31: (108), **33:** 11, 20–23
families summary **33:** (9), (20)
"flying" **33:** (47)
giant devil **33:** 52
golden cow-nose **33:** *38–39*
Haller's round **33:** 44, *45*
Japanese devil 33: 52–53
"jumping" **33:** (47)
lesser electric **33:** 22
manta 32: 9, **33:** 12, 34, 36, 50–51,
   52, **40:** 32, 34
marbled 33: 14, 24–25
ribbon-tailed **33:** *35*
shovelnose **33:** *32–33*
sleeper **33:** (20)
spotted eagle 33: 46–49
stingray *see* stingray
thornback 33: 28–29
torpedo *see* torpedo ray
Who's Who **33:** (9)
ray-finned fish 31: 42–43, **33:** 60
Who's Who **31:** (43)
razorbill 12: 98, (98), 100, 101,
   110–111
razorfish **39:** 26, 50, 51
grooved **39:** *50–51*
recolonization **3:** 14, 35; **7:** 33
Recurvirostra **13:** 29
   americana **13:** 72
   andina **13:** 72
   avosetta **13:** 72, 76–81, 84; **18:** (56)
   novaehollandiae **13:** 72
Recurvirostridae **13:** 72
red ape *see* orangutan
Red Lists of Threatened Species (IUCN)
   1: 16
redband **35:** 73
redcap (oranda) **34:** 50
red-eye (rudd) **34:** 84, (86)
redfish **39:** 21
redhead **14:** 72
redpoll **16:** 76, 77
redshank **13:** 30, *31*, 84
redside
   Lahontan **34:** 74
redstart
   American 17: 88, 90–93
   black **18:** 44
   common **18:** 44, *45*
Redunca
   arundinum **6:** 62
   fulvorufula **6:** 62
   redunca **6:** 62
Reduviidae **24:** *38–43*
reedbuck
   bohor **6:** 62
   mountain **6:** 62
   southern **6:** 62

reedfish **31:** 44, 49, 50
reedhaunter **20:**80
reestablishment **3:** 31, 93
refection **9:** 29, *29*
reflex bleeding **25:** 58
reforestation **4:** 91
Regalecidae **35:** 82, 105, 108–109
Regalecus **35:** 108
   glesne **35:** 82, 108, *108*, 109
   kinoi **35:** 108
   russelii **35:** 82, 108
regeneration, of land **10:** 89
Regina **48:** (93); **49:** 12
reindeer 6: 10, 12, 20–25
reindeer moss **6:** 22–23
reintroduction **1:** 46; **2:** 41, (56), 69;
   4: 87, 88, 90–91; **5:** 34;
   6: 45, (66), 91; **7:** 29, 107
Reithrodontomys
   hirsutus **7:** 81
   megalotis **7:** 80–81
   paradoxus **7:** 81
   rodriguez **7:** 81
   spectabilis **7:** 81
relic populations **49:** (67)
religious ceremonies **5:** 25
relocation **5:** 34
Remipedia **28:** 9, (14)
remora 33: *36–37*, 51, *53*, **40:** 9, 32–33
repopulation **1:** 61, 75
reproduction **1:** 12–14
   see also embryonic diapause;
implantation/fertilization; breeding
Reptantia **28:** 56
reptiles 44: 8–17
   classification of species **44:** 15
   coloration **44:** 12
   declining species **44:** 16
   eggs **44:** *12*, 14, 104–105, (105)
   evolution **44:** 10–11, *10*
   flying, evolution **44:** *10*
   food and feeding **44:** 14–15
   form and function **44:** 11–12
   habitats **44:** 12–13
   hearts **44:** *12*
   origins **44:** 10–11
   as pets **44:** (16–17)
   reproduction **44:** 13–14
   skin modifications **44:** *13*
   temperature regulation **44:** 8–10
   winged **44:** (45)
Reptilia **44:** 8, 9
resource sharing **48:** (61)
respiration, cutaneous **41:** 8, (12), 33,
   68–69; **42:** 10; **43:** 13–14
Rhabdophis **49:** (76)
   tigrinus **49:** (39)
Rhacodactylus **45:** 12
   ciliatus **45:** 12
   leachianus **45:** 9
   trachyrhynchus **45:** 12
Rhacophoridae **42:** 10; **43:** 22, (66), 100
Rhacophorinae **43:** 100
Rhacophorus **43:** (62), 100, 104–105,

   (105); **44:** (45); **45:** (42)
   arboreus **41:** *9*
   pardalis **43:** *101*
   reinwardtii **43:** 104–105
Rhadinea **49:** 16
   flavilata **49:** 16
Rhadinesthes decimus **35:** 85
Rhadinocentrus ornatus **38:** 57
Rhadinoceraea micans **27:** *18*
Rhagio scolopaceus **23:** 59
Rhagionidae **23:** (59)
Rhagoletis completa **23:** 88
Rhagonycha fulva **25:** *34–35*
Rhamdia **37:** 85, 87
   quelen **37:** (89)
   quelen urichi **37:** (89)
Rhamnophis **49:** 36
Rhamphichthyidae **31:** (108); **33:** (100)
Rhamphocottidae **39:** 76–81
Rhamphocottus richardsoni **39:** 79
Rhampholeon **44:** 56, 57, 58, 65, 78
   spectrum **44:** 57, 78–79
Rhamphorhynchus **44:** *10–11*
Rhaphidophoridae **23:** (21)
Rhaphirrhinus phosphoreus **24:** *89*
rhea 11: 18, 19, 40
   common 11: 16, 34–35
   greater (common) **11:** 16, 34–35
   lesser **11:** 16, *18*, 34
Rhea americana **11:** 16, 34–35
rhebok, gray **6:** 62
Rheidae **11:** 16
Rheinardia **11:** 45
   ocellatacruentus **11:** 44
Rheithrosciurus macrotis **7:** 36
"rhenanids" **33:** (10)
Rheobatrachus **42:** (85), 92, 97
   silus **42:** 14, 94, 102–103
   vitellinus **42:** 94, 102
Rheocles
   alaotrensis **38:** 56
   derhami **38:** 54
   lateralis **38:** 56
   sikorae **38:** (56)
   wrightae **38:** (56)
rheocles
   blue-finned **38:** 54
   sicora **38:** (56)
   slender **38:** 56
   Wrights's **38:** (56)
Rhetus periander **26:** *35*
Rhicnogryllus lepidus **23:** *17*
Rhigus horridus **25:** *110–111*
Rhina **33:** (27)
Rhinastus latesternus **25:** *104–105*
Rhinatrema **41:** 21
Rhinatrematidae **41:** 21
Rhincodon typus **32:** 12, 38–41, 78
Rhincodontidae **32:** (12), (30), 38, (40)
Rhinecanthus
   aculeatus **39:** *8*, 100, 103
   assasi **39:** 103
   rectangulus **39:** 105
Rhineura floridana **46:** 105, *109*, (109)

Rhingia campestris **23:** *76–77, 78*
Rhinidae **33:** (9), 27, (27)
Rhiniodontidae **32:** (30)
Rhinobatidae **33:** 8, (9), 27, (27)
Rhinobatoidea **33:** (27)
Rhinobatos **33:** (27)
   rhinobatos **33:** 32–33
   typus **33:** *32–33*
rhinoceros 5: 8, *8*, 9, 11, 12
   black 5: 28, 33, (34), 36–39
   giraffe **5:** 8
   grass (white) **5:** 28, 29, 30–35
   greater Indian (Indian) **5:** 28, 40–41
   Indian 5: 28, 40–41
   Javan **5:** 28
   northern white **5:** 34
   rhinoceros family 5: 28–29
   southern white **5:** 34, *35*
   square-lipped (white) **5:** 28, 29, 30–35
   Sumatran **5:** 28, *29*
   white 5: 28, 29, 30–35
   woolly **5:** 28
Rhinoceros
   sondaicus **5:** 28
   unicornis **5:** 28, 40–41
Rhinocerotidae **5:** 28
Rhinocheilus **49:** 11
   lecontei **49:** *10*; **50:** (25)
Rhinochimaeridae **33:** (55)
Rhinocoris
   albopilosus **24:** *14*
   tristis **24:** *42*
Rhinocryptidae **19:** 75
Rhinoderma
   darwinii **42:** 14, 38; **43:** 8–9
   rufum **43:** 9
Rhinodermatidae **42:** 10; **43:** (11)
Rhinoleptus **48:** 18
   koniagui **48:** 19
Rhinolophidae **9:** 87
Rhinolophus hipposideros **9:** 106–107
Rhinomuraena **33:** 82
   ambonensis **33:** 82
   quaesita **33:** *63*, 82
Rhinophis **48:** 28, 29
Rhinophrynidae **42:** 10
Rhinophrynus dorsalis **42:** 8, 22–23, 92, 98; **43:** 16
Rhinopithecus roxellana see Pygathrix roxellana
Rhinoplax vigil **19:** 48
Rhinoplocephalus **48:** 87
Rhinopomatidae **9:** 86
Rhinoptera **33:** (36)
   bonasus **32:** (18)
   steindachneri **33:** *38–39*
Rhinopteridae **33:** (9), 36
Rhinoptilus
   africanus **11:** 98
   chalcopterus **11:** 98
   cinctus **11:** (103)
Rhinoraja **33:** (26)
Rhinotyphlops **48:** 18
   caecus **48:** 20

   schinzi **48:** *20–21*
Rhipidura hypoxantha **17:** 66
Rhizoprionodon **32:** 55
Rhizostomae **21:** 43
Rhodeus **34:** 66
   amarus **34:** 66
   ocellatus ocellatus **34:** *67*
   sericeus **34:** 66, *66, 67*
   sericeus amarus **34:** 66
   sericeus sinensis **34:** 66
Rhodogastria **26:** *89*
Rhombophryne testudo **42:** (108)
Rhombozoa **21:** 32, 35
Rhopalidae **24:** 58–59
Rhopalus subrufus **24:** *58*
Rhyacichthyidae **40:** 94–99
Rhyacichthys
   aspro **40:** 99
   guilberti **40:** 99
Rhyacosiredon **41:** 56
Rhyacotriton **41:** 27
   cascadae **41:** *9*, 50–51
   kezeri **41:** (51)
   olympicus **41:** *50–51*, (51)
   variegatus **41:** (51)
Rhyacotritonidae **41:** 27
Rhynchobatus **33:** (27)
   djiddensis **33:** 32
Rhynchobdellae **21:** 94
Rhynchocephalia **44:** 8, 9, 18
Rhynchocinetes **28:** *11*
   durbanensis **28:** *66–67*
Rhynchocyon
   chrysopygus **9:** 59, 62–63
   cirnei **9:** 59
   petersi **9:** 59
Rhynchogale melleri **1:** 98
Rhynchohyalus natalensis **35:** 25
Rhyncholestes raphanurus **10:** 14
Rhynchomeles prattorum **10:** 27
Rhynchorhamphus **38:** 77
Rhynochetidae **11:** 92
Rhynochetos jubatus **11:** 92, 96–97; **14:** 82; **19:** 8
Rhysella approximator **27:** *24–25*
ribbonbearer **39:** 9, 15
ribbonfish 35: 105, 106–107, **36:** 96
   blackflash **35:** 106
   festive **39:** 15
   peregrine **35:** 82, 106, *106*
   polka-dot **35:** 106, *107*
   scalloped **35:** *106–107*, 107
   tapertail **35:** 107
   unicorn **35:** 104
ricebird *see* sparrow, Java
ricefish 34: 61, **38:** 50, 64–69
   Japanese **38:** 65
   Javan **38:** *69*
   Javanese **38:** (68)
   Malabar **38:** 64, 65, 67, 68, 69
Richardsonius
   egrenius **34:** 74
ridgehead **39:** 12, 13
riflebird **19:** (109)

   magnificent **19:** 106, 108
   paradise **19:** 106, 108
   Victoria's **19:** 106, *106*, 108
Riftrida **21:** 77
rinderpest **6:** 73, 77, 85
Rineloricaria **37:** 104, 110
ringing of trees **7:** 37
ringtail *see* possum; raccoon
rinkhals **50:** 9, 14, (30), (39)
   African **48:** 17; **49:** 100
Riodinidae **26:** 34–37
Riopa **46:** 8
   fernandi **46:** 34–35
Rioraja **33:** (26)
Riparia riparia **15:** 94, 100–103; **18:** 13
Rissa
   brevirostris **12:** 74
   eburnea **12:** 74
   furcatus **12:** 74
   rosea **12:** 74
   tridactyla **12:** 74, 80–85
Rissola marginata **36:** 25
Ristella **46:** 8, 9
Rivulidae **38:** 79
rivulines 38: 78–83
Rivulus **38:** 79
   marmoratus **38:** (82)
rivulus
   marmorated **38:** (82)
   ocellated **38:** (82)
Rizocephala **28:** 9
roach 34: 73, 84–87
   Black Sea **34:** 87
   compared with rudd **34:** (86)
   Danube **34:** 87
   Kutum **34:** 87
   pearl **34:** 84
   roach/rudd hybrids **34:** (87)
   Siberian **34:** 84
roadrunner 20: 46–47
   greater 20: 46, 56–61
robin
   American 16: 59; **18:** 44, (50), 52–53, 79
   Australian **18:** (50)
   bush- **18:** (50)
   European 11: (49); **18:** 44, 45, 46–51, 52, 54
   Japanese **18:** (50)
   Pekin **18:** (50)
   Ryukyu **18:** (50)
robin-chat **18:** (50)
rockcod **39:** 64
rockfish **39:** 53, 59, 61, 64, 65, 66, (67)
   offshore **39:** 61
   quillback **39:** 65
   rougheye **39:** 65
   silver-gray **39:** 65
   yelloweye **39:** 65
rockhare *see* hare, greater red rockhare
rockhead **39:** 80
rockling **36:** 32, 36, (37)
rock-nuthatch **18:** 64, *64*
Rocky Mountain spotted fever **29:** *32,*

(32)
Rocky Mountain tick fever **7:** 14
Rodalia cardinalis **25:** (56)
rodents 1: *10;* **7:** 8–15
  cavylike 8: 8–11
  evolution **7:** *12*
  expansion **7:** 11
  extinct **7:** 11–12
  mouselike 7: 16–19
  porcupinelike 8: 8–11
  squirrel-like 7: 16–19
Roeboides **38:** 35
roker **33:** 28
Rollandia rolland **14:** 16
roller 15: 86–87; **18:** (18)
  African broad-billed **15:** 92
  azure **15:** 86
  bean-leaf (long-tailed skipper) **26:** *62*
  blue-throated **15:** 86
  cinnamon **15:** 86
  eastern broad-billed 15: 86, 90–93
  European 15: 86, 88–89, 90, (92)
  lilac-breasted **15:** 86, *87,* (93)
  racket-tailed **15:** 86
Romalea microptera **23:** *28*
Romerolagus diazi **8:** 64
Rondeletia
  bicolor **39:** 14
  loricata **39:** 14, *14*
Rondeletiidae **39:** 12–15
rook 18: 90, 93, 108–109
ropefish 31: 44–51, 52
rorquals **3:** 55, 106, 107
rosefinch **16:** 77
  great **16:** 76
rosefish
  blackbelly **39:** (67)
Rosema **26:** *80*
Rostratula benghalensis **14:** 96
Rostratulidae **14:** 96
Rostrhamus
  sociabilis **15:** 8, 28–29
  plumbeus **15:** 28
Rostroraja **33:** (27)
Rotifera **21:** 32, 68–69
rough fish **34:** 94
rough hound **32:** 46
roughy **39:** 9, 16, 20, 21
  orange **39:** 21
roundhead **40:** 22, 25
Rousettus aegyptiacus **9:** 92–93
Royal Society for the Protection of Birds
  (RSPB) **12:** 85; **13:** (77)
rubberlips **40:** 36
rubythroat, Siberian **18:** 44, (50)
Rudarius exelsus **39:** 104
rudd 34: 46, 68, 84–87
  compared with roach **34:** (86)
  golden variety of **34:** (86)
  rudd/roach hybrids **34:** (87)
ruff **13:** 30, *31,* 33
ruffe **40:** 16
Rukia ruki **18:** 68
rumen **6:** 8

ruminants 5: 11, 12; **6:** 8–9
  pseudoruminants **5:** 70
Rupicapra
  pyrenaica **6:** 62
  rupicapra **6:** 62, 108
Rupicaprini **6:** 108
Rupicola
  peruviana **19:** 80, 88
  rupicola **19:** 80, 88–93
Rupicolidae **19:** 88
Rutilus **34:** 68, (87)
  alburnoides **34:** 87
  arcasii **34:** 87
  frisii **34:** 87
  meidingerii **34:** 87
  pigus **34:** 87
  rutilus **34:** 73, 84, *84–85*
Ruwenzorornis, johnstoni **16:** 38
Rynchopidae **12:** 74, 77
Rynchops
  albicollis **12:** 74
  flavirostris **12:** 74
  niger **12:** 74, 96–9

S

abella pavonina **21:** *97*
sabellids **21:** *34–35*
sable, American **1:** 48, 50
sablefish **39:** 53
saccopharyngid **33:** 65
Saccopharyngidae **33:** (62), 94–95
Saccopharyngiformes **33:** 62, (62)
Saccopharynx **33:** 65
  harrisoni **33:** 94
  lavenbergi **33:** 95
Sacculina carcini **28:** 26
Sacoglossa **30:** 18, (43)
sacoglossans **30:** (43)
Sacoglossus **21:** 79
sacred animals **4:** 59, (66); **9:** 91
saddleback **20:** 100
Sagitta elegans **21:** 79
Sagittariidae **15:** 8; **20:** 8, 11
Sagittarius serpentarius **11:** 93, 95;
  15: 8; **20:** 8, 30–35
Saguinus
  fusciollis **4:** 86
  imperator **4:** 86, 94–95
  imperator imperator **4:** 94
  imperator subgrisescens **4:** 94

  oedipus **4:** 86
saiga **6:** 62
Saiga tartarica **6:** 62
sailfin **34:** 88
sailfish **40:** 108
  Atlantic **40:** 109, 110
Saimiri
  boliviensis **4:** 72
  sciureus **4:** 72, 78–79
saki
  bald-faced **4:** 72
  bearded **4:** 72
  buffy **4:** 72
  Guianan **4:** 72, *73*
  monk **4:** 72
  white-nosed **4:** 72
salamanderfish **35:** 8, (36)
salamanders 41: 9–12, (17), 26–29
  alpine **41:** 28, (91), 92, (103), 105
  American mole **41:** 88
  Anji **41:** 36
  Asiatic 41: 27, 36–37
  Barton Springs 41: 73, (81), 82–83
  black-bellied 41: 74–75
  Blanco blind **41:** 73, (83)
  blind cave **41:** 29
  blue-spotted **41:** *57,* (57), 58
  bromeliad **41:** 69
  brook **41:** 27, (29), 88, *88–89,* 92
  California slender **41:** 73
  cascade torrent 41: *9,* 50–51
  Caucasian **41:** 92–93
  cave **41:** 27, *37,* 68, 70, *92*
  Chinese **41:** 37
  Columbia torrent **41:** (51)
  Corsican brook **41:** 96, (97)
  Cumberland plateau **41:** 85
  dusky **41:** 69, 86
  dwarf **41:** 69
  ensatina **41:** 68, *70–71, 92*
  European 41: 27, (29), 88–93
  European cave **41:** 72
  fertilization **41:** 12
  food and feeding **41:** 26–27
  four-toed **41:** *70*
  gold-striped **41:** 93, *93*
  green **41:** 72
  imitator **41:** *72–73,* 73
  Inyo Mountain slender **41:** 73
  Jefferson **41:** 56, *57,* (57)
  Jordan's **41:** 72, *72–73*
  Lake Lerma **41:** 63
  Lake Pátzcuaro **41:** 63
  Lanza's alpine **41:** (103)
  larvae **41:** (29)
  life cycle **41:** *28*
  long-tailed **41:** 80
  long-toed **41:** 56, 59
  lungless 41: (12), 27, (29), 68–73, 93
  Luschan's **41:** (91), 92, (103), 105
  Mabees's **41:** 56
  marbled **41:** *57, 59*
  Mexican mole (axolotls) **41:** 18, 27,
    28, 29, 56, 58, 59, 60–63;

46: (111)
miniature 41: 27, 27–28, <u>76–79</u>
mole 41: 27, 29, (29), 44, <u>56–59</u>, *92*
mud **41:** 86
northwestern **41:** 44
northwestern mole **41:** 57, (58)
Ocoee **41:** (75)
Oklahoma **41:** (81)
palm (miniature) **41:** 27, 27–28, <u>76–79</u>
pedogenesis **41:** 28–29
pedomorphosis **41:** 28–29, (83)
Pyrenean brook 41: <u>96–97</u>
red 41: <u>86–87</u>, 91
red-backed **41:** 87
Red Hills **41:** 68
reproduction **41:** 27–28
respiration **41:** 26
ringed **41:** 57
San Gabriel Mountain slender **41:** 73
San Marcos **41:** (83)
Sardinian brook **41:** 96, (97)
seal **41:** (75)
seepage **41:** 70
Siberian **41:** 36, 37
silvery **41:** (57)
slimy 41: <u>84–85</u>
southern torrent **41:** (51)
spectacled **41:** 93
spotted **41:** 56, *57*, 58
stream **41:** 36, *36*
streamside **41:** 56
Tellico **41:** 85
Texas **41:** (81), (83)
Texas blind **41:** (83)
three-lined 41: <u>80–81</u>
torrent **41:** 27, (29), 50–51, *50–51*
Tremblay's **41:** (57)
tropical palm **41:** *77*
two-lined **41:** (81)
white (olms) **41:** 14, *26–27*, 27, <u>48–49</u>
worm **41:** *69*
see also amphiumas; fire salamander; giant salamanders; hellbender; olm; sirens; tiger salamander
Salamandra **41:** 88, (103); **43:** 45
algira **41:** (103)
atra **41:** 28, (91), 92, (103), 105
atra aurorae **41:** (103)
corsica **41:** (103)
infraimmaculata **41:** (103), (107)
lanzai **41:** (91), 92, (103)
luschani **41:** (91), 92, (103), 105
salamandra **41:** (17), 27, 88, 92, <u>102–107</u>, (107); **42:** 26
Salamandrella **41:** 36, (37)
Salamandridae **41:** *26–27*, 27, 36, 88
Salamandrina **41:** 88
terdigitata **41:** 93
Salangichthys microdon **35:** *30*
Salangidae **35:** <u>30–31</u>
Salanoia concolor **1:** 98
Saldidae **24:** (23)

salema **40:** 40
Salilota australis **36:** *52*
saliva **9:** 17, 21
poisonous **9:** 8, 11, (32), 39
Salmo **34:** 85, 111
carpio **35:** (69)
ferox **35:** (69)
hucho **35:** (51)
marmoratus **35:** (69)
nigripinnis **35:** (69)
salar **31:** *21*, **35:** (51), <u>52–57</u>
stomachicus **35:** (69)
trutta **35:** 35, <u>66–71</u>, (68), 73
trutta aralensis **35:** (68), (70)
trutta fario **35:** *66*, *66–67*, 67, (68), 68, *70–71*, 74
trutta lacustris **35:** (68), 70
trutta macrostigma **35:** (68), (70), 71
trutta oxianus **35:** (68), (70)
trutta trutta **35:** 67, (68), 69
salmon 35: <u>8–9</u>, 26, 32, (51), **36:** 85
Aral **35:** (68)
Atlantic 35: (51), <u>52–57</u>
chum **35:** (65)
coho **35:** (65)
Danube 35: <u>48–51</u>
kamchatko **35:** 73
kokanee **35:** 58, *60–61*, (61)
pink **35:** *64–65*, (65)
red **35:** 58
rock (dogfish) **32:** 22, 46, 47
Sebago **35:** (54)
sockeye 35: 9, <u>58–65</u>, (61), 73
summer **35:** 73
Tigris **34:** 19
Who's Who **35:** (9)
Salmonella **23:** 108
salmonete **35:** 111
Salmonidae **35:** 9, 26, (51), **36:** 16, 85
Salmoniformes **35:** (9)
salp 31: <u>22–23</u>, 25
Salpornis spilonotus **17:** 82
salt glands **12:** (75); **14:** 53–54
Salticidae **29:** 39, <u>74–77</u>
Saltuarius **45:** (47)
cornutus **45:** 20, <u>46–47</u>
Salvelinus **35:** <u>46–47</u>, (51)
alpinus **35:** 46, *47*
alpinus erythrinus **35:** 46
confluentus **35:** 46
fontinalis **35:** *46*, 47, 66, 67
leucomaenis leucomaenis **35:** 46
leucomaenis umbrius **35:** 46
malma **35:** 46
malma krascheninnokova **35:** 46
malma malma **35:** 46
malma miyabei **35:** 46
namaycush **35:** 46, 66
Salvethymus **35:** <u>46–47</u>
svetovidovi **35:** 47
sand devil **32:** 105
sand diver **35:** *95*
sand dollars **30:** 93, 104, 108, *109*
sand eel

Korean 39: 26, <u>28–29</u>
sand gaper **30:** 62
sand hoppers 28: <u>44–45</u>
sand lance **39:** 28, 29
sand puppy *see* mole rat, naked
sand tiger **32:** 35
sanddab
Pacific **39:** 90
Sandelia **40:** 58
bainsii **40:** 59
capensis **40:** 59
Sander lucioperca **40:** 9, 16
sanderling **11:** 15; **13:** 30, (32)
sandfish (fish), Indo-Pacific **40:** 99
sandfish 46: 10, 12, <u>36–39</u>; **49:** (24)
sandgrouse
Burchell's **16:** 8, *8–9*
Lichtenstein's **16:** 8, *9*
Namaqua **16:** 8, *9*
Pallas's 16: 8, <u>10–11</u>
pin-tailed **16:** 8, *9*
sandgrouse family 16: <u>8–9</u>
Tibetan **16:** 8
sandperch **40:** 12, 19
red-spotted **40:** *18–19*
sandpiper 12: 74; **13:** 75; **14:** 98
buff-breasted **13:** 30, 33
common 13: 30, <u>44–47</u>
pectoral 13: 30, 33, <u>62–63</u>
purple **13:** 30, 33
sandpiper family 13: 8, <u>30–33</u>
spoon-billed 13: 30, <u>48–49</u>
Terek **13:** 30
Tuamotu **13:** 30, 31, (33)
white-rumped **13:** 30
white-winged **13:** 30, (33)
sandplover, Kittlitz's **13:** 8
sandroller **36:** 16, 17
sandsucker **38:** 17
saola **6:** 62
sapsucker, yellow-bellied **16:** 53, 67; **18:** 8
saratoga 31: 82, 86, 93, <u>98–99</u>, 101
gulf **31:** *82–83*, 83, 84, 98, *98*
spotted **31:** 83, 84, 98, *98–99*, 99
Sarcodina **21:** 13, <u>18–21</u>
Sarcogyps calvus **20:** 8
Sarcomastigophora **21:** 13
Sarcophaga carnaria **23:** *112, 112–113*
Sarcophagidae **23:** <u>112–113</u>
Sarcophilus
harrisii **10:** 27, <u>28–31</u>
laniarius (*harrisii*) **10:** 27, <u>28–31</u>
Sarcopterygii **33:** 60, (61)
Sarcoramphus papa **20:** 8
Sarda sarda **40:** 106
Sardina **36:** *86–87*, 105, 111
pilchardus **36:** *98*, 106
sardine **32:** 59, 83, **36:** 50, 98, 102
European **36:** *98*
"large-mouthed" **34:** 69
Pacific **36:** *84–85*, *102*, 111
Sardinita
bocagrande **34:** 69

de Tempelmene **34:** 70
Sardinops **36:** 111
  sagax **36:** *84–85, 102*, 111
Sargasso Sea **33:** 67, 70, 72, 73, 88,
  36: (68)
sargassum fish **36:** 64, (68), *68–69*
Sargocentron rubrum **39:** *20*, 21
Sarpa salpa **40:** 40
Sartor respectus **38:** 20
sashimi **36:** 25, **40:** 107, (110)
Satan **37:** 15
  eurystomus **37:** 16
Saturniidae **26:** *9–10*, 70–73
  defense **26:** (72)
Satyridae **26:** 46–47
satyrs 26: 46–47
  marbled whites **26:** *47*
  mating **26:** 47
  mountain beauty **26:** *46–47*
  scotch argus **26:** *46*
saupe **40:** 40
Sauresia **46:** 52
Sauria **44:** 8, 9, 25
Saurida **35:** 94
  flamma **35:** *94*
  gracilis **35:** *94*
  suspicio **35:** 96
Sauromalus **44:** 30, 52, (54), 82
  hispidus **44:** *54–55*
  obesus **44:** 34, (54)
  varius **44:** *54*
saury 38: 50, 70–75
  Atlantic **38:** 74
saury pike **38:** 74
sawbelly **39:** 16, 20, 21
sawfish 32: 108, **33:** 10, 16–17, 27
  Atlantic **32:** 110
  common **33:** 16
  freshwater **33:** 18, *19*
  great-tooth 33: 18–19
  long-tooth **33:** 16
  narrow **32:** 108, 110
  small-tooth **33:** *16–17*
  smoothtooth **32:** 108, 110
  southern **32:** 108, 110, **33:** 18, *19*
sawflies 27: 12
  and allies 27: 14–21
  colon **27:** 9
  defensive measures **27:** 19–20
  European iris **27:** *18*
  feeding **27:** 17–18
  hazel **27:** *20–21*
  and humans **27:** 20
  larvae **27:** 18–19
  lime-green **27:** *16*
  maternal care **27:** (17)
  as pests **27:** 20
  spitfire **27:** *19*
  striped bracken **27:** *17*
sawtailfish
  ribbon **35:** 89
sawwing, Fanti **15:** 94
scale insects **24:** 106–111
  cottony cushion **24:** *106;* **25:** (56)

as pests **24:** 109–110
  soft **24:** 106, *107*
  tortoise **24:** 106
  wax **24:** 106
  woolly insects **24:** 110
scales **49:** 10
  polishing **49:** (14), 61
scallops
  and allies 30: 58–59
  Atlantic bay **30:** *58*
Scandentia **1:** *10;* **9:** 58
Scapanorhynchidae **32:** (74)
Scapanorhyncus **32:** 90
Scapanus orarius **9:** 40
Scaphidura oryzivora **18:** 74
Scaphiophryne **42:** 105, *105*, 109
Scaphiophryninae **42:** 104, 108
Scaphiopus **42:** 40, *40–41*
  bombifrons **42:** 44
  couchi **42:** 44–45, 73
  hammondi **42:** 44
Scaphirhynchinae **31:** (52), 53, 68
Scaphirhynchus **31:** 68, *69*
  albus **31:** 68–69
  platorynchus **31:** 53, 68, *69*
Scaphopoda **30:** 9, 10, 16–17
Scaphura **23:** *15*
Scapteriscus vicinus **23:** 23
Scarabaeidae **25:** 76–89
Scardinius **34:** 46, 68, (87)
  acarnanicus **34:** 87
  erythrophthalmus **34:** 84, 86, *86, 87*
  erythrophthalmus racovitzai **34:** 86
  graecus **34:** 86
  racovitzae **34:** 86
  scardafa **34:** 87
Scaridae **34:** 102, **40:** 9, 88–89
Scarus
  chameleon **40:** *89*
  ferrugineus **40:** 88
scat 40: 42–43
  African **40:** 43
  common **40:** 42, 43, *43*
  green **40:** 43
  red **40:** 43
  spotbanded **40:** 43
  spotted **40:** 42, *43*
Scathophaga stercoraria **23:** *98, 98–99*
Scathophagidae **23:** 98–99
Scatophagidae **40:** 42–43
Scatophagus
  argus **40:** 42, 43, *43*
  argus atromaculatus **40:** 43
  multifasciatus **40:** 43
  papuensis **40:** 43
  rubrifrons **40:** 43
  tetracanthus **40:** 43
Scaturiginichthys vermeilipinnis **38:** (56),
  59
scaup **12:** 66, 70
  greater **12:** 66, *68*
scavengers (breams) **40:** 40
Scelidotherium **9:** 64
Sceliphron

fistularum **27:** *78–79*
  fuscum **27:** 79
Sceloporus **44:** 85
  jarrovi **44:** 85
  malachiticus **44:** *82–83*, 85
  olivaceus **44:** *27*
  poinsettii **44:** 85
  undulatus hyacinthinus **44:** 85
Scelotes **46:** 8, 11
Scenopoeetes dentirostris **19:** 100
scent gland **17:** (16)
schelly **35:** 38, 40
Schilbe
  mandibularis **37:** (40)
  maramoratus **37:** 41
  mystus **37:** *38*, 41
Schilbeidae **37:** 30, (32), (34), 38–41
Schinderia
  pietschmanni **40:** 99
  praematura **40:** 99
Schindler's fish **40:** 99
Schinia masoni **26:** 94
Schistometopum **41:** 21
  thomense **41:** 21
Schistosoma mansoni **21:** *83*
schistosomiasis **21:** (83), (85); **30:** 46
Schizodonta **30:** 9, 50, 60–61
schizogony **21:** 14
schooling **32:** 72, **33:** 48–49, *99*, **36:**
  100, 101, 102, 103
Schoutedenella **43:** 12
Schuettea
  scalaripinnis **40:** 43
  woodwardi **40:** 43
Sciaenidae **39:** 54, **40:** 11, 12–19
Sciaenops ocellatus **40:** 19
Scincidae **44:** (23), 25, (26), 28, 84;
  46: 8
Scincus **46:** 8
  scincus **44:** 27, 84; **46:** 10, 12, 36–39;
  49: (24)
Sciomyzidae **23:** 94–95
Sciuridae **7:** 12
Sciurognathi (sciurognaths) **7:** (8), *12*,
  16–19; **8:** 8
Sciuromorpha **7:** 8
Sciurus
  carolinensis **7:** 34, 38–41
  niger **7:** 34, 46–47
  vulgaris **7:** 34, 42–45
Scleractinia **21:** 43
Scleropages **31:** 84, 93, 98–99
  formosus **31:** 82, 90, 95, 96–97, 99
  jardinii **31:** 82, *82–83*, 98, *98*
  leichardti **31:** 82, 98, *98–99*
Sclerorhynchus **33:** 10
Scliorhinus canicula **33:** 30
Scolecomorphidae **41:** 21
Scolecomorphus **41:** 21
Scolecophidia **48:** 18
Scolecophis atrocinctus **49:** 109
Scoliidae **27:** 36–37
Scolopacidae **13:** 8, 30, 75
Scolopax **15:** (52)

bukidonensis **13:** 30
Scolopendra cingulatus **22:** *22–23*
Scoloplacidae **37:** 11, 97
Scolopostethus affinis **24:** (45)
Scomber **40:** 11
   japonicus **40:** *104–105*
   scombrus **40:** *104*, 106
Scomberesocidae **38:** 70–75
Scomberesox saurus **38:** 74
Scomberomorus **40:** 106
   concolor **40:** 107
Scombridae **31:** (47), **38:** 50, **39:** (10),
   40: 104–107, 108
Scopelogenys tristis **35:** 82, 103
Scophthalmus rhombus **39:** 90
Scorpaena
   porcus **39:** 61
   scrofa **39:** 61
Scorpaenichthys marmoratus **32:** 102,
   39: 76
Scorpaenidae **39:** 8, 53, 58–67
Scorpaeniformes **39:** 52–53
   families summary **39:** (52)
Scorpaenodes hirsutus **39:** 62
Scorpaenopsis **39:** *52–53*, (62)
   cirrosa **39:** 61
Scorpiones **29:** 16–19
scorpionfish 35: 101, **38:** 50, **39:** 11,
   53, 58–67, 71
   Ambon **39:** *66*
   black **39:** 61
   crested **39:** 70
   decoy **39:** 64
   hairy **39:** 62
   large-scaled **39:** 61
   leaf **39:** 61, *64–65*
   midwater **39:** 66
   pygmy **39:** 61
   spiny crown **39:** *52–53*
scorpionflies 22: 104–108
   common **22:** *106–107*
   snow **22:** 104–108
scorpions 1: (102); **29:** 8, 9, 16–19;
   49: (63)
   African emperor **29:** *16*
   anatomy **29:** 16–17
   body **29:** *17*
   false **29:** *20*
   mating **29:** 18–19
   microwhip **29:** (29)
   stings **29:** (18)
   tailed whip 29: 28–29
   tailless whip 29: *15*, 26–27
   water 24: 20–21
   wind (sun spiders) **29:** 34–35
scoter **12:** 66; **14:** 52, 53
   black **12:** 66
   surf **12:** 66
   velvet **14:** 52, *53*
   white-winged **12:** 66
Scotobleps **43:** 12
Scotopelia **15:** 56
   peli **15:** 50, 56–57
scrub fowl, dusky **11:** 44, 49

scrub jays **49:** 96
scrub typhus **29:** (32)
scrub-bird 11: 104–105
   noisy 11: 104, 105, 110–111
   rufous **11:** 104, *104*, 105
Scudderia **23:** *12–13*
sculpin 35: 44, **39:** 11, 76–81
   Baikal **39:** 77, 78
   Bear Lake **39:** (78)
   blob **39:** 80
   blotch-bodied polar **39:** 80
   deep-sea **39:** 77
   dwarf **39:** 77
   flat **39:** 78
   grunt **39:** 79
   Klamath Lake **39:** (78)
   Pacific staghorn **39:** *78*
   pygmy **39:** (78)
   red **39:** 77
   rough **39:** (78)
   sailfin **39:** 80, 81, *81*
   short-headed **39:** 77
   shorthorn **39:** 76
   Shoshone **39:** (78)
   silver-spotted **39:** 80
   slender **39:** (78)
   Utah Lake **39:** (78)
   web **39:** 80
   whip **39:** 80
   Wood River **39:** (78)
Scutelleridae **24:** 70–71
Scutiger **42:** 34
   boulengeri **42:** 34
Scutigera coleoptrata **22:** 22
Scutigerella immaculata **22:** (15)
Scutisorex somereni **9:** 28
scuttle bugs (whirligig beetles)
   25: 26–27
Scyliorhinidae **32:** (12), (42), 58
Scyliorhinus **32:** 46, 57
   canicula **32:** 10, 46–47, 57
   capensis **32:** 57
   retifer **32:** 46
   stellaris **32:** 46, 57
Scyllarides haanii **28:** 83
Scyphozoa **21:** 43, 50–55
scythebill **17:** (29)
   black-billed **17:** 28, *28*, (29)
Scythrops novaehollandiae **20:** 46,
   54–55
Scytodes
   globula **29:** 58–59
   thoracica **29:** 58
Scytodidae **29:** 58–59
sea anemones 21: *34–35, 42,* 56–61;
   28: (97), 99
   aggression **21:** (59)
   anatomy **21:** 57
   beadlet **21:** *56, 59*
   burrowing **21:** (58)
   and clownfish **21:** (61)
   fireworks **21:** *57*
   frilled **21:** *56*
   magnificent **21:** *61*

sea bass *see* bass
sea butterflies **30:** 36, 37
sea canary *see* beluga
sea cow
   Steller's **3:** 46, 47, *47*, 53
   see also dugong
sea cucumbers 30: *91, 92–93, 93,*
   110–113; **36:** 22, *22–23*, 23
   armored **30:** *111*
   Cuvierian organs **30:** (113)
   defense **30:** (113)
   plate and anchor spicules **30:** (111)
sea devil **36:** (76), 82, 83
   black **36:** 82
   giant **36:** 77
   toothy **36:** 82
   triplewart **36:** 77
sea dragon
   leafy **31:** *9*
sea fans **21:** 66–67
sea grass **3:** 46, 52
sea hares **30:** *36, 36–37,* 37
sea horse 31: 42, **38:** 50, **39:** 8, 10,
   26–27, 36, 38–47
   Cape **39:** (46)
   for Chinese medicine **39:** 45, (46)
   as curio **39:** 45, 46
   Denise's pygmy **39:** (40)
   Knysna **39:** *40,* (46)
   long-snouted **39:** *39, 40–41*
   pot-bellied **39:** 38
   "pregnant" male **39:** *47*
   pygmy **39:** *27*
   short-snouted **39:** *47*
   smallest known **39:** (40)
sea lemon **30:** *38*
sea leopard *see* seal, leopard
sea lilies 30: 92, 94–97
   orange **30:** 96
sea lion 1: *10;* **3:** 8–13, 64
   Australian **3:** 9, *11*
   California 3: 9, *13,* 18, 20–23
   Galápagos **3:** *9*
   New Zealand **3:** 9, 12
   Steller's 3: 9, 12, 18–19
sea monkeys **28:** (20)
sea mouse **21:** *99*
sea nettles **21:** 55
sea potato **30:** 108–109
sea raven **39:** 80
sea roach **28:** *46*
sea robin **39:** 53, 54, 55, 56, 57, 72
   African armored **39:** 57
   armored **39:** 56, 57
   northern **39:** 56, 57
   striped **39:** 56
sea slater **22:** *9;* **28:** *46, 49*
sea slugs 30: 38–43
   nudibranch **30:** *21*
   opalescent **30:** *10–11*
   pyjama **30:** *40–41*
sea snakes 33: 81; **49:** (82); **50:** 9, 10,
   44–49, 80
   beaked **50:** 47

eyelash **50:** 46
Hardwicke's **50:** 46
Lake Taal **50:** (47)
Merton's **50:** 44
olive **50:** *44–45*, 46, *48–49*
Stokes's **50:** 46
turtle-headed **50:** 44, 46, *46–47*, 47–48
yellow-bellied **48:** 25; **50:** 45, 47, (48), 49
sea spider **22:** *8*
sea squirt 31: 22–23, 25, 31, 42, **36:** 22, **39:** 29
sea vase **31:** *22*
sea toad **36:** (73)
sea urchins 30: *91, 93,* 104–109
Aristotle's lantern **30:** 93, 106
common **30:** *105*
hatpin **30:** *106*
pedicellariae **30:** (107)
regular (rounded) **30:** *104*
slate pencil **30:** *105*
spines **30:** 104–106
sea wasp **21:** *52*
seabream 40: 40–41
"cleaner fish" **40:** 40
common **40:** *40*
two-banded **40:** 40
white **40:** 40
see also bream
seadragon **39:** 38, 40, 41, 42, 43
leafy **39:** (42), *44*
ribboned **39:** (42)
weedy **39:** *10–11*, (42)
seal 1: *10*; **3:** 8–13, 64; **7:** 12
Antarctic fur **3:** 9, 12
Baikal **3:** 9, *10–11*
Cape fur 3: *8*, 9, 16–17
Caribbean monk **3:** 9
circus tricks **3:** (23)
common (harbor) **3:** *8*, 9, 40–41
crabeater 3: 9, 11, 36–37, 38
eared **3:** *8*, 9, *9*, 10, 11, *13*
fur **1:** (11)
gray 3: 42–43
harbor 3: *8*, 9, 40–41
harp 3: 9, 12, 44–45
Hawaiian monk 3: 9, 30–31
leopard 3: 9, 11, 37, 38–39
monk **3:** 9
northern elephant 3: 9, *12*, 32–35
northern fur 3: 9, 12, 14–15
phocid **3:** 9–10, 11
ringed **2:** 86–87
saddleback (harp) **3:** 9, 12, 44–45
southern elephant 3: 32
southern fur (Cape fur) **3:** *8*, 9, 16–17
seamoth 39: 26, 36–37
brick **39:** 36
dwarf **39:** 36, *36*
Hawaiian **39:** 36, 37
longtail **39:** 36
sculptured **39:** 36
slender **39:** 36, *37*

"winged" **39:** *10*
Searsia **35:** *9*
seasnails **30:** 26
violet **30:** *29*
seastar, horned **30:** *91*
Sebastapistes fowleri **39:** 61
Sebastes
aleutinus **39:** 65
borealis **39:** 65
goodei **39:** 64
levis **39:** 65
maliger **39:** 65
marinus **39:** *58*
paucispinis **39:** 64
ruberrimus **39:** 65
serriceps **39:** 64
Sebasticus marmoratus **39:** (67)
Sebastidae **39:** 64
Sebastolobus alascanus **39:** (67)
secretary bird 11: 93, 95; **15:** 8, 12; **20:** 8–9, 11, 30–35
sedge darner **22:** *51*
seedeater, white-collared **16:** 62
Segestria senoculata **29:** 63
Segestriidae **29:** (63)
Sehirus bicolor **24:** 66–67
Seiurus aurocapillus **20:** 80
Selasphorus
flammula **16:** 44
rufus **16:** 44
sasin **16:** 44
Selene **40:** 35
Selenidera culik **19:** 56
Selenostomidae **39:** 38–47
Seleucidis melanoleuca **19:** 106
Selvinia betpakdalaensis **7:** 102
Semaeostomae **21:** 43
Semaprochilodus taeniurus **38:** 19
Semibalanus balanoides **28:** 22
Semicassis labiata **30:** 30
Semilabeo prochilus **34:** (92)
Semionotidae **31:** (72), 73
Semionotiformes **31:** 72–75
families summary **31:** (72)
Semioptera wallacii **19:** 106
Semiotus insignis **25:** *43*
semizygodactylism **16:** 38; **17:** (22)
Semnopithecus **4:** 40
entellus **4:** 40, 64–67
geei see *Trachypithecus geei*
hypoleucos **4:** 40
obscurus see *Trachypithecus obscurus*
Semnornis
frantzii **19:** 56, 70
ramphastinus **19:** 56, 70–71
Semotilus atromaculatus **34:** 78–79
sengi **9:** 58
Senoculidae **29:** 93
senses, bird **11:** 13
Senticolis triaspis **49:** 10, (43)
Sephanoides sephanoides **16:** 44
Sepia **30:** *77–78*
apama **30:** *77*
latimanus **30:** *78*

officinalis **30:** (78)
pharaonis **30:** *76–77*
sepia dun **22:** *38*
Sepidium tricuspidatum **25:** *72–73*
Sepiidae **30:** 72
seps (plated snake lizards) **45:** 101
seps (three-toed skinks) **46:** 20–23
Sepsidae **23:** (99)
Sepsis fulgens **23:** *98–99*, (99)
Serengeti Plains **6:** 84, (85)
Sergeant Baker fish **35:** *78–79*
Sericulus **19:** 102
aureus **19:** 100
chrysocephalus **19:** 100
seriema 11: 93; **14:** 90; **19:** 8
black-legged **11:** 92
crested 11: 92, 94–95
red-legged (crested) **11:** 92, 94–95
Serinus
canaria **16:** 76
totta **16:** 76
serow **6:** 108
Japanese **6:** 62
mainland **6:** 62
Serpentes **44:** 8, 9; **48:** 9
Serranidae **39:** (10), 109, **40:** 9, 12–19
Serranus **40:** (16)
Serrapinnus kriegi **38:** 35
Serrasalmus **38:** (45), 46
gibbus **38:** 46
irritans **38:** 44
manueli **38:** 42
Serrivomeridae **33:** (62)
serval 2: 10, 46–47
servalines **2:** 46
Sesia apiformis **26:** 104
Sesiidae **26:** 104–105
Setifer setosus **9:** 24
Setonix brachyurus **10:** 48, 68–69
Setophaga ruticilla **17:** 88, 90–93
sewellel **7:** (29)
sewin **35:** 66, (68)
sexual dichromatism **23:** 25
sexual dimorphism **17:** (37)
shad **36:** 98, (101)
African **36:** 89
allis **36:** *100–101*
Atlantic **36:** (101)
gizzard **36:** 87
ilisha **36:** 88, 89
Indo-Pacific **36:** 89
Twaite **36:** (101)
shag **12:** 48, 83
European **12:** 44, *48*
imperial **12:** 44, *48*
spotted **12:** 44, *48*
shanny **40:** *90*
shark 31: *14, 26, 42, 46, 70,* **32:** 8–25, **33:** 8, 10, **36:** 97, 104, **37:** 8, **39:** 111, **40:** 32, 34, *35,* 102, 103
African nurse **32:** 35
American saw **32:** 109
angel 32: 10, 24, 36, 104–105
angular angel **32:** 25

Apollo **34:** 57
Atlantic angel **32:** 106
Atlantic nurse **32:** 34, (40)
attacks on stingrays **33:** 34, 36
Australian **32:** 107
Australian swell **32:** 59
Bahamas saw **32:** 109
Bahamian saw **32:** 109
Bala **34:** 57
balloon **32:** 58
bamboo **32:** *31*, 33
barbeled cat **32:** 56
basking 31: 70, **32:** 12, 22, 25, 38,
    74, 76, 77, 78–81, (81), 93
bigeye thresher **32:** 82, 83
black **34:** 56
black-spotted cat **32:** 56
blacktail reef **32:** 50
blacktip **32:** 15, 22, 25
blacktip reef **32:** 50
Bleeker's Apollo **34:** 57
blind **32:** 30, 32, 45
as "bloodhounds" **32:** 15
blotchy swell 32: 58–59
blue **32:** 25
blue gray **32:** 32
blunthead **32:** 64
bluntnose cow **32:** 101
bluntnose sixgill 32: 20, 25, 99,
    102–103, (103)
bonnethead (shovelhead) **32:** *73*
Borneo **32:** 25
bramble **32:** 47, 55
breeding **32:** 16–18
broadnose sevengill **32:** *99*
brown cat **32:** 32
bull 32: 20, *20–21*, 22, 24, 52–55,
    (55)
bulldog **32:** 28
bullhead 32: 10, 26–27, 28
California angel **32:** 107
California horned **32:** *27*
California swell **32:** 59
carpet 32: 10, 30–33, 38, 75
cat **32:** 46, 47
chain cat **32:** 46
Chinese **34:** 94
cobbler carpet **32:** 37
Colclough's **32:** 32
collared **32:** 100
collared carpet **32:** 30, 33
common angel 32: 106–107
common saw **32:** 109, 110
common thresher **32:** 82, 83
cookiecutter **32:** 20, 92, 93
cow 32: 45, 98–99, 100, 109
crested horn **32:** 26
crocodile **32:** 74
cub **32:** 52
death **32:** 84
distribution **32:** 19–20
dogfish 32: 26, 45, 92–93
doglike bamboo **32:** 30
draughtboard **32:** *43*, 59

dusky **32:** 25
dwarf lantern **32:** 92
eel **32:** 100
egg layers **32:** 18–19
electronic sensors **32:** 15
endangered species **32:** 25
epaulette **32:** *32*
external organs **32:** *9, 14*
families summary **32:** (12)
fox thresher **32:** 82
freshwater 34: 54–57
frill **32:** 100
frilled 32: 10, 45, 98–99, 100–101,
    108
frilled-gilled **32:** 100
Ganges **32:** 20, 25
ghost **33:** 54, 58, *59*
giant sleepy **32:** 35
goblin **32:** 10
goblin 32: 74, 90–91
graceful **32:** 50
gray nurse **32:** 25, 35
gray reef 32: 22, 24, 48–51, (51)
great hammerhead **32:** 68, 69, 102
great white 32: 10, *10–11*, 12, 16,
    24, 25, 43, 54, 60, 74, 77, 84–89
greater-spotted cat **32:** 46
Greenland **32:** (66)
ground 32: 10, 42–45, 45, 52, 74
gulper **32:** 26
gurry **32:** 96
hammerhead 32: 20, 22, 24, 55,
    68–73, 102
harlequin **34:** 56
horn **32:** 18
internal organs **32:** *14*
iridescent **37:** 41, 42, *42–45*, (45)
Isabel's swell **32:** 59
Japanese angel **32:** 107
Japanese saw **32:** *11, 108–109*, 109
kitefin **32:** 25
Lake Nicaragua **32:** 52, 53
lantern **32:** 92, 94, 95
largetooth cookiecutter **32:** 93
lemon **32:** 16, (18), 55
leopard **32:** *8*
leopard cat **32:** 56
lesser-spotted cat **32:** 46, 47
little saw **32:** 109, 110
livebearering **32:** 19
long-finned Apollo **34:** *56–57*
long-nosed blacktail **32:** 48
longnose saw 32: 109, 110–111
mackerel 32: 10, 35, 38, 43, 45,
    74–75, 91
mako **32:** 22, 24
Malaysian **34:** 57
mallethead **32:** 69
Mediterranean angel **32:** 106
megalodon **32:** (13)
megamouth 32: 20, 74, 76–77, 93
monk (angel) **32:** 105
nurse 32: 16, 26, 29, 30, 33, 34–35,
    36

oceanic whitetip **32:** 24, 66
one-fin **32:** 56
ornate angel **32:** 107
Pacific angel **32:** *105*, 107
Pacific sleeper **32:** 92, 96, 97
paroon **37:** 44, *44–45*
pelagic thresher **32:** 82, 83
pigeye **32:** 20
plain **34:** 56
"playing dead" **32:** (18)
populations **32:** 23
Port Jackson 32: 26, 28–29, 43
Portuguese **32:** 93, 97
purple **34:** *55*
pyjama 32: 56–57
ragged-tooth **32:** 35
rainbow **34:** 56
red-finned **34:** 56
red-spotted **34:** *55*
red-tailed black **34:** *17*, 18, 55, 56, 57
reef **32:** (18), *54–55*
requiem **32:** 55, 93
reticulated swell **32:** 58
rough **32:** 47
ruby **34:** *54–55*, 56
sand **32:** 35
sand tiger **32:** 19, *23*, 25, 74, *75*
sandbar **32:** (18), 22, 25, 55
saw 32: 10, 108–109
scalloped bonnethead **32:** 69
scalloped hammerhead **32:** *68–69*, 69,
    70–71, 72
school **32:** 25
scoophead **32:** 69
sensing vibrations **32:** 14
sevengill **32:** 98, 99
sharpnose **32:** 55
sharpnose sevengill **32:** *98–99*, 99
short-nosed blacktail **32:** 50
short-tail nurse **32:** 35
shortnose saw **32:** 109, 111
"shovel nose" **32:** 90
shovelhead (bonnethead) **32:** *73*
silver **34:** (56), 57
silvertip **32:** *44–45*, 51
sixgill **32:** 98, 99
sleeper **32:** 26, (66), 92, 94, 96
"Sleepy Joe" **32:** 59
slender lantern **32:** *93*
smalleye hammerhead **32:** 69
smalltooth thresher **32:** 82
smooth hammerhead **32:** 69
smoothback angel **32:** 25
soupfin **32:** 22, 25
southern saw **32:** 109, 111
speartooth **32:** 25
spined pygmy **32:** 12, 92
spitting **32:** 35
spotted ragged-tooth **32:** 35
striped cat **32:** 56
swell **32:** *42–43*, 57, 58–59
tawny nurse **32:** 24, 35, (40)
teeth **32:** *11, 12, 61, 85, 101*
thintail thresher **32:** 82

threat behavior **32:** (50)
thresher 32: 14, 25, 74, 77, *82–83*
tiger 31: *12*, **32:** 24, 54; **32:** 60–63
tricolor **34:** 57
"unicorn" **32:** 90
variegated **34:** 56
velvet belly lantern **32:** *19*
West African nurse **32:** (40)
whale 32: 12, 25, 30, 31, 33, 38–41, 78, 80
whiptail thresher **32:** 82
white-finned swell **32:** 59
whitefin hammerhead **32:** 69
whitetip reef 32: *15*, (18), *24–25*, 36, 64–67
whitetip soupfin **32:** 25
Who's Who **32:** (9)
winghead **32:** 69
yellow-spotted cat **32:** 57
Zambezi **32:** 52, 53
zebra **32:** 30, *32–33*, 36, (40)
zebra horn **32:** 26
see also dogfish
shark fins **32:** 22, *22*, 63, (80)
shark meat **32:** 22, *39*
sharkminnow
 tricolor **34:** 57
sharksucker **40:** *32, 33*
 shearwater 12: 8, 25, 29, 31, 64; **20:** (14)
 Audubon's **12:** 28
 great **12:** 28
 Manx **12:** 28, (30), 106
 short-tailed **50:** (40)
 sooty 12: 28, 38–39
sheatfish 37: 30–37, 39
sheathbill 13: 93
 black-faced **13:** 90, *92*, 93
 snowy 13: 90, 108–111, *111*
sheep 1: 15; **5:** 11, *11*; **6:** 60–63
 American bighorn 6: 100–103
 barbary **6:** 62
 blue **6:** 62
 desert bighorn **6:** 100
 domestic **6:** 62, 63
 Orkney Island Soay **6:** *63*
 wild **6:** 63
sheep strike **23:** 109–110
sheepshead
 Atlantic **40:** 40
shelduck, paradise **14:** 52
shells 30: (93)
 ark, and relatives **30:** 53
 auger **30:** 35
 bubble, and allies 30: 36–37
 burrowing razor **30:** (70)
 carpet **30:** 62, 67–68
 coat-of-mail *see* chitons
 coin **30:** 63–64
 cone 30: 32–35
 elephant's tusk 30: 16–17
 file **30:** 58, 59
 harp **30:** *34*, 35
 hatchet **30:** 62, 63

helmet **30:** 26, *30*
jewel box **30:** 62, 67
laver spire **30:** *29*
miter **30:** 35
mollusk **30:** 9, (10)
olive **30:** 35
otter **30:** 70–71
pullet carpet **30:** *67*
razor 30: 62–71
textile cone **30:** *33*
top 30: 22–25
turban **30:** 22, 25
venus **30:** 62, 67–68
wavy top **30:** *24*
wedge **30:** 62, 68–70
shiner 34: 68–71
 beautiful **34:** 69
 blacktail **34:** *70*, (71)
 bluehead **34:** *69*
 cardinal **34:** 70–71
 Conchos **34:** 69
 Cuatro Ciénegas **34:** 69
 golden **34:** 68, 85, (87)
 large-mouthed **34:** 69
 Ouachita Mountain **34:** 70
 phantom **34:** 70
 prosperine **34:** 69
 red **34:** 53, *68*, 71, 97
Shinisaurus **46:** 70
 crocodilurus **44:** 30; **45:** 93; **46:** 70, *70–71*, 72–73, 101
shipworms **30:** 71
shivers **32:** 72
shoaling **33:** (49), **35:** 28, **36:** 43, *84–85*, *92–93*, **38:** *30–31*, *62–63*
shoebill **12:** 45; **14:** 22, 32, *33*
shortraker **39:** 65
shoveler **11:** *8*; **14:** 54
 northern **14:** 52
shovelfish **31:** 70
shovelheads **28:** 84
shrew 1: *10*; **9:** 8, 9, (10), 11
 African forest **9:** 28
 American short-tailed 9: 30–33
 American water 9: 36–37
 armored **9:** 28, 29
 desert **9:** 29
 elephant **9:** 10
 Etruscan **1:** (11); **9:** 28
 Etruscan white-toothed 9: 28, 38–39
 Eurasian common 9: 34–35
 Eurasian pygmy **9:** 28, *29*
 Eurasian water **9:** 28, *29*
 forest **9:** 28
 greater white-toothed **9:** *8–9*
 Indian house **9:** 28
 least **9:** 28
 northern (American) short-tailed **9:** 28, 30–33
 piebald **9:** 28
 pygmy white-toothed **9:** 8, 28
 shrew family 9: 28–29
 Tibetan water **9:** 28

see also elephant shrew; otter shrew; tree shrew
shrew mole 9: 40, 41
 American 9: 54–55
 Asiatic **9:** 42
 Gibb's (American) **9:** 54–55
 inquisitive **9:** 40
shrew mouse **8:** 102
 branch **8:** 102
 variable **8:** 102
shrike 17: (13), (39), 66, 98, 109, (109); **19:** (74)
 brubru **15:** 104
 chat- **15:** 104
 fiery-breasted bush- **15:** 104
 fiscal **15:** 104, 105
 four-colored bush- **15:** 104
 gray-headed bush- **15:** 104, *104*
 great gray (northern) **15:** 104, 105, *105*, 106; **18:** 59
 loggerhead **15:** 104, (105)
 olive bush- **15:** 104
 red-backed 15: 104, 106, 108–111; **20:** (48)
 shrike family 15: 104–107
 woodchat **15:** 104, *104*
 yellow-billed **15:** 104, 106
shrike-vireo, chestnut-sided **17:** 98
shrimpfish 39: 11, 26, 50–51
 speckled **39:** *50–51*, 51
shrimps 28: 60–69
 Baikal **28:** *44–45*
 banana **28:** *63*
 boxer **28:** 63, 64, *64*, 65, 67–68
 brine (fairy) **28:** 16–21
 brown **28:** *60*
 California mantis **28:** *38–39*
 clam (fairy) **28:** 16–21
 cleaner **28:** (67)
 clown mantis **28:** *38*
 Coleman **28:** 65
 common **28:** *60*
 emperor **28:** 57
 fairy 28: 16–21, *42–43*
 flat-browed mud **28:** *80*
 freshwater **28:** (64)
 ghost 28: 80–81
 giant deep-water opossum **28:** *36–37*
 glass (ghost) **28:** 80–81
 harlequin **28:** *35*
 harlequin mantis **28:** *38*
 helmeted **28:** (17)
 hingebeak **28:** *11*
 mantis 28: 38–41
 Mono Lake **28:** (19)
 mountain **28:** *37*
 mud 28: 80–81
 mussel 28: 32–33
 northern **28:** *60, 68*
 opossum 28: 42–43
 pink possum **28:** *43*
 pistol **28:** 63, (63)
 or prawns **28:** (60)
 sex-change **28:** (68)

snapping **28**: (63)
tadpole (fairy) **28**: _16–21_
vibrant Indonesian mantis **28**: _40_
shubunkin **34**: _42_, 49
American **34**: 49
Bristol **34**: 49
Japanese **34**: 49
London **34**: 49
Sialia
currucoides **18**: 54
mexicana **18**: 54
sialis **18**: 44, _54–57_
Sialis lutaria **22**: _98_, 98–99
siamang **4**: _8_, 36, 37
Sibine see Acharia
Sibon **49**: 16, (99)
Sibynomorphus **49**: (99)
Sicalis auriventris **16**: 62
sicklebill
black **19**: 106, 108
buff-tailed **19**: 106, (109)
white-tipped **16**: 44, _45_
Sicus ferrugineus **23**: _82_
sidewinder 48: 11–12, (58); **50**: 9, 54,
55, _104–105_
American **50**: 51, 66, 70
Siebenschlafer **7**: 104
sierra-finch, red-backed **16**: 62
sifaka
diademed **4**: 96
golden-crowned **4**: 96
Verreaux's **4**: 96
sight **11**: 13; **14**: 109; **15**: (52)
Sigmoceros lichtensteinii
see _Alcelaphus lichtensteinii_
Sigmoria aberrans **22**: 21
Sign Language, American **4**: 13, (16), 27
silk
casting **29**: (101)
production **29**: 43, (44)
spiders' use of **29**: 45
silky-flycatcher **18**: 30
Silpha **25**: _31_
tristis **25**: _28_
Silphidae **25**: _28–31_
Silurana **42**: 46, 48
Silurichthys sanguineus **37**: 32
Siluridae **33**: 100, **37**: _30–37_, (32)
Siluriformes **33**: 20
Silurus **42**: 46
aristotelis **37**: 30
electricus **37**: 63
glanis **37**: 11, 30, _30_, 33
soldatovi **37**: 32
silver angel **37**: (108)
silver dollar 38: _42–47_
hard-bellied **38**: 45
silverbiddy **40**: 36, 37
silverfish 22: _31_, _36–37_
silverside 34: 72, **38**: 30, 31, 50, 52,
_60–63_
marine sailfin **38**: 59
sailfin **38**: 59
shoaling **38**: _62–63_

tusked **38**: (59)
simakobu **4**: 40
Simenchelys parasitica **33**: _65_, 85
Simias concolor
see _Nasalis concolor_
Simoselaps **50**: 15
australis **50**: (25)
Simuliidae **23**: (53)
Simulium **23**: 52
single-celled life 21: _12–15_
Siphamia fistulosa **40**: 30
Siphonaptera **22**: 30, _110–113_
Siphonophora **21**: 43
siphonophorefish **39**: 14, 15
Siphonops **41**: 21
annulatus **41**: (20), _20–21_, 21
Siphonostomatoida **28**: 9
Sipodotus wallaci **18**: 60
Sipuncula **21**: 32, 77, 78
Siren **41**: _52–55_
intermedia **41**: (54), _55_
lacertina **41**: _26–27_, _52_, _53_, (54)
Sirenia **1**: _10_; **3**: 47; **5**: (12)
Sirenidae **41**: _26–27_, 27, 29, (54)
sirens 41: 26, 27, 29, _52–55_
dwarf **41**: _54_, (54)
greater **41**: 52, _52_, _53_, 55
lesser **41**: 52, 55, _55_
siskin
Cape **16**: 76
Eurasian **16**: 76, _76_, 80
Sisor rhabdophorus **37**: (49)
Sisoridae **37**: _48–51_
Sisorinae **37**: (51)
Sistrurus **50**: 101
catenatus **48**: 17; **50**: 9, 54, _106–107_
Sitta **17**: (91); **20**: 80
canadensis **18**: 64, _66–67_
carolinensis **18**: 64
europaea **18**: 64
ledanti **18**: 64
magna **18**: 64
neumayer **18**: 64
pusilla **18**: 64
pygmaea **18**: 64, 67
victoriae **18**: 64
Sittasomus griseicapillus **17**: 28, _32–33_
Sittidae **18**: 64
sitting patches **4**: 39, 52, 58
skate 31: 42, (108); **32**: 9, 59, 86, 104,
33: 8, 10, 15, _26–27_
blue 33: _12–13_, 27, _30–31_
California **33**: 26
common **33**: 30
families summary **33**: (26–27)
flapper **33**: 30
gray **33**: 30
legskate **33**: 26, (26)
softnose **33**: 26, (26)
true **33**: (27)
skate wings **33**: 31
skeletons **11**: _8–9_, 9–11; **31**: _14_, 15, _15_
Skiffia francesae **38**: _106_, 109
skimmer 12: 74, 77

African **12**: 74, 77
black 12: 74, 77, _96–97_
Indian **12**: 74
skin trade **1**: (23), 69, 72, 74; **2**: 33, 36,
37, 39, 47, 100, 111; **3**: 12,
15; **5**: 91; **6**: 66; **10**: 56, 91;
45: 96; **46**: (85), (90), 99;
47: 105
see also fur trade
skinks 44: (23), 25, 28, 30; **45**: (85), 99;
46: _8–15_; **48**: 77
African legless **49**: (25)
Australian blue-tongued **46**: 13
Australian stump-tailed **44**: 27
barrel (three-toed) **46**: _20–23_
Berber 46: 10, _28–29_
black-sided **46**: 11
blind burrowing 46: _32–33_
blue-tongued 46: 15, _40–43_
Bojer's **46**: 11
broad-headed **46**: _14–15_
brown ground **46**: (11)
Cape 46: _30–31_
Cape Verde giant **46**: (67)
casque-headed (crocodile) **46**: _48–49_
casque-headed (_Tribolonotus
novaeguineae_) **46**: 9
cat **46**: 9
common fire (fire) **46**: _34–35_
crocodile 46: _48–49_
cylindrical (three-toed) **46**: _20–23_
diet and feeding **46**: 13–14
diving **46**: 9–10
European limbless **44**: (26)
Fernand's fire (fire) **46**: _34–35_
fire 46: _34–35_
five-lined 46: _13_, _26–27_, 61
Florida sand **46**: 12, 21
Gidgee (spiny-tailed) **46**: _24–25_
golden (Berber) **46**: 10, _28–29_
Great Plains **46**: (13)
green blood **46**: 9
Indian **46**: 14
keeled **46**: 9
lidless **46**: (11)
lifestyle adaptations **46**: 9–10
mangrove **46**: 14
medicinal **46**: (37)
monkey-tailed 46: 9, 15, _16–19_
New Guinea water **46**: 8
northern blue-tongued **46**: 40, _42_
orange spotted (Berber) **46**: 10, _28–29_
oriental brown-sided **46**: 14
Pecos **46**: (13)
pink-tailed **46**: _12–13_
pink-tongued **46**: 14
rainbow **46**: 10
Roux's blind dart **46**: 33
sandfish 46: 10, 12, _36–39_; **49**: (24)
Schneider's (Berber) **46**: 10, _28–29_
silvery dwarf burrowing **46**: 11
Smith's dwarf burrowing **46**: 11
Solomon Islands great (monkey-tailed)
46: 9, 15, _16–19_

South African dart **46:** (11), 12
Southeast Asian snake **46:** (11)
speckle-lipped **46:** *11*
spiny-tailed 46: 8, <u>24–25</u>
Stokes's (spiny-tailed) **46:** 8, <u>24–25</u>
striped **46:** *12*
stump-tailed 46: 9, *10*, 14, 15,
    <u>44–47</u>
Tanimbar blue-tongued **46:** 40
three-toed 46: <u>20–23</u>
Togo fire (fire) **46:** <u>34–35</u>
Travancore **46:** (11)
water **46:** 9
zebra (monkey-tailed) **46:** 9, 15,
    <u>16–19</u>
skipjacks (click beetles) **25:** <u>42–45</u>
skipper **38:** 74
skippers 26: <u>62–65</u>
long-tailed **26:** *62*
skua 12: 17, 37, 69, 74, 76; **13:** 65,
    109, 111; **15:** (26)
brown **12:** 74
Chilean **12:** 74
great 12: *9*, 43, 74, <u>92–95</u>
south polar **12:** 74
skunk 1: 34
Andes **1:** 32
hooded **1:** 32
pygmy spotted **1:** 32
striped 1: 32, <u>84–87</u>
western hog-nosed **1:** 32
western spotted **1:** 32
skylark 18: 22, <u>24–27</u>, 28–29
oriental **18:** 22
sleeper **40:** 94, 96
Chinese **40:** 99
fat **40:** 97, 98
spotted **40:** 97
striped **40:** 97
tailface **40:** 97
sleeping sickness **21:** (17); **23:** (103)
sleepyhead **38:** 17
slickhead
long-snouted **35:** *9*
slimehead **39:** 9, 16, 20, 21
slimy **40:** 34, 35
slipmouth **40:** 34
sloth 9: 64–65, 65–66, 66, (66)
brown-throated three-toed (three-
    toed) **9:** 65, <u>72–73</u>
giant ground **9:** *64*
Hoffmann's two-toed **9:** 65
maned three-toed **9:** 65
southern two-toed **9:** 65
three-toed 9: 65, <u>72–73</u>
slow worm 44: 28; **45:** *99*; **46:** 50, 51,
    <u>56–59</u>, (61)
European **44:** (26)
habitats **46:** 57–59
reproduction **46:** 59
tails **46:** (58)
slugs 30: <u>44–49</u>
banana **30:** *49*
great gray **30:** *48–49*

terrestrial **30:** 44, 45, 48–49
    see also sea slugs
smell, sense of **11:** 13; **12:** 28–29;
    16: (17); **20:** (14); **34:** (75)
smelt 35: 8, 22, <u>26–29</u>
Arctic rainbow **35:** 26
Atlantic rainbow **35:** 26, 29
as candles **35:** (28)
delta **35:** *27*, 29
European **35:** 27, (28)
Japanese **35:** 26, 29
Kunashir **35:** 29
lonfin **35:** 26
pond **35:** *27*, 29
pygmy **35:** 29
sand **38:** *60*, 62
strange pike **35:** *99*
surf **35:** 26, 27, 28
Smilodon fatalis **2:** 10
Sminthillus limbatus **42:** 9
Sminthopsis
    aitkeni **10:** 38
    crassicauda **10:** 27
    dolichura **10:** 38
    gilberti **10:** 38
    murina **10:** <u>38–39</u>
    virginiae **10:** 27
Smithornis capensis **20:** 74
smolt (salmon) **35:** 53, (54), *56–57*
snaggletooth **35:** 84, 85, (88), *88–89*
snailfish 39: 53, *82–83*
tadpole **39:** 83
tidepool **39:** 83
snails 30: <u>44–49</u>
dune **30:** *46*
European grove **30:** *18–19*
freshwater **30:** *19*, 44
garden **30:** *45*
giant African land **30:** *48*
great pond **30:** *44*
South Pacific **30:** (48)
terrestrial **30:** 44, 45, 46–48
wandering **30:** *45*
water **30:** 45–46
    see also seasnails
snake charmers **50:** 30
snake cults **50:** (55)
snake venom **48:** 15; **50:** 8, 10–11
composition **50:** 10–11
delivery of **49:** (39)
mambas **50:** 16
medicines from **50:** (11)
venom glands **50:** (21)
snakebites **50:** (8), 38
snakefish **31:** 44, 49, 50
snakeflies 22: <u>100–101</u>
Texas **22:** *100*
snakehead (fish) **40:** <u>64–65</u>
African **40:** 65
Ceylon **40:** *64–65*, 65
Chinese **40:** 64
dark African **40:** 65
frog **40:** 64, 65
giant **40:** 64, 65

Indian **40:** 65
light African **40:** 65
rainbow **40:** 65
red **40:** 64, 65
smooth-breasted **40:** *64–65*, 65
spotted **40:** 65
striped **40:** 65
snakelet **40:** 22
snakes 1: (102), 109; **9:** 16; **20:** (58);
    44: *13*; **48:** *8–17*
Aesculapian **49:** 10, 45
African burrowing 49: <u>106–107</u>
African egg-eating **50:** 58
African mole **48:** 109
African sand 49: <u>60–61</u>
American burrowing (American
    sunbeam) **44:** 101; **48:** <u>38–39</u>
American snail-eaters 49: <u>98–99</u>
American sunbeam 44: 101;
    48: <u>38–39</u>
anatomy **48:** (13)
arrow **49:** 28
Asian crab-eating **49:** (51)
Asian keelback **49:** (39)
Asian mangrove **49:** (22)
Asian pipe **48:** 30, 31
Asian reed **49:** 8
Asian slug 49: <u>90–93</u>
Asian snail-eating (Asian slug)
    49: <u>90–93</u>
Asian sunbeam **48:** *29*, 31, 38
Atlantic salt marsh **49:** (81)
Aurora house **49:** 12, *69*, (69)
Australian copperhead **50:** 15
Australian hooded **48:** 87
Balkan whip **49:** 29
banded sand **49:** 25
banded snail-eater **49:** *16–17*, *98–99*
bandy-bandy **50:** 15
Bibron's stiletto 49: 106, <u>110–111</u>
bicolored quill-snouted **49:** *106–107*
black-headed **48:** 87; **49:** 11, (63),
    108, 109; **50:** 14
blue **48:** *95*
blunt-headed **49:** 16
bockadam **49:** 15
brown **49:** 12, 13, (86); **50:** 14
brown cat (Asian brown tree)
    49: <u>20–23</u>
brown house 49: 12, <u>66–69</u>; 50:**62**
bush **49:** 11; **50:** 17
Cape centipede-eater **49:** 108,
    108–109, 109
cat **49:** (39)
cat-eyed **43:** 61; **49:** 16
cave racer **48:** 85
centipede-eating 49: 106, <u>108–109</u>
Central African house **49:** (69)
Central American centipede **49:** 109
Central American sunbeam **48:** 31
chicken (yellow ratsnakes) **49:** 40, *41*,
    42, (43)
coachwhip **49:** 10
collared (grass) **42:** 63, 71; **49:** <u>74–79</u>

color **48**: 8–9
common egg-eating 49: 30–35, (67), 68
common slug eater **49**: 93, (93)
corn 49: 10, (43), 46–47
crayfish **49**: 12
crowned **50**: 14, (35)
Cuban wood 48: 78–79
dark-green (western whip) **49**: 28–29
defense **48**: 15–17
dice **49**: (76)
distribution **48**: 14
Duerden's stiletto **49**: *107*, 111
dwarf pipe **48**: 28, 30
earth **49**: 12
East African egg-eater **49**: 33, (35)
egg-eaters **49**: 11, (35), 91
egg eating, mechanics of **49**: (32)
egg shapes **49**: (45)
Ethiopian house **49**: (69)
European hooded **50**: 14
European Montpellier **49**: 15, 61
European smooth **48**: 87
European worm 48: 19, 20, 26–27
evolution **44**: *10*
families **48**: 8, 9
feeding **48**: 14–15
fierce (inland taipans) **50**: 42, 43
Fisk's house **49**: 13, (69)
flowerpot (Brahminy blind snakes)
    48: 19, 20, 24–25
flying **43**: (62); **44**: (45); **49**: 11
as food **48**: (43)
four-lined **48**: (97); **49**: 10, 45
fox **49**: (43)
frog-eating **43**: 80
frog-eating viperine **42**: (31)
Galápagos **48**: *14*
giant **48**: (110)
gopher **49**: 10–11
green **49**: 11
ground 49: 62–63, 109
Hampton's slug **49**: 90
harlequin **49**: 106
hissing sand **49**: 15
hook-nosed **49**: 11, (63)
horseshoe **49**: 29
house **49**: 12–13
100-pace (Chinese copperhead)
    50: 50, (97)
indigo **49**: 11, 52
in Ireland **50**: (81)
iridescent earth (sunbeam) **48**: 36–37
on islands **48**: (14), (76)
Italian Aesculapian **49**: 45
Jackson's centipede-eater **49**: 107,
    109
Kelaart's earth (shield-tailed) **48**: 28,
    (31)
Key ringneck **49**: 97
kukri **48**: (39); **49**: 12
ladder **49**: 45
leaf litter **49**: 16
leaf-nosed **48**: (39); **49**: 11

leopard **49**: 10, 44–45, (51)
lifestyle and habitat **48**: 13–14
locomotion **48**: 10–12
long-nosed **49**: *10*; **50**: (25)
long-nosed whip (long-nosed vine)
    48: 12; **49**: 18–19
lyre **49**: 11
mangrove **49**: (22), (39)
markings **48**: 8–9
marsh **49**: 12
mole **49**: 13, (54); **50**: 32
montane egg-eater **49**: (35)
montane slug **49**: 90–91, *91*, *92–93*
mud **49**: 16
mussuranas **49**: 16
Namib sand **49**: *60–61*
Natal purple-glossed **49**: 107
New Guinea forest **50**: (21)
North American mud **48**: 109
northern bandy-bandy **50**: 15
oak (gray ratsnakes) **49**: 40, 42, (43)
olive house **49**: 68, (69)
organ pipe shovel-nosed **49**: 25
paradise flying (paradise tree)
    49: 26–27
pilot black (black ratsnake) **50**: 88
pinewoods **49**: 16
plain blunt-headed **43**: 61
prairie ground (ground) **49**: 62–63,
    109
prairie ringneck **49**: (96)
primitive 48: 28–31, 49
purple-glossed **49**: 109
racers **49**: 10, 29, (39)
rainbow **49**: 16
rear-fanged tree dwellers **49**: 11
red-bellied **49**: (86)
red (South American) pipe **48**: 28,
    30, 31, 34–35
red-tailed pipe 48: 32–33; **50**: 21
reed **49**: 16; **50**: 21
regal ringneck **49**: 95, (96), 97, *97*
reproduction **48**: 17
rhombic egg-eater (common egg-
    eating) **49**: 30–35, (67), 68
ribbon **49**: (89)
ringed (grass) **42**: 63, 71; **49**: 74–79
ringneck 49: 16, 94–97; **50**: 14, (35)
rough green 49: 58–59, 73
sand **44**: 41; **48**: *16*; **49**: 13, (63);
    50: 17
San Diego gopher **49**: *8–9*
sand racer **49**: *14–15*
sand swimmers **49**: 24, (25)
scales **48**: 9–10
senses **48**: 12–13
Seychelles house **49**: (69)
sharp-tailed **50**: (35)
shield-nosed **50**: 14
shield-tailed **48**: (31)
shovel-nosed **49**: 11, 62, (63); **50**: (25)
shovel-snouted **49**: (39)
size and shape **48**: 8
skaapstekers (sheep stabbers) **49**: 15,

61; **50**: 33
skin **48**: 9–10
slug-eating **49**: 13, 16
small-scaled stiletto **49**: 110
smooth green **49**: (59), (86)
snow corn **49**: *47*
Sonoran ground (ground) **49**: 24, (51),
    62–63, 109
South American parrot **49**: 26
South American pipe 48: 28, *30*,
    31, 34–35
South American snail-eater **49**: 90
southern brown egg-eater **49**: (35)
spotted house **49**: (69)
spurs **48**: (49)
stiletto **49**: 106, 107; **50**: 9, (21), (35)
sunbeam 48: 36–37
Swazi rock **49**: (69)
teeth **49**: (11)
tentacled 49: 15, 64–65, (73)
toad-eating **42**: *68*
twig **43**: 103; **49**: 11, (39)
two-colored **50**: (21)
two-headed (red-tailed pipe)
    48: 32–33
variable stiletto **49**: 110
variegated slug-eater **49**: (93)
venomous 50: 8–11
wart (file) **48**: 40–41; **49**: 13, (82);
    50: (35), 37, 62
West African egg-eater **49**: 30, (35)
western keeled **49**: 10
western ribbon **49**: (89)
western shovel-nosed 49: 24–25
western whip 49: 28–29
whip **49**: 10, 13; **50**: 14
white-bellied mangrove **49**: 15
white-spotted slug **49**: *90*, 91
wolf **49**: 13
wood (dwarf boas) **48**: 44, 47, 79,
    105
yellow-bellied house **49**: (69)
see also blind snakes; boomslang;
    coral snakes; file snakes; garter
    snake; grass snake; hognose
    snake; king snake; milksnake;
    ratsnake; rattlesnake; sea
    snakes; thread snakes; tiger
    snake; tree snake; vine snake;
    water snake
snapper 32: 67, **39**: 109, **40**: 36–37
bluestripe **40**: 39
emperor **40**: *37*
freshwater **40**: 36
majestic **40**: 36
pygmy **40**: 36
yellowtail **40**: *36*
snares **4**: 24, 53
snipe 13: 31, 50–51, 59, 75; **18**: (10)
Chatham **13**: 30
common **13**: 30, 50–51
giant **13**: 30
great **13**: 30, 33
painted *see* painted snipe

snipefish 39: 11, 26, 50–51
longspine **39:** 51
slender **39:** 50
snook 40: 12–19
snorer **38:** 17
snow tunnels **11:** (68)
snowcap **16:** 44, (45)
snowshoes **8:** (78)
Snyderidia **36:** 23
soapfish **32:** 66
soaring **15:** (33)
sociability
ants **27:** 40
Hymenoptera **27:** 11–12
sockeye *see* salmon
Solaster papposus **30:** 98
soldierfish **39:** 9, 16, (20), 21
big scale **39:** *21*
spinycheek **39:** (20)
sole 39: 11, 92–95
American **39:** (94)
American Dover **39:** 89, 91, 92
American freshwater **39:** 92
butter **39:** 91
common **39:** 92, 93, (94)
deepwater **39:** (93)
Dover **39:** 89, *93*
drab **39:** 92, *92*, 93
English **39:** 90
estuary **39:** 92
European Dover **39:** 89, 92
habitats of **39:** (93)
Klein's **39:** (93)
lemon **39:** 89
petrale **39:** 90
rex **39:** 90
rock **39:** 90
saltpan **39:** (93), *95*
small-headed **39:** *94–95*
tongue *see* tongue sole
zebra **39:** (93)
Solea solea **39:** 89, *93*
Solegnathus **39:** 41, (46)
Soleidae **39:** 92–95
Solenidae **30:** 50, 68
solenodon **9:** 8, 9, (10), 11
Cuban **9:** 9
Hispaniola **9:** 9
Solenodon
cubanus **9:** 9
paradoxus **9:** 9
Solenodontidae **9:** 9
solenogasters **30:** (13)
Solenopsis invicta **49:** (103)
Solenostomidae **39:** 26, 38–47
Solenostomus
armatus **39:** 42
cyanopterus **39:** 42
paradoxus **39:** *42–43*, 45
Solifugae **29:** 34–35
solitaire **18:** 44
Townsend's **18:** 44, *44*, 45
Solpuga **29:** *34*
Somateria **12:** 70; **14:** 52

fischeri **12:** 66
mollissima **12:** 66, 72
spectabilis **12:** 66, 72–73
Someticus bohemani **25:** *19*
Somniosus
microcephalus **32:** (66), 96–97
pacificus **32:** 96
sonaghen **35:** (69)
sonar **3:** 83
songs **16:** (67); **19:** (58); **20:** (44)
countersinging **16:** (70)
courtship **18:** 39, 40
duets **18:** 75; **20:** 86, *87*
gibbons **4:** 36, 39
mimicry **11:** 104, 109; **18:** 39–40;
20: (91)
song flights **13:** 13–14, 33; **18:** 23,
25–26
territorial **16:** (70); **18:** 23, 25–26, 45,
48–50, 53
whale songs **3:** 99–100, 105
Sonora
aemula **49:** (63)
episcopa **49:** (63)
michoacanensis **49:** (63)
semiannulata **49:** (51), 62–63, 109
Sonorini **49:** (63)
Sooglossidae **42:** 10; **43:** 10–11, 87
Sooglossus
gardineri **42:** 9; **43:** 10, *10–11*
pipilodryas **43:** 10
sechellensis **43:** 10, (11)
Sorex
araneus **9:** 34–35
minutus **9:** 28
palustris **9:** 36–37
Soricidae **9:** 9, 58
Sorosichthys **39:** 21
Sorubim lima **37:** 85
souffie **34:** 78
sound production **11:** (109); **22:** 30
fish **36:** (42), (44), 57, **39:** 105
millipedes **22:** 18
spiny lobsters **28:** (84)
southern beauty **33:** 58, *59*
spadefish **31:** 70
spadefoot toad 42: 10, 20, 34, 40–41,
76; **43:** 34, 82, 86
American **42:** 92, 95
Asian **42:** 34, 35
Australian **42:** 92–93
common 42: 42–43
Couch's 42: 44–45, 73
European **42:** 92, 95
plains **42:** 44
western **42:** 40, *41*, 44
Spalacopus cyanus **8:** 30
Spanish dancer **30:** *40*
Sparassidae **29:** 66–67
Sparidae **40:** 40–41
sparrow 16: 100–101
American tree **16:** 62
desert **16:** 100
European tree **16:** 100

golden **16:** 100
hedge *see* dunnock
house 16: 62, 100, 108–111;
18: 42, 57; **20:** 87
Java 16: 90, 98–99
New World 16: 62–63, 100
song **16:** 62
Spanish **16:** 100
tree **16:** 100; **18:** 13, (57)
sparrowhawk **15:** 11, 12, *13*
northern **15:** 8, 38
Spartocera fusca **24:** *54*
Sparus swinhonis czerskii **40:** 40
Spatangus purpureus **30:** *104*
Spathobathis **33:** 8
Spathodus **40:** 68
spatuletail, marvelous **16:** 44, *45*, 47
spawning
salmon **35:** *62–63*, *64–65*
trout **35:** *70–71*
Spea **42:** 40
spearfish **40:** 108
Mediterranean **40:** 110
roundscale **40:** (110)
speciation **50:** 59
species
cryptic (hidden) **41:** (51)
definition **48:** 88
Speirops lugubris **18:** 68
speirops, black-capped **18:** 68
Spelaeogriphacea **28:** 34, 37
Speleomantes **41:** 27, 68, 70, 72, 73
Speothos venaticus **2:** 50
Speotyto cunicularia **15:** 50
sperm competition **22:** 48
spermaceti **3:** 86, 87, 89, 91
spermatophore **22:** 11
Spermophilus tridecemlineatus
7: 34, 54–55
Sphaeramia nematoptera **40:** *30–31*
Sphaerium **30:** *61*
Sphaerodactylinae **45:** 8, 11, (27)
Sphaerodactylus **45:** 8–9, 10, (36)
ariasae **44:** 24
elegans **45:** 26–27
notatus **45:** 26
Sphecidae **27:** 76–83
Sphecius speciosus **27:** (82), *82–83*
Spheniscidae **12:** 8
Spheniscus **12:** 10
demersus **12:** 8
humboldti **12:** 8
magellanicus **12:** 8
mendiculus **12:** 8, 18–19
Sphenodon
guntheri **44:** 18–23
punctatus **44:** 8, 18–23
Sphenodontia **44:** 18
Sphenomorphus **46:** 8
Sphenophryne **42:** 104
palmipes **42:** 105, (111)
Sphiggurus
insidiosus **8:** 12
vestitus **8:** 12

Sphingidae **26:** 66–69
Sphodrolestes **24:** *15*
Sphodros **29:** 50, 51
  atlanticus **29:** *50–51*
Sphongophorus guerini **24:** *90*
Sphyraena
  afra **40:** 102
  barracuda **40:** 102, *102–103*
  chrysotaenia **40:** 102, *102*
  guachancho **40:** 102
  pinguis **40:** 102, 103
  putnamae **40:** *103*
Sphyraenidae **38:** 52, **39:** 109, **40:** 9, 102–103
Sphyrapicus varius **16:** 53, 67; **18:** 8
Sphyrna **32:** 55, 68
  corona **32:** 69
  couardi **32:** 69
  lewini **32:** 69
  media **32:** 69
  mokarran **32:** 68, 69, 102
  tiburo **32:** *73*
  tudes **32:** 69
  zygaena **32:** 69
spiderhunter
  long-billed **19:** 94
  spectacled **19:** 94
  streaked **19:** 94, 98–99
spiders 29: 8, 9, 36–45
  anatomy **29:** *35–36, 38–42*
  anemone sea **29:** *12*
  aquatic **29:** (110)
  arrow-shaped thorn **29:** *109*
  Asian bird-dropping **29:** *70*
  banana **29:** 111
  bark **29:** *108*
  bird-eating (tarantulas) **29:** 46–47
  black-lined orchard **29:** 103
  brown **29:** (59)
  bugs living with **24:** (33)
  bull's horn **29:** *109*
  buzzing **29:** (81)
  cellar **29:** *60, 99*
  classification **29:** 38
  cobweb **29:** *40*
  comb-footed 29: 89–101
  crab 29: 68–73; **42:** 82
  daddy-longlegs 29: 60–63
  dead-leaf jumpers **29:** (77)
  death's head **29:** (108)
  decoy **29:** 106–107
  Diard's heavy jumper **29:** *41*
  European buzzing **29:** *42–43*
  European water **29:** (110)
  false wolf **29:** 93
  feather-footed 29: 56–57
  fence-post jumper **29:** *74–75*
  fisher **29:** *89*
  flat wolf **29:** 93
  flower **29:** 71–72
  funnel-web 29: 48–49
  garden **29:** *110–111*
  giant crab (huntsman) **29:** 66–67
  gladiator (net-casting) **29:** 54–55

  goldenrod **29:** 71–72
  gossamer 29: 112–113
  grass (sheet-web weavers) **29:** 94–97
  green lynx **29:** *80–81*
  hammock-web (gossamer)
    29: 112–113
  house **29:** *95*
  huntsman 29: 66–67
  jumping 29: *39,* 74–77
  lynx 29: 78–81
  mating **29:** 42–43
  meadow stilt **29:** *103, 104*
  money (gossamer) **29:** 112–113
  mothercare **29:** *98,* (99)
  mouse **29:** (81)
  net-casting 29: 54–55
  nursery web 29: 88–93
  ogre-faced (net-casting) **29:** 54–55
  orb-weaving **42:** 82
  pirate **29:** *83*
  purse-web 29: 50–51
  rafter **29:** *60, 61, 62–63*
  red widow **29:** *100*
  rusty wandering **29:** *87*
  sea **22:** *8;* **29:** 8, *12–13*
  silk-city **29:** (101)
  silk production and use **29:** 43, (44), 45
  six-spotted fisher **29:** 88–89
  snake's back **29:** *63*
  spear-fanged **29:** (59)
  sperm induction **29:** (42)
  spider families **29:** 36
  spiny **29:** *108–109*
  spiny flag **29:** *111*
  spitting 29: 58–59
  stick **29:** 57
  sun 29: 34–35
  trap-door **29:** (49)
  tube-web **29:** (63)
  two-tailed 29: 64–65
  wandering 29: 86–87
  wasp **29:** *106*
  wedding-present **29:** *42, 88,* (91)
  whip (tailless whip scorpions)
    29: 26–27
  widow **29:** 100–101
  wind (sun) **29:** 34–35
  wolf 27: (61); **29:** 82–85
  see also silk; tarantulas; weavers
spikefish 39: 84, 97, 98–99
  fleshy-lipped **39:** 99, *99*
  longsnout **39:** 96, 98
  reticulate **39:** 98
  shortsnout **39:** *98*
  trumpetsnout **39:** 98
Spilocuscus
  kraemeri **10:** 74
  maculatus **10:** 82–83
  papuensis **10:** 74
Spilogale
  gracilis **1:** 32
  pygmaea **1:** 32
Spilopsyllus cuniculi **22:** 110–111

Spilostethus pandurus **24:** *11*
Spilotes pullatus **49:** 11
Spinachia spinachia **39:** 29, *33*, 35
spinebill
  eastern **20:** 88
  western 20: 88, 94–95
spines **9:** 13, 15, *16–17*
  see also quills
spinetail
  pale-breasted **20:** 80
  white-browed **20:** 80, *81*
  yellow-throated **20:** 80
spiny mammals **8:** 12
spinyfin **39:** 21
spiny-finned fish 33: 106, **38:** 50, (51), **39:** 8–11
  Who's Who **39:** (9)
spiny-skinned animals 30: 90–93
Spirinchus thaleichthys **35:** 26
Spirobranchus giganteus **21:** 98–99
Spirostreptida **22:** *16*
Spirotrichea **21:** 13
spirula **30:** (80)
Spirula spirula **30:** (80)
spittlebugs (froghoppers) **24:** 78–79
Spizella arborea **16:** 62
splitfin **38:** 106
Spondylus **30:** 52
sponges 21: *28–29,* 34–35, 36–41
  azure vase **21:** *36–37*
  barrel **21:** *40*
  body forms **21:** 36–38
  brown tube **21:** *36*
  classes of **21:** 35
  cloud **21:** *39*
  coralline **21:** (40)
  orange puffball **21:** *37*
  red **21:** *39*
  reproduction **21:** 39–40
  structure **21:** (38)
  yellow tube **21:** *40–41*
spookfish **35:** 24, 25
  brownsnout **35:** 24, 25
spoonbill 14: 22, 28, 32, *33*
  black-faced **14:** 32
  roseate 14: 32, 42–43; **19:** 36
spoonbill **31:** 70
Sporophila torqueola **16:** 62
Sporozoa **21:** 13
sprat **36:** 98, 106, 107, 111
  Amazon **36:** 98
Spriggina **21:** 35
springbok 6: *8–9, 61,* 62, 96–97
springfish **36:** 18, **38:** 110, (111)
  Railroad Valley **38:** 111
  White River **38:** 111
springhaas *see* springhare
springhare 7: *12,* 18, 20–21
springtails 22: 28–29
spy-hopping **3:** 71, 96, 107
Squalidae **32:** (12), 26, 47, 55, (92)
Squaliformes **32:** 92–93
Squaliolus laticaudus **32:** 12, 92
Squalus acanthias **32:** *16–17, 93,* 94,

102
Squamata **44**: 8, 9, 25; **48**: 8, 9
Squatina
  acanthoderma **32**: 105
  australis **32**: *104*, 107
  californica **32**: 107
  guggenheim **32**: 25
  japonica **32**: 107
  oculta **32**: 25
  squatina **32**: 106
  tergocellata **32**: 107
Squatinidae **32**: (12), 36, (104)
Squatiniformes **32**: <u>104–105</u>
squawfish **34**: 16
  Colorado **34**: 19
squeaker (fish) **37**: 8, 70, 71, 73
  polkadot **37**: *70–71*
  see also catfish, squeaking
squids 3: 87, (88), 91; **30**: <u>76–83</u>
  California market **30**: *83*
  dumpling **30**: *80–81*
  eyes **30**: (86)
  giant **30**: (82)
  Mexican giant Humboldt **30**: *82*
  ram's horn *see Spirula spirula*
  short-finned **30**: *82–83*
Squilla **28**: *38*
squirrel 7: 11, *12*, 13, 15
  African ground **1**: 101
  African pygmy **7**: 34
  American gray (gray) **7**: 34, 36,
    <u>38–41</u>, 43–44, 47
  American red **7**: 42
  Arctic ground **2**: *65*
  black flying **7**: 34, *36*
  black giant **7**: *36*
  black-striped **7**: *36*
  Cape ground **7**: *36–37*
  colonial ground **7**: 36
  eastern flying (southern flying)
    7: 34, <u>60–61</u>
  eastern fox 7: 34, <u>46–47</u>
  Eurasian red 7: <u>42–45</u>
  European red **7**: 34
  flying **7**: 8, 13, 17, 34, *37*, (37);
    10: (76); **45**: (42)
  gray 7: 34, 36, <u>38–41</u>, 43–44, 47
  gray-cheeked flying **7**: *36*
  ground **7**: 18, 19, 34, 36
  Harris' antelope **7**: *8–9*
  horse-tailed **7**: *36*
  Indian giant 7: 34, <u>62–63</u>
  Javanese flying **7**: *36*
  Low's **7**: *36*
  Malabar (Indian giant) **7**: 34, <u>62–63</u>
  Mindanao flying **7**: 34
  northern flying **7**: 61
  northern striped palm **7**: 34, *35*
  pale giant **7**: *36*
  plantain **7**: *36*
  Prevost's **7**: *36*
  pygmy **7**: *36*
  red **7**: 41
  red-cheeked flying **7**: 34, *36*

red giant flying **7**: *36*
scaly-tailed **7**: *12*, 17, (19)
slender **7**: *36*
South African ground **7**: *10*, *36–37*
southern flying 7: 34, <u>60–61</u>
spotted giant flying **7**: *36*
squirrel family 7: <u>34–37</u>
thirteen-lined ground 7: 34, <u>54–55</u>
three-striped ground **7**: *36*
tree **7**: 17, 34, 35, 36
tufted ground **7**: *36*
squirrelfish **39**: 9, 16, (20), 21
  common **39**: 21
  redcoat **39**: *20*, 21
squirrel-like rodents 7: <u>16–19</u>
squirt *see* sea squirt
Sri Lanka, frogs **43**: (101)
St Peter's Fish **39**: (24)
St Peter's thumbprint **36**: (40)
stabilimenta **29**: 107–108
Stagmatoptera septrionalis **22**: *76–77*
stainers 24: 11, <u>48–49</u>
stances **5**: 9–10
standardwing, Wallace's **19**: 106, 108
Staphylinidae **25**: <u>32–33</u>
Staphylinus olens **25**: *32–33*
starfish 30: *91*, 92, <u>98–103</u>
  candy cane **21**: *64*
  crown-of-thorns **30**: (102–103)
  stomach eversion **30**: 92, 100, 102
starfrontlet **16**: (45)
  rainbow **16**: 44, 46
stargazer **31**: (108), **39**: 28, **40**: 19;
  40: 91
starling 13: 68; **18**: (80), (81)
  Bali **18**: 82
  chestnut-tailed **18**: 82
  European 18: 32, (41), 57, 79, (81),
    82, 83, <u>84–87</u>
  red-winged **18**: 82, 83
  rose-colored **18**: 82, *83*
  Samoan **18**: 82
  shining **18**: 82
  starling family 18: <u>82–83</u>
  white-cheeked **18**: 82
stars
  basket 30: <u>98–103</u>
  brittle 30: <u>98–103</u>
  feather 30: *93*, <u>94–97</u>
  rosy feather **30**: *94*
Staurois **43**: 82, 84
Stauromedusae **21**: 43
Steatocranus causarius **40**: *68–69*
Steatoda grossa **29**: 99
Steatomis caripensis **15**: 78
Steatornithidae **15**: 78
steenbok **6**: *61*, 62
steenbras
  white **40**: 40
Stefania **43**: 41, (45)
Steganopus tricolor **13**: 72
Stegobium paniceum **25**: (53)
stegosaur **44**: *10–11*
Stegostoma

fasciatum **32**: 36, (40)
Stegostomatidae **32**: (12), (30), 33, (40)
Steindachneria argentea **36**: *32*, 37
Steindachneriidae **36**: <u>32–37</u>
Stelgidopteryx serripennis **15**: 94
Stellula calliope **16**: 44
Stelopolybia pallipes **27**: *72*
Stemonosudis
  bullisi **35**: 99
  elegans **35**: 99
Stenella longirostris **3**: 55, <u>76–77</u>
Stenocara gracilipes **25**: *68–69*
Stenodus **35**: <u>38–41</u>, (41)
  leucichthys **35**: 38, 39
  leucichthys leucichthys **35**: 39
  leucichthys nelma **35**: 39
Stenolaemata **21**: 69
Stenopalmatus fuscus **23**: *20*
Stenopelmatidae **23**: <u>20–21</u>
Stenopodidea **28**: 56, <u>60–69</u>
Stenopterygians
  Who's Who **35**: (79)
Stenopus **28**: *64*
Stenorhynchus seticornis **28**: *103*
Stenorrhina **49**: (63)
Stephanitis pyri **24**: *28*
Stephanoberycidae **39**: <u>12–15</u>
Stephopaedes **42**: 56, (60)
  anotis **42**: (60)
Stercorariidae **12**: 74, 76; **13**: 65
Stercorarius **12**: 76, 92
  longicaudus **12**: 74; **13**: (36)
  parasiticus **12**: 74
  pomarinus **12**: 74
Stereochilus **41**: 68, 71
sterlet 31: 53, (56), 60, <u>62–63</u>
  captive bred **31**: (63)
Sterna
  antillarum **12**: 74
  caspia **12**: 74, <u>90–91</u>
  forsteri **12**: 74
  fuscata **12**: 74
  hirundo **11**: (49); **12**: 74, (89); **13**: 79
  paradisaea **11**: 15; **12**: 74, <u>86–89</u>;
    13: 63
  sandvicensis **12**: 74
Sternidae **12**: 74, 75
Sternoptychidae **35**: 78, <u>90–91</u>
Sternoptyx diaphana **35**: 90
Sternopygidae **33**: (100)
Sternopygus **33**: 103
Sternorrhyncha **24**: 8, 10, 12, 13, 15
Sternotherus **47**: (31)
  minor **47**: 10
  odoratus **47**: (31), 47
Sternotomus variablis **25**: *92*
stick insects (walkingsticks) **22**: <u>52–57</u>
  giant **22**: 55
  titan **22**: *52*
stickleback 38: 50, **39**: 10, <u>26–27</u>, 28,
  29, <u>30–35</u>, 43
  Amur **39**: 34
  Aral **39**: 34
  armored **39**: 38, *38*, 43

blackspotted **39:** 33
brook **39:** 34, 35
fifteen-spined **39:** 29, *33*, 35
four-spined **39:** 34, 35
Greek nine-spined **39:** 26, (35)
Greek ten-spined **39:** (35)
nine-spined **39:** 30, (32), 33, *34*
Sakhalin **39:** 34
Santa Ana **39:** 33
sea **39:** 35
smoothtail nine-spined **39:** 34
southern nine-spined **39:** 34
ten-spined **39:** *30–31*
three-spined **39:** 26, 29, 30, *30*, 31,
    31, (32), *32*, 33, *33*, 34, 35
Stigmatogobius sadanundio **40:** 95, *95*
Stigmodera rufolimbata **25:** 47
Stilosoma extenuatum **50:** (35)
stilt 13: 72–75
    banded **13:** 72–73, *74*
    black **13:** 72, 73–75
    black-necked **13:** 72, (85)
    black-winged 13: 72, 79, 82–85
    pied **13:** 72, 75, (85)
    white-backed **13:** 72, (85)
Stiltia isabella **11:** 98
stingaree **33:** (34)
stingfish **39:** 61, 66, 67
    gray **39:** 66
    orange-banded **39:** 67
    weedy **39:** 61
stingray 32: 55, **33:** 10, (11), 34–40
    antenna **33:** *35*
    Atlantic, barb **33:** *11*
    black-spotted **33:** *36–37*
    camouflage **33:** *42–43*, 43
    common 33: 40–41
    families summary **33:** (34–36)
    motoro **33:** 42, *42–43*
    ocellate river 33: 42–43
    pelagic **33:** 34
    river 33: (34)
    round 33: 38, 44–45
    smooth **33:** *8–9*
    southern **33:** *14–15*, 37
    sting **33:** (36)
    whiptail **33:** 34, (34)
stint, little 13: 30, 56–57
Stipiturus mallee **18:** 60
Stizostedion
    (Sander) vitreum **35:** (12)
    vitreum glaucum **35:** (12)
stoat 1: 19, *32*, 34, 36, 40–43
stockfish **36:** (36)
Stolonifera **21:** 43
stomach stones **3:** (27), 91
Stomatopoda **28:** 34, 38–41
Stomias **35:** 85
    brevibarbatus **35:** 86
    longibarbatus **35:** 86
Stomiidae **35:** *80*, 84–89
Stomiiformes **35:** 78
    families summary **35:** (79)
stonecat **37:** 15, 16, 21

stone-curlew, beach
    see thick-knee, beach
stonefish 38: 50, **39:** 8, 11, 52, 53,
    58–67
    estuarine **39:** 52, 58, *58*
    pitted **39:** 59
stoneflies 22: 80–81
    European **22:** *80*
    giant **22:** *80–81*
stones
    as hammers **1:** (74); **4:** 31–32, (31)
    in the stomach **3:** (27), 91
stones, swallowing **12:** 8; **14:** 54
Storeria **49:** 12, 13, (86)
stork 12: 45; **14:** 22, 32–33; **18:** (10);
    20: 11, 35
    Abdim's **14:** 32, (39)
    black **14:** 32
    greater adjutant **14:** (36), (39)
    marabou 14: 32, 36–39
    white **14:** 32, *33*
    wood 14: 32, 34–35, 37
storm-petrel 12: 29, 31, 93; **20:** (14)
    ashy **12:** 28
    black **12:** 28
    European **12:** 28, *31*
    Leach's 12: 28, 42–43
    Swinhoe's **12:** 28
    Wilson's **12:** 28, 31, *31*
stotting **6:** 35, 97; **8:** 32
strandings, on shore **3:** (59), 66, 67, 96
straptail **36:** 37
Stratiomyidae **23:** 56–57
Stratiomys
    longicornis **23:** *57*
    potamida **23:** *56–57*
streamerfish **35:** 108
Strepera
    fuliginosa **20:** 100
    graculina **20:** 55, 100
    versicolor **20:** 100
Strepsiptera **22:** 30; **25:** (14)
strepsirhines *see* primates, lower
Streptopelia **16:** 13
    decaocto **16:** 12
    senegalensis **16:** 12
Streptoprocne zonaris **15:** 70
stridulation **9:** 27; **22:** 18, 30, 87; **50:** 77
Strigidae **15:** 50, 51
Strigocuscus
    celebensis **10:** 74
    pelengensis **10:** 74
Strigops habroptilus **16:** 22; **20:** 36,
    42–45
Strix
    aluco **15:** 50, 54–55
    nebulosa **11:** 13, (68)
    occidentalis **15:** 50
    occidentalis caurina **41:** (45)
    seloputo **15:** 50
Strongylogaster lineata **27:** *17*
Strongyloides **21:** *88*
Strongylopus **43:** 83
    grayii **43:** 83, *87*

Strongylura **38:** *73*
    kreffti **38:** 73
    raphidoma **38:** 73
Stronogobiops nematodes **40:** *97*
Strophurus **45:** 44
Struthidea cinerea **20:** 100
Struthio camelus **11:** 8, 16, 20–25,
    34, (109); **12:** 8; **20:** 31
Struthionidae **11:** 16
Strymon
    martialis **26:** 28
    melinus **26:** *31*
Stumpffia
    pygmaea **42:** 104
    tridactyla **41:** (17)
sturgeon 31: 43, 48, 52–57, 74, 88,
    32: 90
    Atlantic **31:** (56), *58*
    Baltic (common) 31: 53, 54, 58–59,
    67
    lake 31: (56), 60–61
    little **31:** 53
    osetra **31:** (57)
    pallid 31: 68–69
    Russian **31:** *52–53*, (57), 66, 67
    sea (dogfish) **32:** 22, 47
    sevruga **31:** (57), *57*, 66
    ship **31:** 56
    short-nosed **31:** 67
    shovelnose **31:** 53, 68, *69*
    starred **31:** (57), *57*, 66, 67
    stellate **31:** (57), 66
    Syr-Dar shovelnose **31:** 56
    whiptail **31:** *43*
    white **31:** 52, 54, *56*
Sturisoma **37:** 110
Sturnella
    magna **18:** 74
    militaris **18:** 74
Sturnia
    malabarica **18:** 82
    pagodarum **18:** 82
    roseus **18:** 82
Sturnidae **18:** 82
Sturnus
    cineraceus **18:** 82
    vulgaris **13:** 68; **18:** 32, (41), 57, 79,
    82, 84–87
Stygichthys typhlops **38:** 8
Stygnobrotula latebricola **36:** 27
Stylasterina **21:** 43
Stylephoridae **35:** 82, 105
Stylephorus chordatus **35:** 82, 105
styloglossus **5:** (12)
Stylommatophora **30:** 18, 45, *47*
suboscines **20:** 74, 80
subspecies **49:** (53)
subungulates **5:** (12)
sucker 34: 11, 12, 88–89
    Asian **34:** 94
    blackfin **34:** 99
    blue **34:** 13, 94, 99
    carp **34:** 89
    Chinese **34:** 94

Chinese high-fin **34:** 94
Chinese sailfin 34: 12, 13, 88, 89, 94–95, 99
chub **34:** 99
flannelmouth **34:** 98
harelip **34:** 96, 99
hog **34:** 99
longnose **34:** 12, 94
Lost River **34:** 96
Modoc **34:** 96
North American 34: 94, 96–99, 100
razorback **34:** 96, *96*, 97, 98, (98), 99
redhorse **34:** 99
Roanoke hog **34:** 99
sailfin **34:** 94
shortnose **34:** 96
Snake River **34:** 96
spotted **34:** *96–97*, 99
topsail **34:** 94
torrent **34:** 99
white **34:** *98–99*
suckermouth **37:** 73
Sucuriji gigante **48:** 64
Sudis hyalina **35:** 99
Sula
    dactylatra **12:** 44
    granti **12:** 44
    leucogaster **12:** 44
    nebouxii **12:** 44; **18:** (56)
    sula **12:** 44
"sulfur bottom" *see* whale, blue
sulfurs (whites) **26:** 22–27
    mass migration **26:** 26
    orange **26:** 22
    ultraviolet markings **26:** 25
Sulidae **12:** 44, 47; **18:** (56)
sun stars **30:** 98
sunbathing **16:** 94; **17:** 77; **19:** 62; **20:** (21), 57, 63
sunbird 18: 68; **20:** 74, 88
    black **19:** 94
    fork-tailed **19:** 94, 95
    golden-winged **19:** 94, *95*
    greater double-collared **19:** 94, *95*
    malachite 19: 94, 96–97
    olive-backed **19:** 94
    plain-backed **19:** 94
    plain-throated **19:** 94
    purple-rumped **19:** 94
    red-tufted **19:** 94, 96
    regal **19:** 94
    scarlet **19:** 94
    shining **19:** 94
    sunbird family 19: 94–95
    superb **19:** 94
sunbird-asity **20:** 74
    common **20:** 74
    yellow-bellied **20:** 74
sunbittern **11:** 92; **14:** 90
Suncus etruscus **9:** 28, 38–39
Sundasalangidae **35:** 30–31
Sundasalanx praecox **35:** 31
Sundasciurus
    hippurus **7:** 36

lowii **7:** 36
    tenuis **7:** 36
sunfish 32: 78, **34:** 53, **40:** 26–29, 86
    banded pygmy **40:** 29
    blue-barred **40:** 28
    bluegill **37:** 18, **40:** *26–27, 27*
    bluespotted **40:** 26
    Everglades pygmy **40:** 28
    giant **39:** 111
    green **40:** *26*
    longear **40:** 26
    mola ocean **39:** 111
    ocean **39:** 11, 97, 110, *110*, 111, *111*
    Ofefenokee **40:** 29
    pygmy **40:** 26, 28, (28)
    "satellite" **40:** 27, 28, 86
    sharptail **39:** 111
    slender **39:** 110, 111
    "sneaker" **40:** 27, 28, 86
    spring pygmy **40:** 29
Supercohort **1:** *10*
supercooling **49:** (85)
sureli **4:** 41
    banded **4:** 40
    grizzled **4:** 40
surfperch **40:** 12
    livebearing **40:** (17)
surgeonfish 32: 51, **40:** 9, 100–101
    powder-blue **40:** 100, *101*
surgery
    animal parts for human surgery **5:** 79
    testing surgical techniques **4:** 13
Suricata suricatta **1:** 98, 100–105
suricate *see* meerkat
Surnia ulula **15:** 50
Sus
    barbatus **5:** 74
    scrofa **5:** 74, 76–79
sushi **39:** 108, **40:** (110)
suslik, thirteen-lined *see* squirrel,
thirteen-lined ground
Sutorectus **32:** 37
    tentaculatus **32:** 37
swallow 15: 71
    American cliff **15:** 94
    bank 15: 94, 100–103; **18:** 13
    barn 15: 94, 95, 96–99
    Japanese **40:** *53*
    northern rough-winged **15:** 94
    swallow family 15: 94–95; **20:** 87
    violet-green **15:** 94, *95*
    white-backed **15:** 94, 95
swampfish **36:** 18, *19*
swan 14: 52, 53, 54, 80
    black **14:** 52, *55*, 56
    black-necked **14:** 52, *52*, 56
    mute 11: 14; **14:** 52, 56–59; **18:** (81)
    trumpeter **14:** 52
    whooper **14:** 55, 56
swan upping **14:** (58)
sweetfish **35:** 29
sweetlips **40:** 36, 37
    harlequin **40:** 37
    oriental **40:** *10–11*, 37

western Indian Ocean **40:** 37
sweet-oils (ithomiids) **26:** 56–57
swift 15: 11, 70–71, 94
    African black **15:** 70
    African palm- **15:** 70, *71*
    alpine **15:** 70, *71*
    chimney **15:** 70, 71
    cloud **15:** 70, 71
    crested tree **15:** 70, *71*
    Eurasian 15: 70, 71, 72–75
    fork-tailed **15:** 70
    great **15:** 70
    lesser Antillean **15:** 70
    lesser tree **15:** 70, *71*
    mustached tree **15:** 70, *71*
    needle-tailed **15:** 70
    pallid **15:** 70
    short-tailed **15:** 70
    silver-backed needletail **15:** 70
    sooty **15:** 70
    tree **15:** 71
    Vaux's **15:** 70
    white-chinned **15:** 70
    white-rumped **15:** 70
swiftlet 15: 71
    Himalayan **15:** 70
    Indian 15: 70, 76–77
    Indian edible nest (Indian) **15:** 70, 76–77
    Philippine **15:** 70
    Seychelles cave **15:** 70
    Tahitian **15:** 70
swim bladder soup **40:** (18)
swimming therapy **3:** 74
switchtail **31:** 53
swordfish 31: 42, **32:** 63, 86, 93, **39:** (10), **40:** 11, 107, *108–109*, 108–111
    spear-billed **38:** 50
swordtail 38: 94–105
    "Helleri" **38:** 100
    hybrid **38:** (100)
    lyretail **38:** (96)
    lyre wagtail **38:** 99
swordtails (swallowtail butterflies) **26:** 16–21
    fivebar **26:** *16–17*
Sylvia **17:** 60, 61
    atricapilla **17:** 60
    borin **20:** (48)
    communis **17:** 60
    curruca **17:** 60
Sylvicapra grimmia **6:** 62, 80–81
Sylviidae **17:** 60
Sylvilagus
    aquaticus **8:** (93)
    audubonii **8:** 64, (93)
    bachmani **8:** 64
    dicei **8:** (93)
    floridanus **8:** 64, 90–93
    insonus **8:** (93)
    palustris hefneri **8:** 64
    transitionalis **8:** (93)
Sylviorthorhynchus desmursii **20:** 80

Sylviparus modestus **17**: 70
Symbion pandora **21**: *69*
symbiosis **6**: (73)
symbiotic relationships **17**: (21);
     42: 110
symmetry, pentameric **30**: 90, 110
Sympetrum sanguineum **22**: *46*
Symphorichthys spilurus **40**: 36
Symphoromyia **23**: (59)
Symphurus **39**: 94
     normani **39**: 95
     rhytisma **39**: 95
Symphyla **22**: 14, *15*
symphylans **22**: (15)
Symphysodon **37**: (108), **38**: (40), **40**: 68
     aequifasciatus **40**: (71), *71*, 78
     aequifasciatus aequifasciatus **40**: 79
     aequifasciatus axelrodi **40**: 79
     aequifasciatus haraldi **40**: 79
     discus **40**: 79
Symphyta **27**: 8, 9–10, *12*, 14–21
Sympterygia **33**: (26)
Synagrops bellus **40**: 15
Synallaxis albescens **20**: 80
Synanceia
     horrida **39**: 52, 58, *58*
     verrucosa **39**: 52, 58
Synaphobranchidae **33**: (62), 65, 84–85
Synaphobranchus **33**: 84
     kaupi **33**: 85, *85*
Synapsida **44**: 10
Synaptolaemus cingulatus **38**: 20
Synaptula **30**: *112–113*
Synaptura
     kleinii **39**: (93)
     lusitanica nigromaculata **39**: (93)
     salinarum **39**: (93), 95
Synbranchidae **33**: 106, (106)
Synbranchiformes **33**: 106–107
Synbranchus **33**: (106)
     marmoratus **33**: 106
Syncarida **28**: 9, 34
Syncerus caffer **6**: 62, 70–73
Syncope **42**: 104
syndactylism **18**: (18); **19**: (82)
syndactyly **10**: 75, (94)
Syngnathidae **38**: 50, **39**: 8, 10, 26, *27*,
     36, 38–47
Syngnathus watermeyeri **39**: (46)
Synodontidae **35**: 79, 94–97
Synodontis **37**: 71, 75
     acanthomias **37**: 73
     angelicus **37**: 70–71
     decorus **37**: *8–9*
     multipunctatus **37**: 73, *74–75*
     nigriventris **37**: 70, *70*, *72–73*,
          39: (86)
     petricola **37**: 73
     schall **37**: 73
synodontis
     cuckoo **37**: *74–75*
     even-spotted **37**: 73
     gray **37**: 73
     Payne's **37**: 71

Synodus **35**: 95
     intermedius **35**: *95*
     variegatus **28**: *30;* **35**: *96–97*
Synthliboramphus antiquus **12**: 98
syrinx **11**: (109)
Syrphidae **23**: 76–81
Syrrhaptes **16**: 8
     paradoxus **16**: 8, 10–11
     tibetanus **16**: 8
Systelommatophora **30**: 18, 45
Systoechus **23**: *71*

Tabanidae **23**: 58–61
tabanids **23**: 58–61
     blood feeding **23**: 61
     feeding **23**: 61
     larvae **23**: 61
     mating **23**: 58–60
Tabanus
     atratus **23**: *60*
     sudeticus **23**: *60*
     trimaculatus **23**: *58*
tabbigaw **32**: 28
Tachina fera **23**: *104, 106*
Tachinidae **23**: 104–107
Tachybaptus
     dominicus **14**: 16
     ruficollis **14**: 16
Tachycineta thalassina **15**: 94
Tachycnemis seychellensis **43**: 11, 18
Tachyeres
     brachypterus **12**: 66
     leucocephalus **12**: 66
     patachonicus **12**: 66
     pteneres **12**: 66
Tachyerini **12**: 66
Tachyglossus aculeatus **10**: 110–111
Tachymarptis melba **15**: 70
Tadarida brasiliensis **9**: 100–103
Tadorna variegata **14**: 52
tadpole fish **36**: 53, *53*
tadpoles **41**: 8, 13
     crowned **42**: (60)
Taenionotus triacanthus **39**: 61, *64–65*
Taeniopoda auricornis **23**: *28*
Taeniura **33**: (34)
     lymma **33**: *35*
     meyani **33**: *36–37*
tahr, Himalayan **6**: 62

tail biter **38**: 13
tail
     streamers **15**: (86), (99); **19**: 38
     used as prop **18**: 8; **19**: 58
taimen **35**: (50)
     Sichuan **35**: (50)
taipans 50: (8), 9, 15, 42–43, 95
     coastal **50**: 9, 42, *42*, 43
     inland **50**: 42, 43
takh *see* horse, Mongolian wild
Takifugu **39**: 108
     niphobles **39**: *109*
     rubripes **39**: 109
takin **6**: 62, 108
Takydromus **45**: 58, 59
     sexlineatus **45**: 80–81
talapoin **4**: 40, *41*, 43
talking **16**: (28), 37
Talpa **41**: 56
     europaea **9**: 40, 44–47
     streeti **9**: 40
Talpidae **9**: 9
tamandua **9**: 68
     southern **9**: 65
Tamandua tetradactyla **9**: 65
tamaraw **6**: 62
tamarin 4: *8*
     bearded emperor **4**: 94
     black-chinned emperor **4**: 94
     black-faced lion **4**: 88
     black lion **4**: 86, 88
     cotton-top **4**: 86, *87*
     emperor 4: 86, 94–95
     golden-headed lion **4**: 88
     golden lion 4: 86, 87, 88–91
     lion **4**: 86
     saddleback **4**: 86, 95
     tamarin family 4: 86–87
tambaqui **38**: 45
Tamias
     sibiricus **7**: 48
     striatus **7**: 34, 48–49
tanager **17**: 89; **19**: 70, 74
Tanaidacea **28**: 9, 34, (51)
Tanaidomorpha **28**: 34
tanaids **28**: (51)
Tanakia **34**: 66
Tandanus tandanus **37**: 67
tang **40**: 100
     Achilles **40**: 100, *100*
     blue **40**: 101
     yellow **40**: 100, 101
Tanichthys albonubes **34**: 62, *62–63*,
     (65), 72
Tantilla **48**: 87; **49**: 11, *48–49*, (63), 108,
     109; **50**: 14
     relicta **50**: (35)
Tanysiptera galatea **14**: 100
tapertail **35**: 105
tapetail **39**: 9, 15
tapetum lucidum **2**: 10–12; **4**: 85,
     106, 107
tapeworms 21: 80–85
tapir 5: *8*, 11, 12

Baird's **5:** 62, *62*, 63
Brazilian 5: 62, 63, <u>64–65</u>
Malayan **5:** 62, 63, *63*
mountain **5:** 62, *63*
South American (Brazilian) **5:** 62, 63, <u>64–65</u>
tapir family 5: <u>62–63</u>
Tapirus
bairdii **5:** 62
indicus **5:** 62
pinchaque **5:** 62
terrestris **5:** 62, <u>64–65</u>
Taraba major **19:** 72
tarantulas 29: <u>46–47</u>
red-knee **22:** *9*
Mexican red-knee **29:** *46*
tarantulas **42:** 110; **49:** (63)
Tardigrada **21:** 32; **22:** 12–13
Tarentola **45:** (29)
mauretanica **45:** <u>28–29</u>
Taricha **41:** 88, 91, (92)
granulosa **41:** 44, <u>108–109</u>
rivularis **41:** 89, 92, 108
torosa **41:** *90–91*, 108
Tarletonbeania crenularis **35:** 81, 102
tarpon 36: 86
Atlantic 33: <u>98–99</u>
tarsier **4:** 11, 106, 107
pygmy **4:** 106, 107
spectral **4:** 106, *107*
western **4:** 106, 107, *107*
Tarsipes rostratus **10:** 74, <u>102–103</u>
Tarsius
bancanus **4:** 106
pumilus **4:** 106
spectrum **4:** 106
Tasmanian devil 10: (24), 27, <u>28–31</u>
Tateurndina
ocellicauda **40:** 98
tattler, wandering **13:** 30
Taudactylus **42:** 92, 94, *94*, 95, (97)
Tauraco
corythaix **16:** 38
hartlaubi **16:** 38
leucolophus **16:** 38
leucotis **16:** 38
livingstonii **16:** 38
Tauroma auricornis **25:** *97*
Taurotragus
derbianus **6:** 62, <u>76–77</u>
derbianus derbianus **6:** 76
derbianus gigas **6:** 76
oryx **6:** 62, 76
Taxidea taxus **1:** 32, <u>76–77</u>
Taxodonta **30:** 50
taxonomy **21:** <u>8–11</u>
Tayassu
pecari **5:** 88
tajacu **5:** 88, <u>90–91</u>
Tayassuidae **5:** 88
tayra **1:** 32; **4:** 89
Tealia lofotensis **21:** *56–57*
Tectocoris diophthalmus **24:** *70–71*
teeth **31:** 79, **32:** *11, 12, 61, 85, 101*,

35: (51), *82–83*, **36:** (66),
38: *43*, (44)
aardvark **9:** 65, (66), 78–79
bats **9:** (85), (95)
pharyngeal **31:** 82, **34:** 40, *40*
selenodont **6:** 9
Tegenaria duellica **29:** 95
tegu 44: 25; **45:** 82, 83, 84, <u>94–97</u>;
47: 45
black-and-white **45:** *84–85*, 94
crocodile **45:** 83–84
reproduction **45:** 95–96
Teiidae **44:** 25, (26); **45:** 61, 82, 83
Teius **45:** 82
teledu **1:** 32
Teleostomi **33:** 60, (61)
Telephorous
olivaceus **15:** 104
quadricolor **15:** 104
telescopefish 35: 79, <u>92–93</u>, 96
Telescopus **49:** 11
Telestacea **21:** 43
Telicomys **7:** 11–12
tellins (wedge shells) **30:** 62, 68–70
Telmatherina
antoniae **38:** 59
celebensis **38:** 59
Telmatherinidae **38:** <u>54–59</u>
Telmatobiinae **42:** 76
Telmatobius **42:** 76
culeus **41:** (12); **42:** 11, *78*, (78)
patagonicus **42:** (78)
Telostylinus **23:** *85*, (85)
Temera **33:** (20)
Temnotrogon roseigaster **19:** 34
temperature
body **11:** (13), 21, 38; **16:** 46
regulation (lizards) **45:** 70
temperature-dependent sex
determination (TDSD)
41: (27); **45:** 14, 15–17,
25, 37; **47:** (19), 46, 59, 73
tench 34: 46, <u>80–83</u>
color variations **34:** (83)
golden **34:** *82–83*
Tenebrionidae **25:** <u>68–73</u>
tenguzame **32:** 90
tenrec 8: 12; **9:** 8, 9, 11
aquatic **9:** 24, 25, *25*
common 9: 24, <u>26–27</u>
four-toed rice **9:** *24*
greater (common) **9:** 24, <u>26–27</u>
greater hedgehog **9:** *24*, 25
large-eared **9:** 24, 25
lesser hedgehog **9:** 24, 25
long-tailed **9:** *24*, 25
pygmy shrew **9:** 24
rice **9:** 24, 25
spiny **9:** 25
streaked **9:** 24, *24–25*
tailless (common) **9:** 24, <u>26–27</u>
tenrec family 9: <u>24–25</u>
Tenrec **9:** 9
ecaudatus **9:** 24, <u>26–27</u>

Tenrecidae **9:** 9, 11, 24
Tentaculata **21:** 43
Tenthredo **27:** 9
mesomelas **27:** *16*
Tephritidae **23:** <u>88–91</u>
Terathopius ecaudatus **15:** 8, <u>36–37</u>
Teratolepis fasciata **44:** 30; **45:** (10)
Teratoscincus **45:** 9, (10)
microlepis **45:** *8–9*
terciopelo 50: (8), 9, (52), <u>92–93</u>, (111)
Teredinidae **30:** 71
Teretrurus **48:** 28
termitaria **22:** (64)
termites 2: 50, 76, 110–111; **6:** 87;
9: 64, 66, 69; **10:** 34;
22: <u>62–67</u>; **27:** 11, 40, 41
colonies **22:** 63–65
compass **22:** (64)
defense **22:** (67)
feeding **22:** 65–66
fungus gardens **22:** (64), 65, 67
mounds **6:** 88, *88–89*
nasute soldier **22:** 62
nests **22:** (64)
western subterranean **22:** *62–63*
tern 12: 64, 74, 75; **13:** 71, 84;
14: (74); **15:** (68)
Arctic 11: 15; **12:** 74, <u>86–89</u>; **13:** 63
black **12:** 74, 88
Caspian 12: 74, <u>90–91</u>
common **11:** (49); **12:** 74, *77*, (89);
13: 79
Forster's **12:** 74
Inca **12:** 74, 75
least **12:** 74
roseate **12:** 79
Sandwich **12:** 74
sooty **12:** 74, *77*
whiskered **12:** 74
white **12:** 74, *76*
white-winged **12:** 74
Terpsiphone **17:** 67
corvina **17:** 66
paradisi **17:** 66
viridis **17:** 66, <u>68–69</u>
Terrapene **47:** 28
carolina **47:** *11*, <u>74–75</u>
terrapin
helmeted **47:** 41, (42)
pan-hinged 47: <u>40–43</u>
serrated hinged **47:** *43*
Seychelles mud **47:** 42
yellow-bellied **47:** 42
territorial behavior
attacking own young **14:** (59)
defense **12:** (85), (95); **13:** 27;
14: 98–99; **17:** (16); **20:** (34)
display **11:** 96–97, *97*; **12:** 25, 27;
14: (12); **15:** (92); **18:** 50;
20: 58
display copulations **20:** 66
display flights **13:** 24, 41–42, 84;
15: (92)
etiquette **18:** (107)

for feeding **17:** (49)
fighting **11:** 43, 54, *56–57*, 89–90, *90*; **12:** (85), (107); **14:** (12), (59), *93*, 95; **16:** 52–53, *55*, (74); **17:** (109); **18:** 41, 50; **19:** 11; **20:** (34)
gaining territory **18:** (107)
hierarchies **20:** 110–111
marking **11:** (39)
mobbing **15:** (67)
queuing system **13:** 97
refusing to leave **19:** 77–78
size of territory **11:** 14; **15:** 11; **18:** 53
song **18:** 23, 25–26, 45, 48–50, 53
song duels **16:** (70)
warning calls **11:** 24, (62); **14:** 8, (12), 30; **18:** 16
Tessaratomidae **24:** (64)
Testudines **44:** 8, 9; **47:** 8, 9, 28
Testudinidae **47:** 9, 80, (81)
Testudo **47:** 80
graeca **47:** 80, (81)
hermanni **47:** 80
horsfieldii **47:** (83)
marginata **47:** 80
Tetanocera **23:** 94
assogans **23:** 95
Tethya aurantia **21:** *37*
tetra 38: 14
adonis **38:** 30
African 38: 30–31, 36
African silver **38:** 30
albino **38:** 40
black **38:** 41
black neon **38:** 40, *40*
black wedge **38:** 9
blackspot Congo **38:** 31
bleeding heart **38:** *38–39*, 41
blind **38:** 8
blind cave **38:** 8, 35
bloodfin **38:** *34–35*
blotchy arrowhead **38:** 48, 49
blue **38:** 35
blue Congo **38:** 30
boodfin **38:** 35
bristly mouthed **38:** 49
cardinal **38:** 8, 35, 37, *37*, 39
cheirodon **38:** 37
Columbian predator dwarf **38:** 23
Congo **38:** 30, *30–31*
copper **38:** 8
croaking 38: 48–49
darter **38:** 14, 15, 17, 33
diamond **38:** 40
diamondhead **38:** 40
discus **38:** 35, (40)
false neon **38:** 40
false silver **38:** 37
garnet **38:** *9*
golden neon **38:** 40
green neon **38:** 40
male black phantom **38:** *41*
Mexican **38:** 8, 35, 36
naked **38:** 41

neon **38:** 8, 35, 39
one-banded African **38:** 15
one-lined African **38:** 15, *15*
orange-red dwarf **38:** 30
"parasitic" **38:** (40)
predator 38: 32–33
pretty **38:** *9*
red Congo **38:** 31
redfin Congo **38:** 31
sailfin **38:** 32, *32*, 33
silver **38:** 37
silver dollar **38:** 35
silver-tipped **38:** 8
South American 38: 36–41
splashing 38: 8, 22–23
swordtail **38:** 48, *48*, 49
three-lined **38:** 15
three-spot **38:** 35
Uruguay **38:** 35
Weitzman's predator **38:** 32, *32*
white **38:** 41
yellow Congo **38:** 31
yellow neon **38:** 40
Tetrabranchia **30:** 74–75
Tetracerus quadricornis **6:** 62
Tetradactylus **45:** 98, 101
Tetragnatha
extensa **29:** *103, 104*
montana **29:** *102*
Tetragnathidae **29:** 102–105
Tetragonopterus **38:** 35
argenteus **38:** 37
chalceus **38:** 37
Tetrao
tetrix **11:** 44, 68
urogallus **11:** 44
Tetraodon
biocellatus **39:** 109
cutcutia **32:** 58, **39:** 109
fluviatilis **39:** 109
mbu **39:** 109
schoutedeni **39:** 109
Tetraodontidae **39:** 11, 96, 97, (102), 108–109, 110
Tetraodontiformes **39:** 96–97
families summary **39:** (96)
Tetraonidae **11:** 44, 48
Tetrapturus
audax **40:** (110), *111*
georgii **40:** (110)
Tetrastichus galactopus **27:** 25
Tetrax tetrax **11:** 84
Tetrigidae **23:** 34–35
Tetrix subulata **23:** *34, 34–35*
Tettigoniidae **23:** 12–15
Tevniida **21:** 77
Thalassarche
cauta **12:** 28
chrysostoma **12:** 28
melanophrys **12:** 28, 62
Thalassema neptuni **21:** *78*
Thalassenchelys
coheni **33:** 77
foliaceus **33:** 77

Thalassinidea **28:** 56, 80–81
Thalassius **29:** *92*
Thalassophis anomalus **50:** (45)
Thalassophryne **36:** 55, 59
Thalassophryninae **36:** 55
Thaleichthys pacificus **35:** (28)
Thaliacea **31:** 22–23
Thamnomanes **19:** 73
schistogynus **19:** 72
Thamnophilidae **19:** 72
Thamnophilus
doliatus **19:** 72, 76–79
nigriceps **19:** 72
Thamnophis **49:** 12
butleri **49:** (86)
hammondi **49:** *12*
marcianus **49:** (89)
proximus **49:** (89)
sirtalis **41:** 108; **48:** 17, 109; **49:** (29), 84–89
valida **49:** (89)
Thanasimus formicarius **25:** *40*
thanatosis **43:** 9
Thaumatichthyidae **36:** 74–83
Thaumatichthys **36:** *77*
Thecadactylus rapicauda **45:** 11
Thecanephria **21:** 77
Theclinae **26:** 29
Thecosomata **30:** 18
Thecostraca **28:** 9
Thelenota anax **30:** *110–111*
Theloderma **43:** 100
horridum **43:** (76)
Thelotornis **49:** 11
capensis **43:** *103*; **49:** (39)
kirtlandii **49:** (39)
Themos olfersii **27:** 17
Theragra chalcogramma **36:** 50
Theraphosidae **29:** 46–47
Thereva annulata **23:** *65*
Therevidae **23:** (65)
Theridiidae **29:** 98–101
Theridion
impressum **29:** (99)
sisyphium **29:** *98,* (99)
thermals **15:** (33), 37, (98)
Thermobia domestica **22:** *36*
Thermosbaenacea **28:** 34, 37
Theromyzon tessulatum **21:** *110–111*
Theropithecus gelada **4:** 40, 62–63
Thetetra japonica **26:** 66–67
thetisfish **39:** 66
thick-knee 13: 91, 101
beach 13: 90, (93), 106–107
bush **13:** 90, (93)
Eurasian **13:** 90, (93)
great **13:** 90
Peruvian **13:** 90
Senegal **13:** 90, (93)
Thoburnia
atripinnis **34:** 99
rhothoeca **34:** 99
Thomisidae **29:** 68–73
Thomomys talpoides **7:** 26–27

Thoracica **28:** 9
Thorius **41:** 68
   arboreus **41:** (17)
thornbacks **33:** 27, (27)
thornyhead **39:** 64, 65, (67)
   shortspine **39:** (67)
Thorococharax securis **38:** 29
thrasher **20:** 82
   brown **18:** 36, *36*
   Cozumel **18:** 36, 37
   crissal **18:** 36
Thrasops **49:** 36
thread snakes **44:** 15; **48:** 18–21, 105; **50:** (25)
   Blandford's **48:** 20
   Texas 48: 20, 22–23
   western **48:** *19*, 23
threadfin **38:** 52, **40:** 36, 37
   Indian **40:** 39
threadtail **35:** 82, 105
threatened species (fish) **31:** 20, **35:** 41
   Aral trout **35:** (70)
   Baltic sturgeon **31:** 58, 59
   barbels **34:** 31
   barbs **34:** (29)
   belugas **31:** 66, 67
   carps **34:** 35
   chubs **34:** (78)
   dace **34:** (78)
   delta smelt **35:** 27
   freshwater catfish **37:** (19)
   galaxiids **35:** 33, 35
   gobies **40:** 94
   Greek nine-spined stickleback **39:** (35)
   lake sturgeons **31:** 61
   mudminnows **35:** 21
   rainbowfish **38:** (56)
   Ryukyu ayu-fish **35:** 29
   sculpins **39:** (78)
   sea horses **39:** (46)
   sharks **32:** 20–25, 78, 79, 87
   shiners **34:** 69, 70
   silver shark **34:** (56)
   silversides **38:** (63)
   sterlet **31:** 63
   tetras **38:** (41)
   totoaba **40:** (18)
Threskiornithidae **14:** 32
Thrichomys apereoides **8:** 30
Thripophaga dorbignyi **20:** 80
thrips **22:** 84–85
   tube-tailed **22:** *84*
   western flower **22:** *84*
thrush **11:** 13; **15:** 19; **17:** (39), 60; **18:** 36, (81); **20:** 84
   ashy ground **18:** 44
   hermit **18:** 44, 45
   Siberian ground **18:** 44
   song **18:** 44, *45*
   thrush family 18: 44–45; **19:** (74)
   wood **18:** 44, *44*
Thryonomyidae **7:** *12*; **8:** 31
Thryonomys
   gregorianus **8:** 30

swinderianus **8:** 30
Thryothorus
   felix **17:** 52
   ludovicianus **17:** 52
Thryssa setirostris **36:** (92)
thunder bugs (thrips) **22:** 84–85
Thunnus
   alalunga **40:** 107
   albacares **40:** *105*, 106
   maccoyii **40:** 107, *107*
   obesus **40:** 107
   thynnus **40:** (10), 106, 107
thylacine **2:** 80; **10:** 24, 26, 28, 36–37
Thylacinidae **10:** 24, 26
Thylacinus cynocephalus **10:** 27, 36–37
Thylamis
   elegans **10:** 14
   pallidior **10:** 14
Thylogale
   stigmatica **10:** 48
   thetis **10:** 48
Thymallus **35:** 42–45, (45)
   arcticus **35:** 42, 44, 45
   arcticus arcticus **35:** 44, (45), *45*
   arcticus baicalensis **35:** 44
   arcticus grubii **35:** 44
   arcticus pallasi **35:** 44
   brevirostris **35:** 44
   nigrescens **35:** 45
   thymallus **35:** 42, *42*, *43*, 44
   yaluensis **35:** 45
Thyropteridae **9:** 87
Thyrsoidea nacrura **33:** 78
Thyrsopsocus **22:** 86–87
Thysania agrippina **26:** 93
Thysanoptera **22:** 30, 84–85
Thysanura **22:** 30, 36–37
tiang **6:** 88
Tiaris canora **16:** 62
Tibicen
   canicularis **24:** *81*
   plebejus **24:** 80
Tibificida **21:** 94
tiburón **32:** 53
tick-bite fever **29:** (32)
ticks **6:** 18; **7:** 14; **29:** 30–33
   diseases **29:** (32)
   hard **29:** *31*
   hedgehog **29:** *30*
   wood **29:** *32*
tiger **2:** 10, 20–25
   Bali **2:** 21
   Bengal **2:** 21, *21*, *22*, 23
   Caspian **2:** 21
   Chinese **2:** 20, 21
   Indochinese **2:** 21
   Javan **2:** 21
   Siberian **2:** 20, 21, 22–23
   Sumatran **2:** 21
   Tasmanian *see* thylacine
   white **2:** *23*, (23)
tiger salamander **41:** 56, 57, 59, 60, 63, 64–67
   Arizona **41:** 64, 66

   barred **41:** 64, *64–65*, 65
   blotched **41:** 64, 66
   California **41:** 56, *67*, (67)
   eastern **41:** 64, 65, 66
   North American blotched **41:** *28–29*
tiger snake **49:** 11
   Australian 50: 38–41
   black **50:** 38, *38*
   Chappell Island **50:** (40)
   common **50:** 38
   mainland **50:** 38
tigerfish **38:** 30, *30*, **39:** 60, **40:** 36
   finescale **40:** 36
   four-barred **40:** 36
   South American **38:** 24, *25*
tiger-horses **5:** 52
tigers (moths)
   ithomiids **26:** 56–57
   plain **26:** *60*
Tigrisoma lineatum **14:** 20
Tilapia zillii **37:** 18
tilapia
   redbelly **37:** 18
Tiliqua **46:** 8, 13
   scincoides **46:** 15, 40–43
   scincoides intermedia **46:** 40, *42*
Tiluropsis **33:** 97
Tilurus **33:** 97
timemas **22:** 52, (55)
Tinamidae **11:** 40
tinamou
   Andean **11:** 40
   elegant crested 11: 40, 42–43
   great **11:** 40
   highland **11:** 40, *41*
   little **11:** 40
   Magdalena **11:** 40
   ornate **11:** 40
   tinamou family 11: 40–41
   undulated **11:** 40, *41*
Tinamus major **11:** 40
Tinca tinca **34:** 46, 80–83
Tingidae **24:** 28–29
Tingis ampliata **24:** *28–29*
tinselfish **39:** (25)
   spotted **39:** (25)
   thorny **39:** (25)
Tipula
   maxima **23:** *42*
   oleracea **23:** *39*
   paludosa **23:** *38*, 42–43
Tipulidae **23:** 42–45
tit **17:** 70–73, (76); **18:** 64
   blue **17:** 70, *71*, 72, (72)
   bush **17:** 70, *70*
   coal **17:** 70, (72), (73)
   crested **17:** 70, *73*
   Eurasian long-tailed **17:** 72
   great **17:** 70, *70*, 72, (72), (73); **18:** 69
   long-tailed 17: 70, 72–73, 80–81
   marsh **17:** 70, 77
   pygmy **17:** 70
   red-headed **17:** 70, *70*
   sultan **17:** 70, *70*

willow **17:** 70, *70*, 76, 77
yellow-browed **17:** 70
Titanus giganteus **25:** 90
titi
　dusky **4:** 72
　masked **4:** 72
　yellow-handed **4:** 72
titmouse **11:** (15)
　tufted **17:** 70, *70*
toad crossings **41:** *16*; **42:** 63
toadfish 32: 66, **36:** 8, 25, <u>54–59</u>, 77,
　39: 54, 109
　American oyster **36:** 54, *54*
　grunting **36:** *58–59*
　large-eye **36:** *56*
　venomous **36:** 54, 55
toadlets
　Australian 42: 10, <u>92–97</u>, <u>100–101</u>
　Bibron's **42:** 97
　gold **42:** *79*, (79)
　red-backed **42:** 101
　red-crowned **42:** 100, 101
　three-toed **42:** 10, (79)
toado
　clown **39:** 109
toads 41: 12–13; **42:** <u>8–15</u>
　adapting to environment **42:** 12
　African clawed 42: 46, <u>52–55</u>, (69);
　　43: 51
　African live-bearing **42:** 56
　alpine **42:** 34
　American **42:** *60–61*, 68
　American oak **42:** 59
　Arizona **42:** 57
　Asian black-spined **42:** 56
　Asian horned 42: 9, 10, <u>34–35</u>,
　　<u>36–39</u>, 40, (89); **43:** 86
　bell (midwife) **42:** 10, 14, 25, <u>30–31</u>,
　　<u>32–33</u>; **43:** (11)
　Blomberg's **42:** (38), 56, (65)
　body forms **42:** 9–10
　Brongersma's **42:** 71
　brown (Malaysian) tree **42:** 58, <u>72–73</u>
　burrowing **42:** 22
　bush **42:** 56, 60
　Cameroon **42:** (38), 56
　cane 42: 12–13, 56, <u>64–69</u>;
　　46: 85; **50:** 43
　Cape platanna **42:** (53)
　Chirinda **42:** (60)
　clawed 42: 10, 23, <u>46–49</u>, 69; **50:** 57
　Colorado river **42:** 57, (65)
　common **42:** *11*, 12, (18)
　common midwife (midwife) **42:** 10,
　　14, 25, <u>30–31</u>, <u>32–33</u>; **43:** (11)
　common platanna (African clawed)
　　42: 46, <u>52–55</u>, (69); **43:** 51
　corroboree **42:** 100, *100*, *101*
　Costa Rican golden **41:** *14–15*
　crucifix **42:** *93*
　defense **42:** 58
　dwarf clawed **42:** 46, *48*
　eastern narrow-mouthed
　　42: *110–111*, (111)

Eurasian green **42:** 55
European common 41: (17);
　42: 56, 59, <u>62–63</u>
European fire-bellied **42:** 25–26, (25),
　26
European natterjack **42:** 57
extinct **41:** 17
fertilization **41:** 12
fire-bellied 41: (92); **42:** 10, (22),
　<u>24–27</u>
fire-bellied harlequin **42:** 74
flat-headed **42:** 60
food and feeding **42:** 12–13, 58
or frogs? **42:** (8)
giant (cane) **42:** 12–13, 56, <u>64–69</u>;
　46: 85; **50:** 43
giant fire-bellied **42:** *25*, 26
giant river **42:** (65)
golden **42:** *12*, 73
gold nugget (gold toadlets) **42:** *79*,
　(79)
Great Plains narrow-mouthed
　42: <u>110–111</u>
green 42: 44, <u>70–71</u>
habitats **42:** 11, 12
harlequin 42: 10, 57, 58, 60, <u>74–75</u>;
　43: 73
helmeted water **42:** 76
horned **42:** 10, 35
Iberian midwife **42:** 30, *30*, 31
Karoo **42:** 57
Kinabalu dwarf **42:** *58*
lazy **42:** 34
life cycles **42:** 13–14
live-bearing **42:** 60
Majorcan midwife **42:** *31*, (31)
Malaysian tree 42: 58, <u>72–73</u>
marbled tree **42:** (73)
marine (cane) **42:** 12–13, 56, <u>64–69</u>;
　46: 85; **50:** 43
Mauritanian **42:** 71
midwife 42: 10, 14, 25, <u>30–31</u>,
　<u>32–33</u>; **43:** (11)
miter **42:** 38, 56, *57*
Mueller's clawed **42:** 55
natterjack **42:** *59*, 71
northern corroboree **42:** 100
oriental fire-bellied 41: 18, *19*;
　42: 9, 26, <u>28–29</u>
paradise **42:** 57
Pinocchio **42:** 56
platanna **42:** 46
rain **42:** 56
red-bellied **42:** 57
reproduction **42:** (12), 13–14, 58–60
river **42:** 58, (65)
rococo **42:** (65)
saddle-back **41:** (17)
short-legged **42:** 34, (89)
slender **42:** 57
Sonoran desert **42:** 44
Sonoran green **42:** 57
South American horned **42:** (38)
southern midwife **42:** 31

spiny **42:** 34
stream **42:** 60
Surinam 42: 10, <u>46–49</u>, <u>50–51</u>;
　43: (11)
survival **42:** 14
swamp **42:** 58
tongues **42:** (22)
toothed **42:** 34
true 42: 10, <u>56–61</u>
western (Great Plains) narrow-
　mouthed **42:** <u>110–111</u>
yellow-bellied **42:** (25), 26, *26–27*, 27
Yosemite **42:** 73
see also spadefoot toad
Tockus **18:** 48–49; **19:** 51
　camurus **19:** 48
　erythrorhynchus **19:** 48
　flavirostris **19:** 48
　nasutus **19:** 48
toddy **1:** 95
toddy cat *see* civet, common palm
Todidae **19:** 42, 43
Todirhamphus
　pyrrhopygia **14:** 100
　sanctus **14:** 100
　veneratus **14:** 100
Todirostrum maculatum **17:** 30
Todus
　angustirostris **19:** 42
　mexicanus **19:** 42
　multicolor **19:** 42, <u>46–47</u>
　subulatus **19:** 42
　todus **19:** 42
tody 19: <u>42–43</u>
　broad-billed **19:** 42
　Cuban 19: 42, <u>46–47</u>
　Jamaican **19:** 42
　narrow-billed **19:** 42
　Puerto Rican **19:** 42, *42*
Tomaspis inca **24:** *79*
tomcod **36:** 38, 39, (51)
Tomeurus gracilis **38:** 68, 94
Tomistoma schlegelii **44:** *8–9*; **47:** *94–95*
tommie *see* gazelle, Thomson's
Tommy **32:** 84, **38:** 68, 94, 95, 96
tommygoff (terciopelo) **50:** (8), 9, (52),
　<u>92–93</u>, (111)
Tomopterna **43:** 82, *84*, 86–87
Tomopterninae **43:** 82, 86–87
tongue sole **39:** 94
　Norman's **39:** 95
　patchtail **39:** 95
tonguefish **39:** 88, 94, 95
tongues **11:** 12–13; **19:** 18, 61, 94;
　20: (90)
　as "teeth" **31:** 82, (90)
Tonicella lineata **30:** *15*
Tonna perdrix **30:** *26–27*
tool users **1:** (74); **4:** 10–11, (16), 31–32,
　(31); **18:** 64, 92; **19:** 105
toothcarp **38:** (88), 106
　Andean **38:** 89
　Corfu **38:** (88)
　Spanish **38:** (88)

Valencia **38:** (88)
tope **32:** 22, 25
topi 6: 62, (85), 88–89
topknot **39:** 90
topminnow 38: 84–85
  barrens **38:** 84
  saltmarsh **38:** 84
  thready **38:** 68
Tor **34:** 20–21
  khudree **34:** 21
  mussalah **34:** 21
  polylepis **34:** 20
  putitora **34:** 8, 19, 20, 21
  tambra **34:** 21
  tambroides **34:** *20–21*, 21
  tor **34:** 20, *20*, 21
torafugu **39:** 109
Torgos tracheliotus **20:** 8, 24–27
Torpedinidae **31:** (108), **33:** (9), (20)
Torpedinoidei **33:** 20–23
  families summary **33:** (20)
Torpedo **33:** (20)
  californica **33:** 22
  marmorata **33:** 14, 24–25
  nobiliana **33:** *20–21*, (22)
  torpedo **33:** *23*
torpedo **38:** 17
torpedo ray **33:** (20)
  Atlantic **33:** *20–21*, (22)
  blind legged **33:** (23)
  common **33:** *23*
  Pacific **33:** 22
  spotted **33:** 24, *25*
torpor **7:** 80; **9:** 20–21, 29, 38, 82, 102; **10:** 40, 85, 103; **15:** (75), 95; **16:** (51); **20:** (73)
tortoises 47: 80–83
  Aldabran **47:** 30, *89*, (89)
  Bell's hingeback **47:** 80
  Berlandier's gopher **47:** 90, 90–91
  Bolson **47:** 90, 91, (91)
  Burmese brown **47:** 82
  Chaco **47:** 82
  desert gopher **47:** 90
  elongated **47:** 82
  eroded hingeback **47:** 80
  evolution **44:** *10*
  Galápagos giant 44: 16; **47:** 84–89
  giant **46:** (67); **47:** (81), (89)
  gopher 47: 90–91
  Hermann's **47:** 80
  Home's hingeback **47:** 80, *81*
  horned **47:** 83
  Horsfield's **47:** (83)
  leopard 47: 80, 92–93
  marginated **47:** 80
  Mediterranean spur-thighed **47:** 80, (81)
  pancake **47:** 81
  plowshare **47:** 82
  radiated **47:** 82, *82*
  red-footed **47:** 82
  saddleback **47:** 87–88
  speckled Cape **47:** 81

spurred **47:** 80
star **47:** 82
Texas desert **47:** 91
yellow-footed **47:** 82, *82–83*
tortoiseshell **47:** 22
totoaba **40:** 11, (18)
Totoaba macdonaldi **40:** 11, (18)
toucan 11: *14*; **19:** 50, 56–59
  keel-billed 19: 56, 60–65
  plate-billed mountain **19:** 56
  rainbow-billed (keel-billed) **19:** 56, 60–65
  toco **19:** 56, *59*
  yellow-throated **19:** 61
toucanet
  emerald **19:** 56
  Guianan **19:** 56
tourism **3:** 51, 71, (94), 95; **5:** 39; **9:** 53, 101
  whale watching **3:** (57), 71, 95, 104
Toxicocalamus buergersi **50:** (21)
toxins **41:** 91; **42:** 58; **43:** 80–81
Toxocara vitellorum **21:** *91*
Toxorhynchites moctezuma **23:** *48*
Toxostoma **18:** 36; **20:** 82
  crissale **18:** 36
  guttatum **18:** 36
  rufum **18:** 36
Toxotes **40:** 44
  blythii **40:** 45
  chatareus **40:** *44*, 45
  jaculatrix **40:** 45
  lorentzi **40:** 45
  microlepis **40:** 45
  oligolepis **40:** 45
Toxotidae **38:** 50, **40:** 9, 44–45
Tracanthidae **39:** 96
Trachelophorus giraffa **25:** *106–107*
Tracheloptychus **45:** 98, 101
Trachelyopterus **37:** 83
  galeatus **37:** *82*
Trachichthyidae **39:** 9, 16–21
Trachinidae **39:** 28, **40:** 19
Trachinocephalus **35:** 95
Trachipteridae **35:** 82, 105, 106–107
Trachipterus
  altivelis **35:** 107
  arawatae **35:** 106
  fukuzakii **35:** 107
  trachipterus **35:** 82, 106, *106*
Trachurus **40:** 34
Trachydosaurus rugosus **44:** 27; **46:** 8, 9, *10*, 14, 15, 44–47
Trachylina **21:** 43
Trachyphonus **19:** (58)
  erythrocephalus **19:** 56
  vaillantii **19:** 56
Trachypithecus
  geei **4:** 40
  obscurus **4:** 40
Trachyrhynchus **36:** 28
trade, in parrots **16:** (35)
Tragelaphus
  buxtoni **6:** 62

  scriptus **6:** 62
  strepsiceros **6:** 78–79
tragopan **11:** 46
  satyr **11:** 44
Tragopan **11:** 46
  satyra **11:** 44
Tragulidae **6:** 10
Tragulus **6:** 48
  javanicus **6:** 10, 48
  napu **6:** 10, 48–49
trahira 38: 8, 24–27
  giant **38:** 25
Tramitichromis brevis **40:** 72
transparents (ithomiids) **26:** 56–57
Trapezonotus arenarius **24:** *44*
Trechalea **29:** *93*
Trechaleidae **29:** 93
tree dwelling **2:** 31
tree shrew 1: *10*; **5:** (10); **9:** 10, 58–59
  common 9: 59, 60–61
  pen-tailed **9:** 58, *58*, 59
  Philippine **9:** *58*
  pygmy **9:** *58*, 59
tree snake
  Asian brown 49: 20–23
  Blanding's **49:** *22–23*, (39)
  blunt-headed (blunt-headed vine snakes) **42:** 82; **49:** 16, (71), 90, 104–105
  golden **49:** *11*
  Kirtland's **49:** (39)
  long-nosed (long-nosed vine) **48:** 12; **49:** 18–19
  paradise 49: 26–27
treecreeper
  brown (American) **17:** 82
  common 17: 82, 84–87
  Eurasian (common) **17:** 82, 84–87
  short-toed **17:** 82, *82*, 83, 86, 87
  spotted **17:** 82, *82*
  treecreeper family 17: 82–83
treefish **39:** 64
treefrogs 42: 8, 9–10, *10*, (22); **43:** 28, 32–39, (49)
  African foam-nesting 43: 102–103
  African gray **43:** (66)
  Afro-Asian 42: 10; **43:** 100–101
  American gray **43:** 36
  American green 43: 48–49, 51
  Asian brown **43:** 100, (105)
  Australian **42:** (18); **43:** 32
  bony-headed **43:** 32, (76)
  breeding **43:** 36
  brown **43:** 104
  calls **43:** 35–36
  Central American **43:** (35)
  cinnamon **43:** 100
  color **43:** 34–35, (35)
  common European 43: 46–47
  crowned **43:** *38–39*, 39, (76)
  Cuban 43: 50–51
  dainty green **43:** 57
  Effinger's **43:** (76)
  environmental adaptations **43:** 33–34

file-eared **43:** *101*
foam-nesting **43:** (20)
frilled **43:** 105
giant (Cuban) **43:** 50–51
gray (African foam-nesting)
    43: 102–103
gray (*Hyla versicolor*) **43:** 36, 107
green (common European) **43:** 46–47
green (White's) **43:** 32, 54–57
harlequin **43:** *101*, 105
jade **43:** 105
Jamaican brown **43:** 38
Japanese **41:** *9*
leaf-nesting **49:** 16
Madagascan **43:** 100
magnificent **43:** 54, 57
map **43:** 37
marbled **43:** *36–37*
ornate **43:** *23*
Peter's **43:** (66)
red-eyed **43:** 57, *57*
satellite males **43:** (36)
shovel-headed **43:** 38
vslender-legged **43:** 38
    southern gray **43:** 36
    squirrel **43:** 51
    stripeless **43:** 46, *46–47*, (47)
    tiger-striped **43:** *34–35*
    water loss **43:** 57
    white-lipped **43:** 54, *54–55*, 57
    White's 43: 32, 54–57
treehoppers 24: 15, 90–95
    ants and **24:** (93)
    mating **24:** 94
    Mexican **24:** *92–93*
    parental care **24:** 93–94, 94 (95)
    pronotum **24:** (91)
treerunner, white-throated **20:** 80
Tremarctos ornatus **2:** 82
Trematoda **21:** 77, 81, 82–83
trembler, brown **18:** 36
Treron calva **16:** 12
Tretioscincus **45:** (85)
trevally
    giant **40:** 34
    golden **40:** *35*
    razor **40:** 35
trey pra **37:** 44
Triacanthidae **39:** 98–99
Triacanthodes ethiops **39:** *98*
Triacanthodidae **39:** 98–99
Triacanthus biaculeatus **39:** 99
Triadobatrachus **41:** 14
Triaenodon obesus **32:** *15*, 36, 64–67
Triakidae **32:** (42)
Triakis semifasciata **32:** *8*
Trialeurodes vaporariorum **24:** *98*, 99
Triatoma sanguisuga **24:** *41*
Triatominae **24:** (41)
tribal warfare **4:** 30
Tribolonotus **46:** 8
    gracilis **46:** 48–49
    novaeguineae **46:** *9*
Tricanthodidae **39:** 84, 96

Trichechus
    inunguis **3:** 47
    manatus **3:** 48–51
    senegalensis **3:** 47
Trichinella spiralis **21:** *88–89*
Trichius fasciatus **25:** *86*
Trichobatrachus **43:** 12
    robustus **42:** 11; **43:** 12, *15*, (15)
Trichochermes walkeri **24:** *96–97*
Trichodectes canis **22:** 88
Trichodes
    apiarius **25:** *40–41*
    ornatus bonnevillensis **25:** *41*
Trichogaster **40:** 61, (62)
    trichopterus **40:** 63
Trichoglossus ornatus **16:** 22; **19:** 12,
    16–19, 21
Trichogramma semblidis **27:** *26–27*
Trichomonadida **21:** 13
Trichomycteridae **37:** 11, 84, (91), (94),
    94–95
Trichomycterus maculatus **37:** *95*
Trichophthalma jaffueli **23:** 69
Trichopsis **40:** 61, 63
Trichoptera **22:** 30, 102–103
Trichosurus
    caninus **10:** 74
    vulpecula **10:** 74, 78–81
Trichys fasciculata **8:** 12
Tridacna **30:** (65)
    crocea **30:** (65), *66*
Tridacnidae **30:** 50
Tridactylidae **23:** 35
trigger *see* triggerfish
triggerfish 39: 8, 11, 96–97, 99,
    100–105
    Arabian **39:** 103
    black **39:** 103
    black-finned **39:** 103
    blackbar **39:** *100*, 103
    clown **39:** 103, *104–105*
    orange-green **39:** 103
    orange-lined **39:** 103
    outrigger **39:** 104
    painted **39:** 103, 105
    Picasso **39:** *8*, 103, 105
    queen **39:** 103
    red-lined **39:** 103
    red-toothed **39:** 103
    stone **39:** 104
    undulate **39:** *101*, 103
    "urchin cruncher" **39:** (103)
    wedge-tailed **39:** 105
    white-banded **39:** 103
    whitebar **39:** 103
Triglidae **39:** 11, 53, 54–57, 66
Trigona fulviventris **27:** *108–109*
Trigonalyoidea **27:** (23)
Trigonoceps occipitalis **20:** 8, 24
Trigonostigma
    espei **34:** 64
    hengeli **34:** 64
    heteromorpha **34:** *60–61*, 64
trilobites **28:** (13)

Trimeresurus **50:** 54, 59, 91
    albolabris **48:** *12*; **50:** *54*, 108, 110
    borneensis **50:** 110
    brongersmai **50:** 110
    canton **50:** 110
    flavoviridis **50:** (8), 110
    karanshahi **50:** 110
    malcolmi **50:** 110
    popeiorum **50:** 50, 108–111
    puniceus **50:** 110
    purpureomaculatus **50:** 111
    sumatranus **50:** *110–111*
    sumatranus malcolmi **50:** (108)
    tibetanus **50:** 111
    vogeli **50:** 110
Trimmatom nanus **40:** (10), 94
Trimorphodon **49:** 11
Trinectes maculatus **39:** 92
Tringa **13:** 30–31
    flavipes **13:** 30
    melanoleuca **13:** 30, 66–67
    totanus **13:** 30, 84
Triodon macropterus **39:** 108
Triodontidae **39:** 96, 97, 108–109, 110
triok, Tate's **10:** 74, (77)
Trionychidae **47:** 9, 10, 28, 60
Trionyx **47:** 10
triplespine 39: 96, 97, 98–99
tripletail **40:** 36
    Atlantic **40:** 36
tripodfish
    blacktip **39:** 99
    long-spined **39:** 99
    longtail **39:** 99
    short-nosed **39:** 99
Tripodichthys blochii **39:** 99
Tripostheus elongatus **38:** 29
Triprion **43:** 33, 38
Tripterygion
    delaisi **40:** 93
    melanurus **40:** 93
Trisopterus
    luscus **36:** *11*, *44–45*
    minutus **36:** *50–51*
Triturus **41:** 88, 91, (111)
    alpestris **41:** 89
    cristatus **41:** (92)
    palmatus **41:** 89
    vulgaris **41:** *29*, 89, 110–111
triungulins **25:** (14), 65–66
Trixiphichthys weberi **39:** 99
Trochilidae **16:** 44; **19:** 43; **20:** (73)
trochophore larva **21:** (76), 101
Trochozoa **21:** 32, (76)
Troginae **25:** (81)
Troglodytes **17:** 57
    aedon **16:** 71; **17:** 52
    troglodytes **17:** 52, 54–55; **20:** (48)
Troglodytidae **17:** 52; **18:** 36
Trogloglanis pattersoni **37:** 15
trogon 18: (18)
    African **19:** 34
    American **19:** 34
    Asian **19:** 34

Baird's **19:** 34
bare-cheeked **19:** 34
collared 19: 34, <u>40–41</u>
Cuban **19:** 34, 36
elegant **19:** 34, *35*
Hispaniolan **19:** 34
Javan **19:** 34
Narina **19:** 34, *36*
Philippine **19:** 34
red-headed **19:** 34, *34*
scarlet-rumped **19:** 34, *34*
Sumatran **19:** 34
trogon family 19: <u>34–37</u>
violaceous **19:** 34, *37*
Ward's **19:** 34
white-tailed **19:** 34, *34*
Trogon
  bairdii **19:** 34
  collaris **19:** 34, <u>40–41</u>
  elegans **19:** 34
  violaceus **19:** 34
  viridis **19:** 34
Trogonidae **19:** 34
Trogoniformes **19:** 34
Trogonophidae **46:** 102, 103, 104, 105
Trogonophis, weigmanni **46:** 104, *104–105*, 105
trophallaxis **27:** *41–42*, (42), 56, 70
tropicbird 12: 44, 45, 47–48, 63
  red-billed **12:** 44, *47*
  red-tailed **12:** 44, *47*, 59
  white-tailed 12: 44, *47*, <u>58–59</u>
  yellow-billed (white-tailed) **12:** 44, *47*, <u>58–59</u>
Tropicranus albocristatus **19:** 48
Tropidodipsas **49:** (99)
Tropidolaemus wagleri **50:** 9, 111
Tropidophiidae **48:** 9, 44, 47, (79)
Tropidophis **48:** 105
  melanurus **48:** <u>78–79</u>
Tropidophorus **46:** 8, 9
Tropidurinae **44:** 80
trout 34: 85, 111, **35:** 8, 9, 26, 32, (51), **36:** 85
  Amu-Darya **35:** (68), (70), 71
  Aral **35:** (68), (70), 71
  blue-dotted hill **34:** 65
  brook 35: <u>66–71</u>
  brown 35: 35, <u>66–71</u>, 73, 74, (75)
  bull **35:** 46
  coast angel **35:** 73
  coast range **35:** 73
  coral **40:** 16
  Danube **35:** 48
  European river **35:** 48
  European sea **35:** 67
  "fish from heaven" **35:** (75)
  Galway sea **35:** 66, (68)
  golden **35:** (75)
  Golden Trout Wilderness **35:** (75)
  hill **34:** 65
  Kamloops **35:** 73, 74
  lake 35: 46, <u>66–71</u>
  "large spotted" **35:** (68), 71

Little Kern golden **35:** *75*
  marbled **35:** (69)
  mountain **35:** 33
  Orkney sea **35:** 66, (68)
  Pacific brook **35:** 46
  rainbow 35: <u>72–77</u>, (77)
  red-spotted Rocky Mountain **35:** 46
  river **35:** *66–67*, 67, (68)
  salmon **35:** 66, (68), 70, 73
  sea 35: <u>66–71</u>, (75)
  silver **35:** 73
  South American **38:** 35
  spotted mountain **35:** 33, 36
  steelhead **35:** 72, 73, (77)
trout char
  western brook **35:** 46
trout-perch 36: 8, <u>16–17</u>
  blunt-nosed **36:** 16, *16*, 17, *17*
  Columbia **36:** 16
true bugs 24: <u>8–15</u>
  anatomy **24:** 10–11
  defense **24:** 14–15
  development **24:** 13–14
  families **24:** 8
  life cycle **24:** 13–14
  see also bugs
true crabs 28: <u>102–113</u>
  anatomy **28:** 102–104
  communication **28:** 113, (113)
  feeding **28:** 108
  as human food **28:** 113
  land crabs **28:** 105–106
  larvae **28:** (108)
  migrations **28:** 106–108
  mineral supplements **28:** (105)
  predator avoidance **28:** 108–109
  reproduction **28:** 112–113
  swimming **28:** 102–104
  walking sideways **28:** (104)
  see also crabs
truffles **5:** 79
trumpet, triton **30:** *27*
trumpeter 14: 82; **39:** *48–49*
  common 19: 8, <u>10–11</u>
  dark-winged **19:** 8, *8*
  gray-winged (common) **19:** 8, <u>10–11</u>
  green-winged **19:** 8
  pale-winged **19:** 8, *9*
  trumpeter family 19: <u>8–9</u>
  white-winged **19:** 8
trumpetfish 39: 10, 26, <u>48–49</u>
  Caribbean **39:** *48–49*, 49
  Chinese **39:** *48*, 49
trunkfish **32:** 66, **39:** 106
Trygonoptera **33:** (34)
Trygonrrhina **33:** (27)
Tryngites subruficollis **13:** 30
Trypanosoma cruzi **8:** 27
trypanosomes **21:** 17
Trypeta serratulae **23:** *89*
tsessebe **6:** 88
tsetse flies **21:** (17)
tuataras 44: *8*, 9, *13*, <u>18–23</u>
  and birds **44:** 20–21

breeding **44:** 13, 14, 22
  Brothers Island **44:** 23
  conservation **44:** 22–23
  defense **44:** 22
  evolution **44:** *10*
  tails discarded **44:** 22
Tubastrea **21:** *64*
  faulkneri **21:** *62*
tube-eye **35:** 82, 105
tubemouth **39:** 28
tubenoses 12: 8, <u>28–31</u>, 45; **39:** 29
tuberculosis, bovine **1:** 81; **10:** (80)
tubesnout 39: 10, 26, <u>28–29</u>
tubeworm **21:** *28*
Tubulidentata **1:** *10*; **5:** (12); **9:** 65
tuco-tuco **7:** *12*; **8:** 9–10, 11, 28–29, *31*
  forest **8:** 30
  strong **8:** 30
tularemia **8:** 81, 93
tumblebugs **25:** 76, 78
tuna 3: 69, 77; **31:** (47), **32:** 63, 93, **38:** 50, **39:** (10), 111, **40:** <u>104–107</u>, 108
  bigeye **40:** 107
  northern bluefin **40:** (10), 106, 107
  skipjack **40:** 106
  southern bluefin **40:** 107, *107*
  yellowfin **40:** *105*, 106
tunnels, foraging **7:** 15, 100–101
  see also burrows
tuns **30:** 26
  Pacific partridge **30:** *26–27*
Tupaia
  glis **9:** 59, <u>60–61</u>
  minor **9:** 59
Tupinambis **45:** 82, 83, 84, (96); **47:** 45
  teguixin **45:** *84–85*, <u>94–97</u>
tur
  east Caucasian **6:** 106, 107
  west Caucasian **6:** 106, 107
turaco
  great blue **16:** 38, 41, <u>42–43</u>
  Hartlaub's **16:** 38, *38*
  Knysna **16:** 38, *40*
  Livingstone's **16:** 38, *40*
  Ross's **16:** 38, *40*
  Ruwenzori **16:** 38
  turaco family 16: <u>38–41</u>
  white-cheeked **16:** 38, *38*
  white-crested **16:** 38, *39*
Turbellaria **21:** 81–82, (81)
Turdidae **18:** 36, 44; **19:** (74)
Turdus
  merula **18:** 44
  migratorius **16:** 59; **18:** 44, 47, <u>52–53</u>, 79
  philomelis **18:** 44
  pilaris **18:** 44, <u>58–59</u>
  torquatus **18:** 44
turkey 11: 49
  Australian brush **11:** 44
  brush **11:** 48, 49
  common 11: 44, 49, <u>76–81</u>
  ocellated **11:** 44, *48*, 49, 81
  wild (common) **11:** 44, 49, <u>76–81</u>

turkeyfish **39:** 60, (61)
Turnicidae **11:** 92
Turnix
　suscitator **11:** 92
　sylvatica **11:** 92
　tanki **11:** 92
　varia **11:** 92
turnstone 13: 30
　ruddy 13: 30, 68–71
turretfish **39:** 106
Tursiops truncatus **3:** 55, *72–75*
turtles 44: *13*; **47:** 8–11
　African yellow-bellied mud **47:** 41
　Alabama red-bellied **44:** *8*
　alligator snapping 47: 30, *46–51*
　anatomy **47:** 9–10, *10, 11*
　arrau **47:** *30–31*, 45
　Asian leaf 47: 78–79
　big-headed 47: 42, 56–57
　body parts **47:** 10, *10–11*
　box **47:** 28
　Brisbane short-necked **47:** 38
　Central American river 47: 62–63
　cogwheel **47:** (31)
　common mud **47:** 31
　common musk **47:** (31), 47
　common snapping 47: 47, 52–55
　East African black mud (pan-hinged terrapin) **47:** 40–43
　eastern box 47: *11*, 74–75
　eastern painted **47:** 66, *66–67*, (68)
　European pond 47: 72–73
　evolution **44:** 10
　flatback **47:** *14–15*
　Florida box **47:** *74–75*
　fossils **47:** 9
　freshwater 47: 28–31
　green 47: 18–21, 73
　hawksbill 47: (15), *22–23*
　Hope Valley ("Old 1844") **47:** (75)
　Kemp's ridley **47:** 12, 14, (15)
　Krefft's river 47: 38–39
　leaf (Asian leaf) **47:** *78–79*
　leatherback 47: 9, *24–27*
　loggerhead 47: *8–9, 15, 16–17*, 54
　loggerhead musk **47:** 10
　long-necked **47:** 28
　Malagasy big-headed **47:** 41–42
　marine 47: 12–15, 54
　matamata 47: 10, 34–37
　midland painted **47:** 66, (68)
　mossbacks **47:** (49)
　mud **47:** (42)
　musk **47:** (31)
　neck retraction **47:** 9–10
　North American wood **47:** *30*
　oblong snake-necked 47: 32–33, 38
　olive ridley **47:** *13*
　painted 47: 66–69
　pancake **47:** 60–61
　pig-nosed 47: 58–59
　pitted-shelled (pig-nosed) **47:** 58–59
　pond slider 47: 70–71
　red-bellied **47:** *29*

　red-eared slider **47:** *70–71*
　scorpion mud **47:** 64–65
　sea **47:** (15)
　senses **47:** 10–11
　side-necked **47:** 9, *30*, 32, (42)
　sliders **47:** 10
　snake-necked **47:** 10, 83
　snapping **47:** (50)
　South American river **47:** 45
　southern painted **47:** 66, 68, (68), *69*
　spiny **47:** (31)
　spiny softshell 47: 60–61
　spotted 47: 76–77
　stinkpot (common musk) **47:** (31), 47
　tracking/tagging **47:** (15), 17, 23, (25)
　Vietnamese leaf **47:** *79*
　West African black **47:** *41*
　western painted **47:** 67, *67*, 68, (68)
　yellow-margined box **47:** *29*
　yellow mud 47: 64–65
　yellow-spotted river 47: 44–45
　see also terrapin
tuskfish **40:** 84
　harlequin **40:** *85*
tusks **3:** 26, 84–85; **5:** 14, 17, 26, 66, 72, 74, 80–81, 86, *87*
　see also ivory
twighoppers, net-winged **24:** 95
twisted-winged insects **25:** (14)
Tydemania navigatoris **39:** 99, *99*
Tylos granulatus **28:** 49
Tylosurus crocodilus **38:** 73
Tylototriton **41:** 88, 91
　taliangensis **41:** *26–27*
　varrucosus **41:** *91*
Tympanocryptis **44:** 32, 34
Tympanoctomys barrerae **8:** 30
Tympanuchus cupido **11:** 44, *74–75*
Tyndall scattering **43:** (35)
Typhlacontias gracilis **46:** *33*
Typhlonarke **33:** (20)
　aysoni **33:** (23)
Typhlonectes **41:** 21, 24–25; **43:** 45
　natans **41:** *24–25*
　relatives **41:** (24)
Typhlonectidae **41:** 21, (24)
Typhlophis **48:** 18
Typhlopidae **44:** 15; **48:** 9, 18, 19, (35); **50:** 15
Typhlops **48:** 19, 20
　vermicularis **48:** 19, 20, 26–27
Typhlosaurus **46:** 8, *32–33*
Typhlotriton **41:** 68, 71
typhoid **23:** 103
typhus **7:** 14, 74
Tyranneutes virescens **19:** 80
Tyrannidae **17:** 28, 30; **19:** 80
tyrannulet **17:** 30
　black-fronted **17:** 30
Tyrannus forficata **17:** 30
tyrant, short-tailed pygmy **17:** *29*, 30
Tyria jacobaeae **26:** *90*
Tyto alba **15:** 50, 64–69; **18:** (57)
Tytonidae **15:** 50, 53

U

uakari
　bald (red) **4:** 72, 80–81
　black **4:** *9*, 72
　black-headed **4:** 80
　red 4: 72, 80–81
　white (red) **4:** 72, 80–81
uaru **37:** (108), **38:** (40), **40:** 68, (71)
Uaru **37:** (108), **40:** 68
　amphiocanthoides **38:** (40)
Uca **28:** (113)
　annulipes **28:** *112–113*
Uegitglanis zammaranoi **37:** 55
ula-ai-hawana **20:** *99*
uli, po'o **20:** 98
Uloboridae **29:** 56–57
ultraviolet protection, snakes **50:** (63)
Uma **44:** 82
　notata **44:** *80–81*; **50:** 105
Umbonia spinosa **24:** 90, *90–91*
Umbra
　krameri **35:** 21
　limi **35:** 21
　pygmaea **35:** 21
umbrellabird 19: 83
　Amazonian 19: 80, 86–87
　bare-wattled **19:** 86, 87
　long-wattled **19:** 86, 87
Umbridae **35:** 20–21
Umfolozi park **5:** 34
Uncia uncia **2:** 34–35
Uncisudis advena **35:** 99
Ungaliophis **48:** 47
　panamensis **48:** *47*
ungulates (hoofed mammals) **5:** 8–13
　even-toed **1:** *10*; **5:** 10, 88
　odd-toed **1:** *10*; **5:** 10, *11*, 43
unicornfish **35:** 104, **40:** 101
　Vlaming's **40:** *101*
　whitemargin **40:** 101
Unionidae **30:** 50, 60, (61)
Unken reflex **41:** (92); **42:** *26–27*, (27), 28
Upeneichthys vlamingii **40:** *38*
Upeneus taeniopterus **40:** 38
Uperoleia **42:** 92, 93
Upogebia affinis **28:** 80
uptail **32:** 84
Upucerthia

dumetaria **20:** 80, 82–83
harterti **20:** 80
Upupa epops **17:** 8, 14–19; **19:** 48
Upupidae **17:** 8, 9
Uracentron **44:** 81, 82
azureum **44:** 84–85
Uraeginthus
granatina **16:** 90
ianthinogaster **16:** 90
Uraeotyphlidae **41:** 21
Uraeotyphlus **41:** 21
Uranoscodon superciliosus **44:** 82
Uranoscopidae **31:** (108), **39:** 28, **40:** 19
Uratelornis chimaera **15:** 86
Urbanus proteus **26:** 62
urchin *see* hedgehog, European
Uria
aalge **12:** 98
lomvia **12:** 98
Urobatis **33:** (34)
halleri **33:** 44–45
Urocerus gigas **27:** 15
Urochordata **21:** 32
Urocolius
indicus **20:** 68
macrourus **20:** 68, 72
Uroconger **33:** (91)
Urocyon
cinereoargenteus **2:** 50
littoralis **2:** 50
Urodela **41:** 8, 27
Urogale everetti **9:** 59
Urogymnus **33:** (34)
Urolophidae **33:** (9), (34), 38
Urolophus **33:** (34)
Uromastyx **44:** 32, 33, 36, 37, (54), 55
acanthinurus **44:** 52–55; **50:** 70
aegyptia microlepis **44:** 9
ornata **44:** 53, (54)
Uropeltidae **48:** 9, 28, 29
Uropeltis **48:** 28
grandis **48:** (31)
philippinus **48:** (31)
Uropetala cavorei **42:** 19
Urophycis **36:** 36, (37)
floridana **36:** 34–35
Uroplatus **44:** 28, 30; **45:** (10), (21), 47
fimbriatus **44:** 30, 30–31; **45:** 20–21
Uropsilus investigator **9:** 40
Uropygi **29:** 28–29
Urotrichus **9:** 54
Urotrygon **33:** (34)
Ursus
americanus **2:** 82, 90–93
arctos **2:** 82, 92, 94–97
maritimus **2:** 82, 84–89
melanoleuca **2:** 98
thibetanus **2:** 82
Uta **44:** 82, (109)
stansburiana **44:** 24, 84, 105, 108–109; **45:** 57; **50:** 1

vaccination, against rabies **2:** (67)
Vaejovis boreas **29:** 19
vairone **34:** 78
Valamugil cunnesius **38:** 53
Valencia
hispanica **38:** (88)
letourneuxi **38:** (88)
Valenciennellus tripunctulatus **35:** 90
Valvifera **28:** 34
Vampyromorpha **30:** 72, (75)
Vampyroteuthis infernalis **30:** (75)
Vampyrum spectrum **9:** 86
Van Leeuwenhoek, Antonie **21:** 9, (12)
Vandellia cirrhosa **37:** (91), 94, 95
Vanellus **13:** 9
armatus **13:** 8, 20–21
cinereus **13:** 8
indicus **13:** 8
senegallus **13:** 8
spinosus **13:** 8
vanellus **13:** 8, 22–25
Vanessa
atalanta **26:** 38
cardui **26:** 38–39
Varanidae **44:** 25; **46:** 54, 82, (83)
Varanus **46:** 82–85
acanthurus **46:** 86–87
albigularis **46:** 82, 83, (84), 85
bengalensis **46:** 88–91; **50:** 31
brevicauda **46:** 82, 85
caudolineatus **46:** (84)
dumerilii **46:** (84)
exanthematicus **46:** 82–83
giganteus **46:** 84
gouldii **46:** 82, 92–93
griseus **46:** 39, 83; **50:** 70
indicus **46:** 82, (85)
kingorum **46:** 82
komodoensis **44:** 24, 24–25; **46:** 82, 94–97
mertensi **46:** 82
niloticus **46:** 83, (83), (85), 98–99
olivaceus **46:** (84)
prasinus **46:** 82
rusingensis **46:** (83)
salvadorii **44:** 24; **46:** 84, (84), 85, (85), 94
salvator **46:** 82, 83, (85), 89, (89), (90)

varius **46:** (85)
Varecia
variegata **4:** 96, 104–105
variegata rubra **4:** 104
variegata variegata **4:** 104
Vargula **36:** 59
Variola louti **40:** 16
veiltail **34:** 49
Velia caprai **24:** 18, 18–19
velifer
sailfin **35:** 82
spinyfin **35:** 82
Veliferidae **35:** 82, 105
Veliidae **24:** 18–19
velvetfish 39: 11, 53, 68–71
orbicular **39:** 68
red **39:** 68, 71, 72
threefin **39:** 69
Weber's **39:** 70
Vema **30:** 13
vendace **35:** 38, 40
Veneridae **30:** 50, 67–68
Venerupis senegalensis **30:** 67
venom
beaded lizards **46:** (78)
see also snake venom
venomous fish **33:** (11), **37:** (57), **39:** 52, 58, 59, (61), (62)
Ventrocercus urophasianus **11:** 44
Venustria superba **24:** 84–85
Vermicella **50:** 15
Vermivora
bachmanii **17:** 89
celata **17:** 88, (93)
peregrina **17:** 88, (93)
Vespa crabro **27:** 63
Vespertilionidae **9:** 87
Vespicula depressifrons **39:** 67
Vespidae **27:** 62–75
Vespula
germanica **27:** 74–75
vulgaris 68, 73
Vestiaria coccinea **20:** 98
Vestimentifera **21:** 77
Vibrio **36:** (79)
vibrissae **8:** 56
Vibrissaphora **42:** 34
Vicugna vicugna **5:** 92, 110–111
vicuña 5: 92, 93, 110–111
Vidua fischeri **16:** 90
Viduinae **16:** 90
Villa modesta **23:** 70
Villosa vibex **30:** 60–61
vine snake 49: 14, (18)
American **49:** 52
blunt-headed 42: 82; **49:** 104–105
leaf-nosed 49: 70–73
long-nosed 48: 12; **49:** 18–19
Madagascan **49:** 72–73
savanna **49:** (39)
vinegaroons (tailed whip scorpions) **29:** 28–29
giant **29:** 28
"violon de mer" **33:** 32

Vipera **50**: 55
  ammodytes **49**: (73); **50**: 52, <u>78–79</u>
  aspis **49**: *29*; **50**: (78), (85)
  berus **48**: 17, 25; **49**: 28, 52, 55;
    50: 9, 50, *53*, <u>80–85</u>, 109
  berus bosniensis **50**: 80
  berus sachaliensis **50**: 80
  latasti **49**: (73); **50**: (78)
  latifii **50**: (85)
  sachalinensis **50**: 80, (85)
  seoanei **50**: 80, (85)
  ursinii **50**: 53, *85*, (85)
  xanthina **50**: 79
viperfish **35**: 87
  Dana **35**: 86, (86)
  Sloane's **35**: *84–85*, 86, (86), *87*
Viperidae **48**: 9, 15; **50**: 9, 50
Viperinae **50**: 50, 51
vipers 48: 15; **50**: 9, <u>50–55</u>
  African rhinoceros **49**: (73)
  Arabian horned **50**: 71
  asp **49**: 29; **50**: (78), (85)
  Burton's carpet **50**: 74, 75
  carpet 50: (8), 14, 52, 53, 58,
    <u>74–77</u>, 103
    Central American eyelash **49**: (73)
    desert horned (Sahara horned)
    48: *9*, 12; **49**: 34; **50**: 9, 51,
    52, 58, <u>70–71</u>, 77
  Eurasian **50**: 55
  eyelash 48: (97); **49**: (51); **50**: 9,
    10–11, 59, <u>90–91</u>
  Fea's **50**: 50, *57*, (57)
  Gaboon 48: 8; **50**: 9, 51, 61, <u>64–65</u>
  Lataste's **49**: (73); **50**: (78)
  Latifi's **50**: (85)
  lowland swamp **50**: 58
  meadow (Orsini's) **50**: 53, *85*, (85)
  Mediterranean nose-horned **50**: (78)
  Milos **50**: 79
  North African desert horned **49**: (73)
  northern (adders) **48**: 25; **49**: 28;
    50: 9, 50, <u>80–85</u>
  nose-horned 50: 52, <u>78–79</u>
  Old World **50**: 53
  Orsini's **50**: 53, *85*, (85)
  Ottoman **50**: 79
  painted (Burton's) carpet **50**: 74
  Peringuey's **50**: 51
  rhinoceros **50**: 52, 65
  riverjacks (rhinoceros vipers)
    50: 52, 65
  Russell's 50: (8), 9, (11), <u>72–73</u>
  Sahara horned 48: 12; **50**: 9, 51,
    52, 58, <u>70–71</u>, 77
  Sahara sand **50**: 71
  Sakhalin Island **50**: (85)
  sand (nose-horned) **50**: 52, <u>78–79</u>
  saw-scaled (carpet) **49**: 33, *33–34*;
    50: (8), 14, 52, 53, 58, <u>74–77</u>,
    103
  sedge **50**: *51*
  Seoane's **50**: 80, (85)
  temperature regulation **50**: (53)

tree **50**: 91
West African carpet **50**: *75*
white-headed **50**: (57)
white-lipped pit **48**: *12*
see also bush viper; pit vipers
vireo 17: (39); **19**: (74)
  bell's **17**: 98
  red-eyed 17: 98, <u>100–103</u>
  solitary **17**: 98, *98-99*, 104
  vireo family 17: <u>98–99</u>
  white-eyed **17**: 98
  yellow-throated 17: 98, <u>104–105</u>
Vireo
  bellii **17**: 98
  flavifrons **17**: 98, <u>104–105</u>
  griseus **17**: 98
  olivaceus **17**: 98, <u>100–103</u>
  solitarius **17**: 98, 104
Vireolanius melitophrys **17**: 98
Vireonidae **17**: 98
virgin birth *see* parthenogenesis
Virginia **49**: 12
viscacha **7**: *12*; **8**: 28
  mountain **8**: 28
  northern **8**: 30
  plains **8**: 28, 30
viscacha rat **8**: 29, 30
  plains **8**: 30
visual **20**: 38
  vocal **11**: 30, (62); **13**: (79);
    14: 30–31; **18**: (99); **20**: 72
  unison **14**: 86–87
  see also songs; communication
vivaria **43**: 73
Viverra
  megaspila **1**: 88
  tangalunga **1**: 88
  zibetha **1**: 88
Viverricula indica **1**: 88
Viverridae **1**: 18, 88, 98
viviparity **25**: 99; **42**: 60, (85); **46**: 14,
  (22), (43), 47
vocalization
  skinks **46**: (49)
  turtles **47**: 73
voladora **38**: 23
vole 7: 13, 17, 65
  bank **7**: *14–15*
  field 7: <u>92–93</u>
  north European water (water)
    7: 9, <u>98–99</u>
  short-tailed (field) **7**: <u>92–93</u>
  southern red-backed 7: <u>94–95</u>
  water 1: 54; **7**: 9, <u>98–99</u>
Volucella bombylans **23**: *79*
volutes **30**: 35, *35*
Vombatiformes **10**: 75
Vombatus ursinus **10**: 74, <u>98–101</u>
vomeronasal organ **5**: 62, 65
Vormela peregusna **1**: 32
Vorticella **21**: *24–25*
Vulpes
  bengalensis **2**: 50
  cana **2**: 50

chama **2**: 50
corsac **2**: 50
lagopus **2**: 50, <u>70–73</u>
rüppelli **2**: 50
velox **2**: 50, <u>68–69</u>
velox herbes **2**: 69
vulpes **2**: 50, <u>64–67</u>
zerda **2**: 50, <u>74–75</u>
Vultur **15**: 24
  gryphus **15**: 8; **20**: 8, *16*
vulture 11: 13, (13); **20**: <u>8–11</u>
  African white-backed **20**: 8, *9*
  American black **20**: 8, (11), 12, 15
  bearded *see* lammergeier
  Egyptian **11**: (25); **20**: 8, *10–11*, (11)
  Eurasian black **20**: 8
  greater yellow-headed **20**: 8
  hooded **20**: 8, 24
  king **20**: 8, *10*, (11)
  lappet-faced 20: 8, (11), <u>24–27</u>
  lesser yellow-headed **20**: 8
  New World **11**: 13; **15**: 12; **20**: 8–11
  Old World **15**: 12; **20**: 11
  palm-nut 20: 8, <u>28–29</u>
  red-headed **20**: 8
  turkey 15: 24, (26); **20**: 8, (11),
    <u>12–15</u>, 17
  white-headed **20**: 8, 24

W

wagtail 15: 94; **17**: 51
  cape **17**: 44, 45
  forest **17**: 44, 45
  gray **17**: 44
  Madagascar **17**: 44, 45
  mountain **17**: 44
  pied 17: 44, <u>46–49</u>; **20**: (48)
  wagtail and pipit family 17: <u>44–45</u>
  white (pied) **17**: 44, <u>46–49</u>; **20**: (48)
  yellow **14**: (50); **17**: 44, *44*, 45
wahoo **40**: 106
"walking" fish **36**: (14), <u>64–65</u>
walkingsticks 22: <u>52–57</u>; **49**: (78)
  defense **22**: 56–57
  giant thorny **22**: *57*
  Macleay's specter **22**: 57
  slender-bodied **22**: *52–53*
  2-striped **22**: *52–53*
Wallabia bicolor **10**: 48
wallaby 10: <u>48–53</u>

banded hare **10:** 48, *51*
Bennett's (red-necked) **10:** 48, 64–65
bridled nail-tailed **10:** 48, *50*
lesser forest **10:** 48
northern nail-tailed **10:** 48
Papuan forest **10:** 48
prettyface **10:** 48, *51*
Proserpine rock **10:** 48, *50*
red-necked 10: 48, 64–65
ringtailed rock (yellow-footed rock)
  10: 48, 70–71
rock **10:** 51
rufous hare **10:** 48, *51*
spectacled hare **10:** 48
swamp **10:** 48, *49*
toolache **10:** 53
whiptail **10:** 48, *51*
yellow-footed rock 10: 48, 70–71
wallaroo **10:** 60–61
common **10:** 48, *50*, 60
hill **10:** 48, *50*
walleye **35:** (12)
wallowing **5:** 38, 69, 71, *71*, *76–77*, *83*
walrus 3: *8, 9, 10, 11*, 24–29
want *see* mole, European
wapiti *see* elk
warbler 17: (39), 70, (76)
African sedge **17:** 60
Arctic **17:** 60, *60*
Bachman's **17:** 89
bay-breasted **17:** 88, (93)
black-and-white **17:** 88, (91)
Cape May **17:** 88, 93
Cetti's **17:** 60
garden **20:** (48)
grasshopper **17:** 60, 61
great reed **17:** 60, 61; **20:** *49*
hooded **17:** 88, (91), (93)
Kirtland's **17:** 88, *88*, 89
marsh **18:** (41)
melodious **17:** 60
New World warbler family
  17: 88–89, 98
northern parula **17:** 88, *88*, 93
Old World warbler family
  17: 60–61, 89
orange-crowned **17:** 88, (93)
pine **17:** 88, (93)
prothonotary **17:** 88, *88*
red-faced **17:** 88, *88*
reed **17:** 60, 61, *61*; **20:** (48), *49*,
50–51
scrub **17:** 60
sedge **17:** 60, 61
Tennessee **17:** 88, (93)
willow 17: 52, 60, 62–65
Wilson's **17:** 88, (91), (93)
wood **17:** 89; **19:** 70, (74)
yellow **17:** 88, *89*, 93
yellow-rumped **17:** 88
warbling-finch, ringed **16:** 62
warfarin **7:** 75
warthog 5: 75, 80–83
common **5:** 74

desert **5:** 74
washing bears **1:** (24)
Washington Convention *see* Convention
  on International Trade in
  Endangered Species of Wild
  Fauna and Flora
waspfish **39:** 53, 67
cockatoo **39:** 67
ocellated **39:** 65
sailfin **39:** *60*
wasps 27: 8–13
alder wood **27:** *14–15*
cicada-killer **27:** (82)
cuckoo 27: 34–37
digger 27: 36–37
feeding **27:** (73)
fig **27:** (33)
gall 27: 32–33
German **27:** *73, 74–75*
hornets **27:** 63
horse guards **27:** 79–80
hunting (solitary) **27:** 76–83
ichneumon 27: 22–31
jewel (cuckoo) **27:** 34–35
mason **27:** 64
mass provisioning **27:** 66, 79
nectar-gathering **27:** 69
nest cooling **27:** (69)
nest defense **27:** 75
nests **27:** 66–69
paper (social) **27:** *11*, 62–75
parasitic (parasitoids) **27:** 22–31
potter (social) **27:** 62, 64–66
progressive provisioning **27:** 66, 79
ruby-tailed (cuckoo) **27:** 34–35
slender digger **27:** (37)
social 27: 62–75
solitary 27: 76–83
spider 27: 58–61
spider-hunting (spider) **27:** 58–61
thread-waisted sand **27:** *13, 77,
  80–81*
wild carrot **27:** 31
wood (sawflies) **27:** 14–21
yellow jacket **27:** *66–67*, 72–73
water balance, snakes **48:** (99)
water bears **22:** 12–13
water boatmen (backswimmers)
  24: 24–27
lesser **24:** (27)
water dog **38:** 30
water dragon, Asian **48:** (58)
water fleas 28: *11*, 16–21; **41:** 62
water loss **43:** (66)
water measurers **24:** (19)
water moccasins **50:** (89)
"water monkey" **31:** 92
water reabsorption **5:** 96
water scorpions 24: 20–21
water snake 49: 12, (83); **50:** 15
American mangrove **49:** (51)
banded **49:** 80–81, (81)
broad-banded **49:** (81)
brown **49:** *82–83*

dog-faced **49:** 15
Florida **49:** (81)
Florida green **49:** *82–83*
green **48:** 109
Gulf salt marsh **49:** 81, (81), (82)
homalopsine **48:** 33
keeled-bellied **49:** 15
mangrove **49:** (81), 82
North American **49:** (76)
northern **49:** 83
southern 49: 80–83
water stick insects (water scorpions)
  24: 20–21
water striders 24: 16–17
small (ripple bugs) **24:** 18–19
water vascular system **30:** 91–92, 96
water
from diet **11:** 21; **16:** (30)
provided by parents **16:** *8, 9, 11, 11*;
  20: 35
waterbuck 5: *75*; **6:** 62, 92–93
defassa **6:** 93
waterbug **22:** 68
waterdogs (mudpuppies) **41:** *26–27*, 27,
  29, 46–47, 49
wattlebird
  New Zealand 20: 100–101
yellow **20:** 88
waxbill
black-crowned **16:** 90, *91*
violet-eared **16:** 90, *90*
waxbill family 16: (18), 62, 90–91
waxwing 11: 15
Bohemian 16: (84); **18:** 30, 32–35
cedar **18:** 30, 32, (35), 41
Japanese **18:** 30, *30*, 31
waxwing family 18: 30–31
weasel
African striped **1:** 32, *34*
European common (least) **1:** 19, 32,
  34, *35*, 36–39
least 1: 19, 32, 34, *35*, 36–39
long-tailed **1:** 32, 36
North African banded **1:** 32, *34*
Patagonian **1:** 32, *34*
short-tailed *see* stoat
weasel family 1: 32–35
weather fish **34:** 106
weaver 16: 100–101; **18:** (81); **19:** *50*
black-headed (village) **16:** 100,
  102–105
buffalo **16:** (104)
sociable **11:** *8*; **16:** 100, (104)
viduine **16:** 90
village 16: 100, 102–105
V-marked (village) **16:** 100, 102–105
weavers (spiders)
cobweb (comb-footed spiders)
  29: 98–101
funnel (sheet-web) **29:** 94–97
grass funnel **29:** *97*
lace 29: 52–53
large-jawed orb 29: 102–105
leaf lace **29:** *53*

orb 29: *43*, 106–111
   pygmy hackled-web **29:** (53)
sheet-web 29: 94–97
weaving **16:** 104, (104), (105)
web spinners 22: 82–83
webbed fingers **4:** 71
Weberian apparatus **34:** (10), **37:** 8,
   38: (10)
wedgefish **33:** 27, (27)
weedfish
   yellow-crested **40:** (93)
weever
   barfaced **40:** 19
weeverfish **39:** 28, **40:** 19
weevils 25: 104–111
   acorn **25:** *104*
   big-foot **25:** *104–105*
   boll **25:** (110)
   clay-colored **25:** *110*
   cloverleaf **25:** *104*
   destructive habits **25:** 109–110, (110)
   eight-humped **25:** *106*
   emerald **25:** *105*
   fungus **25:** 104
   giraffe-necked **25:** *106–107*
   hazel leaf-rolling **25:** *109*
   larvae **25:** 109
   oak leaf-rolling **25:** *109*
   pest control **25:** 110
   primitive 25: 112–113
   reactions to danger **25:** 110
   reproduction **25:** 105–109
   toothpick (primitive) **25:** 112–113
   twelve-spined **25:** *110–111*
   zygopine **25:** *107*
Weil's disease **7:** 14, 74
wels **37:** 11, 30, *30*, 32, 33, *33*, 34,
   36, (36)
Westafrikanischer knochenzüngler
   31: 86
wetas (king crickets) **23:** 20–21
wetlands **1:** 24
Wetmorena **46:** 52
whale 1: *10*, (11), 14; **3:** 54–59; **5:** (10),
   66; **7:** 12; **31:** 106–109, 107,
   110, 111
   baleen **3:** 54–55, 56, 58
   big-nosed **31:** 106
   blue 1: (11); **3:** 54, 55, (57), 58,
      98–101
   bowhead 3: 55, 108, 110–111
   dorsal-banded **31:** 107
   dwarf sperm **3:** 55
   gray 3: 55, *57*, (57), *59*, 92–97
   humpback 3: 55, (57), *58*, 102–105;
      36: 102, *102–103*
   killer 3: 37, 39, 55, 62–65, 83, 94,
      96
   long-finned pilot 3: 55, 66–67
   minke 3: 55, 106–107
   northern bottlenose 3: 55, 90–91
   northern right **3:** 109
   pygmy right **3:** *54*, 55
   pygmy sperm **3:** 55

right **3:** 55
short-finned pilot 3: 66
southern right 3: 55, 108–109
sperm 3: 55, 57, 58, 86–89
   white *see* beluga
whale meat **3:** 59, 67
whale songs **3:** 99–100, 105
whale watching **3:** (57), 71, 95, 104
whalefish **39:** 13
   flabby **39:** 9, 12, 13, 14
   orangemouth **39:** 12, 14
   red **39:** 12, 13, 14
   redmouth **39:** 12, 14, *14*
   velvet **39:** 12, 13
whaler
   freshwater **32:** 52
   river **32:** 52
   Swan River **32:** 52, 53
whaling industry **3:** 58, 89, 91, 93, 101,
   105, 107, 108
wheatear, northern **18:** 44
whelks 30: 32–35
   common **30:** *32*
   common northern Atlantic **30:** *19*
   dog **30:** *32, 34–35*
   waved **30:** *32*
whimbrel **13:** (15), 16, 30, (36)
whippoorwill 15: 78, 82–83
whippy **39:** 80
whiptail (fish) **36:** 28
   toothed **36:** *28–29*
whiptails (lizards) **44:** 25, (26), 30;
   45: 82–85; **50:** 105
   breeding **45:** 84
   coastal **45:** *90*
   conservation **45:** 84–85
   desert grassland 45: 83, 88–91
   food and feeding **45:** 84
whistlepig *see* woodchuck
whistling-duck *see* duck, whistling-
White Cloud Mountain fish **34:** (65)
white death **32:** 84
white fish **38:** 62
white pointer **32:** 84
whitebait **36:** 111
   fisheries **35:** (35)
   Tasmanian **35:** 33, (34), (35)
white-eye 18: 68–69; **38:** 93
   chestnut-flanked 18: 68, 70–71
   cinnamon **18:** 68, *68*
   crested **18:** 68
   Javan **18:** 68, 69
   oriental **18:** 68, *68*
   Truk **18:** 68
   yellow-spectacled **18:** 68
whitefish 35: 9, 38–41, **36:** 12, 13
   Acadian **35:** 41
   Bear Lake **35:** 39
   Bonneville **35:** 39
   common **35:** *38*, 40
   lake **35:** 38, 40, (41)
   mountain **35:** 39, *39*
   pygmy **35:** 39
   round **35:** 40, (41)

whiteflies 24: 98–99
   greenhouse **24:** *98*
   rain-forest **24:** *98*
whiteness in mammals **8:** (84)
whites 26: 22–27
   cabbage whites **26:** (24)
whitethroat **17:** 60, *60*, 61
   lesser **17:** 60
whiting **35:** 66, (68), **36:** 33, 38, *46–47*
   blue **36:** 33
whitling **35:** 66, (68)
Whittaker, Robert **21:** 9
whydah
   Jackson's **16:** 100
   straw-tailed **16:** 90
wigeon, American 14: 52, 72–75
wildcat 2: 10, 13, 48–49
   African **2:** *12*
   European **2:** *12*
wildebeest 5: 12, 47; **6:** 95
   black 6: 62
   blue 6: 62, 82–85
wildfowl 14: 52–81, (62)
willet **13:** 30, 31, *32–33*
Wilsonia **17:** (91)
   citrina **17:** 88, (91), (93)
   pusilla **17:** 88, (93)
wings
   of birds of prey **15:** (9)
   claws on **20:** 47, 67, (67)
   elongated feathers **15:** 84, 85, *85*
   as flippers **12:** 8, *13*
   for hovering **16:** *50*
   of migrating birds **17:** (64); **18:** 28
   for silent flight **15:** 52
   for soaring **15:** (9)
   for speed **15:** (9)
   used for swimming **11:** 8; **12:** 98;
      14: 8, 108–109
winkles and relatives 30: 26–31
Winteria telescopa **35:** 25
wip **39:** 80
wiretail, Des Murs' **20:** 80
wireworms (click beetles) **25:** 42–45
   false **25:** *71*
wobbegong 32: 10, 30, 33
   banded **32:** 37
   cobbler **32:** 37
   Japanese **32:** 37
   northern **32:** 37
   ornate **32:** 37
   spotted **32:** 37
   tasseled 32: 36–37
wolf 2: 9
   Ethiopean **2:** 50, *52*
   Falkland Island **2:** 50, *53*, (53)
   gray 2: 50, 53, 54–57, 59
   maned **2:** 50, 53
   marsupial *see* thylacine
   Mexican **2:** 54
   red **2:** 59
   Tasmanian *see* thylacine
   timber (gray) **2:** 50, 53, 54–57, 59
wolffish **38:** 25, *25*

wolverine 1: 18, 32, *35*, <u>56–57</u>
wombat 10: (10), 77, 93
  common 10: 74, 75, <u>98–101</u>
  northern hairy-nosed **10:** 74, (101)
  southern hairy-nosed **10:** 74, *101*,
    (101)
woodcat **37:** 83
  common **37:** *82*
  midnight **37:** *82–83*
  zamora **37:** *82–83*
woodchuck 1: 87; **7:** 34, <u>50–51</u>
woodcock **13:** 31; **15:** (52)
  Bukidnon **13:** 30, (33)
woodcreeper 17: <u>28–31</u>; **19:** 74
  barred **17:** 28
  buff-throated **17:** 28, *28*
  lineated **17:** 28
  long-billed **17:** 28; **19:** (29)
  montane **17:** 28
  olivaceous 17: 28, (29), <u>32–33</u>
  plain-brown **17:** 28, *28*
  scimitar-billed **17:** 28; **19:** (29)
  spot-crowned **17:** 28
  striped **17:** 28
  strong-billed **17:** 28, (29)
  tyrannine **17:** 28
  wedge-billed **17:** 28, (29)
  white-chinned **17:** 28, (29)
woodlice **28:** *46–47*
  common **28:** *48–49*
  common striped **28:** *46–47*
woodpecker 11: 10, 12, (15); **17:** (22);
  18: *18*, (19), 64; **19:** 36, 58,
  76
  black **18:** 8
  chestnut **18:** 8, *10*
  Eurasian green (green) **18:** 8, <u>20–21</u>
  gila **18:** 8, *9*
  great spotted **18:** 8, *11*
  green 18: 8, <u>20–21</u>
  ground **18:** 8, (11)
  ivory-billed **18:** 8, 11, 14
  pileated 18: 8, <u>14–19</u>
  Syrian **18:** 8, 11
  three-toed **18:** 8
  woodpecker family 18: <u>8–11</u>; **19:** 56
woodstar, little **16:** 44
woodswallow 20: 100–101
  ashy **20:** 100
  dusky **20:** 100
  little **20:** 100
  masked 20: 100, <u>108–109</u>
  Papuan **20:** 100
  white-backed **20:** 100
wool production **5:** 104, 105, (106),
  108, 111
World Conservation Union **31:** 20, 21,
  37, 63, 97, **32:** 25, **34:** 22,
  (28), (56), 96, (104), **35:** 21,
  26, 29, 33, 41, (70), **37:** (19),
  38: (63), **39:** (35), 40, (46),
  (78)
  see also IUCN
World Conservation Union *see*

International Union for the
  Conservation of Nature
worm lizards 41: 20; **44:** *8*, 10, 11;
  46: <u>102–105</u>
  ajolote 46: 104, <u>110–111</u>
  black and white (sooty) **46:** 102,
    <u>106–107</u>
  Cape shovel-snouted **46:** 104, 105
  checkered **46:** 104, *104–105*, 105
  European (Iberian) **46:** 102, <u>108–109</u>
  Florida **46:** 105, *109*, (109)
  Iberian 46: 102, <u>108–109</u>
  keel-headed **46:** 102
  Mexican (ajolote) **46:** <u>110–111</u>
  short-headed **46:** 105
  sooty 46: 102, <u>106–107</u>
  tunneling techniques **46:** *103*
  white **46:** 104–105, *105*, 107
wormfish **40:** 99
wormlike invertebrates 21: <u>76–79</u>
worms 9: (46)
  acoelomate **21:** 77
  acorn **21:** *30–31*, 79
  annual festival **21:** (104)
  arrowworms **21:** 79
  beard 21: <u>92–93</u>
  bootlace **21:** 86
  bristleworms **21:** *99*
  candystripe flatworms **21:** *80*
  Christmas tree **21:** *98–99*
  coelomate **21:** 77
  deuterostomian coelomate **21:** 77
  earthworms *see* earthworms
  feather-duster **21:** 100–101
  fire (bristleworms) **21:** 99
  flatworms 21: <u>80–85</u>
  gordian (horsehair) **21:** 77–78, *77*
  green phoronid **21:** *74*
  horsehair **21:** 77–78, *77*
  horseshoe 21: <u>74–75</u>
  innkeeper **21:** 78
  palolo **21:** *101*
  peacock **21:** *97*
  polychaete **21:** *97*
  proboscis (ribbon) **21:** <u>86–87</u>
  pseudocoelomate **21:** 77
  ragworms *see* ragworms
  ribbon 21: <u>86–87</u>
  roundworms 21: <u>88–91</u>
  sand mason **21:** *97*
  scale **21:** *98*
  segmented 21: <u>94–97</u>
  spiny headed **21:** *76*, 77
  spoonworms **21:** 78
  tapeworms 21: <u>80–85</u>
  threadworms (roundworms) **21:** <u>88–91</u>
  velvet **22:** 13
  wireworms (click beetles) **25:** <u>42–45</u>
  zebra flatworms **21:** *81*
woundfin **34:** 53, 71
wrasse 33: 51, **39:** (10), **40:** 9, 12, 53,
  <u>84–87</u>, 89, 101
  bicolor cleaner **40:** 84
  bluestreak cleaner **40:** *86*, 90

  cleaner **33:** (82), **40:** 84, 86, 90
  razor **40:** *87*
  redlip cleaner **40:** 84
wreckfish **40:** 15
wren 17: (39); **18:** 36
  bicolored **17:** 52, (57)
  cactus 17: 52, <u>56–59</u>
  Carolina **17:** 52
  common (winter) **17:** 52, <u>54–55</u>, 57;
    20: (48)
  giant **17:** 52, (57)
  happy **17:** 52
  house **16:** 71; **17:** 52
  marsh **17:** 52, *53*
  northern (winter) **17:** 52, <u>54–55</u>, 57;
    20: (48)
  winter 17: 52, <u>54–55</u>, 57; **20:** (48)
  wren family 17: <u>52–53</u>
  Yucatan **17:** 52, (57)
wriggler **40:** 99
wrybill 13: 8, <u>26–29</u>
wryneck 18: 8, <u>12–13</u>
Wyeomyia **23:** *48*
Wyulda squamicaudata **10:** 74

X

Xanthocephalus xanthocephalus
  18: 74, 80
Xanthomyza phrygia **20:** 88
Xanthopan morgani praedicta **26:** *55*
Xantusia **45:** 54, (57)
  henshawi **45:** <u>56–57</u>, (107)
  vigilis **45:** 55, (57)
Xantusiidae **44:** 25, 28; **45:** 54
Xenaploactis cautes **39:** 69
Xenarthra **1:** *10*; **9:** 64–66
Xenentodon cancila **38:** *74–75*
Xenobalistes punctatus **39:** 104
Xenobatrachus **42:** 105
Xenocalamus **49:** 106
  bicolor **49:** *106–107*
Xenoconger
  fryeri **33:** 77
  olokun **33:** 76
Xenodermatinae **49:** 8, 16
Xenodermis javanicus **49:** 16
Xenodon rhabdocephalus **42:** *68*
Xenodontinae **49:** 8, 16, 96
Xenolepidichthys dalgleishi **39:** (25)
Xenomystus **31:** <u>104–105</u>

nigri **31:** 104, *104*, 105
Xenopeltidae **48:** 9, 28
Xenopeltis
  hainanensis **48:** 31
  unicolor **48:** *29*, 31, 36–37
Xenophidion **48:** (79)
Xenophrys **42:** 34, 35, 55
Xenophthalmichthys danae **35:** *8–9*
Xenopoecilus **38:** 67
  oophorus **38:** 65, *66–67*
  poptae **38:** 65
  saranisorum **38:** 65
Xenopsylla cheapis **22:** *113*
Xenopus **42:** 23, 46, 48, 49, 55; **50:** 57
  gilli **42:** (53)
  vlaevis **42:** 46, 52–55, 69, (69); **43:** 51
  muelleri **42:** 55
Xenosauridae **44:** 25; **46:** 54, 70
xenosaurs 46: 70–71
Xenosaurus **46:** 70–71
Xenotoca eiseni **38:** *108–109*
Xenotyphlops **48:** 18
  grandidieri **48:** 19
Xenus cinereus **13:** 30
Xestobium rufovillosum **25:** *53*, (53)
Xestospongia testudinaria **21:** *40*
Xiphias gladius **32:** 86, **40:** 108,
  108–109
Xiphiidae **39:** (10), **40:** (107), 108–111
Xiphocolaptes promeropirhynchus
  17: 28
Xiphophorus **38:** (100)
  helleri **38:** (96), *99*, *100*
  maculatus **38:** *51*, 109
Xiphorhynchus
  guttatus **17:** 28
  obsoletus **17:** 28
Xiphydria camelus **27:** *14–15*
Xyleutes ceramicus **26:** *105*
Xylocopa **22:** *35*; **27:** 100–101
  nigra **27:** *101*
Xyphosia miliaria **23:** 89, 90
Xyrauchen texanus **34:** 96, *96*, 98
Xysticus cristatus **29:** *68–69*, *70–71*

yak 6: 74–75
  wild **6:** 75
yapok *see* opossum, water
yellow cheek **34:** 16, 19
yellow-finch, greater **16:** 62
yellowfish
  banded **39:** *50*
yellowhammer **16:** 62
yellowlegs 11: (15)
  greater 13: 30, 66–67
  lesser **13:** 30, *32*
Yellowstone National Park **6:** 66, 67
yellowthroat, common 17: 88, 94–97
Yersinia pestis **7:** 76
Y-loach **34:** (104)
yolk sac (fish) **35:** *76*
Yponomeuta padella **26:** *112–113*
Yponomeutidae **26:** 112–113

Zacco **34:** 65
  platypus **34:** 65
Zalophus californianus **3:** 9, 20–23
Zamenis **49:** 10
Zanclistius elevatus **40:** 55
Zanclorhynchus spinifer **39:** 71
zander **40:** 9, 16, 17
Zaniolepis
  frenata **39:** 75
  latipinnis **39:** 75
Zanobatidae **33:** (9), (27)
Zanobatus **33:** (27)
Zaphobas **25:** 71
Zapteryx **33:** (27)
zebra 2: *8–9*; **5:** 12, *12–13*; **6:** (85), 95
  Burchell's (plains) **5:** 42, 46–51
  common (plains) **5:** 42, 46–51

  Grèvy's **5:** 42, (44), 52–53
  mountain **5:** 42
  plains 5: 42, 46–51
  zebra family 5: 42–45
Zebrais **39:** (93)
Zebrasoma flavescens **40:** 101
Zeidae **39:** 9, 22–25
Zenaida macroura **16:** 12, 20–21
Zenarchopterus beauforti **38:** 77
Zenopsis
  conchifer **39:** 23
  nebulosus **39:** 23
Zeugopterus punctatus **39:** 90
Zeus faber **39:** 9, 22, *22*, *23*
Zoantharia **21:** 43
Zoanthidea **21:** 43
zokor **7:** 15
zona **38:** (56)
Zonitis sayi **25:** *66–67*
Zonocerus elegans **23:** 27
Zonosaurus **45:** 98, 101
Zonotrichia melodia **16:** 62
zoogeography **21:** (33)
Zoogoneticus quitzeoensis **38:** *111*
zoology **21:** (33)
Zoomastigophora **21:** 13, 16–17
Zoothera
  cinerea **18:** 44
  sibirica **18:** 44
Zopheridae **25:** *73*
Zopherus nodulosus **25:** *73*
Zoraptera **22:** 30, (83)
zorilla **1:** 32, 34, *34*
Zorotypus hubbardi **22:** (83)
Zosis geniculatus **29:** *56–57*
Zosteropidae **18:** 68
Zosterops
  erythropleurus **18:** 68, 70–71
  flavus **18:** 68
  lateralis **18:** 68
  palpebrosus **18:** 68
  wallacei **18:** 68
Zu
  cristatus **35:** *106–107*, 107
  elongatus **35:** 107
Zygaena
  graslini **26:** *109*
  lonicerae **26:** *109*
Zygaenidae **26:** 108–109
zygodactylism **16:** 22; **17:** 20, (22);
  18: 8, *18*, (18); **19:** 58; **20:** 46
Zygoptera **22:** 42